T0209691

Teaching IN THE DARK

A MEMOIR

GENÉT SIMONE

BALBOA.PRESS
A DIVISION OF HAY HOUSE

Balboa Press books may be ordered through booksellers or by contacting:

Balboa Press
A Division of Hay House
1663 Liberty Drive
Bloomington, IN 47403
www.balboapress.com
844-682-1282

Print information available on the last page.

Interior Graphics/Art Credit: Gordon R. Pierce

ISBN: 979-8-7652-4428-9 (sc)
ISBN: 979-8-7652-4429-6 (hc)
ISBN: 979-8-7652-4430-2 (e)

Library of Congress Control Number: 2023914436

Balboa Press rev. date: 09/18/2023

For my students, past, present, and future.

There are stories from that time that have never left me.
I feel inexorably called to share them.
They are not my stories. They are our stories.
They are asking to be told.
~ Anne Parker, *Stories from the Origin*

CONTENTS

PART FIVE: SPRING THAW

PART SIX: LEAVING

AUTHOR'S NOTE

This is the story of my first year as a high school teacher—a year most anyone in the profession would describe as *cringeworthy*. I decided to add a slight twist of pressure by accepting employment in the amazingly remote community of Shishmaref, Alaska.

The events in this book are true, supported by my own journals and photos, school yearbooks and newspapers, and letters I wrote to friends, who graciously gave them back to me years later, saying, "You should write a book!"

While I have tried to accurately portray the landscape, culture, and customs of Shishmaref, I know that my perspective is that of an Outsider. For that reason, I sought guidance from a few Shishmaref residents on certain sections of this book but am aware of the possibility that I may still have inaccurately described aspects of their lives and culture. I accept full responsibility for any errors.

The people in this book are real. I have changed names and altered aspects of their personalities and appearance to protect their privacy. If any reader believes they know someone in these stories, I hope they will smile and send that person a little blessing for having made such a lasting impression on my life.

ACKNOWLEDGEMENTS

I have been writing this memoir in my mind for almost four decades, and actively writing it for four years. During that tenure, countless people guided and supported me toward publication. I want to thank my friends, and former students and colleagues who heard my stories and urged me to write them down. Their persistence kept this book alive.

Deep gratitude goes to Ingrid Ricks, author and teacher at Hugo House in Seattle, whose excellent workshop and personal coaching guided me into the world of memoir. I am also thankful for the team at Balboa Press who provided guidance and support through the multiple twists and turns of publication.

Special thanks to my Airbnb hosts on Whidbey Island - Stephanie and Paul, Lois and Julio, Genie and Rich - and my dear friends Trish and Mike Zimburean in Lake Stevens, for providing quiet spaces where I could immerse myself in research and writing. Those long weekends were critical for making steady progress.

Gratitude to the Discovery Channel and the Tweto family—Jim, Ferno, and their daughter Ariel—who were featured in *Flying Wild Alaska*. I watched the series to remind myself what it's like to travel by bush plane. I am awed by the steadiness, courage, and humor that bush pilots bring each day to their work—flying people and cargo through all kinds of weather and over challenging terrain. No one carried the essence of "bush pilot" better than Jim Tweto. Tragically, as I was putting the finishing touches on this manuscript, I learned that Jim died on June 16, 2023, along with his friend and outdoor guide Shane Reynolds. Jim's Cessna 180 crashed after it failed to gain altitude upon take-off in a remote area near Shaktoolik. Their deaths are a sobering reminder that flying is both beautiful and dangerous. They will be missed.

A variety of industry experts helped bring authenticity to parts of this book, happily researching and supplying factual data: Will Gooding, Customer Service at Alaska Commercial Company in Nome, AK, for prices of goods back in the 1980s; Luchie Manlangit at Diomede School, for confirming details about Little Diomede Island (with thanks to Frank Stanek for helping make the connection); the Museum of the North in Fairbanks, for research on Melvin Olanna, world-renowned Shishmaref artist; the *Nome Nugget*, for sending articles about Libby Riddles winning the Iditarod Dogsled Race in 1985; David Olson, Pilot and Director of Operations with Bering Air, located in Nome, Alaska, who kindly provided useful details about planes, flare pods, and the challenges of flying in and out of Shishmaref and Little Diomede Island in the 1980s; Seattle Public Library for assistance with retrieving articles about the history of schooling for Native people in Alaska and access to their archives; Amy Vinlove, Director of Education at University of Alaska, Fairbanks, for providing information about preparatory coursework given to new teachers heading into bush communities; and Jason Whipple, Publication Specialist II at the Division of Community and Regional Affairs, Department of Commerce, Community, and Economic Development, in Anchorage, for research and permission to use the aerial photo of Sarichef Island.

I am so grateful to Richard ("Rich") Stasenko and his wife, Rachel Walliq Sinnok Stasenko, for their insights and corrections on portions of my manuscript. Rich traveled to Shishmaref as a teacher in the 1970s, where he met and married Rachel, a Shishmaref Native. They are the parents of Suzzuk Huntington, currently the Superintendent of Mt. Edgecumbe High School in Sitka, Alaska.

Suzzuk provided information about Shishmaref dialect. She is actively studying and working toward revitalizing the local language.

There is no way I could have pulled this book together without the incredibly talented and fun-to-work-with women at Allegory Editing: Andrea Karin Nelson, Elena Hartwell (Taylor), and Amy Cecil Holm. Andrea convinced me about the importance of good editing, and agreed to pitch my project to Elena, who showed me how to write with increased clarity and confidence. Through examples, prodding, and her great sense of humor, Elena offered vital guidance about the arc of my story and how to keep the momentum going. Amy was my eagle-eye proofreader who gave terrific advice on word choice and grammar. Her knowledge of the Chicago Manual of Style is simply jaw-dropping.

I am indebted to the teachers throughout my life who, whether they knew it or not, were like lighthouse keepers, illuminating my pathway into the teaching profession: Rita Sobcoviak (John Long Middle School, Grafton, Wisconsin); Marilyn Englander (Vail Mountain School, Colorado), Dr. Dorothy ("Dottie") Engan-Barker (Minnesota State University, Mankato), and Lee Worley (Naropa University, Colorado).

And, to my family, I want to express my gratitude for supporting me when I suddenly pulled up the stakes and flew so far away. Regardless of distance, they supported me through all the months I was in Shishmaref and through all the years it has taken for me to bring this book to fruition …

To my paternal grandmother, Carol Pierce ("Nana") who changed the trajectory of my life with a simple phrase and a bowl of ice cream.

To my mother, Maritta Florkovski Pierce, for her many thoughtful care packages and sense of humor that both fed and emotionally carried me through the ups and downs of living in a remote Alaskan community.

To my father, Gordon R. Pierce, for his unceasing support and polite encouragement to "write that book, will ya?!" Papa (and wife

Peggy) provided valuable insights and feedback on my manuscript, helping me shape the flow and cadence of my stories. An architect and artist in his own right, my dad lovingly provided the artwork found in this book: the maps and the replica of my Sorel boots.

To my sister, Juliet Pierce Kent, an exceptional artist and intuitive writer, who cheered me through the inevitable stumbling of early drafts and then gave valuable feedback on word choice and writing conventions.

To my brother, Todd Winslow Pierce, an environmental entrepreneur, and award-winning photographer, for his companionship and vital work on the images found in this book. Todd scanned my old photos and prepared them beautifully for production.

Finally, I want to thank my life partner and wife, Mary Lanza, who stood by my side every step of the way. She graciously gave me the space and time to disappear for days into my writing and editing, picking up the slack around the house and encouraging me when I felt stuck or overwhelmed. For that, and so much more, Thank you, Mary. You're simply the best, and I love you with all my heart.

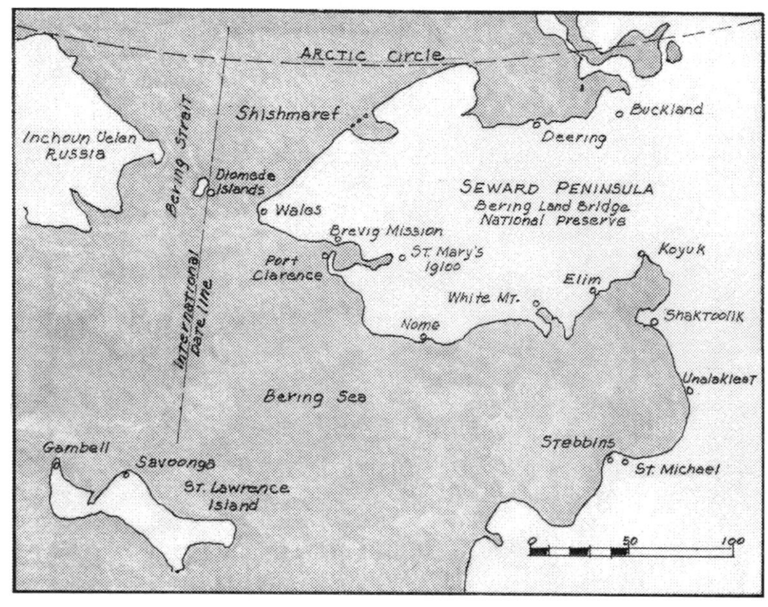

Map 1: Alaska's Seward Peninsula in relation to Russia, International Dateline, and Arctic Circle

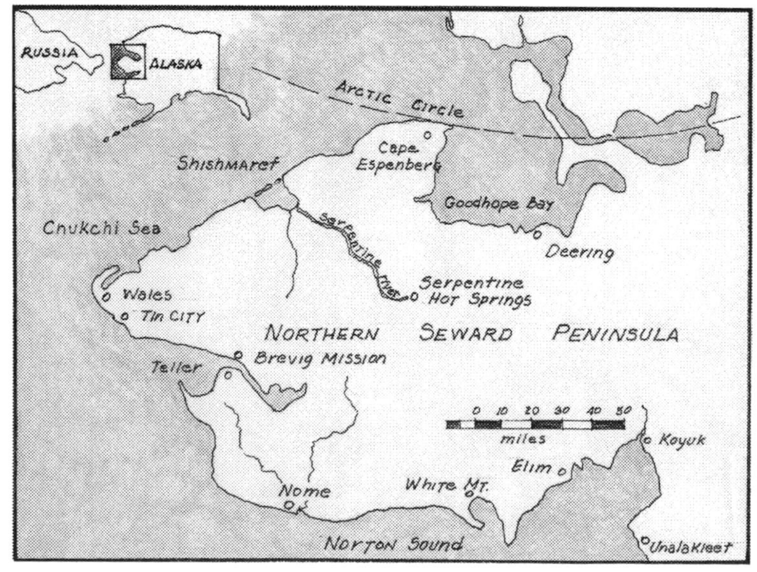

Map 2: Close-up of Seward Peninsula

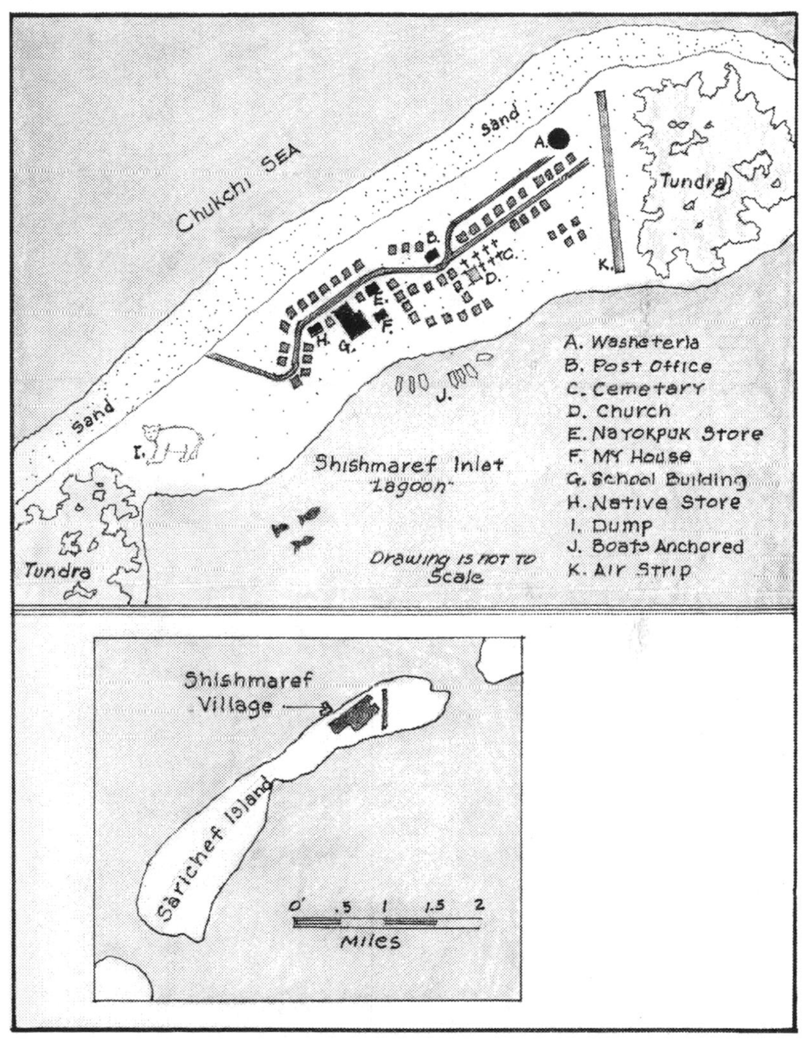

Map 3: Close-up of Shishmaref and Sarichef Island, redrawn from author's original

PART ONE

UP IN THE AIR

ONE

THE SURPRISE

Our small plane shuddered unexpectedly, bumped up in altitude, then dropped again. My stomach was empty but growing increasingly queasy with every creak of the fuselage as the wings dipped this way and that. Far below, glimpses of Arctic tundra came and went as we flew through cloud banks and fog.

Our departure from the Nome Airport was less than an hour ago. Our pilot, Steve, acted like this bucking bronco ride was typical travel. I, on the other hand, didn't know how much longer I'd be able to maintain composure before letting out a primal scream. With every jolt, I instinctively grabbed the back of his seat. It was low, like an old Chevy car seat, and so close that my knees pressed into it. I hadn't been to church in a while but was making up for my absences with some serious turbo-charged prayer. The prayers started innocently, but within half an hour, my well-intentioned pleas for safe passage devolved into a surprising matrix of devotion and rather unladylike swearing between clenched teeth. Lots of *sweet jeee-sus* and *oh-my-god-effing-help-me!*

The precariousness of our situation wasn't aided by the fact that our pilot called his passengers "souls" when confirming our status with the control tower. He said something like, "Flight x-er 9-er ready for takeoff. Three souls on board." The word had the discomforting effect of describing us in a rather ethereal manner, as if we had already perished in a plane wreck. I found it odd that he didn't include himself in his soul count, so I had watched him closely as he taxied us down Nome's runway, turned sharply to face us into the wind, and increased power to the engines until everything, including my head, buzzed like a swarm of angry bees.

The intimacy of the small vessel amazed me—the passengers were squished in with the cargo, nets, and straps. I had never been seated so close to a pilot, within an arm's reach of his dashboard of dials. Steve's hands flashed through a series of well-practiced motions, flipping a switch here, turning a knob there, lining everything up to launch us into the heavy gray sky. I felt everything about the plane inside of my body: the wheels grabbing the tarmac, the shimmy and shake of the aircraft, the disconcerting squeaks as if the plane (and me by extension) had second thoughts about getting off the ground.

Steve was a quintessential Alaskan guy, sporting a heavy-duty Carhartt jacket and steel-toed boots. He looked content but tired, and probably hadn't seen a shower in days. Stubble outlined his strong jaw, and his scraggly brown hair had a deep crease in back, marked by the edges of his battered baseball cap.

The other two passengers, Carl and Ned, were returning to their native village after a short visit to Nome. The men had similar Alaska-Guy attire, complete with worn baseball caps. Carl's had an Alaska flag patch, and Ned's read CAT. I had no idea what that meant but was too shy to ask.

Before boarding, I had stood with the two men on the tarmac, watching Steve as he dipped in and out of the aircraft loading supplies. Judging by their breath, Carl and Ned had enjoyed their own share of dipping, but in a saloon. Carl was especially tipsy and kept leaning into Ned's shoulder, forcing Ned to shrug him upright again.

Then there was me, the third soul and only female on board, a recent college graduate newly minted for the teaching profession. Job prospects for high school English teachers weren't good that year, so I'd settled on bussing tables at a café in Seattle and fussing over the lack of more rewarding work. But one sunny morning in mid-July, I spied the following words in the newspaper: "WANTED. TEACHERS IN ALASKA. Full Time. Call to apply."

I'd nearly choked on my coffee. It hadn't occurred to me to look for a teaching job out of state, and certainly not in Alaska. Would they accept a Washington State teaching certificate?

Alaska was a huge place. A wild place. A place impossibly far away. Yet there was something unmistakably alluring about it. Images of polar bears on ice floats came to mind. Vast stretches of wilderness with untouched, sparkling freshwater streams. Glaciers, forests, and snowcapped Denali, the tallest mountain in North America. The power of those places spoke to me. They whispered in my heart like a lover I didn't know I had.

But the implications of my chosen career terrified me. I had no real experience, and I knew that I didn't know anything. Adding this venture into unknown territory terrified me even more. Yet here I was, hurtling in a tin can with wings to a small village on the north-facing coast of the Seward Peninsula.

When I announced my new job to friends and family, their initial congratulatory sentiments were quickly followed by, "Wait a minute. *Where* are you going?"

Pronouncing Shishmaref was challenging to the untrained tongue, and I grew weary having to spell it out, so I started replying with North of Nome. Most people had heard of Nome—something about a gold rush in the 1800s and an annual dogsled race. I had to admit, that's about all I knew, too. When the job offer came, I said a hasty yes, even though I had no clue where that yes would be taking me. My only comfort was knowing that I'd be teaching high school English, a class called Consumer Math, and one titled Graphic Communications. I understood English, but the other two were a mystery.

To offset my uncertainty about the future, I spent half of my last Saturday in Seattle at an Army Navy Surplus store, purchasing gear that might at least make me look on the outside like I knew what I was doing. It was a profitable afternoon for the store owner as well as for me. I emerged victorious and drenched in sweat from trying on down parkas and pants, flannel shirts and long underwear, and boots called Sorels.

I'd never heard of Sorels, but the clerk—when he saw me raising an eyebrow at the price—assured me they were worth the money.

"Let's have you try this pair first." He held out a petite pair of women's boots.

I shook my head and pointed at a pair of men's. I'd heard that Alaska was a rugged place—one that required sturdy footwear with tank-like treads. The women's looked suitable only for traipsing along paved city park trails.

The men's boots were hot and heavy, but they made me feel like I meant business. Maybe I'd buy a baseball cap when I got to the village.

Prior to boarding, Pilot Steve sized up his souls and cargo and decided to board me first. Row Two, Seat One. Carl plopped himself into Seat Two, buckled up, leaned back, and pulled his cap over his eyes.

Ned took the only other seat available, up front with Steve. He was surprisingly alert and grew more animated when he learned that I was going to be the new English teacher in his village. That information prompted a cascade of opinion about how I should manage students in my classroom. With each piece of advice, Ned leaned back and offered me a Jolly Rancher candy from a large cellophane bag.

"Don't let 'em get off too easy!" Ned yelled over the loud engine noise. "Those kids, you can't spoil 'em. Ya gotta be tough. Real strick!"

He repeated these words multiple times, pointing his finger at me and then poking Steve in the shoulder. "Ain't that right, Steve?"

Steve was only half-listening. He nodded in feigned agreement but shook his head whenever Ned held out his bag. "Wanna candy?"

Half an hour later, Ned's counseling session ended. Thank God. I had run out of responses to assure him that I'd be tough, alright, and had plenty of candy, thank you. I'd already sucked and crunched through two watermelon candies and one green apple, and I had a few more tucked in my coat pocket: orange, grape, and one that was deep red and looked suspiciously like it might set my mouth on fire.

Ned began to doze in and out of consciousness, and Steve focused on navigating the single-prop plane through a continuous mass of thick, white clouds. I peered down and tried to catch a glimpse of ground to get my bearings whenever I wasn't grabbing the seat in front of me and exhaling a prayer, a curse, or both.

I was deep in thought, reflecting on the previous three weeks of preparations and the hundreds of decisions I'd made so far. Quitting my café job, backing out of my apartment lease, and selling my car. I'd had to pack and store or throw away everything but the bare essentials. I was exhausted, and I hadn't even reached my destination.

Steve's voice startled me back to reality.

"Okay, we're making our descent! Be there soon!"

He dropped us under the thick layer of clouds, allowing a sweeping view of the land below. Through streaks of rain on the windows, the village of Shishmaref appeared in the distance.

OH MY GOD. What have you done?

The words fell out clean, and I realized it was me who had uttered them. To myself, to anyone. Maybe to God, if he was still listening. Wanting to be sure, I repeated them louder, taking cover behind the brain-rattling vibration of the plane.

OH. MY. GOD.

There'd been times in my life when I spoke to Yours Truly in third person to distance myself emotionally from a situation that appeared catastrophically larger than I could handle. Third person language helped me examine my predicament from a parallel reality and thus figure out what the heck to do. This time, the question flew out of my reaction to seeing Shishmaref for the first time.

Contrary to what I had been led to believe during my job interview in Seattle, Shishmaref wasn't a village on the coast of the Seward Peninsula. It was an island. *An island on the coast.*

How could I have missed that vital piece of information? Maybe my brain was fried after answering a seemingly endless series of questions like, "Why do you want to be a teacher?" and "Do you like camping?" I followed John, one of the interviewers, to a map of Alaska that had been taped to a wall in the hotel's hallway.

"This is where we're thinking of sending you." He placed a finger down. John's hand was browner than mine, and strong. His silver ring glistened under the ceiling lights. The name was hard to read. I stepped closer and squinted.

"Shishmaref." John looked at me and smiled. In that moment, I was dumbfounded by John's nonchalant pronouncement that they were sending me anywhere. But his words confirmed that I'd been hired. *Hired*! I had made it through two rounds of interviews and had just been handed my first real teaching job. This despite being fresh out of college with no teaching experience save for two rounds of student teaching, which I had nearly failed.

All this time, I'd been thinking that Shishmaref sat along the coast of the Chukchi Sea. Which it did, by the looks of what lay a few thousand feet below. But there was no mistaking the bodies of water surrounding what looked like a very thin and vulnerable stretch of land.

Sarichef Island (looking southeast). Photo Credit: Environmental Services Limited under contract with the Alaska Department of Community and regional Affairs, Division of Community Planning

I thought back to when John pointed on the map. *That was it.* His finger must have covered the large body of water on one side, so the village looked like it was part of the mainland. Now, from the air, I understood. Shishmaref was surrounded by ocean. I'd known I was being sent to a remote village, but I didn't know it was going to be *this* remote.

A new thought popped into my head: *Well, now you've really done it.*

I fought the urge to scream out loud, "No one said it was a frickin' island!" But I didn't want to be the laughingstock of the village, nor the topic of countless retellings Steve would undoubtedly enjoy with future souls. "Can you believe it, there was this one girl—a teacher of all things—who didn't know the village was on an island!"

I felt ridiculous. Embarrassed. But what could I do? I was on a plane that would soon land on that island, the final stop at the end of a series of one-way tickets from Seattle to Juneau, Juneau to Anchorage, Anchorage to Nome, and Nome to Shishmaref. There was no turning back.

A flash of the sun's reflection on the ocean's surface shifted my attention to the impressive landscape below and out to every horizon. *Stop your whining,* my Inner Coach interjected. *Now's your chance to take all this in.*

My eyes traced the contours of the island's unusual shape—long and thin on the north end, indented in the middle, and wider and rounder to the south. A misshapen lima bean. The tundra had a copper sheen to it, with patches of green and black. The mottled landscape stopped abruptly at the edge of a massive body of water on the island's western side: the Chukchi Sea—ominous in its expansiveness and steely presence under the heavy gray sky. Repeating lines of whitecapped waves rolled onto the island's north-facing shore.

We approached from the east, flying high over the large body of water that John's finger had obscured. Several skiffs lay anchored near the shoreline, huddled together and far away from where the sea flowed through narrow channels at the island's north and south ends. It didn't seem far across to the mainland, but who knew how deep that water was? Or how cold? A sense of isolation began creeping in.

I looked out past Carl's slumped figure to distant hills on the mainland, the height of which I couldn't gauge. They were probably taller than they appeared. As my friends in Juneau mentioned during my short stopover, everything in Alaska is bigger than it looks. They recounted a popular joke: Two men are sitting in a bar. One's from Texas, the other from Alaska. The Texan is droning on and on about the size of his property. "I can get in my truck and drive for *hours* without reaching the end of it," he boasts. The Alaskan shrugs and says, "Yeah, I used to have a truck like that."

As we descended, dozens of small, square structures on the island came into view. Most were gray and brown, with a sprinkling of reds, greens, and blues. They were clustered just to the south of the indented middle, with a few in rows along two main streets. Other structures dotted the village's edges in less linear fashion. At the north end, a black road cut a perpendicular line across the island: the airstrip.

Ohmygod, we are so gonna die. The airstrip isn't long enough! We're gonna run out of pavement and whiz into the ocean on the other side.

But we weren't landing. Not yet. With no explanation, Steve continued flying high above the island, heading us over the Chukchi Sea. What the hell was he doing? I kept my eyes on the village as he turned the plane sharply back toward the mainland once more. My rear end pressed down, and my hand instinctively grabbed his seat. I shifted my weight to counter the plane's steep angle and found myself in the surprising position of looking almost straight down to the ground. I spotted drying racks with black things hanging on them and small shacks dotting the landscape. *Outhouses?*

"Letting them know we're here!" Steve's voice called out. He seemed to be enjoying his little tour.

"Yeah!" Ned perked up and turned to me with a toothy grin. "Buzzin' the village!" He laughed and slapped Steve playfully on the arm.

We passed over the rooftops, signaling to villagers below that a plane load of boxes and bags, two tipsy guys, and a brand-spanking-new teacher were arriving shortly. If anyone expected something, this was notice to come and get it.

Steve leveled out and flew us over the largest building on the island. It was mustard yellow and had a brown roof. It looked new. He leaned back and jabbed a finger downward. "The school!"

A wave of relief nudged my earlier sense of doom. School was the one place that made sense to me.

A few people walked on the sandy streets, while several others darted about on four-wheelers. Anticipation and dread filled me, followed by excitement.

But how were we going to land?

Steve flew the plane inland for several minutes and then arced northwest, back toward the island, bringing us full circle. He started a rapid descent over the large lake-like body of water, dropping us steadily closer to its surface and providing an unnerving view of the dark waves. The skiffs came into view. We were flying so low that I could see assorted items laying in them. A brown tarp, a blue cooler. A pair of rubber boots. Something small and silver glistened. *Keys in the ignition?*

Steve brought the plane lower and lower, levelling out at the height of the island's bluff, which couldn't have been more than five feet in elevation. It felt inevitable that the plane's wheels were going to clip that edge and snap off. We'd slide all the way down the pitifully short black landing strip on the plane's belly, sparks flying.

The plane's tail swung left, and the wings flexed. I gripped my tiny armrests and squeezed my eyes shut. But then I felt the plane's tail sway again. I cracked one eye open. If we were going to crash, maybe it was better to see the catastrophe as it unfolded—the struts and wheels shearing off, a cartwheel of wings, and then a tangle of strapped-in bodies littering the ground amidst a scattering of Ned's Jolly Ranchers.

My god, we're landing sideways.

I glanced again at Steve. Cool as a cucumber. One second before the wheels touched down, he deftly turned the steering mechanism and aligned the plane's nose straight down the runway. We landed with a bump on one wheel, then the other. I lurched forward with the sudden impact, nearly smacking into the back of Steve's head. Carl, who had been sleeping through everything, jolted awake.

Steve taxied past a line of unevenly spaced orange traffic cones and continued rolling toward the runway's end as if to say, "See? Plenty of room to land!" Then, he turned the plane around and rolled us back to the middle.

My relief over a safe landing was quickly replaced with a disconcerting awareness of impending exposure. *Where's the terminal? Isn't there an airport? Like a hangar or someplace to get out of the rain?*

But there was no shelter, just a cluster of four-wheelers on the sand and men standing by. The welcoming committee. No airport building, no hangar. No terminal at the terminus.

Steve switched off the engine and removed his headset. "Welcome to Shishmaref!"

The propeller ground to a halt, the silence followed by a strong gust of wind that whistled around the craft.

"Best move fast." Steve nodded toward the sea and a long line of darkening clouds. "A squall's coming."

He hopped out, walked around to Carl's side, and swung open the door. Carl slid out, shook hands with Steve, and ambled toward the four-wheelers, presumably looking for a ride home. As Steve helped Ned deplane, I scooted across Carl's seat and stepped down. My legs wobbled, but my Sorels landed me solidly on the asphalt. It was bumpy and cracked. The wind was sharp and whisked the light brown sand across the ground like a fast-moving snake slithering for cover. Granules lodged themselves into every crevice.

The air smelled of salt and something else. Metal? Blood? The rain blew sideways and stung my face. I turned and pulled up my hood, bemoaning the fact that my parka was shoved deep inside one duffel bag and out of reach.

Steve re-entered the plane and started unhitching cargo and handing boxes out a side door to the waiting men. I caught the words "produce" and "fragile" scrawled on some of them. Canvas bags and my own belongings got rougher treatment. Steve held them out and whoever received them tossed them to one side and onto the ground. Thud! Thud! A thin line of sand quickly formed along their edges.

The men's rapid decisions for distribution prompted me to do the same or risk my belongings getting intermingled and allocated throughout the village. I doubted there was an airline customer service desk to help sort things out. It would be up to me to knock on doors. "Hello, have you seen my blue duffel with an Alaska Airlines tag?"

I corralled my large backpack, duffel bags, and box of books, then looked around. *Now what?*

The sound of an approaching vehicle caught my attention. A pickup truck driving fast down the sandy street, heading for the plane. Two men sat in the cab with a third perched in the truck's bed. It skidded to a halt and the passenger door flung open. A large man stepped out. He was not native to the village, but White, like me. Up to this moment, I had been feeling rather invisible, but the man held my gaze as he approached.

"You one-uv the teachers?" He stopped, politely positioning himself to block the wind and rain. He wore large round glasses that drooped low on his cheeks, and a large drooping mustache. He looked like a human walrus. A friendly walrus.

"Yes!" I yelled over the sound of the four-wheelers starting up and heading back to the village. "I'm Genét. High School. English." The wind flung my words up and away.

"I'm Ken. Principal. Welcome to Shish'mref!"

His voice was deep and welcoming. We shook. My hand disappeared into his, which was surprisingly warm. I relaxed. *The principal is here! He's come to drive me to my new home. Finally! I have a host for this last leg of my journey.*

But Principal Ken's next words imploded those expectations.

"I'm catching this flight out. Goin' to Nome and gettin' the wife n' kid. Back in a few days."

All I said was "oh!"

It felt like a silly response, but that's all I had. The relief I'd just felt with his handshake disappeared. The principal wasn't coming to get me, he was *leaving* me. He was getting on the plane and leaving. But before I could ask the one prominent question that had been floating around in my head since buzzing the village (*Which house is mine?*), Principal Ken lumbered to the plane and hoisted himself into the front passenger seat, likely still warm from Ned. He turned and waved, and I instinctively waved back. I felt like I was saying goodbye to a friend. My friend, the school principal. The man with the answers.

See me in a few days?

I stood next to my pile of belongings, which now looked painfully inadequate despite weeks of shopping, packing, and repacking to make everything fit. The fabric on one duffel bag was soaking through, so I picked it up and did the only thing I could think of: keep moving. That meant trying to hang anything with a strap over my shoulders, grabbing the rest in hand, and starting to walk into town. Someone, somewhere, would tell me where I was going to live, right?

But my idea quickly unraveled. There was no way I'd be able to manage everything on my own. From the air, the houses looked close to the airstrip. Now, they looked a mile away. I was in the middle of the Texas versus Alaska joke, and it wasn't funny.

"Need a lift?" The voice came from one of the men who had dropped off the principal. He patted the top edge of the truck bed.

"Sure!" I looked past them to the village. "But I don't know where I'm going."

"You a teacher?"

My obvious displacement and box of books must have given me away.

"Yes. High School. English." The words sounded fake. *Was I really going to be teaching high school? And here? And why did I feel the need to identify grade level and primary subject area?* This internal query was answered with a large drop of rain that hit me square in the forehead.

"Hop in. We'll take you."

Consoled that the man understood my predicament, I brushed away the drop and moved quickly away from the plane. Depending on the direction Steve turned his craft, I stood a good chance of being covered in a whip of wetness and dirt.

The driver started up the truck as I hoisted my duffel bags and backpack into the bed. I turned to retrieve the books and groceries I'd purchased in Nome between flights, but the man who had offered the ride reached them first.

"Thanks," I said, then cringed as he unceremoniously tossed everything into the back. At least every belonging was accounted for, and I could get out of the icy rain. The thighs of my pants were soaked through.

I moved toward the truck's cab just in time to see the man who'd offered me a ride jumping into the passenger seat and closing the door. His face looked back at me from the side mirror, and he jerked a thumb over one shoulder to signal that my place was in the truck bed. Of course. That's where he'd ridden from the village, so now it was my turn.

A roar from the plane's engines caught my attention, and I turned to witness the departure of the little craft that had carried Carl and Ned and me across the hundred miles of tundra and water from Nome to this sandy, windswept spot on the planet.

It only took a minute for Steve to taxi to the end of the runway and turn north into the wind and toward the sea. The plane's propeller increased to a blur of blades, and the vessel picked up speed and rumbled past. Steve had flipped his cap around, his face fixed on the controls. Principal Ken waved from his shotgun seat and smiled his big walrus smile.

At that moment, I understood what was meant by "a sinking heart." It started with a lump in my throat, followed by a tug in my chest. My heart thump-thumped so hard that I placed my hand over it, sure that if I didn't, it would beat out of my body and fly away on the wind. Then came the strangest feeling that I was sinking into the earth in direct opposition to the plane's rapid launch into the sky. My legs were like logs, my head like cotton candy.

Strong winds from the north lifted the craft almost straight up, as if it had been pulled back with a huge rubber band and released high into the air. The plane's tail shifted left, then right, and then steadied over the ocean waves as Steve turned toward Nome. The sky, the sea, the tarmac, the air—everything grew still. No sound. All that remained was dark gray dampness and cold.

When I flew over the Mendenhall Wetlands from Juneau the day before (*was that just yesterday?*) I had a similar visceral experience of a throat lump and thump-thumping heart, but that rose from anticipation and hope for what lay ahead in my journey as a new teacher. Now, all I felt was dread and abandonment. Everything I had ever known was flying away out of reach.

An involuntary moan escaped my lips. I wanted to yell, "Wait! Come baaack! I changed my mind!" I wanted the world to freeze, to stop completely so I could catch my breath and process what was happening. I wasn't ready for what might come next. All I wanted was a fistful of one-way tickets back home. Or anywhere, for that matter, as long as the ride included a big comfy jet with free wine and tiny bags of peanuts.

But the world didn't freeze. My face, however, was starting to. Rain pelted down harder, almost sideways, hitting me under my upstretched chin.

The men in the truck waited patiently, likely sensing that I needed a moment to process the plane's departure. Perhaps they had witnessed the same behavior from other new teachers. Not wanting to delay them further, I stepped on the back bumper and swung myself into the truck bed, quickly scanning for where to sit. There were puddles of water everywhere.

That's when I saw the leg of a deer laying on top a piece of blue tarp. Or was it caribou? It was as long as my arm. On one end, a ball of white bone peeked out from a mass of light gray fur. At the other end was a black hoof, glistening from the rain. I had never been this close to a wild animal's leg, especially one without the rest of the animal's body. It looked like a front leg. Poor thing. I nudged it with my boot, then lowered to a semi-squat on top of the wheel well. The rain plinked on the cold metal and pitter-pattered as it hit the tarp.

I made eye contact with the driver, who'd been watching my various maneuverings from his rearview mirror. With one hand firmly grasping the rail, I squared my shoulders and gave him a thumbs-up that I was ready to go.

Wherever that was.

TWO

THE FUTURE COMES OUT TO GREET ME

Providence moves in mysterious ways. This time, it threw me headfirst into an Alice-in-Wonderland wormhole, figuring it'd be fun to see me trying to navigate half-squatting, half-sitting in the back of an open pickup truck in freezing Arctic rain, sharing space with my luggage and a reindeer-caribou leg, and completely in the dark about where the guy behind the wheel was taking me.

My muscles tensed as the truck slowly sashayed through waves of sand, then picked up pace on harder patches. The rain was now at my back, allowing me a look around without having to blink water from my eyes.

Near the airstrip, houses were scattered far apart. But now they clustered together as if looking for safety against the elements. The structures were uniform in size and shape—cracker-box structures known as HUD Housing, short for United States Department of Housing and Urban Development. It seemed an odd label, given the traditional definition of "urban," with sidewalks and driveways, shopping malls and 7-11s.

We moved slowly past small wood homes beaten hard by the wind and stained by rain and salt air. Leaning against their sides and inside the porticos were extra pieces of lumber, rebar, and other construction materials. If anything caved in or fell over, there was plenty laying around to fix it.

I grasped the cold, wet metal edge of the truck bed with one hand and tried to keep my hood on with the other. My hands were strong, but one miscalculated bump and I'd be airborne. I thought of kneeling, but the truck bed was hard and unforgiving, and I didn't think I'd be able to hold that pose. If I lost my grip, I'd probably topple onto that leg. Moose? Antelope? My mind continued to flip through a host of four-legged forest creatures who might be roaming this place that, from what I could see, had no forests.

The thin line of a smile crept to the corners of my mouth. This was typical of me, being caught unawares, leaping before I looked. And this time, I had leaped big time, going through weeks of preparation yet somehow missing the memo about living on an island and now, not even knowing where on said island I'd be sleeping at the end of the day.

The back window of the cab slid open. "You doin' alright?"

I nodded, mouth closed, afraid I'd chip a tooth with the truck's bouncing.

Our pace was slow, that of a comfortable jogger. We passed more houses and small shacks. Between them I caught sight of about ten husky dogs chained to tall posts. They yipped and barked at our presence. Some pranced in tight circles; others stared. It was a shocking sight for me, so many dogs tethered to posts. But now was not the time to process that. The truck slowed, and I spied a sign: SPEED LIMIT 15. Good to know.

The truck turned down a slight hill, out of the wind and alongside the large building Pilot Steve had identified as the school. Years of traffic had formed a gully in the sand. It drifted up on either side, resting against rusted oil drums, snow machine carcasses, and a couple shipping containers that looked like they had been dropped from the air and left where they landed.

We slowed at one corner of the school, took a hard left, and jerked to a stop in front of a lime-green one-story box-of-a-house with wood siding. The man who'd relegated me to "cargo class" got out and unhinged the tailgate. I handed my bags to him, wincing each time he dropped one onto the wet sand, then hopped down myself. Our eyes met—mine blue, his onyx. He nodded without a word, pulled his collar against the rain, and re-entered the cab. The driver put the truck in gear and continued a short distance, then disappeared around a corner.

For the first time in several days, I was alone. I stood for a moment in the street, studying the structure. *Was this it? Home?*

The greenish paint was peeling, giving the building a gray hue. Gray sky reflected in a small rectangular window next to the door. Nailed to the window frame was a small thermometer, angled so the occupant could check the temperature before venturing outside. Judging by the current chill in what was now mid-August, the mercury likely vacillated between Cold to Freezing to "I'd go back inside if I were you."

The house looked weary, like it had been sitting in the same spot under protest, enduring decades of harsh weather and tenant neglect. I suddenly remembered one sentence in my teacher contract, something about housing being provided at nominal cost. In other words, rent would be deducted from my paycheck. How much, I didn't know.

I moved my belongings out of the middle of the street and approached the wooden steps. The bottom one was buried in sand. A small porch with cracked and uneven boards rested against the siding.

And then I saw another one.

Another disembodied leg.

On the porch.

You have got to be kidding me. *What's with these animal legs?*

Moose leg, deer leg, whatever leg. It looked just like the one in the truck bed. Maybe the grumpy luggage handler thought it'd be funny to toss the leg when my back was turned? I poked it with my boot to the sand below. I'd deal with it later. Then I reached for the doorknob.

That's when I saw the padlock.

A big 'ol industrial strength padlock on the front door.

Principal Ken's words came back to me. "I'm headin' to Nome. Back in a few days."

The air felt colder. The sky darker. Was this the right house? Did my driver assume I had a key? Was a key mailed to me in Seattle, but I missed it? Did Principal Ken have the key?

These questions flew around in my head like a swarm of irritated gnats. A discomforting resentment toward my school leader rose in my throat and mixed with the scent of sea. Pungent, sharp with salt and sand, and intermingled with what I could only assume was the smell of decaying things. Of rotten fish and musky animal hides.

This was absurd. Maybe there was a back door. I walked around one corner but found only one small window set high and, curiously, covered with foil.

I peeked along the backside of the structure. No door. Large metal drums blocked further exploration, so I retraced my steps and studied the portable across the street. It was identical—same size, shape, and color. Maybe I was supposed to live there? My taxi guys didn't exactly point to one or the other. Maybe I had misunderstood. I rescued my box of books from the wet ground and carried it with me twenty paces. Another sandy porch, another padlocked door.

Maybe I should try the school? Someone might be in there who would know the whereabouts of a key. I walked across the sandy lane and up the metal-grated stairs of the school, box of books under one arm like a salesperson peddling wares.

One pull of the handle told me that the school was locked. I turned and looked across the street at the deer leg portable. With all the uncertainty swirling in my head at this moment, one thing was sure: my commute to work was going to be short.

I marched back down. This house *must* be it. I stared at the padlock. Bolt cutters weren't on the school district's packing list, but I had a Swiss Army knife. It had been my constant companion since high school, and I made special mention of it during the second interview after being prompted, "Tell us more about your love of camping."

At the time, I thought the committee was truly interested in my adventures.

"Sure! I love camping! I'm a mountain girl. I've done day hikes and overnights. Colorado, Washington, Oregon. I always keep my Swiss Army knife handy."

I'd meant the latter as a joke, not realizing the committee was attempting to ferret out a more accurate truth about who I was. Specifically: Is this person sitting before us able to handle getting dropped on an island where she …

1) doesn't know a soul
2) has to find her teacher housing without a map
3) must negotiate not one, but *two* deer-or-whatever legs and
4) figure out how to get past the padlock without having a key?

Check, check, checkity-check.

I wondered if the villagers were hiding in their homes right now, peeking out to see how the blond newbie was managing these challenges. "If she figures all this out, she'll be fine."

The lock stumped me. Maybe I could pick it. How hard could it be? Burglars on TV opened locks in a jiffy, so why not me? I dug out my Swiss Army knife and tried the small blade, but it didn't fit. Was there something smaller? I pulled out the tiny plastic toothpick. No, that would just snap off in the mechanism.

I stood back and examined the lock in its entirety.

Maybe I should just unscrew the whole damn thing from the side of the house.

The men had dropped me off without a second glance, and Principal Ken left me in the lurch. I might be accused of damaging school property, but so what? They owed me.

I opened the Phillips screwdriver. It fit beautifully.

A few anxious and hard, squeaky turns later, the entire padlock mechanism was in my hand. All the while, I prayed no one would pass by. But the streets were quiet. The doorknob turned and I let myself in.

PART TWO

BOOTS ON THE GROUND

THREE

HOME

Letting myself in meant shoving the door and stomping on a sand dune inside the entryway. With each stomp, I fell more in love with my boots. Definitely worth the price.

The house was dark, and the air was cold and stale. But it was dry. I brought my things inside and flipped a light switch. A pale ceiling light flickered to life, revealing a small kitchen with brown cupboards, a gray Formica counter, a sink and stove, and a refrigerator. Gold metal stripping separated the kitchen's gray-brown linoleum from the brown carpet in the living and dining area, which held a maroon Formica-topped table and four chairs, diner-style with metal frames and brown plastic seats. There was also a brown plaid couch and coffee table. A small TV perched high on a shelf.

I ventured further, looking for signs that I was indeed in an unoccupied unit. It felt silly; the place was padlocked. But I still called out, "Hello?"

No answer.

The interior looked tired. And it replicated the brown furniture and carpet of my apartment in Seattle with stunning accuracy. Even the poster of Mt. Rainier was identical. Maybe there'd been a sale.

The only difference was the sand. The wind had blown miniature alluvial fans of the stuff through a gap at the base of the front door and across the linoleum flooring, totally unchecked. Each step I took was accompanied by a crunch. My parents had raised me to remove outer footwear upon entering a dwelling, but even they would forgive me in this circumstance.

I nudged the thermostat from fifty degrees Fahrenheit to sixty. I would have gone further but was afraid of asking too much of the heater and blowing the place up.

The bathroom had a small sink and cabinet, a bathtub, and a toilet. But it was a toilet unlike any I'd seen. There was a toilet seat, but instead of being attached to a porcelain bowl, it sat on top of a cone-shaped metal can that was bolted to the floor.

Another stretch of linoleum led into two bedrooms at the end of the hallway. Both had a bare mattress with a wooden frame and a wood dresser with an attached mirror. I caught my reflection and paused, taken aback by the bags under my eyes and the state of my clothing. *I look as tired as this place.*

I spent a moment in each bedroom, closing my eyes to sense their energy. Whichever room I chose was going to be my sanctuary—likely the only space where I'd have privacy and inner security in this very different world.

The room on the right felt the best, but that foil on the window had to go. What the heck? The previous occupants must have missed "How to Properly Decorate a Bedroom Day" in Home Economics class. It only took a minute to reach up and pull off the thin silver covering. I crunched the foil and tucked it in a pocket.

I was still unsure if this dwelling was intended to be occupied by me, but I could settle in, if only for the night. I returned to the front room, brushed the sand from my belongings, and carried them to the bedroom I'd staked out, resisting the urge to unpack in case someone showed up and said, "Oops! There's been a mistake. This building's condemned! There's another place down the street for you."

But I couldn't wait for that vision to become a reality. If this was going to be my new home, I needed to make it more habitable. There was no other choice. My German ancestry, strong Protestant work ethic, and being born under the astrological sign of Virgo meant I had a near obsession for organizing and cleaning spaces. It was becoming rapidly clear that living here was going to be a constant challenge.

First task—the floors.

I found a broom in the entryway. Its straw bristles were stiff, but they gradually flexed as I worked through the kitchen. The living room carpet posed a new challenge. No vacuum on the premises. The broom would have to do.

Slowly and methodically, I worked a thin line of sand from the far end of the living room to the linoleum in the kitchen, like I was raking leaves on a brown shag lawn. It was a tedious task, but twenty minutes later, I was flicking the three-inch pile over the threshold and onto the porch, then over the edge to cover the deer-or-whatever leg that had greeted me. Mission accomplished.

The wind had already covered my earlier footprints with a fresh layer of sand. No doubt I'd be repeating this exercise, and often. Plugging the gap under the door would help. Note to self: Get weather stripping.

I set the broom against the wall and noticed the water heater, quiet witness to my efforts. Strange place for that, an unprotected corner in a house quite absent of insulation. But there must be a reason. People had been living here for a very long time, and they'd figured out what worked. I would have to do the same.

My sweeping workout warmed me up. I took off my coat. But why did my legs feel cold? I nudged the thermostat toward seventy and searched for heat registers to make sure nothing was blocking them. I walked throughout the house, my eyes trailing the sideboards. I even moved the couch. Nothing.

That's when I realized the top hairs of my head always prickled when I walked through a certain part of the living room. I looked up and spotted the heat register. What the heck? Who put heat registers in the ceiling? I grabbed a chair for a closer look. Sure enough, a stream of warm air was coming through the slats. I opened them wide, reveling for a moment in the warmth, then set my sights on the kitchen.

It was difficult to wedge the broom into corners; I'd have to make peace with that. The countertops, stove, and top of the fridge were layered with grime and sticky to the touch. I opened the refrigerator. It was empty, save for a rock-hard box of baking soda. At least it worked, and the former tenants had cared enough not to leave behind a carton of milk.

There was a box of Wheaties in one cupboard. It had been opened, but the shelf-life was still active. I popped a flake of cereal in my mouth. It was stale but might soften with milk. I set it aside and reached for the Wheat Thins. Expired in May. A second cupboard held a collection of bone white Corning Ware dinner plates with their signature blue flower design, an open bag of Gold Medal flour, and a handful of sugar packets.

And on it went. Crackers, rice, spaghetti noodles, spices, Lipton tea, cocoa powder—all abandoned, as if some island Bigfoot creature had scared my predecessors and forced them to flee the scene. The only way to make sense of it all was to separate everything into two piles: Maybe and Dead.

I continued my inventory with the lower cabinets and drawers, finding an equally mismatched jumble of silverware and pots and pans. The kitchen counter now looked like a sad garage sale.

I tossed the larger Dead pile into a trash can in the corner and looked around for a cloth to wipe the shelves before setting the Maybe items back in. I was about to sacrifice my one washcloth when I spotted a dehydrated sponge laying behind the faucet. The tap sputtered and ran rusty brown for a moment, then yellow. Then clear.

Gradually, the water warmed. I shifted my weight and heard a sloshing sound, then looked down to see a stream of water emerging from under the cupboard doors at my feet. *I swear, I am never taking off these boots.*

I turned off the tap and opened the door for inspection. *What the …* My mouth fell open. There was no plumbing. No pipe to carry the water from the faucet, down and away and outside. Instead of a normal curved fitting, I was staring at a piece of PVC piping that was open on one end, not connected to anything. A stub.

That's when I found the plastic pail sitting off-center of that stub. Whoever had used it last forgot to place the pail correctly. All the water I'd just run missed it entirely. And, by the looks of the buckled wood down here, they'd missed it plenty, too.

I repositioned the pail and laid eyes on a bottle of Formula 409 cleaner. *Hallelujah.* Formula 409 was all the rage in the 1960s and still popular decades later. Women, expected to do the majority of house cleaning, wanted multipurpose cleaning solutions to make their jobs easier and more efficient. So, scientists (mostly men who wanted to keep that arrangement) worked hard and fast, ultimately deriving a solution that made it possible to clean an entire house with squirts of blue liquid from just one product. They called it Formula 409, because those crafty guys finally succeeded on their 409th try. In this moment, I genuinely appreciated their tenacity.

I shifted to kneeling, sprayed 409 on the floor, and gave it a wipe. A lighter shade of linoleum instantly emerged. *Oh god, now I have to clean the entire floor so it's one color.* I surveyed the room and sighed. *Sure hope this is where I'm supposed to live.*

My stomach growled. Time for a break. Maybe a peanut butter and jelly sandwich. And coffee. Note to self, buy more dinner stuff.

Was the tap water safe to drink? If not, there'd be a warning sign, right?

There was no sign. Given the sparseness of information about living conditions so far, I decided to boil the heck out of it. Within minutes, I had a lovely saucepan of roiling water, scalding enough to kill any germs that might be lurking therein. Strangely, there were no mugs, which meant sipping my first cup of coffee from a bowl. Note to self, buy mugs. And a teapot.

Then I had to go. Number One and Number Two. It had been hours since I arrived in the village, and with all the cleaning, I hadn't stopped to think about how my body was doing.

I walked down the hall to the bathroom and looked more closely at the metal cone-shaped can. The toilet seat and lid confirmed that this was the place to do one's business. There was a pipe running from the back of the cone can to the ceiling. A vent? But there was no plumbing—no water, no handle for flushing. Of course there wasn't. There was no drainage pipe in the kitchen. Why would there be a toilet that flushes?

I was really starting to hate the way I had freely offered up my delight of camping during those interviews. Maybe there was a flush toilet in the school building. I could try another door to gain access, but what if they had the same contraptions over there?

"Well, crap. The hell with it. I'll deal with however this works later."

I couldn't hold it any longer. The sound of my emptying bowels echoed so loudly into the metal can, I was sure any neighbors could hear. "There's that new teacher, crapping in her can."

Thankfully, there was a roll of toilet paper within reach. I hadn't even thought to bring my own TP. And how the heck was I going to deal with my mess? Note to self.

My task complete, I double-checked for a pail underneath the bathroom sink. It was small but would suffice. I ran the water in a slight stream and scrubbed my hands with an old bar of soap. It was cracked and dirty, but it was soap. The water was icy at first, but then it ran warm. I grinned, relieved in more ways than one.

FOUR

FOILED

Shishmaref: Day One.
Time: Almost midnight. Still light outside.
Boots: Still laced up.

In August, Shishmaref gets about eighteen hours of daylight, almost two days packed into one. The slight tilt of the earth would keep the village just shy of perpetual brightness, offering plenty of time to run around outside.

I became acutely aware of this phenomenon as I lay in my sleeping bag and listened to the wind, which mimicked the sound of jets high overhead. The constant stream of imaginary aircraft was accompanied by screams and laughter of children running by my bedroom window like they'd just been released for recess. Up to now, I'd been so obsessed with cleaning that I hadn't paid any attention to sounds outside. Where did all the children come from?

My mind and body ached for sleep after what had been a seemingly endless day of travel and then cleaning my maybe-home. During my own childhood, bedtime came early, even in summer. Every now and then, however, my parents allowed my brother and me to stay up past dark so we could run around the yard and play catch and release with fireflies. Mom gave us mason jars and Dad punched holes in the lids so we wouldn't suffocate the tiny creatures after trapping them and studying their green-yellow lights up close. But soon, always too soon, it was time to let the last firefly go, come in and wash up, and go to bed.

Then it dawned on me. The foil on the window. It wasn't for privacy, but rather to feign darkness so a person could sleep during the Arctic summer months. The panes were too high for anyone to see inside. I couldn't see anything from the inside, either, except for sky. It was just like my basement apartment in Seattle. I swear, those interviewers must have followed me home, looked at my place, and thought, "Yup, she'll fit in just fine. Brown flooring, brown couch, wood paneling, high windows." Checkity-check and checkmate.

I unzipped myself from my warm cocoon, slid my bare feet into my boots, and clomped to the kitchen. Was there any foil, save for the piece I'd ripped off the window? I searched the drawers and cupboards, then turned my attention to the trash can of Dead items. *Was there trash collection here? If so, which days? If not …*

The memory of the deer-or-whatever leg returned, and I wondered if I should dig it up and throw it farther from the house. On the other hand, if there was a dog loose somewhere, he'd think it was a stick and bring it back.

I picked through until I found the tightly wadded piece of foil. When I'd pulled it from the window, I wasn't able to resist a bit of elementary play, and had scrunched it into a compact ball that I launched toward the trash can from different parts of the kitchen and living room, banking it off the walls and throwing it from behind my back until it finally landed in the bucket. Now I bemoaned that folly.

I stood at the kitchen counter and, with surgical precision, methodically picked apart each crease, trying not to tear it. Fifteen minutes later, I had smoothed out a piece large enough to make out the blurry edges of my own reflection.

Now I needed tape.

Tape was not on the list of required supplies. My note to self was getting longer: weather stripping, dustpan, teapot, mugs, toilet paper, sponge, dinner stuff, foil. And now, tape.

I returned to the bedroom and pawed through my belongings. *Band-Aids!* I had slipped a few into my toiletry bag. They might work. I carried a dining room chair to the bedroom and climbed up just as two young girls passed by on the street below. They stopped upon seeing movement from the window. I stared at them, surprised by the sudden attention and then embarrassed with getting caught.

They giggled and clamped their hands over their mouths. I quickly covered the window. Six Band-Aids later (note to self) I accomplished my task of making the room acceptably darker and snuggled back into my sleeping bag.

I would learn a week later that, once school started, curfew for all the kiddos was ten o'clock. There wouldn't be much enforcement of that rule, however, and children of all ages would be out on the streets, and outside my bedroom window, until well after midnight. Clocks might have been masterpieces of human ingenuity, but they were a contrived inconvenience brought to the Arctic by well-intentioned Westerners. Probably Germans. But the Native community knew all too well that daylight would steadily diminish in the weeks to come, and temperatures would dip to dangerous levels. For now, it was best to let the children run around outside and catch their own fireflies.

The children's cheery voices faded away, and I drifted to sleep.

FIVE

FACILITIES

The next day, after coffee, a peanut butter sandwich, and a couple more trips to the strange metal cone-can toilet, I returned to the school. If word was out that the new English teacher was in town, maybe someone had unlocked the doors.

I pulled on the handle and gasped with delight when it opened. The entryway was cold, and the air smelled of sand and old carpet. There were no lights on, save for the glimmer of a green EXIT sign at the far end of the hallway—just enough to illuminate my inaugural tour.

I flipped one light switch and then another, but nothing happened. My footsteps boomed on the worn carpet, signaling a large crawl space underneath. I tried stepping lightly to minimize the sound—not an easy thing to do in my man-boots. I felt edgy in this strange place, all alone with no one around, and not knowing if it was okay for me to be in the building. Perhaps my presence would be considered an affront to the community. Village customs were a mystery, and I didn't want to start the school year as a social outcast—the Goldilocks Teacher who broke into someone's place and set up home, then traipsed through the school uninvited.

I moved in the semi-darkness from one door to the next. They were all locked. I pressed my nose against each window and cupped my hands at the sides of my eyes. Most rooms had a window on the far wall, allowing just enough daylight to see outlines of typical classroom furniture. Student desks, bookshelves, file cabinets, a table or two.

Which of these rooms will be mine?

The thought made my heart flutter. After years of college, the horrible months of student teaching, the blizzard of tasks I dogged through when uprooting my life in Seattle, followed by days of travel and yesterday's Formula 409 flurry, I had finally made it.

I moved along and stopped in front of a large glass trophy case. Even in semi-darkness, the story of Shishmaref's youth was clear. They had winning basketball teams, both boys and girls. On the shelves were silver and gold trophies, medallions, certificates of achievement, and framed black and white photos of teams standing proudly in their uniforms. Some smiled; others looked deadly serious.

Farther down was a small library and a staff room. At the end of the hall was a swinging door. I pushed through, into a small industrial kitchen. The shelves were bare. Pots and long-handled kitchen utensils hung from hooks. Sand crunched under my feet, making me smirk. Even here.

I went through a set of doors labeled GYM. The size of the space surprised me. The building didn't look that big from the outside. The first thing to catch my gaze was a huge mural on the far wall, depicting slabs of Arctic ice jutting from the sea and polar bears frolicking in the snow. One pair played with a large snowball. Another pair stood on their hind legs, snouts up as if playing with the moon overhead. Northern lights cascaded down in a magical screen of green and blue. Even in the dim lighting, it was a mesmerizing display.

Aside from that stunning piece of artwork, the gym was typical, with shiny lacquered flooring and basketball hoops hung high on both sides. Collapsible bleachers lined one wall and musty gym-mat smell lingered in the air. The space felt cavernous, making me step quietly and carefully to avoid leaving black boot marks and antagonizing the janitor.

I spotted a door marked GIRLS. *Hallelujah.* Pushing in, I was greeted by a row of metal lockers and half a dozen bathroom stalls and as many sinks.

Oh god please. I held my breath as I pushed a stall door inward. Sure enough. A toilet. I stepped forward and pushed down the handle.

Oh my god—it flushes. Life suddenly got a lot less complicated. Before leaving the building, I was going to use this toilet whether I had to go or not. Clearly, I had to cease and desist using the cone-can toilet in my maybe-home. Strangely, there didn't seem to be any horrible smell, probably on account of the vent leading up through the ceiling and outside. Still, I had a sneaking suspicion that I was in serious violation of village code for waste removal, and my continued use was going to make it harder to clean out. The canister was bolted to the floor, so I couldn't drag it outside even if I wanted to and—what? Dump my crap in the sand? No, I was going to have to reach in there and mop things up. Which meant I needed more Formula 409 (note to self).

Even though no one else knew what I had done, I was embarrassed, mortified, and grossed out with this dilemma of my own making. But there was no one around to ask for instructions. No one to kindly show me how to gracefully work the contraption. And what would I say? "Hello! I'm new here. Can you come over and tell me how to use this thing?"

I approached a sink and turned a knob. Water sputtered out, brown at first, then gray, then clear. I held a palm under the stream and felt a surge of confidence as it gradually warmed.

My eye caught another door marked SHOWERS.

Wow, this little field trip was getting better by the minute. A shower would feel good. After my workout of cleaning the house yesterday and all the sand lodged in my hair and clothes, I knew I must need a wash but, curiously, I didn't feel dirty. Perhaps my level of acceptance for proper hygiene had shifted to match this new reality. Still, a lather and rinse before bed would be nice. There was a tub in my maybe-home bathroom, but I hadn't wanted to turn on the faucet for fear of how the water might drain—or not. Besides, there were no signs of it having been used; the bottom was grimy and there was no shower curtain.

The door to the showers was locked.

You have got to be kidding me.

I retraced my steps to the gym. If there was a door marked girls, there must be one for boys, right? Sure enough. I pushed through the BOYS door and found a similar arrangement of toilets and sinks, along with a row of urinals. And a door marked SHOWERS.

It opened to a large room with eight shower heads spaced several feet apart. This was promising, but there was no privacy. Did the girls' showers have separate stalls?

My initial exuberance dimmed. I was not a fan of communal showers. My first experience was in middle school, where my classmates casually undressed and traipsed around, wrapped in the school's little white gym towels. I had seen plenty of girl bodies by then, having taken swimming lessons at the local pool, but I was overly self-conscious during that stage of my life. Puberty was unpredictable, mysterious, and terrifying. I always hurried through shower protocol by quickly walking (no running allowed!) into the large, tiled room, getting a spray of water on my head, and retreating as fast as possible.

One day, I'd neglected to pee ahead of time, and my body betrayed me. I lost control and watched in horror as yellow mingled with shower water and headed down the drain. Before I was even out of the locker room, I had earned the nickname "pee pants," even though I wasn't wearing any at the time.

That entire mortifying scene came rushing back as I stood in the boys' shower room. Minutes ago, the space was a glistening gem, but now it was a symbol of my youthful angst. There was no lock on this door, so anyone could walk in unannounced. Maybe I would come early in the morning and bring a very large towel. And pee first.

Wait a minute. Did the shower work? I stepped to one side and turned the knob. It sputtered, but a spray came out, and that was enough. Before leaving, I returned to the girls' locker room, used the facilities, and flushed with satisfaction.

It was time for a tour of the village.

SIX

WALKABOUT

This was going to be my first stroll through Shishmaref, my first trek through uncharted territory. I wanted to walk with an open mind but hadn't even reached the top of the street before projecting expectations about what I might find. What kinds of stores were here? Did they have a coffee shop? Maybe a town square?

Main Street

I knew nothing about Native Alaskan people and how they chose to congregate. But from what I'd seen so far, it was probably too windy and cold to sit on a park bench. And there certainly wasn't going to be any fountain.

It struck me that I had to drop those misplaced notions and accept the fact that I'd be learning about Shishmaref one step at a time. I was sure to miscalculate things and make mistakes. Hadn't I already? But I hoped to understand a little about the people here and what they valued. The coming months would teach me about how things worked, and I'd find my place. I'd find out how I might fit in.

For now, outside and exposed and far from everything familiar, I felt dazed and dull. My boots marched me along the sandy street, but my body floated in a peculiar mix of here, not here. Somewhere in the middle was a creeping awareness that, starting today, this place was going to change me. I could feel the subtle tug of something shifting inside. It rode the wind and merged with the sand in snakelike traces low across the ground. And it dropped from the heavy layers of gray and white clouds. There was no protection, no barrier, no time, no hurry. But whatever It was, It was insistent. It was intimate. And It was coming for me.

This somewhat disorienting vortex was eased by the feel of my Swiss Army knife in my pants pocket. My fingers instinctively curled around the smooth red casing that had warmed from body heat. Its heaviness reassured me.

A gust of wind grabbed at my breath and snapped me to attention. The muscle memory of yesterday's roller coaster plane ride returned. I stomped my boots lightly to ground myself once more. I had no knowledge of the history of this place but felt a mysterious connection to the past—like I was joining a long line of people who had walked here, perhaps for centuries.

I kept on and started to hum. *The bear went over the mountain. The bear went over the mountain. The bear went over the mountain, to see what she could see.*

There wasn't a mountain in sight, but the silly song helped me orient my inside world to this outside world and gave me confidence to keep going. All I needed for today was to find the grocery store. Maybe the post office. The store would provide sustenance. The post office, a lifeline to my former life. I had no cash with me but could at least run reconnaissance and return later with my note to self list.

At the crest of the little hill, I spotted a street sign: MAIN STREET. Close by was a second sign, SEAVIEW LN. I trudged several yards farther, and true to its name, Seaview Lane opened to a breathtaking expanse of the Chukchi sea. It was gray-blue, reflecting an equally gray-blue sky. The horizon blended sea and sky together, obscuring any sense of distance. I kept humming … *to see what she could see.*

There was no sound, only gentle waves curling into shore. This surprised me. I'd expected to hear pounding surf. I walked a bit closer and then the pounding came—not as waves, but as wind. This grand view had a price. With no structures to block it, the wind hit my chest hard. Spray stung my cheeks. The scents of salt, sand, and metal flew through the air and up my nose. The wind was so harsh it made my nostrils flare and my eyes water. Note to self: get ski goggles and a scarf.

North-facing beach with supplies, drying racks, and seawall under construction.

The sand was rock hard in some places and soft in others. A chain of cement blocks stretched down the sandy slope to the water's edge. They were threaded together with steel cables, like large beads forming a blanket of heaviness and protection. A seawall? It didn't stretch very far.

I'd grabbed my camera on the way out the door, expecting to photograph first impressions, but everything seemed jumbled to me; I couldn't find a focal point. I was tempted to drop down to the beach, but it was uncomfortably windy, so I backtracked to Main Street and turned north.

Dozens of modest structures and telephone poles lined the sandy road all the way down to the airstrip where, less than twenty-four hours before, I'd set foot on the island. Less than a day since Principal Ken greeted me and then flew away. All that seemed like a week ago.

I didn't know what to expect about Shishmaref housing, but the dwellings seemed to be constructed only with plywood and looked sorely inadequate for such a harsh environment.

Bright blue and silver oil drums, some standing and some laying on their sides, were scattered between the houses. There were machine parts, wooden sleds, four-wheelers, and an assortment of sheets of plywood and other construction materials piled or leaning. The street looked like a Department of Transportation open house, where people could scavenge whatever they needed for home repair.

I'd seen only a handful of people—the men at the airstrip, Principal Ken for all of two minutes, my truck-taxi guys, and the girls outside my window at midnight. I was on the main drag through town, but it was eerily quiet. No one anywhere. I felt exposed and insecure without a chaperone or tour guide identifying points of interest and making introductions. I was still hoping for a coffee shop, but given the water situation and no indication of any downtown area, that dream of normalcy was quickly fading.

At some point, I'd swapped out "The bear went over the mountain" for the song sung by Julie Andrews in *The Sound of*

Music: "I have confidence in sunshine, I have confidence in rain ..." My thoughts ricocheted like the ball in a pinball machine. *How did I end up here? Where is everybody? What will it be like to teach? How many students are there? What's for dinner?*

These questions (and my humming) came to an abrupt halt when four young girls appeared suddenly from around the corner of one house. They were about ten or eleven years old. Their hair was straight and black, shimmering even without the sun. The girls wore jeans and t-shirts. One of them had on a pink sweatshirt with streaks of dirt, and a rather large drip of snot came from her nose. She made no move to clear it.

"You a teacher?"

This question came from the tallest girl as she twisted a long blade of grass through her fingers, sliding it over and around and starting again.

My heart did a little belly flop. The reality of actually being a teacher seemed incredibly remote—as remote as this village from the nearest McDonald's. I nodded.

"Yep."

"What you teach?"

"High school. English. Math."

The girls scrunched their faces and then burst out laughing.

"Oh, too bad!" said another. "We want you to be *our* teacher!"

I was about to ask them what grades they were in when the drippy-nosed child pointed at my feet.

"Like your shoe pacs."

"My what?"

She squatted and tapped my boots.

"Shoe pacs," she repeated. "You know. Shoe!" She stood and stomped with one foot. "Pac!" She stomped again with such force that the snot released from her nose. She tipped her head forward just in time for it to drop cleanly onto the sand.

The girls giggled and covered their mouths, playfully shoved each other, and moved around me as if I were a boulder in a stream.

They skipped down the street, shouting and flapping their arms like baby birds. This friendly encounter boosted my spirits. Maybe I should have chosen an elementary teaching certificate. I could have been their teacher, one with a plus-size box of Kleenex.

Another gust of sea air convinced me to fasten the button under my chin. I was amazed the girls didn't wear coats or hats. I had on two layers of flannel, a down vest, corduroy Levi's and my trusty Sorels. On my next walkabout, I might add my wool hat, which was bright red and yellow. You could see me coming for miles.

I readjusted my camera strap and nudged it behind one arm. Not yet knowing Shishmaref's cultural nuances, I felt self-conscious taking photos. I didn't want to be known as the disrespectful tourist, a voyeur. For now, it seemed wise to simply take in my surroundings without focusing on details. The simple structures and utilitarian objects strewn about would tell me their story over time and in their own way.

Random thoughts began again. Did everyone have the same water and toilet situation? How did the grass get here? How did oil drums get delivered? And telephone poles? I pictured Pilot Steve strapping them to the top of his plane.

A man appeared far down the street, heading toward me. But then he turned and disappeared. I would have liked to meet another adult yet was scared to do so. A stranger in a strange land.

Ten paces farther, there it was. A prominent structure painted rust-brown and a sign that read NAYOKPUK GENERAL STORE. Mission accomplished. I stepped into a weather-beaten portico, turned the doorknob, and went in. A loud jangle of bells announced my arrival, followed by a man's voice.

"Halloo!"

With mounds of merchandise obstructing my view, I stepped around one shelf and laid eyes on the voice's owner, dressed in a blue- and black-checkered flannel shirt and wearing a baseball cap with BERING AIR stitched above the bill A slew of paperwork was spread out on the counter in front of him.

"Welcome! You must be a teacher!"

"Yeah," I smiled back. "High school. English. Math." We shook hands.

"Pleased to meet you …" He waited for me to finish.

"Oh, sorry. My name is Genét."

"Genét," the man repeated. "Well, I'm Walter. Nayokpuk. Store owner." His Ks came from deep in his throat, seemingly stuck for a moment, then released.

"Have a look around. Just got a shipment of apples." He pointed to a box. "Teachers love apples!"

"Thanks. But I left my list at home. Come to think of it, I won't have any cash until my first paycheck, and I don't know when that'll be. Do you take post-dated checks?

"No cash, no problem. You can have store credit. Pay later. I know you're good for it." He winked. "B'sides, where could you run?"

Relieved of financial pressure, I began to walk methodically up and down the aisles, hoping to spy things from my note-to-self list. Walter busied himself with his papers, leaving me to explore.

My insides jittered from my self-imposed, neurotic pace of the past few days. Walter's store was quiet. No sound of wind, no grocery store music. My motor of emotions shifted down a few gears. In my former life, my modus operandi was to speed through the store and snatch what I needed, hoping not to bump into anyone I knew and be forced to engage in meaningless conversation. I didn't go to the store to talk. I preferred "in and out" in under fifteen minutes.

In Shishmaref, however, it seemed important to visit for a while, which might come easily. There was no rationale as far as I could tell for how Walter arranged things. That meant I'd be constantly asking if an item was in stock.

After several minutes of meandering, I'd located foil, a sponge, and scotch tape, along with items not on my list: a stick of butter, a canister of instant oatmeal, and a box of Carnation Breakfast Bars. If Walter had shopping baskets, they were nowhere to be seen. I cradled my stash and carefully tumbled it onto the counter.

"Well, that's it for now," I announced, feeling exposed once more. I had never been the sole shopper in a grocery store. "Would you have a bag?"

Walter surveyed my pile of goods.

"That's all?" He walked around the counter.

I followed.

"Here, take one of these." Walter brought me to a shelf I'd missed and held out a dish towel. "Teachers always need these. Maybe two."

He turned another corner and called out over his shoulder. "How 'bout batteries? For your Walkman. Got one of those? Batteries run down real quick in the cold."

For the next several minutes, Walter gave me a thorough tour of his establishment, finding items I hadn't planned on getting but would be nice to have.

"Band-Aids, tea—mint flavor, good! Tomato soup, cheese." He paused. "You got bread?" Before I could reply, he added, "How's your sock supply?"

Walter was the consummate businessman, and I was the perfect customer. What I initially intended as a simple scouting mission had morphed into enough supplies to fill two large paper bags. I was about to leave when I realized that Walter hadn't asked me to sign an IOU or show identification.

He saw my confusion. "No problem. Just bring your paycheck when it come. We'll settle up then." He walked me to the door and patted my shoulder as I went through. "See you soon!"

I stepped out to the sand street and blinked at the pale sun, feeling like I'd just emerged from the magical wardrobe in C.S. Lewis's *Chronicles of Narnia*. My arms now loaded with supplies, I was forced to head home. The trek back was quick. Within a few minutes, each item was tucked away in my newly washed kitchen, an act that made the place feel less like a Maybe and more like Home.

SEVEN

NOT IN KANSAS ANYMORE

Thus began my ritual of suiting up in my shoe pacs, slipping a Carnation Breakfast Bar in one coat pocket and my Swiss Army knife in the other, and departing the little gray-green portable for a walkabout. My route passed the school and headed straight for the beach at the top of the rise, to the edge of the Chukchi Sea. From there, I went left or right, depending on my mood or which direction the wind was blowing.

By the third day, with several short walks under my belt, I discovered that heading north and across a patch of open land by the airstrip always resulted in crossing paths with a pack of husky puppies. Somehow, they found me and scampered along as company. The pups had the unique husky markings of white fur on their chests, gray ears, and light brown or black patches. Their eyebrows always seemed to be raised in a sense of exuberant expectancy.

"Hey, lady, where ya going?"

"Can we come?"

"Got a snack for us?"

They yipped and tumbled into each other, running ahead, running behind, running into my legs. The first time I met this charming pack, I reached down to pet one and immediately regretted doing so. My hand smelled like rotting fish for hours. Even Formula 409 didn't remove the odor. From then on, I kept my hands in my pockets.

Husky puppy troupe

The north end of town seemed to have more drying racks. They were constructed with driftwood logs and tied or nailed in the shape of pi signs. They'd been pounded into the sandy ground and stood tall like sentinels. From a distance, the meat hanging from them looked like stiff black rags. At least, I *thought* it was meat. The material didn't look like anything I'd ever seen in the supermarket. But I did spot some fish filets. They had a reddish hue and, with the light shining through them, looked like strips of scarlet stained glass—windows into the souls of fish bodies, now harvested.

Fillets of fish drying

The day before, on the island's southeast side, I came across racks of polar bear hides hanging like rugs to dry in the wind. The hairs were several inches long and bright white with a tinge of yellow. I ran my palm across one hide, imagining the massive animal that used to live in it. Its coarseness surprised me. Someone told me once that a polar bear's coat had two layers. The outer layer was made of guard hairs that were hollow and transparent. When light passed through them, the bear looked white, even luminescent. The hairs' hollow structure also made the bear buoyant—a useful perk in frigid Arctic waters.

I tried measuring the hide using my outstretched arms but fell short by a few feet. How do you kill a bear this size? And why was the hide way out here? Did the locals eat bears? How do you cook a bear? My walkabouts always raised an armload of questions.

The scent of salt from the ocean and the smell of fish and animal carcasses permeated the air. It mingled with a musty metal smell, the way blood tastes after biting one's lip. In another place and time, I might have been repulsed by those strong odors, the grime, the animal skins, and trash laying exposed at the dump for the wind and water to carry away. I would have turned up my nose at these scenes. But Shishmaref was so different from anyplace I'd ever been. It defied comparison, forcing me to accept it on its own terms and accommodate the profound newness, while keeping any critique of it in check. In short, I couldn't stroll into this brave new world called Shishmaref; I had to leap.

Later that same day, I was walking on the north beach again, puppies in tow, and spied something black, partially submerged in the wet sand. As I got closer, I realized it was a seal. Actually, two seals. And they were dead. I shooed away the puppies and stepped closer. Patches of spotted fur confirmed my suspicion. I should have been mortified at the sight and smell of decay, angered by the waste of what seemed like a senseless and untimely death. What happened to them? Where was animal rescue? Up until this point in my life, I had only seen seals at the zoo or on television. In those places, seals were cute and playful, even comical with their half grins and whiskers.

But these seals were not cute. They were covered in sand and missing chunks of flesh. I felt the stability of my childhood beliefs swirling like the tornado that swooped up Dorothy and dropped her in the Land of Oz. She had her little dog, Toto, and I had a pack of bumbling, stinky puppies. And rotting seals on the beach. They were all just part of the scenery.

There was one scene in the village, however, I could not wrap my mind around, and that was the presence of lean huskies chained to posts near some houses. The dogs were tethered close enough to keep each other company, but out of physical reach. Some had access to a doghouse but seemed to prefer exposure to the elements as opposed to cramped quarters with less visibility of their surroundings. They yipped and howled at me as I passed by; one would start and the rest would follow.

I had seen husky dogs before, but these were smaller in stature, just thigh-high. Chained up most of the time, they'd worn deep grooves in the sand. Piles of dog poop were scattered about. There was no hay, no blankets, no beds. Certainly no squeaky toys. I couldn't fathom how the dogs managed in such harsh conditions, never allowed to go inside and plop down on a couch. It bothered me.

In high school, we had a debate about the relativity of values. What was considered cruel to animals in one culture might be deemed normal and necessary in another. I felt conflicted, but who was I to judge this situation? Maybe that's why those stinky, frisky puppies were allowed to romp untethered for the first six months of their lives; it gave them the experience of freedom, if only for a while.

I was nearing home base and decided to dip into the school. Nature was calling, and I wanted to check out the school's front office. Did I have a mailbox?

I pulled the door open and blinked in the bright fluorescent lighting. Someone was here. I approached the office timidly and came upon a woman with her back turned. She had a fistful of papers in one hand and a large manila envelope in the other, which she seemed to be trying to open with her teeth. I cleared my throat to announce my presence.

"Ahh!"

The woman dropped the envelope and turned, eyes wide with surprise.

"Geez, I am so sorry." I backed up. "I didn't mean to scare you."

"It's okay." She picked up the envelope and tossed back her long black hair. "I didn't hear you come in." She paused. "You must be new."

We shook hands, and I offered my usual greeting of name and subject areas.

"I'm Marjorie, but I go by Midge." She chuckled. "It's easier to yell when you need me. I'm the school secretary and doer of all tasks no one else wants to do."

Midge informed me that, since school didn't start until next week, teachers weren't due back until a day or two before orientation. The village was empty because residents were on the mainland, hunting fowl and picking berries.

"Salmonberries." Midge mimicked popping a berry into her mouth and finishing with a kiss of her fingertips. "They're real good!"

That explained the ghost-town feel of the village. I had been given the school start date but had chosen to arrive several days ahead so I had more time to get a lay of the land and prepare for my classes. No one had said that nearly the entire village would be empty of inhabitants.

I asked Midge if she knew which classroom was going to be mine. We walked only a few steps down the hall before she stopped, unlocked a door, and flicked on the light.

"Take your time, move things the way you want." She waved her arm. "But prop the door if you step out and plan to return. It locks automatically. You'll get keys next week."

I stepped into the room. *At last! My own classroom.*

The carpet was gray-blue and seemed in good condition. No linoleum, thank goodness. There was a large chalkboard on the front wall. A few short pieces of white chalk and two erasers sat on its wooden tray. I counted fifteen desks, the kind with a plastic seat and attached Formica desktop. There was a gunmetal gray teacher's desk by the door, an office phone, and a set of plastic filing trays. Two tall metal file cabinets, also gray, stood in one corner. There were two narrow windows. I walked over and peered out. *That's east. Facing the sunrise.* A good omen. A cluster of large cylinder tanks stood like sentries in a field nearby. Water or fuel, I didn't know.

My eyes traveled back to the desk and the large metal bookshelf behind it. Books! Their presence signaled vital information about my prospective curriculum. I had been busy adjusting to the newness of village life, but the mystery of what I was supposed to teach lurked in the back of my mind. Maybe today I would catch some clues.

The first set of books was familiar: *Romeo and Juliet*—classic ninth-grade literature that, thankfully, I had used during my student teaching. I had one "college prep" group and one "remedial." My mentor teacher predicted that the young-love Shakespeare play would flop with the latter. She shook her head. "Don't expect too much. They're lower track. Be strict or they'll run all over you."

She was right. The remedial group challenged me mercilessly, and my mentor teacher had to assert her authority on numerous occasions when students refused to participate, preferring instead to pass notes or deface their desks.

The college prep students, in contrast, came into the room excited to learn. They loved reading and hamming it up during certain scenes. The girls took turns as Juliet and pretended to swoon: "My bounty is as boundless as the sea! … My love as deep!"

They argued about who had more jurisdiction over Romeo and Juliet's love, the Capulets or the Montagues. I was delighted with their youthful energy but scared that my mentor teacher would disapprove of my lack of control. They did get loud on occasion, but I didn't see their exuberance as cause for close supervision. They were learning fine on their own, so I served as cheerleader, prop coordinator, and the person who had to periodically shush them.

Their joy, with or without my input, was the highlight of my student-teaching career. They represented the ever-elusive sweet spot that kept me coming back every day. Maybe the students in Shishmaref would be like that.

How many kids would I be teaching? Were classes small? There were only a few copies of *Romeo and Juliet*, and a couple each of *Old Yeller* and *Of Mice and Men*.

The largest set (ten) was George Orwell's *1984*. How appropriate. It *was* 1984. My mind flashed back to when my high school English teacher entered a dystopian phase and dragged my class through *Lord of the Flies*, *Brave New World*, and *Animal Farm*. She saved Orwell's *1984* for last. Her literature choices were confusing to me. She was a calm and peaceful hippie type who wore peasant blouses and hummed Beatles songs, like "Here Comes the Sun" and John Lennon's "Imagine." I didn't understand her fascination with such depressing books. Maybe she wanted to process those darker moments of humanity to test out how she would navigate reality if any one of the stories came true.

I was the Pollyanna type, believing that people were basically good and could be counted on to rise above personal needs and grievances when necessary. Mine was a simplistic and naïve perspective, but it's how I wanted the world to be. As such, I was largely dismissive of Orwell's prophecy and skimmed the book just enough to get through class discussions and short essays. The reality of a Big Brother watching and controlling the government and the media seemed too far-fetched. Still, I knew I'd breathe a sigh of relief when the calendar turned over to 1985.

The books hadn't been used. No folded corners, no stains. Maybe the previous teacher had decided to skip it. I studied the bright red cover with its title in bold black lettering and image of one large eyeball staring back at me. The summary on the back highlighted unnerving themes of Newspeak. Police State. Systemic Distortion of Truth. *Yikes.* Maybe I'd skip it, too.

My disposition changed when I spied two teacher manuals for guiding students' writing. Curiously, there were no accompanying student texts. My heart beat a bit faster. I needed the structure and content of textbooks to help me sequence instruction, especially this first year. I disliked textbooks as a student, but as a teacher, I coveted the chapter approach and requisite ten questions at the end of each.

Then on the bottom shelf, I found the Holy Grail. A large white binder with ENGLISH CURRICULUM handwritten on the front cover. I scanned the tabs: K-3, 4-8, 9-12 and eagerly flipped to the 9-12 tab. There was nothing behind it.

What the—

I sat down and methodically scanned each page, checking headers to see if the high school curriculum had been misfiled. Or maybe the former teacher had removed the pages and placed them elsewhere for easier use? I walked to the file cabinets on the far side of the room. The top drawer was empty. The next drawer was, too. The clank of metal drawers echoed in the bare room as I slammed each one shut, my emphasis matching my growing angst. But all I found was a piece of notebook paper with sketches of seals on it, and some errant paper clips.

This can't be right. How can they expect that I would come all this way and not have a curriculum guide? It wasn't on the list they gave me. No note that read, "In addition to bedding and long underwear, teachers must bring their own curriculum."

My Inner Coach saw where this negative line of thinking was heading and stepped in. *Just study the early grades and talk to Principal Ken when he returns.*

I took the binder, made a pit stop in the bathroom, and clomped down the school steps in a mood that matched the gray sky. I hated this moment and kicked myself for arriving in the village sooner than necessary. I could have stayed in Seattle longer. I could be sitting in a coffee shop right now, reading to my heart's content. I could have had more time in the library, researching how to live in an Arctic village with more poise than I was currently manifesting.

I stomped as much sand as I could on the porch and entered my abode in stocking feet, then set the curriculum guide on the table and went to the kitchen. Maybe tea and a snack would make this curriculum dive more palatable.

I watched the water in the saucepan slowly come to a boil. The air bubbles increased, along with a steady stream of questions. Was I really cut out for this teaching gig? Or was I fooling myself and over-estimating my aptitude for this heartache of a profession? It was one thing to let a bunch of college prep ninth graders goof off with Shakespeare, and another to roll out an entire curriculum in three different subject areas, two of which I knew nothing about.

The water reached a full boil, yet no answers presented themselves. I pulled out a bag of Lipton tea and a Carnation Breakfast Bar, then added more water to the pan. Just a few more moments of "boiling water contemplation" might offer some resolution to the swirl of questions.

Maybe the English curriculum was in the building. There were still a few days to figure things out. No need to panic. Midge might help. She did say she was "the doer of all things," right? She appeared kind, and she wouldn't think less of me when I asked about Consumer Math textbooks or what the heck was Graphic Communications.

I carried my scalding cup of tea to the table, took a tentative sip, and opened the binder to Kindergarten. When bringing order to chaos, my Virgo Self preferred to start at the beginning. That's what I'd do here, too. I would review what the little kids learned and move forward methodically, grade by grade, following the progression of academic content and skills and building toward what I could expect of high school students. How hard could that be?

EIGHT

VISITORS

The K-8 curriculum ran nearly one hundred pages of single-spaced material. This review was going to be quite the chore. It seemed easiest to first skim headings for each age group before diving into details.

I turned to kindergarten. The little ones did basic lettering and learned to write their names and point at pictures to demonstrate reading comprehension. They identified patterns in rhyming words like cat, hat, mat, and fat. Dog, log, bog. Easy peasy.

First through third grades built on that foundation, tasking kiddos with two- and three-syllable words, writing basic sentences, and practicing capital letters and periods. Students also learned sequencing words, like first, middle, and last, and wrote opinion pieces about why dogs made better pets than cats (or vice versa).

Why didn't I get an elementary teaching certificate? This would be a piece of cake.

I was about to take a sip of tea when I heard an odd sound coming from the outer door.

Pat-pat-pat.

I looked up. Was that a knock? Who could that be? Should I answer? Was it Principal Ken? No, the sound was light, not like heavy knuckles. I froze, unsure what to do. I was on a roll with my curriculum analysis and didn't want to be interrupted. I'd been waiting for this moment for years. Whoever it was could come back later.

The door squeaked open, and I heard shuffling of feet in the boot room.

Pat-pat-pat.

This time, on the inner door.

It creaked open, and the face of a young girl cautiously peeked in. She looked familiar. *Well, this is awkward.* I was clearly within earshot of the door but too rude to answer.

Pat-pat-pat. She tapped the door again, even though we were looking directly at each other. Her face had the roundness of youth and was the color of light chestnut.

"Can we come visit?" The girl's voice was soft. Her eyebrows raised high with her query. She opened the door wider, revealing a pink jacket and grubby blue jeans.

It was one of the girls I'd seen on my walkabout. A second brown face appeared over her shoulder, along with a large pink bubble. It reached considerable size, then *shoop!* It collapsed and went expertly back into her mouth. I caught a whiff of grape Bubblicious.

I wasn't much of a gum-chewer, but I knew about Bubblicious. It appeared at the checkout stands in the late 1970s when I was finishing high school and was all the rage with kids—and adults who wanted to keep acting like kids. Who could resist flavors like watermelon and cotton candy, with the potential of blowing a bubble larger than your own head?

A swirl of emotions kicked up inside of me. I felt annoyed, then guilty and embarrassed for not having the ability to easily invite the girls in. I was like the mean neighbor who turned off the lights on Halloween.

Still, was I a bad person for wanting a little privacy? Maybe. But I'd make a better impression if I didn't reject innocent children. There could be repercussions if the message of a stingy, inhospitable new teacher reverberated around the village. Not a great way to start out the school year. If people thought I didn't like kids, no amount of curriculum know-how was going to make a difference.

I stood up and waved the girls in. They took a few steps and glanced furtively around the bare countertops and sparse living room. I followed their gazes and had to admit that the space looked sad. I had no decorations, no knickknacks or coffee table books. The girls shifted. Sand crunched under their sneakers. I took a deep breath.

What happens during a visit?

I patted a couch cushion, like my grandmother did when she wanted to tell me something special. The girls came in farther and sat close, folding their hands. I moved to a chair, and we studied each other in silence. The girls wore similar attire. Hooded sweatshirts over t-shirts, and jeans worn at the knees. White gym socks poked above their sneakers, too short to bridge the gap to the bottom of their pant legs and revealing brown skin.

"I'm Genét." I patted my chest like I was introducing myself to a tribe member in the deep Amazon jungle.

"I'm Helen." The pink-clad girl patted her chest. "And this is Nora." She patted her friend.

Such adult names.

"What you doin'?" Helen eyed my Holy Grail binder and cup of tea. Wisps of steam curled up, then evaporated.

I brought the opened binder to the coffee table but left the tea. I had already been-somewhat rude about not answering the door, and it might be equally rude to drink tea without offering any to them. *Did kids drink hot tea?*

Helen slid off the couch and plopped to the floor, resting her elbows on the table, and cupping her chin in her hands. She wanted a closer look. Nora followed. They scanned the pages, trying to crack the code of what, to them, must have resembled Egyptian hieroglyphics. Little did they know, just moments ago I had been doing the same thing.

"I'm looking at what I'm supposed to teach this year."

The girls' eyeballs moved back and forth across the opened page. They were seeing, but not comprehending.

"What grade you teach?"

Helen was the leader; she had asked me the same question on the street but had either forgotten my answer or wanted to confirm what I had said before.

"High school. English and Math."

"Oh, too bad." Nora looked concerned. "We want you to be *our* teacher!" She poked Helen in the ribs and giggled.

I was about to ask the girls which grade they were in when Helen sat taller.

"Where you from?"

Before I could respond, Nora blurted, "Got anything to eat?"

Well, this was a surprise. From a shy pat-pat-pat to sprawling on my furniture and floor and asking for food. Not hot tea, which was good—I didn't want to scald their little tongues. I'd be known as the stingy and inhospitable new teacher who gives kids second-degree burns.

"I'm from Seattle, Washington. I'll show you." I started toward my bedroom for a map. It was an unnecessary diversion, but I needed a moment to gear up for this conversation.

"And I have some granola bars." I emerged from my bedroom. "You like granola bars?"

The girls nodded.

There were only three bars left in the box. Note to self.

Helen was back on the couch, laying full out. Her feet dangled over one low armrest. Nora was still on the floor, her legs crooked up and resting on the couch cushions. There was no space left for me to sit. I handed each of them a bar and they rotated the wrapped treats, as if not quite understanding what I had given them. Or maybe they were deciding if they could politely decline the non-kid-friendly snack.

I set the curriculum guide back on the Formica table, sipped my tea, and resigned myself to the fact that my planning period had been unceremoniously displaced. But perhaps I could still make good use of the time with a short geography lesson.

I sat on the floor and unfolded my map of the United States. My eyes naturally moved to Seattle. It was hard to believe that, just one week ago, I was living there, lying in the sun on a grassy knoll near the Ballard Locks and watching yachts float by.

Helen propped herself on an elbow, pulled her wad of Bubblicious out and set it on a corner of the table, then unwrapped the bar with her teeth and chomped into it. Nora sat up and copied Helen's moves. Both girls chewed thoughtfully, looked at me, and nodded. My offering had been accepted. So far, so good.

"This is a map of the U.S." I waved my hand over the map in its entirety. "And this," I placed a finger down and traced the border, "is Washington State."

Helen and Nora squinted and nodded. *Did they need glasses?* I swiveled the map to give them better perspective and continued.

"And here is Seattle, where I lived before coming here. Now, keep in mind that the mapmakers ran out of paper to stretch all the way up to Alaska to show where it really is. It's much bigger than what you see here, like a third the size of the rest of the country. If I took Alaska and laid it on top of these states—I waved my hand over California, Texas, Florida—it would stretch almost the entire distance. Pretty amazing." I paused. "So, they tucked a representation of it down here." I pointed to where Alaska and Hawaii were both set next to the Baja Peninsula.

The girls' eyes glazed over. I had just delivered a major new-teacher error: Too Much Information. I forgot that kids their age were more literal with their thinking, and in most instances, not yet adept with abstract thought. I needed to slow down and, like Julie Andrews teaching the Von Trapp kids "Do-Re-Me," help the girls string together the notes in a song.

I was the same way when I was their age. One day, when riding in the car with my dad, I read a sign along the side of the road that said, DO NOT PASS. We flew right by. My dad didn't even tap the breaks. Alarmed, I blurted out, "Dad! That sign said, do not pass!"

My dad glanced in the rearview mirror.

"No, it's okay. It's a different kind of pass. I'll explain later."

I was confused for months. What's the point of having a road with signs saying not to pass if the drivers just drove past? When it happened again, my dad finally eased my mind by explaining the double yellow line.

The girls took another bite and waited for more.

"Pretend that this drawing of Alaska is actually up here," I tried again, gesturing in the direction of Helen's gum. "It's a lot bigger than it looks." I smiled slightly, remembering the Texan versus Alaskan joke.

The girls looked across the map, squinting at the small font and dizzying array of state colors and interstate highways that spread out like a web strung by a spider on LSD.

I needed to simplify this lesson. Bring it home.

"And Shishmaref is here." I grabbed my pen and inked a little dot on the north-side slanting slope of Seward Peninsula.

The girls gasped.

"It's okay, this map needs to have your village on it."

"Where's Alaska?" Nora asked.

"Well, it's shown here," I pointed at the Baja Peninsula, "but it's really up here." I pointed toward Helen's gum, wondering if I should tape a piece of paper to the corner and draw Alaska where it belonged. My students weren't nodding anymore.

Crap, I am going to make a lousy teacher.

"Where's Nome?" Helen sounded alarmed.

Thankfully, the cartographers considered Nome important enough to mention. I placed a finger there and felt a rush of the memory when John had done the same thing as he pointed to Shishmaref. *Just because I'm pointing doesn't mean they get it.*

"And here's Anchorage." I slid my finger east, hoping that reference would help them gain cerebral traction.

"Have you ever been to Anchorage?" I watched their expressions, so intent and innocent. They were trying.

"No, but we've been to Serpentine Hot Springs and Wales and almost to Nome." Nora scanned the Midwestern states.

"Where's Serpentine Hot Springs?" I leaned in, knowing it likely wasn't labelled.

"Serpentine is over the lagoon and a little ways. We go in the fall to camp and pick berries. In winter, we go to sit in the springs."

Nora giggled. "It's very hot!"

For the next few minutes, I stayed in teacher mode, describing how far Seattle was from Shishmaref, but found myself experiencing the famous Abbott and Costello skit, "Who's On First." Nora simply could not grasp two thousand miles, and Helen insisted that Washington State was, in fact, a city. Had they taken a class in geography yet?

"How far to Washington by sno-go?" Nora spoke again.

"Sno-go?" I looked at Nora. "Like a snow machine?"

"Alaska is a country!" Helen blurted, nodding vigorously as if to convince me.

Note to self: Get a map of Alaska.

Pat-pat-pat.

Helen and Nora looked at the door and then at me. I couldn't tell if they wanted more company to refresh our circular conversation or if they wanted to keep the bumbling teacher to themselves. It felt rude not to answer and equally rude not to invite in the next round of visitors.

I got up, stiff from sitting on the floor, and opened the door. Three girls clustered on the porch, arching their necks to see inside.

"Can we come visit?" More Bubblicious wafted in with them. Original Pink.

I waved them in, wincing at the sound of sand underfoot. The girls piled onto the couch, happy to have found their playmates.

"Got any games?" one asked. I glanced at the Carnation granola bar wrappers on the floor and secretly hoped the newcomers wouldn't ask for food. I'd have to cut my last bar into three parts. *Stingy teacher.*

"Silly, introduce yourself!" Helen elbowed her friend.

"I'm Hilda." The girl who asked about games spoke first. "And that's Jen and Henrietta." She pointed down the row.

"Well, it's nice to meet you. I'm Genét."

Wait. Should I use a more formal teacher name, like Miss Pierce? But I'm not their teacher, exactly. Maybe they call their teachers by first name?

"But you can call me Teach." The words fell out of my mouth without any forethought. They felt strange, but true.

"Got any games?" Hilda asked again. My mind raced. Did I bring any games? Nope, not even a pack of cards. *Stingy, boring teacher.*

"Not really. No games." I shrugged my shoulders. "Games weren't on the list."

Maybe, without games, and with the map lesson going nowhere, the girls would leave and I could get back to my work.

"We know some games!" Helen yelled. "How 'bout patty-cake?"

They all jumped up.

"Here. You. Teach!" Hilda pointed to the carpet in front of her. There were five of them—she had no partner.

I moved as commanded, and the girls took off with lightning speed, clapping their hands, smacking their thighs, and high fiving each other in a dizzying array of motion. I was unprepared and horribly slow. Hilda was dismayed. *Stingy, boring, uncoordinated teacher.*

"Slow down, everyone, so she can learn." Helen felt sorry for me. The girls obeyed, and I managed to complete a few mostly correct rounds. I was just getting the hang of it when one of the girls yelled, "How 'bout Wolf?"

"Yeah, Wolf!" They yelled in unison. This game sounded dangerous. They were upping the ante.

Wolf was a fast-paced game, like tag. I never liked that game. I was more of a marathon runner, not a sprinter. A tortoise, not a hare. I always got tagged and then forgotten in "jail" until the game ended. My classmates knew I'd be tagged again, so why bother releasing me?

Wolf was pretty much the same, and it proved quite a challenge with the coffee table serving as home base in a living room the size of Volkswagen Beetle. The girls made use of the hall, back bedrooms, and the kitchen, steering clear of the bathroom, thank god.

Within half an hour, my day had gone from introspection of "I'm-finally-a-teacher-so-I'll-do-some-planning" to being whomped at patty-cake, tagged unceasingly in Wolf, and otherwise marshaled around my maybe-home by a group of carefree Bubblicious-gum-chewing ten-year-olds.

Fortunately, the game ended quickly, with the girls unceremoniously draped over the couch or laying on the floor catching their breath. I sat on a dining chair by the door. I had a feeling that I needed to ask them to leave but was worried about coming across as, well ... rude. Was there a time limit protocol for visitors? I decided to give it a try.

"Okay, girls," I stretched and feigned a yawn. "Time to scoot. I gotta get going on my course planning again. Thanks for visiting, though. It was fun!"

One by one, the girls tugged each other to standing. Nora stayed sprawled on the couch.

"C'mon, we gotta go," Helen said. Nora sighed and, still holding out, slid off the couch like a slinky and onto the floor. Helen pulled her up and pushed her friend to the door.

"Thanks for the visit!"

"Thanks for coming. Sorry I'm a little slow with your games."

"That's okay," Helen replied. "We'll do it again tomorrow!"

I surveyed the room. Wrappers littered the floor. My U.S. map had somehow gotten jammed between the couch and wall. Two graying globs of Bubblicious sat on the coffee table.

"Well, that was interesting," I said to myself.

I reached for my tea. It was cold.

NINE

RUB-A-DUB

Each time I went to the school building to see if any other teachers had checked in, I found the building open but vacant. My classroom door was also unlocked. Maybe Midge wanted me to feel more welcome in my solitude. But where the heck was Principal Ken? He'd been gone for more than a few days. Maybe his wife made him stay in Nome. In a hotel. With plumbing.

I had the sneaking suspicion that I was starting to look like Pilot Steve. I hadn't yet taken a shower, opting instead for simple sponge baths in the kitchen sink. Maybe I should capitalize on use of the school facilities while no one was there? I took a last swig of coffee, grabbed my bath towel and shampoo, and tromped across the street.

The girls' shower door was still locked. That meant using the boys'.

I tested one of the shower heads. The water came out ice cold. Hoping it would warm up, I quickly undressed and stepped close, gasping with the shock of the cold water on my skin, and alternated between stepping out of the stream and then back in.

As I rubbed shampoo into my scalp, it became clear that the shower not only felt good, it was utterly necessary. My hair was stiff from the salty ocean air, and sand had lodged in various body creases and between my toes. I watched as shampoo suds and sand travelled slowly toward the drain.

Scared to death that someone—especially of the male persuasion—would walk in on me, I started singing, "She'll be comin' round the mountain when she comes," and followed each line with a territory cough—something I learned in college while living in a coed dorm.

I was on the third verse and halfway through rinsing my hair when I felt the pressure weaken. I had overestimated just how much lather a handful of shampoo could make and began rubbing my scalp more vigorously to remove the last of it. But the water was hard.

The shower head dribbled and stopped. Frantic, I moved to another showerhead and turned the knob. Nothing. I tried another. Same. I tried them all. No luck. The water was gone. I touched my hair and looked at my hand. It was covered in honeysuckle-scented suds.

I had never been a person who swears a lot, but my short tenure in this village was bringing out a new side of me. The f-word, s-word, and a few other expletives peppered my speech. I would have to clean up my language before school started. But right here, right now, I let go a whole string of them.

There was only one thing to do. Go home and finish rinsing my head in the kitchen sink. Fortunately, my hair was relatively short and quick drying.

I threw on my clothes, shoved my wet feet into my boots, and trudged home with my heavy bath towel draped around my head. I looked like a grouchy nun.

Two questions burned in my mind: where do people take a shower around here? And where do they wash their clothes?

Back in my kitchen, I set the pail under the PVC stub and was rinsing my head and thinking about how easy bald men had it when I heard a sound.

Pat-pat-pat.

"No effing way," I mouthed the words under my breath.

The front door squeaked open. They were getting bold.

"Just a minute, girls!" I called in the cheeriest voice I could muster. I was out of Carnation bars and not in the mood for visitors.

The inner door creaked open, and Helen's face appeared.

"Hi," I said, smiling faintly. "I was just rinsing my hair."

Helen's eyebrows shot up. I wasn't sure if she was registering surprise or a "duh."

"The showers at school ran out of ... Never mind."

"Can we come visit?"

"It's not the best time." I stood still, afraid to make any move that signaled otherwise. The door creaked open a few more inches, and another girl's face appeared.

"Hi." I offered the same flat demeanor.

They didn't budge. Maybe I could negotiate.

"How about later this afternoon?"

The girls blinked and looked at each other, then simultaneously blew Bubblicious bubbles until they bumped into each other. *Shoop!* The gum went back in. Their eyes opened wide, and they burst out laughing.

"Okay, bye!" They slammed the door.

I followed, curious if the door locked from the inside. There was a button in the knob. I pressed it. It popped back. I pressed again. It stayed.

What if it sticks and locks me out? I had no key. I pushed again and the button popped out. Maybe I'd have to prop the door open whenever I left. Note to self: Find a locksmith.

I turned toward the kitchen window and looked out. The high layer of cirrus clouds promised a mostly clear day. A jangle of thoughts started swirling. What was my problem? Here I was, having opportunities to get to know people but resisting on a regular basis. Maybe I was just nervous. Being social had never been easy for me. I was a loner for most of my life, never feeling like I fit in. I was not a person my classmates thought to invite over to hang out. "Stop being so serious," they'd say. Or worse, "You're weird."

But they were right, I was a bit weird. During my elementary years, I didn't have any close friends, just my older brother. He was kind and taught me useful things like how to do a shoulder roll when jumping from a tree, and how to throw a ball high or hard. We were always playing in the yard and coming up with new games. At school, however, and for no reason I could discern, girls and boys were separated during recess. My only option as a girl was hopscotch or tetherball. I hated hopscotch. There was too much drama and infighting.

"You moved my stone!"

"I did not!"

"You're cheating, I saw you skip a square!"

"Did not!"

The constant stream of accusations slowed the game down so much that everyone forgot whose turn it was and had to start over. I found it exhausting.

Tetherball was better. I had a strong upper body and almost always finished off my line of opponents without challenge. I was weird for wanting to play with the boys, weird for not wanting to play hopscotch, and weird for smashing the tetherball harder than any other girl. Some days, on my own, I whacked the ball around the pole, trying to outdo my moves without knocking myself silly.

In third and fourth grade, recess was a mix of boys and girls, but I was usually picked last for Red Rover or dodgeball, even though I could run through the opposing line like a hot knife through butter. And I could throw the heavy red rubber ball as hard as any boy. Maybe that was the problem. I played like a boy, and no one knew what to do with me.

Most of my childhood was a practice in turning inward, spending my time outdoors alone, riding my bike along country roads, dribbling the basketball and shooting hoops by myself, or hitting the baseball high, dropping the bat, and running after the ball to catch it before it hit the ground. In middle school, my father moved our family to Colorado, where I hiked alone in the mountains and journaled by sparkling streams. The result of my solitary childhood meant that I didn't know how to play with others or negotiate my way through moments of angst while growing up. Maybe hopscotch would have been good practice after all.

But I also prided myself in enjoying my own company, and I jumped for any challenge that seemed like a good time: tennis, squash, racquetball, cross-country and downhill skiing, and a lot of yardwork. I didn't shy away from hard things. I handled them the best I could. I might have been lonely at times, but developing courage and tenacity had certainly helped me get through these past few weeks, right? I'd managed to get here, set up a home, and mostly worked through the terror of a big white binder with no high school curriculum and only five copies of *Romeo and Juliet*.

Yet, in spite of my somewhat positive track record, a truckload of uncertainty lingered. It was a Virgo's worst nightmare: lack of direction, disorder, dirty windows.

I dragged a finger across the windowpane, leaving a streak. Note to self …

"You're just getting settled in," I said quietly. "Give yourself a break."

Two minutes later, wool cap pulled over my damp hair, I headed out the door. Another walkabout was in order.

TEN

WALKABOUT 2.0

Several minutes out of the village, I was heading north and still walking at a fast pace. My stomach rumbled. In my haste, I'd forgotten to pack my last snack bar. Maybe I'd make this a shorter walk and stop at Walter's on the way home. I'd have to come up with cheaper snack options or Walter would be cashing and keeping my first paycheck. When was payday, anyway?

The tide was out a significant distance, inviting me to cross the wide, hard-packed sand to the water's edge, where tiny waves lapped gently. I stopped to catch my breath and turned around. From here, the village was merely a row of tiny boxes, the drying racks like toothpicks on the horizon. I turned north again and spied two Arctic terns. They were hard to miss with their loud squawking. The first time I saw one, I thought it was a seagull. But then it made a surprisingly loud screeching noise—so loud that I ducked, thinking I was getting attacked by a pterodactyl.

Screeches aside, the terns were beautiful, stone white with V-shaped wings, black caps, and pointy red bills. They were elegant and lovely to watch as they floated high on the wind and eyed the water below, then abruptly dove like missiles into the cold sea, hoping to score a fish.

I closed my eyes and listened to the wind. It was soft today and caressed my cheeks. Tears came fast and slid down. I blinked and wiped them away.

Unsure what I was feeling and not really wanting to know, I walked farther, fighting the urge to return home and feed my grumbling stomach. A question appeared: How far would I need to walk to come to terms with what I had said yes to?

I had agreed to live in this village for an entire year, and I was lonely in a way I hadn't felt before, more estranged than ever. More outcast than in the tetherball line or waiting to be picked for dodgeball. Now that the busyness of settling in had ended, a sense of isolation flew in to fill the void. All I had was this. Wind. Water. Walking. No bookstores or coffee shops, no mountains to distract me from the heartache of being on my own.

Just before leaving Seattle, the phone rang in my near-empty apartment. It was a credit collector. I had made the mistake of letting a friend use my credit card at the mall. She owed me four hundred dollars and kept promising to pay me back. But I knew I'd never get it. I told the collector about my new job in Alaska and how I'd be able to repay the debt soon. He coldly accused me of trying to run away.

The irony was not lost on me. At this moment, I would have given anything to run back *to* something, even if that meant returning to my little job at the café, wiping tables and washing dishes. That was safe. Predictable. I should forget about being a teacher. Didn't my map lesson prove that I didn't know what I was doing? Twenty weeks of student teaching had taught me nothing about how to relate to kids or sequence instruction.

My boots kept moving me to the northern tip of the island where the strong ocean current swept around, preventing me from continuing in a straight line over the North Pole and landing somewhere in Europe. That might just be how far I had to hike to get the perspective I needed, to gather my wits and resolve so I could return to my maybe-home portable and start with a fresh attitude. Hiking high in the mountains always helped me process tough situations. I used to hike until my muscles burned. It was a good ache. But there were no mountains here, only endless flatness, where the only burn I felt was in my heart.

I stopped at the edge, where the sand was hard and chiseled, and tried to calculate the distance across the channel to the other shoreline. It didn't seem far. If I'd had a tennis ball, I could have easily whacked it high and watched it bounce on the other side.

But there was no way across. No escape. Even if I ran hard and jumped for it, I'd disappear into the depths. Within a few feet of my boot soles, the land dropped steeply. All that remained was dark icy water, racing by.

I turned back to the village, and my eye caught a small patch of something white on the beach. I veered from my intended path for a closer look. It was a white cone-shaped shell, only an inch long, its thick casing worn by waves slowly grinding into the shallow beach. I peered closely. The shell was curled into itself. Like me. Probably the innermost part of what used to be a larger shell. I brushed off the sand and put it in my pocket.

My return to the village had more focus now, scanning the beach ahead for shells I had missed on my initial walk. Another spot of white caught my eye. A flatter piece of shell. I picked it up and inspected its smoothness, but suddenly felt a wave of lightheadedness—from the long walk, my emotional state, lack of food, I didn't know. I looked around. Like Robert Frost on a snowy evening, there was no place to sit. The dizziness bent me over.

It was an awkward stance, hunched over with my elbows resting on my knees, but the spinning stopped. I focused on the tops of my boots, took a couple of deep breaths, and stood up again. I tossed the flat shell toward the water's edge and set my sights on the village, walking at a more contemplative pace. What was the rush? No one at home to greet me, no dinner to cook, no homework, at least not yet. No visitors, I hoped.

As I walked in this more meditative state, the hard ripples of sand gave way to a smoother beach. My boots barely made a dent. There was no reference point, nothing standing out to command my attention. This slight shift in awareness made me pay attention to smaller things—clumps of grass waving slightly in the wind, pieces of driftwood. Small stones and shell fragments scattered about. They began to shape-shift and morph from ordinary pieces of rock and calcium carbonate into the shapes of animals, like the animal crackers I'd loved as a kid. A polar bear. A seal sitting on its hind flippers. Walrus heads, stampeding caribou, reindeer, a solitary fox. There were ten shades of white and gray and hints of blue, yellow, and pink mixed into the gold and brown and green of the swaying grasses. A feather slowly flitted across the beach and for a moment became a seagull.

I paused again. This entire landscape was very much alive. Maybe this would keep me company. My fingers caressed the smooth white shell in my pocket, now warmed by my own body. There were treasures here if I looked hard enough.

I made a lunch of scrambled eggs, toast, and coffee in my new mug from Walter's. Inspired by my beach walk, I pulled out my journal and wrote.

Walkabout Poem

The sky is as large as a beach ball
Hovering with waving gray clouds.
They stretch from one side to the other
Casting shadows and wonderings about.

With the terns' squawks and chatters above me
My boots wander free on the sand
Leaving barely-pressed tracks all behind me
Till I pause for a brief rest and stand.

The wind beckons over my shoulder
Pulling my face to the west
wave pounding wave like a boulder
Rumbling down, released from its crest.

I wonder which way I might set to
When this ocean turns into ice?
Could I venture this open-end vastness,
And survive any sacrifice?

For now I'm confined to this sand here
That's whistling over my shoes.
The future will show if I stay here
When the winter ice to the shore moves.
—August 1984

ELEVEN

VISITORS 2.0

Midafternoon the same day, I felt rested and grounded. The white binder was out once more, opened to the middle grades. The English curriculum was getting more complex. I slowed my pace to closely study what students were supposed to learn before they arrived in my ninth-grade English class.

It looked like they'd be able to understand main points in a text, analyze themes and rhyming patterns, and explain how a book's setting influenced character and plot. Their writing would demonstrate the skills of summarizing, supporting key ideas, and drawing conclusions. It was a lot. Now that I was on the other side of the desk, I was impressed with how my own high school English teacher so seamlessly moved her classes through material. Teachers were crafty people, and I wanted to be one of them.

But my dreams were short lived. As I turned each page, it became abundantly clear that all my years in college hadn't taught me how to build a portfolio of lesson plans. My professors kept saying that curriculum guides would be provided; they sure got that wrong.

There was only one assignment in a literacy methods class that I remembered as having any worth—a vocabulary book students could create using key words from a favorite novel. I had been reading Zora Neale Hurston's *Their Eyes Were Watching God* but felt that a book of that depth and richness shouldn't be reduced to a vocabulary list. Instead, I'd pulled a copy of one of my Nancy Drew mysteries and created a vocabulary book that included "sneaky," "tough," "unpredictable." It ended up being fun.

With the lack of guidance from my so-called higher education, I'd have to rely once more on my creative impulses and meager classroom supplies. Maybe I'd ask Principal Ken for his permission to order a set of classic literature books. I'd have to act quickly as it might take weeks for them to arrive. The wheels of educational bureaucracy turned maddeningly slow. During student teaching, I'd watched my mentor teacher gnashing her teeth one day, frustrated with the magnitude of forms she had to fill out to purchase a set of workbooks. By the time they arrived, she had given up and moved on to something else. In a place as remote as Shishmaref, I'd probably be grinding my teeth down to my gums.

I took another sip of Earl Grey tea. Walter had suggested it. "Smells good! Got bergamot in it, whatever that is!" He laughed. I didn't know what bergamot was either, but I agreed with him on the aroma, not so much the taste. Honey might help. Note to self.

My mealtimes were all screwed up. It was now almost eight o'clock, and I had skipped dinner. The sun was still high in the sky. Tired of looking through the white binder, I pulled out *Coming Into the Country* to see if I could finally finish it in one last sitting.

Pat-pat-pat.

"You've got to be kidding," I muttered. "This late?!"

I had forgotten to lock the door. I heard it open with a long creak, followed by the sounds of feet and bodies shuffling. The girls were assembling in the outer boot room, and given the length of time it was taking, I calculated there were about five of them. Five pairs of sandy shoes, size six. I could request that they remove their shoes, but the floor was freezing (I still had my own boots on). Then again, maybe the discomfort would nudge them out the door sooner rather than later. *Grumpy, cruel teacher.*

The door creaked closed, but it hadn't been latching properly. I heard the girls trying to shove it harder.

Whomp! The house shuddered.

"Ooooh, quiet!" I heard one girl admonish another. I waited.

Pat-pat-pat.

I sat still as a mouse, wishing I could flee without being seen, lock my bedroom door and pretend to be sleeping, maybe add some fake snoring. I didn't know if I was wearier from their visits or my resistance to them. I mean, they weren't all that bad. I was getting better with hosting, and I was learning some cool patty-cake moves.

I blinked first.

"Yes?"

Helen's face appeared.

"Can we come visit?" She opened the door wider to give me a fair assessment of how many visitors were asking. There were four.

"Sure."

I got up and took what would likely be my last sip of hot Earl Grey tea. The girls shuffled into the dining area. Helen, Nora, and two girls I hadn't met.

"And whom do I have the pleasure of meeting today?"

A new girl blew a tiny pink bubble and popped it.

Helen began. "So, I'm Helen." She patted her own chest. "And Nora." She patted Nora's chest. "And this is Celia and Martha." She reached over and patted their chests for emphasis.

"Well, nice to meet you. I'm Genét." I patted my own chest, playing along. "You can call me 'Teach.'"

"Oooh, what grade you teach?" The girl with the name that started with "M" overcame her initial shyness. I was so humored with Helen's approach to introductions that I failed to listen carefully. *Maddy? Madeline?*

"High school. English."

"Told you!" Helen rolled her eyes and led the girls to the couch. They sat next to each other like birds on a wire. At that moment, I was a little sad that I wasn't, indeed, going to be their teacher. They kept coming back for visits, which said something. We were establishing a connection, even when I was reluctant to do so. I doubted that high schoolers would be coming over for visits. It wouldn't be cool. For the most part, teens were moody and difficult to read.

"Got snacks?"

"Yeah, and pop?"

I answered yes and no. I didn't know the rules for sugar intake, but thought the latter was worse. Would the girls' parents approve of the new teacher feeding their children liquid chemicals? Even if they allowed for that, pop was two dollars a can.

"I have hot tea," I stated. "Earl Grey. But I'm afraid I have no honey."

The girls scrunched their faces in unison.

"Sorry." I shrugged.

Helen placed her gum wad on the coffee table.

Ohmygod, they're all going to do it.

I grabbed a saucer. They must have been chewing their gum for hours. It was the color of Silly Putty, and the Bubblicious aroma was long gone.

"What's that?" Nora pointed at my journal.

"Oh, that's my journal." I said the words casually, trying to leave the impression that my precious book was boring teacher stuff.

"Ooh, can we read it?" Nora grabbed it and started thumbing through the pages.

"Um, no," I held out my hand for her to return it. Thankfully, she did.

"Can we sign it? Like a yearbook?" Nora was persistent. She could probably sense that I didn't want her meddling with my journal, but she wanted to be close to something I valued. Maybe I *didn't* want to be their teacher. I suggested they sign their names on the back instead and handed my journal to Helen. Her behavior had been the most mature, and she would likely understand proper etiquette when handling someone's personal possessions. Helen took the pen and slowly wrote her name in cursive.

Nora snatched the pen from Helen and wrote her own name. Soon, the back of my journal was covered in curly signatures and flowers for a border. It was sweet, and it gave me a second chance to learn their names.

"Hey, how do you spell your name?" Nora snatched the pen from Celia and poised the tip above a blank spot.

I spelled my name slowly, omitting the *l'accent aigu* over my second "e." It was a mark I had started using in college to emphasize pronunciation of my name in French, even though any self-respecting French person would know that an "e" followed by a "t" is pronounced with an "ay" sound. The "t" is silent. Thus, *jouet* (toy) is szoo-way and *poulet* (chicken) is poo-lay.

French grammar sounded flowy and melodic, which is how I wanted to feel too. It was easier on the ear than the harsh "Jeh-NET" I'd grown up with, made even more so by my mother's German accent. When she called my name, it sounded like I was in deep trouble. Granted, I often was. But why be reminded?

Within five minutes, my name, sans *l'accent aigu*, graced my journal in both block print and cursive versions. Celia set the pen down and asked shyly, "Where you from?"

"Yeah, show them the map!" Nora exclaimed. "Maybe we can find Serpentine Hot Springs this time." *Uh-oh. Not the map lesson again.*

I redirected, suggesting that I show the girls some photos instead. Before Nora could object, I went to my bedroom, where I swapped my journal with a handful of photos of family and friends and a couple of postcards from places I'd been. It would have been nice to bring all my photos, but the albums were bulky, and I'd left them with a friend in Seattle, along with my flip-flops, tank tops, and shorts.

The girls sat politely on the couch in the same order, looking content, maybe even a little sleepy. I sat on the floor and started with a postcard of the Space Needle. Remembering that less is more, I skipped the history of the structure being built to look like a spaceship for the 1962 World's Fair and stuck to simpler facts.

"It's about sixty stories high."

The girls looked at each other. *Good grief. Do they even know what a story is—as in a tall building?* I hadn't seen any buildings in Shishmaref over two, maybe three stories. I took a deep breath and attempted to explain.

"You know. A story. Like levels." I pancaked my hands over each other.

Still no response.

"How about floors? Like the school has how many floors?"

Nora and Celia scrunched their faces.

"You mean, like how many floors, like rooms?" Martha suggested.

"Not really." I paused. *They're still at Piaget's stage of Concrete Operational Development. Keep it simple!*

"Well, it's more like when you have stairs, and you go up to a second floor. A second story." I watched their faces carefully.

"Oh, I get it!" Helen took the lead. "Like the church had a second floor. We'd go up there and look down on everybody." She stood up to emphasize a high-low perspective, then promptly sat down again, her face growing serious. "But the church burned down."

"Sorry to hear that." I wanted to ask more but didn't want to get sidetracked.

"So, back to your school. If it's two stories high, and the Space Needle is sixty stories high, how many schools would we need to stack on top of each other to reach the height of the Space Needle?"

The girls adopted thoughtful stances. Helen plopped on the floor, crisscrossed her legs, and rested her elbows on the coffee table, chin in hands. Nora followed. *Have they learned two-digit multiplication yet?* Maybe I needed to get some paper.

"We can come back to that later. The Space Needle is just really tall. And it has a revolving restaur … Never mind." I pulled a photo of Vail and its iconic Clock Tower. "Let's try this one."

One by one, the girls politely looked at photos of Vail, the Colorado Rockies, my brothers and sisters, and my paternal grandparents.

Martha let out a huge yawn, then bolted upright. "Got any games?"

"She doesn't." Nora sighed. "But she knows patty-cake and Wolf!"

Oh Lord, I need to nip this in the bud. It was late and I didn't have the energy for another game of tag. I told the girls to wait a minute and returned to my bedroom for my Hacky Sack. The game was popular in college, and my little leather ball filled with beans was soft and shiny from use. Within a few minutes, I had demonstrated the basic moves of keeping the ball in the air with my feet, knees, shoulders, and head. They watched my moves, saying "ooh!" and "ahh!" and clambered for the ball when it rolled under the dining table.

They were soon playing their own version of Hacky Sack, swinging their legs wildly as if winding up for kickball, then smacking it with their palms. The ball ricocheted off the ceiling and walls, went behind the couch and down the hallway, and somehow ended up in the kitchen sink. There was much giggling and dramatic diving onto the couch. Dust motes floated through the air and glimmered in the light still coming through the living room window.

Play started winding down. I glanced at my watch to subtly signal it was time for this party to end, when Celia yelled, "How 'bout the newspaper game!"

"Yeah!" the others shouted in unison.

The door creaked open, followed by a rapid knock on the inner door. Before I could respond, three more girls walked in.

"Can we come visit?"

There I was, hijacked once more in my own house by a bunch of giggling girls trying to teach the teacher another game. And this one was tough.

"Newspaper" was a memory game using names. Participants stand in a circle, with one person in the middle, holding a rolled-up newspaper. All I had was *Newsweek.* Helen started to go over the rules but Nora interrupted, "That's not how it goes!" It was hopscotch all over again.

Eventually, I understood that the person in the middle called out a player's name, and that person had to say their own name and someone else's name, but the person with the newspaper was supposed to whack one of them before they got the name out. I understood the concept but failed miserably with remembering the girls' names.

It was a dizzying race of blurting out names and getting whacked, which hurt. Magazines are heavier than newspapers, and the girls liked hitting "Teach" the most. Whirling and getting whacked made it harder to distinguish one girl from another. They all started looking the same. Long black hair, dark eyes and skin, pastel jackets, hooded sweatshirts, and worn sneakers.

The girls finally gave up and fell to the floor in mass hysteria. Their heavy breathing subsided, and Helen looked at me, sitting once more in my dining chair. Seeing that I was done with the visit, she rallied her troupe.

"Okay, time to go."

The gaggle of girls complied. I listened to their laughter receding up the street, then looked at the curriculum binder and my cup of cold Earl Grey tea. How on earth did elementary school teachers cover all that material with such rambunctious kids? Maybe teaching the younger ones would be more fun than high school, but I would have to seriously ramp up my classroom management. It was clear that the girls had the upper hand.

I was disappointed that I'd missed another opportunity to plan my coursework. I glanced at my watch. The hands said ten. How did two hours slip by so fast?

I dumped the gray gum into the trash and gave the floor a quick sweep. As the small pile of granules disappeared over the threshold and onto the porch, I realized that the girls' visit was the largest party I had ever hosted in my life. And that felt like a win.

TWELVE

ROOMMATE

The next afternoon, I returned home from a short walk and saw a large black Hefty trash bag sitting on the porch. The front door was open. *That's strange. I could have sworn I closed it behind me.* I stepped into the boot room. The inner door was also ajar. I pulled it open farther and saw several medium-sized packing boxes sitting in the middle of the kitchen floor, alongside a suitcase. I heard a scraping sound, something on metal, and grunting, both of which came from deep inside the house.

"Hello?" I called out timidly. The sounds continued. I smelled cigarette smoke. *A workman? A plumber?* I stepped into the living room and looked down the hallway. The bathroom light was on.

"Hello?" I repeated. The scraping sound stopped, and a woman's head popped out around the bathroom door frame, low, as if she were kneeling. Her eyes were large, like a frog's. A cigarette dangled from her lips. Something clattered to the floor as she grabbed the door frame to pull herself up.

"Oof!" She placed a hand on her lower back. Cigarette ash dangled precariously.

The woman stepped into the hallway. She was older than me and a bit heavier. Curly gray hair cascaded to the collar of a pink button-down blouse, which was untucked over navy polyester pants. The final piece of her ensemble was a pair of battered gray sneakers.

"Hi," I said.

"Hi back." The woman took a long drag of her cigarette, then held it casually over her left shoulder. She reminded me of Cruella de Vil, but without the fur coat and streaked hair.

"I'm sorry, but who …"

"Anne. And you must be … the person who's been living here?"

Ohmygod. She's my roommate. And she's cleaning the toilet cone-can.

I'd been postponing the unsightly task, and now it was too late.

"Oh, geez," was all I could manage.

"So what's your name?" She asked it like a police officer during a traffic stop, then took another drag.

"Um. Genét. High school. English. Math."

She looked me up and down.

"And I am so very sorry." I looked toward the bathroom. "Here, let me …"

Anne stepped aside and I peeked into the small room. Another Hefty bag lay on the floor, along with a roll of paper towels, a scrub brush, and the bottle of Formula 409.

"You're supposed to line it." She nodded toward the Hefty bag. "Just drop one in there and pull it around the edges like a trash can. When it's full, we take it out." She paused. "It's called a honey bucket."

A honey what? I still had a lot of questions.

"Like an indoor outhouse?"

"Yep." She took another drag and glanced down the hallway. "I take it the bedroom on the left is mine."

"Um, yeah."

Anne went to the kitchen. A moment later, I heard water running. She must have done this before, this bush living stuff. I tossed my coat on my bed, rolled up my sleeves, and got to work. Maybe when I finished, I'd bum a cigarette. I didn't smoke but was pretty sure I'd start any day now.

My unsightly task complete, I gathered my tools of the trade and went to the kitchen. The house was quiet. Anne was gone. Maybe she went to the school to check things out. I noticed that the trash can filled with "dead" stuff had been removed. Anne had taken it outside. Apparently, Hefty trash bags were on *her* list, not mine.

A familiar pat-pat-pat sounded on the inner door.

"It's open!"

Nora, Celia, and a new girl tromped into the kitchen.

"Ooh, someone else living here?" The girls sniffed the air and looked at Anne's belongings on the dining table. A pack of cards, a hairbrush, and an ashtray.

I explained that I had just gotten a roommate, to which they scrunched their faces and then plopped onto the couch.

"Why the long faces?" I asked, hoping they understood that expression.

Nora changed the subject. "She's Lilly." She patted her friend on the chest. "Got snacks?"

I broke into a new box of granola bars and tried again. "So, what's going on?"

The three girls leaned back on the couch and chewed quietly, not wanting to divulge the cause of their sullen mood. I sat on the floor, eye-level with the soles of their shoes, which were almost worn through. Nora glanced sideways at her friends, on the verge of telling me a huge secret. Could she trust me?

"School." Nora let out a long sigh.

Celia and Lilly sighed in agreement.

Of course. The Big Event I had worked diligently toward for years—the first day of school that would finally launch my teaching career—was only two days away. I was excited, proud, and terrified. They were none of those things.

"Oooh, you got hole there?" Nora changed the subject and pointed at my ear.

She looked at my ear cuff, an accessory I had picked up in college, along with Hacky Sack and a pair of Birkenstocks. A friend in one of my classes had shown her ear cuff to me. I thought it was cool. She always seemed so sophisticated, even mysterious. I wanted those qualities for myself, too, and hoped an ear cuff would help.

I'd chosen a simple design with a tiny fake diamond post and a thin silver chain attached to a silver cuff that bent gently around the outer part of my ear. I had put it on just that morning.

Nora slid off the couch, knelt, and gingerly poked at it. The other girls came in for closer inspection. I held still, smelling the chocolate nuttiness on their breath.

"There's just one hole. Look." I removed the ear cuff and took out the post. The girls gathered around, exclaiming "Oooh!"

Nora directed me to put the earring and cuff back on, then take it off again. I was learning to be patient with her requests. Nora wasn't being rude; she was curious. After the last visit, I wrote a reflection in my journal:

I've decided to become an ethnographer, like Margaret Mead. Rather than feeling bothered by the girls' visits, I'll welcome them and get some answers to my ever-growing list of questions. These kids don't have a filter. They'll give me straight answers to things like:

- *When a plane buzzes the town, how long does it take to land and how long does it stay?*
- *Can a person get on the plane back to Nome and pay later?*
- *Why do the dogs stay chained up all the time?*
- *What's up with your facial expressions? The scrunching and the eyebrow raising?*
- *Where do people wash up?*
- *When does the ice start moving in?*

Without Helen, the group was more subdued. I decided to postpone my inquiry. The girls and I played two rounds of patty-cake, and with no mention of maps or the dreaded game of Wolf, they left of their own accord.

I stood by the kitchen window and watched them skip down the street, pleased with how my social circle was growing. Nora had taken the initiative to visit me and brought her friends. That was something.

I didn't know it yet, but that was their last visit. Once the girls found out that our space had been invaded by a stranger, the Carnation Breakfast Bar Club came to an end. Which meant I'd have to get my questions answered in other ways.

First photo of me in Shishmaref

PART THREE

AS THE WORLD TURNS

THIRTEEN

FIRST DAY OF SCHOOL

It finally arrived—my very first day as a Real Teacher. My nerves were tender, my mindset resolute. I was quivering inside but still standing.

It was only ten o'clock in the morning. My Inner Coach had been cheering me on through Period One, Consumer Math: "You're doing great! Keep going!"

But there was another voice standing by. I pictured it with arms crossed and lips pursed, its presence making me breathe from the top of my lungs in anticipation of a catastrophe. My chosen profession was turning out to be freaking unpredictable.

I learned at teacher orientation the day before that my one math class was for tenth graders only. It was called Consumer Math—an awkward choice of words in a subsistence culture. The title implied that I had to teach students how to make smart decisions when purchasing things like food or clothing. But here in Shishmaref, people's sustenance came largely from hunting and fishing. They didn't make weekend runs to cash in on discounts and fill up their carts at the grocery store. And from what I could tell by my students' worn out shoes and sometimes ill-fitting pants and sweatshirts, clothes shopping was more of an experience in bartering and hand-me-downs.

Only three of the seven students on my roster came. Their eyes darted around the room and then at me before they slumped into a desk. They were like foxes, anticipating a trap. I tried to put them at ease with a traditional roll call.

"Paula?"

I looked at the two girls. They both shrugged.

"Okay, how about Carol?"

Shrug.

"Tim?"

The one boy didn't move.

"Okay, how about you tell me your names and I'll check you off."

The foxes were trapped. One by one, they revealed their names (Cathy, Darren, Carol) and informed me that it sucked to be in school while their classmates were still on the mainland, hunting ducks and moose.

"And berry picking," Cathy added. "I wish we was still berry picking."

Cathy's use of the word "was" made me cringe, and I made a mental note to review which grade students were supposed to have learned proper verb tenses. For now, I let it slide. I remembered Midge's comment about berry picking and, in retrospect, should have invited more conversation. Besides, I was curious. "What kinds of berries? Do they grow near Serpentine Hot Springs?" "How do you cook a moose?" And, more important for course planning, "When does hunting and berry picking season end?"

But I felt pressured to push dutifully forward, briefly describing Consumer Math as a class where the students would learn how to handle money in the village or in a city like Nome or Anchorage, should they ever go.

At least, that's what I hoped it was about. The textbooks had been delivered less than an hour ago, which gave me only enough time to skim the Table of Contents. I was living a teacher's worst nightmare: totally winging it. Principal Ken dumped the box on my desk in a "Welcome to the Club" kind of way.

Since I hadn't had any time to prepare a lesson, I simply handed out the textbooks and instructed the students to turn to the math problems at the end of Chapter One. They seemed simple enough: double- and triple-digit addition and subtraction.

"Just do the odd-numbered ones as a warm-up, okay?"

"What's odd-numbered?"

This question came from Carol.

"Oh, sorry," I looked at her, confused by her question. "You don't remember the difference between even and odd?"

Carol scrunched her face.

My first teaching moment had arrived. I went to the chalkboard and wrote the numbers one to ten, then explained "even" versus "odd." The kids stared at me, like my second round of visitors had when I asked about stories (i.e., number of floor levels) in their school.

I needed to be more explicit.

"Just do these ones." I circled 1, 3, 5, 7, and 9.

None of the students had brought a notebook or pencil. I ripped three pages from a spiral notebook and rummaged in the drawer for pencils. I found a few but their points were either broken or dull. The kids watched as I cranked the pencil sharpener. It was rough going. The mechanism was bolted close to the wall, making the little handle hard to grasp. The blades needed a serious oil change. With each rotation, it shrieked like a baby fox whose paw was caught in a trap.

Cathy, Darren, and Carol methodically worked through the math problems, then moped out. I felt sorry for their second period teacher, and then realized the same group would be returning soon for English with Yours Truly. Perhaps, by then, they'd be livelier.

During student teaching, I had worked with two tenth-grade classes. They had the same brooding "nothing-you-do-will-make-us-smile" demeanor. Maybe it was an inevitable phase in high school—no longer new and nowhere near finishing. Tenth graders were the invisible middle child. In a word, overlooked. Why should they put energy into anything, if it wasn't going to be noticed?

On the upside, the group's lackadaisical posture made me look like I had excellent classroom management. Ned, my happy-go-lucky plane companion, would have been pleased. I pictured him at the door, smiling, then lobbing a Jolly Rancher candy toward me as reward.

Period Two came and I was about to start roll call, when my carefully choreographed plans came to a screeching halt.

"Are you prejudiced?" a female voice called out. Her tone was not one of curiosity. It was fierce and unapologetic, released without warning like an arrow dipped in poisonous provocation. And it pierced the vulnerable flesh of my new teacher's heart.

I scanned the room, feeling the blood that might help me form a coherent response draining from my prefrontal cortex. A girl in the front row stared at me, her eyes as sharp as the arrow she'd just launched.

There were about twelve students in the room, several short of a full roster. They peered at me through their long bangs or from under the visors of baseball caps, trying to gauge my inner response before an outer one left my lips. Would I defend myself? Would I blush? Get angry? Start to cry and leave the room? Anything was possible.

I was standing in the "Command Spot," front and center, my new grade book with student names cradled in one arm, poised to introduce myself and welcome them to school. It was a scene I had practiced multiple times in the mirror, but I still didn't feel grounded. It surprised me, how difficult it was for me to say my name out loud. Worse, I'd gotten conflicting advice about whether to use a more formal title (Miss Pierce) or just my first name.

My student-teaching advisor had told me to use Miss Pierce. "It garners more respect," he cautioned. "You aren't much older than they are, so you have to separate yourself to maintain control." He peered over his glasses. "Don't *ever* let them use your first name."

But Tim, a third-year teacher in the village, countered that advice. "Don't have them call you Miss Anything. They'll think that *you* think you're better than them."

Tim also wore glasses, but his were as thick as Coke bottles, which made his eyes look bigger and more convincing.

I was just about to introduce myself simply as "Genét" when the girl launched her prejudice question. The Command Spot dissolved beneath my boots. Blood returned to my face, making it flush.

Interestingly, the hiring committee had asked a similar question during my job interview. It was nestled between more mundane requests for me to explain my preference for having running water and how I handled boredom. It caught me off guard then, as well. How had I responded? Something about not intending prejudice or quickly making amends. Was that what I'd said? It felt honest, and the interview committee check-marked their pads, evidently in favor.

Then it hit me. I was being interviewed all over again. Before I could expect students to work with me, they needed to know who I was. I had not yet earned the title of Commander in Chief; I was a defendant on trial, and the jury wanted to hear me take the oath and swear to tell the truth and nothing but the truth, so help me God.

"Um, not that I know of," I answered quietly.

It was true, but it made my knees go weak. I needed to sit down. Attendance could wait.

I rolled my teacher's chair to what was left of my Command Spot, sat down, and took a deep breath. The girl who had asked the question was now at eye-level, still staring. I met her gaze and offered a slight smile, trying to soften the impact of her accusation. Her face was firm, but I caught a glimmer of hope behind her eyes—hope that I was not, in fact, prejudiced against her or her classmates. I scanned the other faces. No one moved. Their blank expressions could have outwitted any opponent in a game of poker. In Vegas.

"You know," I started again, "that same question was asked of me when I interviewed for this job." I paused. "And I'll tell you now what I said then, that I didn't believe I was prejudiced in the sense that I would deliberately judge and harm anyone. But there's a lot I don't know about you or this village, so it's likely that I'll say or do something that comes across that way."

I placed a hand on my chest—an instinctive gesture to show good intention and also calm my heart. *Was that okay to say?*

Maybe I should have asked for clarification. What did she mean by "prejudiced?" Did the students think that I believed they weren't smart? Or were they talking about blatant racism? What could I do to prove my innocence in a trial that had no facts other than the charge itself?

The girl in front seemed to want more but had at least stopped staring. The others glanced at her, then away. One boy started drawing circles on his desktop.

"How about this," I said, folding my hands as if in prayer. "If I offend you, please let me know." I paused. "It sounds like something happened before, like with another teacher?"

I didn't know where I was going, so I stopped. No one responded.

"Let's start over. My name is Miss Pierce … I mean, just call me Genét."

The girl's eyebrows went up subtly, then down. The boy next to her let out an audible yawn, his mouth open so wide I spotted two rows of silver fillings.

"And, to get started," I stood up, "I would love to learn your names."

I retrieved my grade book and checked off the students' names one at a time, repeating what I heard as a sign of respect, but worrying I was making things worse by doing so. My tongue just couldn't quite wrap itself around names like Senungetuk, Kiyutelluk, Ningeluk, and Pootoogooluk.

Halfway through, one girl informed me that students didn't go by those names.

"We have nicknames."

She decides to tell me now.

I glanced at the clock. Thirty minutes to go. *What the heck am I going to do with them for thirty minutes?*

I didn't know where the idea came from, but it was lovely, and it would put all of us out of roll-call misery, deliver accurate attendance, useful information about my students' lives, and provide an authentic assessment of their writing skills and penmanship.

"For today, I want you to write a letter to me …"

"Aww, man!" One boy slumped across his desktop. "We gotta work?"

His colleagues nodded in agreement.

"Don't think of it as work," I countered. "Think of it as a way to share things I ought to know about living here. You know, maybe to help me from inadvertently acting prejudiced." I smiled, hoping they'd appreciate some light humor.

No one had a notebook or writing instrument. I was about to rip more pages out of a used spiral notebook when Midge appeared in the doorway.

"Teachers keep coming to the office."

She held out a packet of looseleaf notepaper and a fistful of sharpened pencils. I mouthed "Thank you" and distributed the supplies, then returned to my desk.

A boy's voice broke the silence. "What you want us to write?"

It was a fair question. My prompt was vague. Write a letter about what, exactly?

I erased my previous lesson about even and odd numbers, and wrote the first thoughts that came to mind:

1. Your name
2. What I should know about living in Shishmaref
3. What you like to do
4. Describe your family

"What name you want?" The same boy's voice called out. His classmates chuckled. "Our school name or our nickname?"

Good grief, is this how the year's going to go? I give one instruction and I get three questions about it?

"Just write the name I called out, and your nickname if you want me to use that instead."

Seated once more at my desk, I felt my heart beating hard. My hands were clammy. *What was I doing here?* I was supposed to be in charge of this group, but they clearly had the upper hand. Thankfully, the students gave in. Soon, I heard the scratch-scratching of pencils, alternating with intermittent, vigorous erasing.

I took advantage of the time by doing my own erasing of their names from my gradebook, then carefully rewriting them and leaving three blank lines between each one for nicknames and notes about distinct features to help me tell them apart. Meeting so many students at once, and for the first time, was more challenging than I'd expected. Their faces were a blur of similarity.

The scratch-scratching slowed. I looked up to witness a couple of boys lowering their heads and closing their eyes. We still had fifteen minutes.

The girls must have sensed the lack of movement. One by one, they looked at their male counterparts, then at me. In unison, they laid their pencils down.

One boy jerked up from his snooze. "Time to go?"

What was his name … Harold? Hank?

The other students heard the word "go" and started getting up.

"Wait, wait." I stood and walked to my Command Spot once more. "There's still a few more minutes."

Thankfully, my command worked, and they sat down.

"How about if we just go around the room and you pick one thing from your letter and share that with me?" I gestured to one girl. *Molly?*

She scrunched her face, then sighed and looked at her paper.

"Well, um. If you're going to be here, it gets real cold. So dress warm. I guess."

I had hoped for more detail but moved on.

"How about you?" I gestured at a boy. *I really need to learn their names.*

"Well, um, it gets real cold here. So you need to stay warm."

The room snickered. I offered a slight smile of acceptance and pointed to another boy.

"Yeah, sure. Um." He scanned the two sentences on his paper. "Hey, well, yeah. It gets real cold here. And we're on an island, so you have to catch a plane to go anywhere."

Everyone laughed. I glanced at the clock again. There was no bell in the school to signal transitions between classes. It was up to each teacher to hold the line.

"Okay, good enough," I announced. "Please turn in your papers and pencils. Leave everything on my desk. See you tomorrow." I wondered which teacher would get this group next, wishing I could see how they handled this kind of group dynamic—resistance to work and a challenging demeanor. I also needed to ask Midge for some trays or baskets so I could collect student work in a more organized manner. My desk was already buried in a mashup of papers.

The girl who dared me with her prejudice question stopped at the door frame and turned.

"I have class this afternoon, too."

I stared at her, not understanding.

"After lunch," she added. "You know, Graphic Communications." Her eyebrows went up and stayed there.

"Oh, yes, got it. See you then!"

I had no idea what she was talking about. I pulled my schedule and traced a finger down the list. There it was: Graphic Communications. I had been so fixated on preparing for English and Consumer Math that I'd neglected to plan for my last class of the day and figured I could bluff my way through until I had time to ask Midge about it.

I swiveled in my chair. *How is it that I already feel three weeks behind? Oh god, what was that girl's name?* I stopped spinning and scanned my roster. I needed to confirm her identity before class, or else I would come across not caring enough to memorize her name. In a word, prejudiced. Was it Donna or Debbie? I knew it began with a D, and there were three girl names that started with that letter. I glanced at the clock again. Only an hour until lunch. Teaching was an unending series of glances.

My three tenth graders, Cathy, Carol, and Darren, returned for English class. They shuffled into the room and sat silently in the same desks.

"Wish we was berry picking." Cathy crossed her arms and scowled.

The goals for tenth-grade English were still a mystery to me, so I skipped the introduction and launched into a repeat lesson of writing a letter to me. Maybe writing about berry picking and hunting moose and whatever else they did when not in school would lighten their mood. I brought their attention to the board and added instructions to date their letter, write a salutation, and sign their work (and print your name, please).

"You have the choice to write for fifteen minutes or fill the page, whichever comes first." The idea appeared suddenly, like a download from the Teaching Gods. It was clever and clear, giving more concrete direction about how much to write, not just what to write about.

I returned to my desk and started erasing, then rewriting names in my grade book, feeling like a teacher again.

Carol raised her hand.

On my way to her desk, I passed Darren, who seemed to have interpreted "filling the page" by over-sizing his letters and using three lines instead of one. He was halfway there. I caught the words *cold* and *hunting*. Darren was testing me. He wanted to see how far I'd let him go. I honestly didn't know and was mildly irritated that the next move was on me to determine the limits for student noncompliance. With no ready answer, I walked past.

"Yes?" I came alongside Carol.

"Do we write on every line, or every other one?"

Another unanticipated question.

Carol's handwriting was faint and wobbly.

"Well, um, I guess every other line is fine. But try to press a little harder, okay?"

Carol nodded, pleased that she didn't have to start over. I passed by Cathy's desk. Her script was also wobbly, but at least it was darker, and I wouldn't have to hold her page up to a light source to make it out.

I vacillated between asking them to read their letters out loud versus collecting them, but I had no other plans except my map introduction. I took the chance and asked for volunteers to read their letter out loud. No response. Cathy, Carol, and Darren sat in silence, looking down. No one moved a muscle. Their obstinance reminded me of fifth grade when my music teacher volunteered me to sing the last line in the popular Christmas carol, "The Twelve Days of Christmas." I simply refused to be the sole voice singing "and a partridge in a pear tree" a dozen times, with classmates snickering and mimicking the flapping of little bird wings.

"Why me?" I'd whined. But my teacher had no good reason, and she couldn't make me do it. I hid my face behind my song book, denying the partridge its moment of holiday cheer.

I imagined my fifth-grade music teacher smirking from the other side of the room and saying something like, "Sucks, doesn't it? Now you know how I felt!" Was there such a thing as teacher payback, where everything I did as a kid was going to come back and bite me?

"Alright." I broke the silence and held out my hand to collect their papers. "This time I'll let you off the hook. We'll do my map introduction instead."

During lunch, I bumped into Midge on my way to the office.

"This came for you." She handed me an envelope.

It was a letter from my friend, Mia. I wanted to read it right then and there, but first I needed to clear up my question about Graphic Communications.

"Yeah, funny name," Midge smiled. "It's newspaper and yearbook. The school newspaper is called *The Northern Lights News*, but we didn't have one last year."

The good news, pun intended, was that I had taken a journalism class in high school. Finally, I had experience to fall back on! My high school had also been small, and the journalism class had only four students. We had a lot of fun investigating interesting stories around the town, interviewing people and doing research on things like new restaurants or the negative impact of aerosols on the environment. My contribution to the news crew was creating filler when content fell short of taking up a whole page. I made crossword puzzles, mazes, and word finds based on themes in our current issue.

Maybe that experience, and the fact that Graphic Communications class was the last one of the day, caused the class to go well. Darlene, the girl who'd asked the "Are you prejudiced" question, had a lot of ideas. So did her classmates Natalie, Sarah, and Molly. The previous year's hiatus had spurred them into action. I spent the hour taking notes and letting them lead.

When class ended, the girls continued their brainstorming on their way out of the building, and I made a beeline for the staff bathroom. Such joy, flushing the toilet and washing my hands. Time to be alone and not be in charge. But the day wasn't over, not by a long shot. I had to read the students' Dear Teacher letters and figure out what the heck to teach tomorrow. Back at my desk, I took a bite of a Carnation Breakfast Bar and began.

The first letter had no name and no salutation.

> *The first thing you should know about Alaska is to not go out during storms or you'll freeze to death. The second is to get along with people. The third thing is you have to learn the land and the culture they live on. I get bored when there is no game to hunt and there is nothing to do except count raindrops. It is exciting when we go whaling. We struck about five gray whales*

> *in about a month or two. And walrus hunting we go about 100 heads, sunk about 50-75 walrus. Also duck hunting can be very exiting it is so fun that we stay out for about a day or so.*

Wow. Going after gray whales? I thought whales lived farther north. Pursuing them sounded dangerous. And, if a person sunk a walrus, how did he or she get it back up again?

I flipped to the next paper, written by Martha.

> *You should know about our village. It's a tiny island about to sink. That's why they put seawall. Population of 300 to 400 people. Springtime, men go hunting walrus and oogruk. Men and ladies look for eggs and carrelling reindeer at Cape Espenberg. Summertime go hunt moose, ducks. And go fishing. Pick berries. Wintertime go hunt rabbits, ptarmigans, foxes, wolverines, caribous. Go riding around with snow machines. Or get ice. Dog teaming with guys with smart dogs.*

Both letters demonstrated problems with grammar and punctuation, but they were informative. I wondered what an oogruk was. *And where was Cape Espenberg?* I picked up another.

> *Dear Teacher,*
>
> *You should know that this place is cold and sometimes warm. Every year we always have long winters and short summers. Its lots of fun going camping in the summer. Theres lots of places to go like 7 mile, 18-mile, hot springs, Serpentine, anywhere around this little island. We have ten people in our family. 5 adults, 5*

children. 4 boys and 4 girls. None of them have any children yet. I have three uncles and six aunts. Playing basketball is fun. Going to pool hall is fun.

Sincerely,
Josey

There were a few short papers with comments like, "The first thing you should know is that Shishmaref is an island. It gets really cold here so be sure to have warm cloths." And "What you should no is that teachers should not give homework because we hunt and fish after school and on the weekends. In winter, we ice fish or hunt for seal. Very busy."

Yes, indeed, these kids sounded busy. I had no idea there was so much hunting, fishing, whaling, and walrus-ing going on. And reindeer? The students' letters were revealing, but I was a tad troubled that school didn't get an honorary mention. I kept reading.

"There is a pool hall and it's fun to play and also play Bingo. We like Bingo. We also are the best basketball team in Alaska. I jokes. But we are the best in the districk"

"Don't walk on ice."

"One thing you should know is we have certain expressions. Raised eyebrows means Yes, frown and scrunch face is No. You got to look quick to see but youll get the hang of it.

So *that's* what the eyebrow thing was all about. My little visitors did it multiple times, but I hadn't caught on. Seeing my daftness, Darlene exaggerated her facial expressions, especially her Scrunch of Disapproval.

Overall, the students' advice was clear: watch where you walk and don't expect us to do any homework. I flipped through the stack again. Many papers had no name, and most had no title for the assignment. I glanced at the board. Sure enough, I hadn't been explicit about those things. I could have sworn I said to write a letter. But maybe they had never learned to write a letter. Why bother? They lived within a five-minute walk of each other.

With my initial perusal of student letters to their teacher complete, I opened Mia's letter and read it through quickly. She had a lot of questions. Mia had been my best friend in college. We both had teaching in common and enjoyed long walks and coffee stops. She'd get a kick out of my adventures on the island. I would write back to her before going home tonight.

I tapped the students' papers to neaten the stack and leaned back. The first day of school was over. It was an out-of-body experience for much of the time, but I had their letters as evidence of progress. The question was how long it would last.

FOURTEEN

DEAR MIA

August 23, 1984

Dear Mia,

Thanks for your letter! My letters must take some time to get to you; I've sent 2 already. Your letter took 3 days to get here. You asked a lot of questions, so here are my answers so far!

Was I nervous about the first day of school? Well, yeah, but I was also super curious about how it was all going to go. Can't believe I am finally a teacher! The kids were sleepy, and one girl asked me straight out if I was prejudiced. That was a surprise. She seemed apologetic after I had a couple of classes with her, because she brought in her yearbook from last year and showed me a photo of a young female teacher who looked EXACTLY like me! Same light-colored hair, same haircut, even a jacket that looked like mine. At first, I thought it WAS me, like someone had snapped a picture without me knowing it.

Once the students saw that I'm a nice person, they opened up more and started talking about that teacher, saying things like, "She was bad. She said we wouldn't amount to anything." So, they probably thought I was that woman's doppelganger, sent to haunt them or something. Glad that got cleared up.

As for the size of the school, it's just like the high school I went to. Small classes and way easier than the masses I had to work with during student teaching. There is enough structure, and I haven't had to do much about discipline, just coax them to do the work, sit up. That kind of thing. One of the 10th graders invited me to play pool after school. I was surprised, because she comes across super moody, is often tardy with no explanation, and distracts easily. I'm trying to figure out the students' writing abilities. Not sure if it's fair for me to compare them to students in the Lower 48, but they do seem a couple of years behind. I think the school's only been here for a couple generations. It'll take time.

What did I do on the first day? Well, first, I couldn't for the life of me remember the schedule. It's a wacky breaking up of the day, with 50-minute periods and 5-minutes in between. Except for the first class, nothing starts at the top of the hour. There's no pattern. So strange. Where else in our lives do we stop learning at 12:20 and start up again at 12:25? And what if I have to use the bathroom at 10:15?

Second, I messed up students' names, left and right. My grade book is a disaster. Teachers received an accounting-style grade book. The lines are so narrow, and my students' names are so long, that I'm using 3-4 lines for each kid so I can get their name down and a few distinguishing characteristics. I started with "Wears glasses" and "NHAP" (for "Never Has A Pencil) but then realized that most of them wear glasses and none ever bring a pencil. So I've settled on "Shortest," "Headphones," "Dimples," "Pink coat," "Just Do It t-shirt" and stuff like that. The kids all have Iñupiat names and Christian names and nicknames. I'm trying to catch nicknames because that's what they call each other.

You asked what my roommate is like. Her name's Anne. She's a lot older than me, and marches to her own drummer. She talks a lot about her experiences in remote environments and her successes there. I wonder, if she is so successful, why didn't she stay where she was? Anyway, she teaches lower grades, so we don't see each other during the day. In spite of a lot of differences, we do share the same snarky sense of humor. Being her roommate is a challenge, though. More on that later.

About calling me … There's no phone in our house, but I can use the school phone in the evening. I'll get the number, but it might be easier for me to call you.

About church: They are rebuilding the old Lutheran church. It burned down several months ago, due to faulty wiring. They've had services in the school gym. No, I haven't gone. I don't really plan to go; it's too mechanical for me, and I feel like I'm intruding. And, yes, the Lutheran pastor is the only one in town.

Well, I promised I'd meet a student at the pool hall for a quick game. It's a little awkward, but I know it's important to hang out with kids. I'll finish this tonight.

~~ 7:50pm – Well, the pool hall had a "closed" sign in the window. Too bad. I'm back at school to plan for tomorrow's classes. I watched Reagan's Nomination acceptance speech. What do you think of him? Anne is outspoken with her disdain. She had a wisecrack for just about everything he said. Living in such close quarters, I know it's not wise to challenge her.

Much love, Me

P.S.: Books I'm reading: *The Hobbit, The Well of Loneliness.*

P.P.S: You asked about prices up here. Let's just say that everything costs twice as much!

FIFTEEN

PARADOX

Journal Entry
Friday, August 31

It's early evening as I write this. The setting sun is bathing everything in golden light. Blues are bluer, greens are greener. Everything is alive with the wind. The sea is deep blue and moves without a sound. The sky goes on forever. It is an orange evening.

It's shocking how life feels so fluid here, harmonious and free—yet, at school, that freedom is precisely what we intentionally try to control with our clocks and our rules. Don't we know, Mother Nature has no curfew? There is a peace curling its tendrils into me; it's palpable and cracking open my mind, releasing a self-imposed pressure in my head that I didn't know was there. I am growing new senses.

I want to tell my students about the shifting going on inside of me, but it's not yet clear what it's about. I am not sure how to reconcile where I am and where I'm from. I'm not sure what to still carry with me.

Maybe I want to say something like, "What I have come to do here in Shishmaref is not to teach you my ways. You have survived just fine without people like me coming to your island and telling you what to do. But maybe you don't have the choice? This is the paradox, where you must learn Outsider ways to avoid being taken captive by them. But I say, learn how to read and write in English so you have the power to use the language for your own defense. It's a double-edged sword. The intrusion creates pathways for innovation and change for the greater good, just as it brings cultural decimation.

Regardless, there is no turning back."

SIXTEEN

ARE YOU IN?

Principal Ken poked his head into my classroom.

"Hey. Computer Training. Tomorrow."

Our school leader often announced meetings in this manner, at the end of a long day, making it sound easy and no big deal. It was no secret that teachers didn't need more to do, so he used an innocent tone. Something a spouse might say to their partner on the way out the door: "Honey, can you pick up a carton of milk on your way home?"

Ordinarily, I enjoyed any kind of training. I loved to learn and never shied away from a challenge. So why did I want to claim my first sick day upon hearing the words "computer" and "training"?

My reaction was based on having used nothing more technically advanced than a typewriter. I typed funny, but I was proficient. My awkwardness stemmed from an experience in high school, when a well-intentioned community member donated a batch of 1940's Smith Corona typewriters. They had round black keys and weighed fifty pounds each. If strapped to dynamite, the machines could have doubled as incendiary devices and been dropped onto unsuspecting enemies. My only satisfaction came when pulling the silver lever to advance my sheet of paper and hearing that *ding*!

What I didn't like was losing skin whenever my pinky slipped into the deep gap between the apostrophe and the question mark. I had strong fingers on account of yard work, but I didn't always aim them right. It hurt like the dickens.

Our typing teacher, Miss Penelope, was a retired librarian. She was old and ornery—mean enough to pack a typewriter with dynamite if the occasion called for it. And determined to teach us how to type without looking at the keys.

"If you look at the keys, you slow down your speed," she warned. Her threat was aimed at the girls, of course. We'd be the ones typing, while the boys ran the store. I wondered if she'd ever read Betty Friedan's *The Feminine Mystique*. I pictured her pulling Betty's book from the library shelf and sticking it in a drawer.

One day, Miss Penelope announced a timed typing test. I was so nervous that I mistakenly placed my fingers one row too high. Instead of typing "The quick brown fox jumps over the lazy dog," I typed numbers and a lot of symbols: 2@35#$7%&! (I peeked). On paper, it looked like I was swearing like a sailor.

I raised my hand to explain my error, and could I start over? But my request was denied. Miss Penelope narrowed her eyes. "It's a timed test. Everyone has to take it at the same time."

I was so mad that I blurted out some words that matched the characters on my paper, which prompted my cranky, ancient, non-women's lib librarian to throw me out of the room. She swung her long, skinny arm toward the door. "Out!"

Our typing class was in a portable, so getting kicked out literally meant outside. She followed me to the door and pointed her bony finger at the metal-grated steps. "Sit here!"

I crossed my arms and turned away as she slammed the door on her way back into Typing Hell.

What a stupid, STUPID teacher.

I had never been kicked out of a class before. I was embarrassed, mortified. And fuming. My jaw clenched. My fingers curled into fists. I wanted to throw rocks. Big rocks. At the portable. Then maybe I'd run away. Maybe I'd find her car in the parking lot and kick the tires.

But then I heard the cheery chirp of a bird nearby and looked around. It was a sunny afternoon. The mountain air was fresh with scents of pine and dry earth. A warm breeze blew. I closed my eyes, leaned back, and listened to the bird's call, and another bird answering back. A smile spread on my face. So what if I flunked that so-called test? At least I wasn't stuck inside with my classmates, typing ridiculous sentences. I could hear the clackety-clack of their fingers typing over and over, "The quick brown fox jumped over the frickin' dog."

After that episode, I never trusted my finger placement. Through four years of college, I defied Miss Penelope and looked at the keys. Contrary to her warning, I was surprisingly fast and accurate, except for the times I became so engrossed in thought that the paper advanced past the roller and it took me ten minutes to realize that I'd been typing on rubber and had to start all over again. But I never typed another accidental row of expletives.

When computers came along, I got scared all over again. I expressed my fears to a college friend who was enrolled in a computer coding class. She gave me a tour of the lab, encouraging me to join her in front of the large cube-like machines. She flipped a switch and waited for it to buzz to life, then typed a row of letters and numbers. I watched, mystified.

"What if I make a mistake? And where's the paper?"

"You delete mistakes." She pointed at the delete button. "It's easy! When you're done, you just press this key and it goes to the printer."

It did sound easy, but I wasn't convinced. I preferred my trusty typewriter. Now, however, I had to face my fears. There was no way out of the principal's training.

The next day after school, I reported to the school library and plopped down in front of one of the oddly shaped cubes. Its screen was black as midnight. A small keyboard extended toward me, along with a small square device that I learned was called a "mouse."

There were cords everywhere, draped over the tables, snaking across the floor and into every available outlet. If the power surged, we'd either get excused or get fried.

The other five high school teachers chatted comfortably, not showing concern. I tried to relax. Maybe today it would make sense. Maybe a miracle would occur, and I'd finally understand what the fuss was all about. This was my chance to start over.

Our tables were arranged in a hexagon shape, which made it convenient for Principal Ken to peer over our shoulders and see how we were doing in Computer 101. Good for him, but the formation prevented someone like me from leaning over and seeing what a colleague typed. Call it cheating, but I considered it a necessary evil if I was going to know what the heck to do. The little white cursor blinked steadily, waiting for a command.

Principal Ken walked slowly and methodically around our cluster, like a Buddhist monk circumambulating a temple. The floor creaked under his weight and emitted a particular squeaky-squeak when he stepped behind me. He cradled a thick training binder in one arm and gestured like an orchestra conductor with the other, reading in cadence with each step.

Principal Ken was from the South. And I mean the *deep* South. His accent was so thick that I sometimes had no idea what he was saying. His I's sounded like "ahhhhs" and he dropped all Gs from the endings of words. "Typing" became "TAH-pin" and words like nothing, going, and hoping were reduced to nothn', gohn', and hopn'. At other times, he added sounds and syllables that didn't even exist. "Consciousness" became "KAHN-sheee-us-ness". "I declare" became "Ah dee-clare-uh."

This was a problem. Not only did I not understand the point of this training, I honestly could not comprehend what our dear principal was saying.

The other teachers kept nodding their heads, but I felt like I was on drugs; I could see his lips moving but couldn't string together a coherent sentence. The other teachers started clicking away on their keyboards, so I tapped on a few keys and used the backspace key to delete them, just to look busy. It seemed wise to refrain from asking what I was sure would be a stupid question. If I waited and watched long enough, maybe I'd figure out what to do. A moment later, the chance came skipping along.

After his third or fourth ring-around-the-rosy, Principal Ken stated, "Ah wahnt ya ta tahp arrrr yooo ee-in."

I stared at my computer screen.

Clickety clack! My colleagues typed something quickly and then stopped, waiting for the next instruction.

I bent down and fiddled with my boot lace in a feigned attempt to buy some time. Afraid to make eye contact and give away my growing sense of terror, I slowly sat up again and summoned a wee bit of courage.

"Could you repeat that?" I double-checked the position of my fingers above the keyboard. The cursor blinked, eager for play.

"Tahp arrrr yooo ee-in."

I didn't move. I had no freaking idea what he was saying. But wait ... maybe ... I dutifully typed "Are you in?"

I waited for Principal Ken's next instruction. Surely, it would soon be revealed what the heck we were doing and "who" was supposed to answer the question of being in. He walked around the tables, nodding and affirming, "Good." "Nice." "Got it."

He walked behind my chair. The floor released a squeak and then fell silent.

I felt Principal Ken leaning over my shoulder, his face close, eyes squinting from behind his thick glasses at my screen. My cursor squinted back.

"Wha-aht the hee-ell is that?"

"I typed 'arrrr yooo ee-in,' like you said." I mimicked his accent in defense. The other teachers laughed out loud, not even trying to shield my wounded ego.

To his credit, Principal Ken kept a relatively straight face, modeling that we do *not* embarrass a colleague who is already embarrassed. But he couldn't hold it.

"Hhmmph!"

His stifled laugh came out like one of those "I refuse to sneeze" sneezes. The training binder tipped precariously.

Duncan, a teacher who likely passed his college coding class with flying colors, leaned toward me and whispered, "He said to type R-U-N." He enunciated each letter and followed with a smile and a wink.

My index finger dutifully tapped the backspace key, erasing "Are you in?" and replaced it with the word RUN.

I imagined myself running. Out of the room, out of the school building. Across the timeless tundra, and all the way to Nome. I'd heard they had a street full of saloons where I could disappear into a dark corner—and where no one would ask me to type anything about a quick brown fox jumping over a frickin' dog.

SEVENTEEN

PILOT BREAD

A few days later, I was in the staff workroom. Duncan, the guy who'd corrected my "are you in" gaffe, sat on a counter and watched me at war with the school's one copy machine. The machine was winning. I just needed ten copies of a three-page, double-sided worksheet for my Consumer Math class. With staples. What should have taken five minutes had stretched into fifteen on account of having to stop every minute and unjam the damn thing. Class start time was minutes away. I still needed seven copies. My inner potty mouth was reaching new proportions.

Duncan had no obvious copying job and made no move to help me other than to suggest that I should stick to copying everything single-sided and forget about staples.

"Keep it simple," he advised. "The machine is old. It's gonna croak any day now."

Keep it simple. He had no idea how hard I was working to do just that. But I didn't want to become known as "She who broke the copy machine, so now we have to wait until Christmas for a technician to get all the frickin' way out here to fix it ... Thanks a lot."

The whole situation flustered me. Every lesson I taught was new. My confidence meter was below zero. I hadn't used the restroom for hours, which was going to make me late for class even if the ancient copy machine quit jamming. And I had Duncan, of all people, watching my meltdown. After my R-U-N debacle, he was the last person I wanted to have witness this event. Another Virgo nightmare: ineptness on display.

But there he was, sitting on the counter and rotating a large disc-shaped cracker with both hands, biting off small chunks from around the edges with his front teeth. He looked like a neurotic squirrel eating a Ritz cracker the size of his own head. He was eating as much of the plain part of the cracker as he could before getting to the middle, which was piled high with peanut butter and honey. It looked disgusting.

Ever since Computer 101 training, Duncan had taken a special interest in me, suddenly appearing in the hall outside my classroom or in the copy room. My interest in his presence was, like his cracker, growing progressively smaller.

"Mmm." He smacked his lips. "I sure love Pilot Bread."

I was in the middle of opening the copier's door number three to extract a piece of paper and only half listening.

"Pilot what?"

Duncan's demeanor shifted from neurotic squirrel to super psychoneurotic squirrel. He repeated my "Pilot what?" so loud I nearly cut a finger on a sharp metal edge. He jumped down alongside me, cradling the remains of his sticky cracker in the palm of one hand.

"You've never heard of Pilot Bread? Pilot Crackers?" A wave of peanut butter breath wafted across my face. He held up his palm so I could see every detail of his cracker-peanut-butter-honey-thing with tiny teeth marks around the edges. It was not a rhetorical question; Duncan was genuinely amazed, bordering on mortified, that I did not know about Pilot Bread.

I stopped trying to extricate a corner of paper that had gotten snagged between two rollers and looked directly at him, my mind a mess of peanut-butter-and-honey thoughts about my upcoming lesson and copy machine obstinance. I glanced at the clock. Three minutes.

Upon answering that no, I had not heard of Pilot Bread, Duncan shook his head and backed up a step. He looked genuinely sorry for me, but also pleased, as if thinking, "This girl needs a class in Arctic Living 101, and I'm her man."

Ben walked in with a handful of papers. Like me, Ben was new to teaching, but he seemed to know what he was doing, always casually strolling through the halls in his Carhartt pants and flannel shirt. His light beard had recently been trimmed. Ben looked at the copy machine with all its doors open and the ripped piece of paper in my hand.

"Uh-oh," he said. "Maybe I should come back later."

Duncan couldn't let it go. "Hey, Ben. Did you know our dear teacher here made it all the way to the Arctic without ever hearing of Pilot Bread?"

"No way! Never heard of it, huh?" He winked at me and then looked at Duncan's hand. "What have you got on it today?"

"Well, quite the mess, it seems." Duncan licked a glob of peanut butter and honey and then unceremoniously popped the rest in his mouth. With his mouth full and hands sticky, he turned toward the sink. These two were oblivious, concerned more about what I ate than in helping me with my copying dilemma. Countdown to class was now two minutes.

Duncan finally swallowed and dried his hands. "Cheese, sardines, pickles. You can dip Pilot Bread in soup or crumble it on your green bean casserole. They come in these huge boxes." He held his hands out like he was showing us the size of a fish he'd just caught. "Last forever. Great shelf life. I just had a case shipped up from Anchorage. Come over to my place and I'll give you one." He smiled broadly.

I hesitated, unsure how to respond and wanting to deflect any iota of interest Duncan thought I might have in him. I looked at the copier, then at Ben. "I gotta get to class. Can you figure this out?"

"Uh, sure." He smiled. "You go on and R-U-N to class."

I was caught between thanking Ben and flipping him off. The window of opportunity was closing fast; I'd deal with it later. No students had arrived yet, so I tossed the three unstapled copies onto my desk and jogged down the hall, hoping I'd figure out how to give my students practice with calculating percentages with only a few worksheets between them.

I was fast learning that having students copy equations off the board didn't work well. Whether on account of sloppy attention or poor eyesight, they usually made mistakes with transcribing, which led to mistakes in their answers. Yesterday, it took me half the period to realize why the kids' answers to simple word problems kept missing the mark.

After a considerable amount of student whining, I realized that Paula had copied several math problems incorrectly. Tim, who always sat next to Paula, copied her paper, rather than looking at the board himself. Then Andrew copied Tim's work. And so it went, around the room.

In my opinion, copying classmates' work was called cheating. But the students were so blatant about it that I didn't know what to do. Should I call them out? Should I let them cheat? Ideas flitted about like the fly who'd been trapped in my room for the last two days. It kept batting its poor body on the window, looking for a path to freedom, yet escaping each time I tried coaxing it toward the door.

The voices in my head were loud. *If they don't think through problems on their own, they won't learn anything. But if they copy Paula when she's doing it right, they might pick up the sequence for solving math problems through osmosis. Maybe they needed the threat of a test, with the desks spaced apart.* I had given a short one a few days before; it freaked them out.

That's when it occurred to me to use worksheets. I had to create them myself, but having preprinted math problems right under their noses would eliminate further copying, right? Each student would have the chance to show me they understood how to calculate sales prices on realistic items from the Native Store, like how much for a flat of twenty-four cans of pop when the original price is twenty dollars with tax, but marked twenty percent off?

That was yesterday. After school I excitedly crafted the worksheets. I felt a surge of renewed optimism. But then the copier killed it.

Maybe I could use the three finished copies and have the students work in groups? Or maybe I could write problems on the board and have students come up one-by-one to calculate the answers? But then the other students would get bored and give up. Or maybe the student I called up first would calculate wrong, further confusing the rest of the class.

By the time I finished washing my hands, my thoughts were a jumble of misfired neurons. Like the fly against the window, they banged around, preventing me from seeing a way out of my dilemma. As I jogged back to my classroom, the only thing that made sense was having students do group work. It might work or it might implode. But I was out of time.

I slowed to a walk and crossed the threshold. Two students were at their desks, heads down on folded arms. I stopped and contemplated my next move. Should I back out on tiptoe and go home? Flick the lights to wake them up? Were they truly sleeping or merely pretending?

The latter had happened more than once. Teenagers were crafty with feigning sleep, nodding off in a moment but then jumping up and scaring the bejeebers out of me when they caught any whiff of being able to leave. They'd slip from their desks and exit the room so fast there was no way to give them a homework assignment. On the upside, if we ever had to quickly evacuate the building, my group would win first prize.

Four more students sauntered in, unable to resist poking their sleepy classmates as they passed by.

"Hey." (Poke)

"Hey!" (Poke back)

Class was on.

"Hey, guys," I started, trying to shake away my last twenty minutes of angst. "You know how you go to the store, and something is on sale?"

No response.

"You know, like when you want to buy some pop but instead of getting one can, you see a whole flat of cans with a sale sign at twenty percent off?" I paused. "So you get a better deal?"

I took a breath, realizing I had violated a cardinal rule in teaching: *Thou must begin class slowly so students can match thine pace.*

It was a rule my mentor teacher consistently advised. "You want everyone on the train with you when it leaves the station," she'd say, shaking her head after I destroyed yet another lesson by starting too fast. "When you rush the first steps, the kids aren't with you, which means you have to stop and back up. It's a waste of time. And use more props. Kids love props."

"What's a flat?" Andrew suddenly showed interest.

"Flat tire!" Charlie blurted, snickering. His jacket collar was askew, making me want to reach out and straighten it. His left shoe was also untied.

"Flat earth!" Tim liked following Andrew and Charlie. The more, the merrier. He used his right hand to wipe back and forth on his empty desktop. "We just learned that in Geography class. The earth is *not* flat, even though when you stand on the beach it sure *looks* flat!"

Snorts and giggles erupted around the room.

I was losing control. These students loved jerking my attention back and forth with their antics. I envisioned Ned at my door, shaking his head and saying, "No Jolly Ranchers for you today." Next to him was my embattled mentor teacher, whispering, "I told her to start slow." Ned would nod. And then she'd add, "and use a prop." Ned would nod again and offer her a red-hot cinnamon.

My mentor teacher was right. I should have used a prop to start this lesson. I could have brought a cardboard box flat with twenty-four cans of pop and made a sale sign, and not be dealing with smart-aleck comments about flat tires and a non-flat earth.

"My uncle gets lots of pop on sale. Only lasts a few days."

This comment came from Andrew. He'd hopped on the train. Hopefully, his classmates would hop on, too. Feeling the chug-chug of the train leaving the station, I smiled and handed out my worksheets, pairing the students in ways I anticipated would work best, given their varied abilities and tendency to distract one another. Charlie and Tim constantly interruped class but stayed oddly focused when together. Andrew went with Carol. He was my "can do" student. He always buttoned his shirts to the top and polished his glasses with Kleenex. Carol was equally studious. She'd hardly say a word in class, but would talk my ear off if I got her alone. Cathy and Paula were the last pair. They looked like twins, even though they'd assured me they weren't. My gradebook had microscopic notations: C<P height, blk glasses …

The students were remarkably adept at moving their heavy desks without actually getting up. I watched them hoist the furniture and half carry, half drag it to sit closer, then flip the worksheets front to back, sizing up how much I expected them to do.

I suggested they take turns. "One of you can do the odd numbers, one can do the even ones. I'll guide you from up front."

"I need a pencil."

"Me too!"

I sighed. "You guys really need to start coming to school with something to write with and something to write on." I said these words with an edge of agitation, frustrated about losing momentum and then frustrated that I could not hide my frustration. My pencil supply had dwindled big time. Soon, I'd be known as "the teacher who uses more pencils than anyone-else so that's why there aren't any left in the frickin' supply room … Thanks a lot."

For the next half an hour, we all worked together. My little teaching train huffed and puffed up the hill. We had just started to calculate the cost of a box of Bubblicious at a fifteen percent discount when a line of ninth graders walked by our open door. I glanced at the clock; the other teacher must have let them out a few minutes early.

My group jumped up in unison and, before I could say anything, foisted their worksheets on me and ran out of the room, flapping their arms and performing little leaps in the air.

And taking their pencils with them.

"You're dismissed," I said as the last one flew out the door. "I guess."

That evening, I told Anne about my Pilot Bread altercation with Duncan. She got up from her game of Solitaire and pulled a large box of Pilot Bread from the cupboard.

"Funny you should ask. Just got this today. Help yourself."

The box was heavy, filled with about twenty crackers stacked against each other like Oreos. I slathered butter on one. The cracker was crumbly and dry, but surprisingly satisfying. Duncan's glob of peanut butter and honey was making sense. The gooeyness provided moisture and probably held the cracker together as he ate it.

I read one panel of the box, muttering quietly to myself. "Sailor Boy. Serving size, one. Thirty-eight to forty servings in a box." Munch. "Same calories as a slice of bread."

"Why do they call it Pilot Bread, when there's a sailor on the box?" I looked at Anne. She paused her play and raised an eyebrow, then took a long drag on her cigarette.

"Well ..." She exhaled slowly through her nose like a dragon and blew the remaining smoke toward the ceiling.

"Sailors are pilots, too."

I took another bite to cover my embarrassment. Should have seen that coming.

Always eager to impart her vast knowledge to anyone within earshot, Anne continued with a string of trivia that, if I ever got to be a contestant on *Jeopardy*, would make me a winner.

"Those crackers are better than bread. They don't get moldy very easily. In the old days, it was called 'hard tack.' Perfect for sailors out at sea for months. Now, hunters, fishermen, outdoorsy types, they all love the stuff." She laid a card on a row. "And now, teachers, it seems."

The next morning, I asked Anne if I could take a couple of her crackers for lunch, promising to replenish her supply.

"Use peanut butter and honey," she advised. "It's messy, but it'll hold you till dinner."

I spread a thick layer of peanut butter on one cracker and a drizzled honey on another, then pressed them together into a big 'ol Pilot Bread sandwich.

"I'll eat this in the copy room," I said, smirking. "In front of Duncan."

EIGHTEEN

KULIZUK

The calendar finally turned to Saturday. I loved Saturdays. For forty-eight hours, no one expected anything from me. I rolled over in my sleeping bag and looked at my travel alarm. Not quite nine o'clock. I yawned and shimmied my arms out for a stretch, listening for signs of Anne, who typically woke before me. The house felt quiet. I slid out of my warm cocoon and gently opened my bedroom door. Anne's door was still closed. Maybe she was still here. I tiptoed past, to the bathroom.

The only lighting in the small space was a fluorescent tube behind a plastic ceiling panel. It never mattered what time of day it was, in here my skin looked pasty, even gray, like I had died and was on *The Other Side* looking back at my former earthbound visage.

I splashed cold water on my face and studied my reflection—a pale, young woman with tousled blond hair and an oversized turtleneck that doubled as a sleeping shirt. I leaned in closer. More creases had formed in my forehead, and there were bags under my eyes. I smiled deliberately to look at the lines at the sides of my mouth. *Is this what I'll look like when I'm an old teacher?*

Anne's cough startled me out of my amusing little game. I wanted to be on my way before she appeared and took over the house with her cigarettes and solitaire. My plan was simple. I'd grab coffee and a breakfast bar, then head to school to work on next week's lessons so they didn't chase after me like a pack of stinky husky puppies. All I needed were rough ideas for each class (with props). I'd polish the lessons tomorrow.

Anne's coughing grew louder, a deep, guttural choking that started with brief bursts and ended with a series of longer gagging sounds. I hated Anne's smoking habit. Couldn't she see how bad it was for her, and how bad it likely was for me? Her smoke permeated everything: my clothes, our kitchen towels, the couch. She never apologized for lighting up, and for some reason, I didn't feel like I had a right to ask her to stop. I wished I had more guts. As a young girl, I had plenty of courage, standing up for myself and others. At the ripe age of eleven, I even punched Daniel Spade on top of the head to get him to stop harassing the Catholic kids who got rides on our school bus each day. . . . and he did. So why couldn't I ask Anne to smoke on the porch? Maybe I couldn't stand the thought of her out there, shivering in the frigid air and cursing me.

Anne's coughing stopped. I dressed quickly: Corduroy pants, a flannel shirt over my turtleneck, and a slightly used pair of wool socks. I tiptoed to the kitchen and pulled on my boots. The floor was always freezing, especially near the front door.

A few minutes later, I was in my usual spot, close to the stove and holding my palms over the saucepan to warm them. This was my morning ritual, my meditation, watching my thoughts rise with the bubbles, then vaporizing.

My jar of instant coffee was almost empty. I'd been thinking of graduating to a coffee maker, a smaller version than the one at school. Maybe Walter could order one for me. A coffee maker would bring an end to this ritual, but watching water dripping into the carafe might be just as captivating.

Only one breakfast bar in the box. I'd save it for later. There were usually some errant snacks in the teacher's lounge, and I might find something there. Coffee in hand, I stepped quietly out the door, wishing I had a longer commute to get emotionally ready for the work ahead. But in less than a minute, I was traipsing up the steps and into the chilly air of the school.

Sure enough, there was a box of granola bars in the lounge. Yesterday's coffee was still in the carafe, so I rinsed the pot, tidied the counter, and went to my classroom.

I was unsure what to plan for my English classes, so I started with Consumer Math. It was getting easier, thanks to the textbook. Students still needed practice with basic math functions, so I could move to the next chapter and review decimals, and maybe assign students to interview community members about costs for equipment parked in various places around the village. How much did one of those big Caterpillar machines cost? Or an oil drum? Their research might provide valuable information about village life, more useful than "it's cold" and "don't walk on ice."

I was quickly learning that teaching was frickin' hard, but planning what to teach, and how, was harder. With no curriculum guide for English, the possibilities were endless. I didn't know where I was going and couldn't sketch out more than a day or two at a time. It was like being lowered into a cave without a headlamp and groping in the dark, praying that a shaft of light from the surface would break through and show me what was up ahead.

But if I persisted with my groping, an idea always seemed to appear. That's all I needed: one good idea to greet me in that dark cavern and grab my hand. If I trusted it, more ideas always came along. They braided together like a guide rope, leading me home. I loved those moments in planning, when things clicked. My stride grew longer and more confident. My Inner Coach usually showed up then, too. *See? You can do this!*

It was my happy place, when I entered a kind of floating reality where time ceased to exist. It was just me and the chalkboard, where I wrote my lessons into life. Once they were scripted on that larger palette, I transferred the ideas to paper.

Saturday mornings were usually quiet at school, allowing me to work in solitude. This morning was no different except for when I heard the front door open and click shut, followed by the sound of boots down the hallway. Then it was quiet again.

Near noon, I needed to stop. I set down my chalk and wiped the residue on my pants. Time for a stroll to Walter's store.

"Good day to you, Teacher!" Walter waved. "What brings you here on a Saturday? I thought teachers slept in on weekends!"

"Well, this teacher's been hard at work," I teased back. "Just taking a break."

"Take your time." He jerked a thumb over one shoulder. "Gotta check stuff in back. Holler when you're ready."

I always started with a quick scan of the front shelves, where Walter positioned specialty items. One day, there was a box of pears. Another time, a large bag of brightly colored bandannas. Walter loved to mix things up.

My list was short: Pilot Bread and a portable snack—something other than Carnation Breakfast Bars. I was getting bored with those but, more importantly, I knew I was racking up quite the tab. My first paycheck was still one week away, the first of October. It had been two months since my severance pay at the café, and I was weary with waiting. It felt rude that the school district forced teachers to wait six weeks before rewarding them for all their hard work. Why not offer a start-up bonus to help make ends meet?

I returned to the front counter with a box of Pilot Bread, a box of Nature Valley granola bars, some instant soup packets, and a jar of strawberry preserves. As I waited for Walter, I imagined all of the different kinds of sandwiches I might make with the Pilot Bread. There was plain butter, peanut butter and honey, peanut butter and jam, maybe even peanut butter and butter (redundant but potentially tasty). I had some cheese. Pilot Bread Pizza?

"What'd you come up with today?"

"Typical teacher food, I guess." I shrugged and smiled. "Do you think you could order a coffee maker for me? One of those Mr. Coffees. A small one."

"Sure, I can do that. But it might take a while." He rang up my items and recorded the sum in his ledger.

"You know," I interjected, "I need to get a bill from you. My paycheck is coming next week, and I need to know if I'll have anything left after paying what I owe you."

Walter flipped through his book, did some mental math, and announced that I was on the hook for about three hundred dollars and change. I gulped. I had only a rough idea what my net pay was going to be. Maybe my soup packets and jam could wait.

Walter guessed my thoughts. "Jam's half-price." He grabbed it before I could protest and slipped it in a bag.

The doorbells jangled, and two men walked in. Walter suddenly changed the subject.

"You need a good Eskimo name."

He studied my face and hair, the latter still tousled from not having done more than run a brush through it. His eyebrows narrowed, registering concern.

"But we have no word for yellow hair." He waited a second for the words to sink in, testing my capacity for teasing in front of an audience of strangers. I appreciated the joke, but my face still flushed. It was true—except for Principal Ken's son, I was the only blond person in the entire village.

"Ah." Walter snapped his fingers. "Got it. Kulizuk."

"Kooly-zook?" I tried to imitate his emphasis on the "ook."

"Yup. Means 'brown hair.' Close enough, huh?"

The two men glanced at Walter, their faces blank. They were neither going to confirm nor deny that Kooly-zook meant brown hair. Since landing in the village, I had been learning that the locals had a dry sense of humor and sarcastic wit. People joked easily but kept a straight face, which made people like me (meaning gullible) wonder if what they said was, in fact, true.

I didn't want to offend anyone by disbelieving them or calling their bluff. But then their eyes would start to squint at the edges, giving way to a gentle, almost shy laugh—pleased to have once more pulled one over on the teacher.

Walter loved teasing me and made me wait uncomfortably long at times before his punch line. I had to trust now that he wasn't giving me a derogatory name in jest, like "hair the color of moose doo-doo."

But maybe being called Kulizuk was better than Smurfette, which is what my little visitors had started calling me. Nora and her classmates spied me one day in the street and yelled out, "Hey, Smurfette!" Then they giggled and ran away.

I passed Midge in the office and asked if she knew what a Smurfette was.

"Some cartoon character." Her eyes crinkled with amusement. "She's got blue skin and yellow hair. Part of that new series kids watch." She paused. "I think she's kind of, how to say … spunky."

I looked at Walter. "Okay, Kulizuk it is. There's so much sand around here that brown hair is what I'll have pretty soon."

The men laughed, and for the first time, I felt a little like I belonged.

I returned to school and worked for the rest of the afternoon, excited about my lesson plan for students to expand their vocabulary by learning how to use a thesaurus. I had two of them in my room. I went to the library to look for more.

The day took an interesting turn when I flipped on the light switch and startled a man sleeping on the floor. It must have been his boots I'd heard earlier in the hallway. He was zipped into a sleeping bag and laying on a gym mat in one corner. The man looked a little older than me, probably in his thirties. He sat up and ran a dirty hand through his greasy brown hair. I caught a whiff of motor oil.

A few minutes of polite conversation later, I'd learned that his name was Jed, and he was a traveling electrician. With no hotel in Shishmaref, the only lodging available to maintenance workers was people's homes, the church, or the school. Jed had been working on the school's circuit breakers, which had been tripping almost every day for two weeks. It always happened during second period. The kids and I would hear a whirring sound, then a click, then the lights went out. The outages were so regular that I'd started planning my lessons around them. At first, I tried to come up with things we could do in the semi-darkness, but it was a hard sell; the kids thought the extra activity was unnecessary. They'd lay their heads down for a nap until we heard a click and the lights returned fifteen minutes later.

Jed and I exchanged polite conversation for several minutes, and I was about to excuse myself, when he asked if I wanted to get high.

"Got a joint." He patted his coat pocket. "Happy to share."

"Oh, geez." I laughed nervously. *Where the heck did he expect to smoke a joint and not get caught?* The cold air outside would hold the acrid aroma at nose level, and the constant wind would blow it all over town.

I told Jed I preferred to keep my boots on the ground, a response that humored him but didn't deliver what he wanted. I had the sneaking suspicion that the shared joint would be leading to something more intimate. Another poor bloke barking up the wrong tree.

"How 'bout a moose steak?" Jed changed his approach. "I got a bull last week outside of Anchorage. Been carrying around a good-sized piece." He used his hands to show the size of a dinner platter. Just need a place to cook it."

"Thanks, but I'm a vegetarian." I turned toward the door.

Jed thought it was ridiculously funny that I was a vegetarian, living in a major meat-eating ecosystem. I countered that I was doing just fine with canned soup, apples, and Pilot Bread.

I couldn't get out of the school fast enough. Hopefully, Jed would be gone tomorrow so I wouldn't have to deal with his odd advances when I returned to finish my thesaurus lesson.

Anne was home, of course, and I filled her in about the traveling electrician who wanted to get me high and then feed me moose steak.

"You turned him *down*?" Anne was shocked.

"Which part?" I was confused.

"The moose!" She stubbed out her cigarette and headed out the door.

Ten minutes later she returned, with a gleam in her eye.

"I invited Jed for dinner. I love a good moose steak."

Before I knew it, Jed was in our kitchen, standing at the stove with his platter-sized piece of moose sizzling in half a stick of butter in our largest skillet.

"There's hardly any fat in it," he explained.

Anne doted on Jed as if he were her own son. She made a pot of rice and heated up green beans from a can. It felt rude for me to disappear into my bedroom, so I sat at the dining table, feigning interest in their meal preparations.

The inevitable moment came when Jed and Anne insisted that I try "just a teeny bite" of moose. My only experience with moose was from watching Rocky and Bullwinkle cartoons as a kid, but I had seen pictures in *National Geographic* magazine and knew that moose were wild, majestic, funny-looking creatures with huge heads and skinny legs. They looked comical but had a mean streak. I wondered how many steaks one moose could make.

Jed and Anne watched as I lifted the fork to my mouth.

It might have been the butter, but I had to admit it was the best bite of meat Kulizuk the Compromised Vegetarian ever had.

NINETEEN

NORTHERN LIGHTS NEWS

Late in the evening one week later, I was alone once more with my lesson planning at school. The building was quiet. No sounds drifted in from outside. No wind. No traffic. No birds. Probably because there were no trees. The cries of seagulls or squawks from Arctic terns high in the air would be too faint to hear.

In my hand was Volume One, Number 1 of *The Northern Lights News*, the school newspaper. It was literally hot off the press. It had taken all afternoon and into the evening for my Graphic Communications team, Darlene, Natalie, Sally, and Molly, to make the two hundred copies on our school's embattled copy machine. Ten pages each, single-sided, no staples. That was two thousand sheets of paper—four reams. The machine started to overheat after fifty copies, forcing us to copy in batches of twenty, followed by twenty minutes to let the machine cool down. I finally sent the girls home and finished myself. In my hand was the last copy to drop into the output tray. It was still warm.

Using the school's one copy machine was risky, but we had no choice. Sending the proof to Nome would have taken two weeks. And our news wouldn't have been new anymore.

The girls had worked hard, brainstorming story ideas and making appointments to interview the new teachers for a segment they titled "Close Encounters."

"It's what we do," Natalie said matter-of-factly. "Lots of new teachers every year."

When it was my turn to be interviewed, she asked about "that little line thingy" over the second E in my first name.

"It's French," I explained, "called 'l'*accent aigu*.' It signals the sound of 'ay' at the end. I'm not sure how to type it, so we'll have to draw it by hand." I grabbed a fine-point black pen and drew a tiny line.

"Cool," said Darlene. "Maybe I'll add that over my second 'e', too." She tossed her hair back and mimicked a French accent. "Darlené!"

It was nearing ten o'clock, and I was ready for bed. But I was proud of our little newspaper and wanted to share it with someone. The first person who came to mind was my friend Mia. She'd appreciate the articles the girls had written about school and goings-on about the town, and I could use the blank sides for writing a more personal letter as a means to ease my loneliness. I straightened the pages and stapled them, then looked once more through the edition before taking my pen to it.

The front-page article was Molly's. She wanted to write a report about the Lutheran church that burned down due to faulty wiring. She took a classmate and interviewed Pastor Dillon, who informed them that volunteers had been coming to Shishmaref for weeks, pitching in to rebuild the church and make it safer. They came from the Pacific Northwest, Lutheran communities in Alaska, even the Midwest. I hadn't ventured near the site but had heard distant sounds of hammering and sawing whenever the wind shifted. The story, which they titled "Willing Hearts and Hands," read, in part,

> It can never truly replace the old one, but it surely will be a fine replica. It will rise to two stories and will be topped with a tall tower. A special ivory and rosewood cross carved by Melvin Olanna will decorate the front of the church's interior, behind

> the altar. Sealskin banners, paintings, and other artwork will decorate the other walls.

I wondered who Melvin Olanna was and what a sealskin banner looked like. Lutheran with Iñuit—such a melting of cultures and, apparently, a labor of love.

The Close Encounters segment with new teacher interviews divulged that most of us enjoyed camping, hunting, and outdoor sports, and we wanted to come to Shishmaref to "try something new." It was interesting to read my own interview responses. I had forgotten that I mentioned a fondness for building airplane models or my dream of one day living on a beach.

The newspaper staff also interviewed high school students who had come to Shishmaref on account of their own village not having a high school. Until I read their report, I didn't make the connection that a couple of my students were from Wales, a village seventy miles south of Shishmaref on the southernmost tip of the Seward Peninsula. I wondered if Wales was a misspelling of the word whale. That point of land would see a lot of whales passing by twice each year, heading south in the fall for warmer waters in Baja and returning north in the spring.

Other news included the list of class officers, the recap of a recent junior fundraiser dance party, and information about the fire station and its 1983 red pickup, complete with a water tank and pump. The girls also reported on the seawall construction and how the new design of cement blocks and steel cables would "last way longer than the sandbags!"

There was also a piece about the new airstrip. How did I not know about that? The island was flat; I should have seen something. Maybe that was the activity I'd spotted on a stretch of the island to the south of town. I usually stayed on the beach. But one day the wind shifted, and I heard the droning of engines. Through my binoculars, I saw a bulldozer ripping into the tundra. So that's what they were doing, building a new airstrip. The bush pilots were probably dancing in their boots. No more unnervingly low approaches over the lagoon or takeoffs over the ocean.

The best news, in my opinion, was the near completion of the Washeteria, a huge water tank and adjoining building on the north end of town. Its presence answered one of the primary questions I'd had since moving to the village: where did people shower and wash their clothes? The Washeteria was no small feat. Its water tank held 1.3 million gallons of water (I had no idea how that happened), but there would be only six showers, six washing machines, and four dryers for a village of about five hundred people. *Did they take reservations?*

Later pages of the newsletter included word searches created by Yours Truly. After hearing about my newspaper experiences in high school, the Graphic Communications staff put in orders for word searches of all the students' and teachers' names. I was overwhelmed with the task at first but realized the puzzles were good practice for learning who was here.

I flipped to the back of page one and wrote the date. Tuesday, September 11, 1984.

Oh my god, tomorrow's my birthday. I had been loosely aware of dates, but with everything going on and my general mental and emotional exhaustion, my birthday didn't seem real. And I had no close friends or family around to remind me. No one asking what kind of cake I wanted. Maybe I'd make my own cake. Pilot Bread with a heap of peanut butter and honey. And twenty-four candles.

Dear Mia,

Well, here's our first issue! The girls did 99% of the work. I am really proud of them! Today was tough, but tonight I can look back and see all of the good things that took place: a kind word, an understood lesson, the sunny sky, being teased. I feel good about what I'm doing, yet there is so much that's new to me, so many challenges to face, emotionally and academically.

I've been writing like crazy in my journal. I'm even reading a book about writing in a journal! I've tried a few new techniques, and a whole new side of my life has emerged. I see patterns of thought in my reflections and how my attempts to get consistency in my classroom are sabotaged by waves of indecision based on my lack of experience. I haven't been here long enough to know what works. Things keep changing. My emotions are all over the place. I bottle them up. Does this even make sense? I'm trying to sort it out as I write here. Tomorrow I will turn 24 years old; I feel like I'm 12 years old one minute and have aged 10 years the next.

I've got a new lesson for all of my kids tomorrow, to take some of the stress out of my day. I'm going to build up their stamina for bringing paper and pencil to class, instead of me always providing it. I created a little personal checklist for each student. If they make it through the week with check marks, they win a prize. I don't know what that will be, but I have two days to figure it out.

Anyway, I took a walk yesterday for four hours, around the edges of the island. On the southeastern side, they're bulldozing like crazy; the plan is to move the dump and build a new airstrip, complete with a little building (air terminal). I hate to see them ripping up the tundra for it. The little airstrip seems to work just fine, and even though I was completely terrorized the first time I landed, there is something romantic about setting down on the cracked and bumpy runway and lugging your bags over sand. The reality of larger planes, however elegant, unsettles me somehow.

Yesterday, two of my ninth graders, Curtis and Jacob, came zooming by on their three-wheeler. Curtis was driving and Jacob was carrying a shotgun. "We're huntin' ducks!" they yelled. They were showing off, probably wanting their teacher to see them capable of doing more than they do in class. They drove off, hootin' and hollerin'. I was amazed at their speed and ability to handle the vehicle without flipping it. It's strange, seeing your students in their natural habitat. With a gun.

I hope the darkness of winter won't depress me too much. I hope I can continue to find beauty in this seeming moonscape. I need to get a flashlight.

Okay, I'm going to bed.

Love, Me

I set down my pen and stretched. Outside the narrow windows of my classroom, a faint light illuminated the oil tanks in the field. The classroom clock pointed toward midnight. Digesting that reality brought a yawn, followed by the thought, *You're going to totally hate yourself in the morning.*

I looked at the date on my letter. *Oh my god. I've been here almost a month.* I counted. Yep. Thirty-one days, if I include D-Day: August 12—the day I landed, broke into the portable, swept out mounds of sand, and set up shop like a pioneer who'd found an abandoned building in a ghost town. The only thing missing was tumbleweeds.

I folded the newsletter and stapled the edges to create a mailer and wrote my friend's address. My return address read simply, Genét, c/o School, Shishmaref, AK 99772.

"Thirty-one days." I said the words out loud, stabbing my metaphorical wooden stake into the ground and declaring my territory as a newbie teacher, up late at night in her first classroom. It felt good. Maybe I would make it after all.

TWENTY

THERE'S A HOLE IN THE TUNDRA

Driving to the dump with a load of trash and honey buckets was a thankless chore, but I didn't mind it this morning. I felt happy and free, driving the school's Ford pickup truck and bouncing on the seat as I rolled over uneven tundra, singing, "Here Comes the Sun."

Then—WHAM!

The truck stopped abruptly, and I lurched forward. The seatbelt snapped hard against my shoulder and the driver's side plunged at an unnervingly steep angle. "Ow! Fuck! What the hee-ell." Without intending, I mimicked Principal Ken's drawl as I yelled. There was nothing out here but miles of grass. What did I hit?

I unbuckled my seatbelt, swung open the door, and stepped out. The tundra glistened from morning rain that had blown through. It was a sea of greens and browns and shades of autumn orange. The grasses waved gently in the breeze, painting a stunning tapestry.

A burst of cold air came from the north, making me zip up my coat. I turned my attention back to the truck. "Well, shit."

Attempts to curb my potty mouth were not going well.

The truck was resting on its frame, with the left front tire almost entirely submerged in an inky-black water hole, one of the thousands that dotted the landscape and which I'd seen from the air on my inaugural flight to the village. The holes were natural openings in the sandy, treeless soil, a result of permafrost melting in small patches and filling with water. And I had driven right into one, clean as the eight ball in a side pocket.

Could I reverse out of it? I leaned down, curious about how deep the hole was and equally scared that the truck's weight might suddenly break through and create an even wider chasm that would swallow the truck and take me with it. The ground appeared solid enough, but reversing was not an option. I had gotten stuck in the snow enough times to know that I couldn't get out of that hole without a tow. Did Shishmaref have a towing service?

I looked toward the dump in the distance. It was too far to carry everything. And there was absolutely no way I was going to make multiple trips with the honey bucket bags that Anne and I had filled together. I nearly threw up the first time I lifted one out of the tin cone can and carried it out the front door, its contents sloshing.

"Just set it by the porch," Anne instructed. "It'll freeze. Easier to haul to the dump." And she was right. The bags did freeze … a little. I scrounged the school for cardboard boxes to set each bag inside—extra protection in case of a leak.

I looked back toward the town. "Shit."

There was no other option. I had to walk back to school and ask Principal Ken for help. I had been trying to be self-sufficient by confidently requesting the truck keys and venturing south without a wisp of fear, even though I had never driven on the island before. All I had been told was to steer clear of the beach. I sure didn't want the tide coming in while I was out there, or I'd be known as "She who drove the school truck onto the beach, where it was swept out to sea … Thanks a lot."

The only sensible option was to follow one of the sandy roads that led out of the village. I had thought it would be smooth rolling the whole way, but when grass replaced the sandy trail, it obscured the road. This was probably the only frickin' hole in the tundra between me and the dump. Stupid hole.

I slammed the truck door, then opened it again to grab the keys. After slamming it once more, I tightened my laces and retraced my path, following the tire tracks back to school. My march was accompanied by a litany of self-condemnation in third person:

You are so stupid!

This is so typical of you, leaping before you look!

No one else would be dumb enough to drive right into a hole!

This stream of less than helpful thoughts was soon replaced with questions of a more anxious nature.

Crap, did I break the truck's axle? How much is that going to cost to fix?

How am I going to get all of the trash and (oh god) the honey buckets to the dump?

Principal Ken would be well within his rights to say no if I ever asked for the keys again. I was probably already the laughingstock of the entire school—the only one to repeatedly jam the copier or run it out of toner, the girl who typed "Are you in?" The nincompoop (literally) who used the honey bucket without lining it.

I trudged hard all the way back and up the metal stairs. It was Saturday, but Principal Ken was in his office, sitting in the same position as when I'd left him less than an hour before. While I didn't want to explain my situation, I was relieved to see him still there. If he had gone home, I'd be wandering around the village, asking, "Do you know where Principal Ken lives?" It was several weeks into the school year, and I still didn't know where he resided. The man was smart, probably keeping his home location secret to prevent newbie teachers like me from showing up in the dead of night and demanding an emergency evacuation to Nome. "Get me a plane out of here, and now!"

I felt a mix of dread with a tincture of hope. Maybe we could get this situation handled without much fuss.

I stood in his doorway. "Um, hi."

"Hey." He pushed his glasses higher on his nose and looked at me. "That was quick."

"Um, well …"

"Oh, man." He teased, rocking back in his chair. "Lemme guess. Ya either got a flat tire, ran outta gas, or it's stuck somewhere."

"Stuck. In a hole." I felt my face grow hot. "I was following tracks, but …"

Principal Ken stood up and stretched. "Well, I probly shoulda warned ya to take the beach. At low tide, it's hard as a highway." He glanced at the clock. "Which it is 'bout now."

I stood in the doorway, unsure what to do next.

"It's okay. Gimme the keys. I'll take care of it." He looked closer. "You okay?"

"Yeah, just got a bit of a jolt." I rubbed my neck and handed the jangle of metal to him, then pointed in the direction of where the truck sat in its (stupid) hole. "I never made it to the dump, so …"

I backed out of his office and headed down the hallway, dreading the thought of the principal handling our honey buckets and equally dreading the thought of returning home so soon. I was sick of home and sick of my classroom. All I had wanted to do this one day was accomplish one stinking task from beginning to end. The dump run certainly qualified. I'd been looking forward to driving the school truck and getting out of town, and had been singing Snow White's seven dwarves' song, "Whistle While You Work" all morning, and imagining the satisfaction of hurling every last box and bag off the tailgate.

I rarely felt satisfied these days. Teaching didn't seem to lend itself to any kind of finality. It was a profession filled with an endless series of loose ends.

I pushed hard on an exit door and clumped down the metal stairs, flipping a coin in my mind. Left or right? Left was the ocean; right was the lagoon. My boots went to the right, signaling that I could at least walk to the island's edge and back. It was one stinkin' task I knew I could finish.

The next day, I learned that Principal Ken commissioned one of the airstrip engineers to drive his enormous Caterpillar tractor to the scene of the crime and pull the school truck out of the watery depths. There was no report about who completed my chore. Truth be told, I didn't want to know.

TWENTY-ONE

ME, NOT ME

Another Friday afternoon, another day of feeling torn. Part of me wanted to give up on this whole teaching venture and get on the next plane to Nome. Another part was trying not to care so much, to reduce my suffering.

The obstacle causing this debate in my head stemmed from the daily dose of student apathy. Their slumpy attitudes reminded me of my own classmates when I was in high school, who did everything they could to get as far away from learning as possible. They complained about reading, they whined about writing, they groaned when a math test was announced. I, on the other hand, couldn't wait to see what the teacher had in store for us.

During student teaching, I ran into the same challenge. My mentor teacher had no sympathy. "Just threaten to lower their grade," she advised. I tried that, but the students acted out even more. One student flipped me her middle finger, right to my face. It was exhausting.

What would it feel like to not care about learning? The idea had crept into my consciousness on occasion, but I always backed away from it, afraid of stoking that fire. After all, what if I pretended not to care and ended up liking that? It might be easier than continuing my self-inflicted workaholic approach. *Maybe Virgos shouldn't be teachers.*

I closed my eyes and imagined showing up on Monday with nothing to write with and nothing to write on. It felt surprisingly good. But I couldn't hold the vision of joyous laziness for long.

Teaching was like the tide. Every day, my desire to teach went away, then returned. It didn't take much. Sometimes, just seeing the words *teacher*, *education*, or *school* pulled me back to shore, confirming that I wanted to be in the thick of it.

I had to admit, if I looked closely enough, there was evidence of the occasional student showing interest all the way through and finishing a lesson. In those moments, I felt like the tide was coming in, carrying all kinds of good stuff with it. I'd be filled with hope and fall in love with the student who tried, who raised a hand. That student gave me hope for the ones who didn't, because maybe another one would try tomorrow.

Unfortunately, the teaching tide went out a little more each day, carrying my heart with it. My desire to be a teacher drifted out of sight, making me sad and then afraid that I had indeed chosen the wrong path. Then I'd get mad and want to climb into my metaphorical motorboat and rip the engine into its highest gear to fly far away across the ocean. Those were the days when I knew I was barely masking my frustration with the students, with myself, with the stupid copy machine.

But then something good would occur—a student saying thank you or deciding the lesson wasn't half bad and coaxing their classmates back on board. Those moments probably happened more often than I wanted to admit, and I might have caught them all if I wasn't always looking for the worst. When I did catch them, they made me want to try one hundred percent again. I would turn my boat back to shore. It was an unpredictable, disorienting boat ride no one had warned me about. No cautionary label on the back of my teaching certificate.

I reflected on my classes in college, the ones that were supposed to guide me into the teaching profession and fill me with confidence and street smarts for what lay ahead. But I couldn't remember a single professor whose lectures or textbooks helped me understand how to navigate the emotional side of teaching, which, to be honest, permeated every twist and turn of the job. They'd given no assignments to help me get to know myself as a teacher, much less a young female teaching kids only a few years younger than I was—teenagers who were going through their own rites of passage as surely as I was going through mine. My prefrontal lobes weren't much more developed than theirs. I still had a few years to go.

I'd come across some files I'd lugged all the way to Shishmaref as proof that I had indeed earned a diploma and teaching certificate. There was also a copy of my college transcripts, representing four years of my life and thousands of dollars spent.

The list looked impressive: Teacher and the Social Order; Human Development; Adolescent Psychology; Developing Reading in the Secondary School; Composition for Secondary Teachers; Survey of Exceptional Children. There were poetry classes and courses on Shakespeare and a slew of survey classes that required the purchase of the Norton Anthology tomes. Thousands of Bible-thin pages covering American Literature, Modern Literature, Renaissance Literature, Victorian Literature. There was litter-a-ture all over the place, and I had waded through all of it.

I had also taken grammar classes. One was titled English Usage. I could write circles around my classmates but earned a C on account of the professor's favorite tool for gauging student understanding: multiple-choice tests. I sucked at those. I had a creative mind, which made it impossible to correctly isolate the correct answer; it appeared that I could make a rational connection between any test question and (a), (b), (c), (d), and All of the Above. It didn't help when I lost all points for the one assignment I actually understood.

Unbeknownst to his students, Dr. Creple (I called him Dr. Crab) despised student work that was torn from spiral notebooks; the ragged edges apparently drove him nuts. But we didn't know, and when it was time to turn in our assignments, everyone ripped out their pages and dropped them on his table. We watched—horrified—as he sorted out the offensive sheets and tossed them in the metal trash can. *Whoomph!* Half the class flunked. I never used a spiral-bound notebook again.

There was another grammar class, this one with Dr. Revelle. She was also dramatic, but not in a passive-aggressive way. She'd enter the classroom with ideas like her hair was on fire and emphasize her zeal by tossing her thick, black-rimmed glasses on the front table and grabbing our attention with the question rumbling about in her own mind.

One day, she hit us with, "Where'd the semicolon come from?"

The rest of the class stared blankly at her, probably crossing their fingers that a homework assignment wasn't coming. But that's exactly what Dr. Revelle did. She assigned a punctuation mark to each of us, and our task was to go to the library right then and there, using class time to find out everything we could about the history of the comma, the hyphen, the period, and so on. I raised my hand for the semicolon. It was frickin' fascinating, and I just knew it was an assignment I would use in the future. People didn't seem to use semicolons much and were missing out on all the fun.

Despite those scattered moments that inspired me as a scholar, it was dawning on me that none of my classes prepared me to be a teacher. Even Adolescent Psychology was a dud. The instructor assigned long, boring chapters out of the textbook, lectured without taking questions, and tested our comprehension with multiple choice tests. I left the university even more confused about my own adolescence and unable to apply (a), (b), (c), (d), or All of the Above to my current circumstances.

I loved to learn, but did that mean I should be a teacher?

There were moments when I felt fully "myself" as a teacher—confident, clear, and breathing easily. But then the grumpy students slunk into the room, unwilling to show even the slightest interest in what I had so painstakingly prepared the night before. In those moments, I tended to lose my bearings. I'd second-guess my lesson and hastily pull something together, totally untested. During one

Consumer Math class, I got so frustrated with students' lack of interest that I assigned twenty math problems and took a walk outside until I calmed down.

"This isn't me," I kept repeating as I turned every corner of the school building.

Thank god there wasn't a fire drill.

I found myself angry at my university for preparing me so poorly, and then I got mad at the people who hired me. The Bering Strait School District—those people. They should have insisted on providing coursework that prepared me to grow into my own Arctic Teaching shoe pacs. They could have offered a short class during orientation, like *Finding the Teacher in You*. Or perhaps classes titled *Literature in the Arctic* or *Grammar for Oral Cultures*. Maybe *Strategies for Teaching Without Electricity*? Or *Managing Teen Moods 101, 102, 103 …*

My frustrations leaked out at home. Anne would shrug her shoulders. "Been there," she'd respond. Seeing my look of despair, she'd add, "Relax! Just be yourself!"

But who was I? My sense of self kept shifting, depending on the time of day, the day of the week, and (as a woman) the time of the month.

I remembered loving certain things about high school, and I thought I could transfer those feelings to here and now. But maybe they weren't enough to cancel out the crappy moments when I felt shunned by classmates or teased for trying so hard. High school was a lonely time. Maybe I had never recovered from that.

I was in a funk, and I knew it. My self-imposed pity swirls dominated more and more of my days. And right here, right now, as Friday afternoon approached, I was wallowing in yet another pile of sourpuss thoughts, feeling like a total failure, when Midge appeared in the doorway.

"Some things came for you."

I blinked out of my reverie, not understanding.

"I made a run to the post office," she explained. "Ron asked me to bring your mail to school. It's on my desk." She smiled, a dimple showing. "Looks like you got some fans."

Curious, I followed Midge to the office. She pointed to boxes on her desk—one from my older brother and one from my mother—and some brightly colored envelopes and a padded mailer.

Grateful, but not in the mood for attention, I picked up the pile in a no-big-deal kind of way and turned toward the door.

"Thanks. I think these are for my birthday. It was a few days ago."

"Your birthday!" Midge almost screamed. "Why didn't you say anything?"

"Yeah, I almost forgot about it myself," I joked. "Been busy." I paused. "But it's okay." I walked back to my room before she could reply and closed the door. I was either going to cry or laugh. I wasn't sure which way my emotions would go. Maybe I could get out of my nasty mood if I opened something.

My older brother's card was clever—a cartoon of an astronaut floating in space and tethered to a rocket. The preprinted greeting inside read, "Happy Birthday to someone who's way out there!" There was no note, just the typical scrawl of his name. In person, my brother, André, was remarkably verbose. Writing, he was as terse as ever.

But his gift spoke volumes. In the box was a small wall-mount thermometer. His timing was uncanny. I hadn't said a word about the broken thermometer that was attached to our house.

One birthday card came from my first college roommate, congratulating me and offering a hearty "Hang in there!" If she only knew.

The other card was from my paternal grandmother. Nana always sent sweet greetings with florals and nature scenes, and she tucked in a few dollar bills "for a little treat." This time, a five-dollar bill—enough for two Carnation Breakfast Bars.

My mood lightened. Maybe another package would lighten it more. I opened the padded envelope from Mia and found a copy of the *Juneau Empire*, Alaska's capitol city newspaper. Mia knew I missed reading the news, so this was a joke. By the time the *Anchorage Times* and the *Nome Nugget* showed up at school, the news was anything but new.

By habit, I turned to the comics and chuckled through Blondie & Dagwood, Peanuts, and Hagar the Horrible. Then I spied the weekly horoscope.

> *August 23-September 24*
> *Focus on business, commercial activity, production and timing. Get a professional appraisal, be aware of property value, don't give up something for nothing. Older individuals may try to intimidate—hold your ground, protect territorial rights.*

The first segment of this premonition seemed to be aimed at the village. Contrary to my initial experiences of desertion and quiet, there was a lot of business going on—city planning, construction, worrying about the seawall. Being an Outsider, I wasn't privy to the details but sensed that people were incredibly busy with surviving and taking care of each other out here.

The last line (Older individuals may try to intimidate) seemed more personal. It might be intended for me, heading home soon to deal with my roommate's idiosyncrasies.

I looked at my mother's box and felt homesick. A lump formed in my throat and tears stung the corners of my eyes. Hearing people's voices close by in the hallway, I decided to wait until I got home, where I could open it in privacy.

For the next hour, I finished grading students' papers, noting that I needed to request they abstain from tearing pages from their spiral notebooks; my professor had been right, those ragged edges were annoying.

I soon reached a stopping point and, packages in my arms, slipped out the door.

The house was quiet. I made a cup of tea and retreated to my bedroom.

My mother's card was handmade, a sketch of a little bird in a tree. Inside, she had written, "Genet, Happy Birthday, I hope you enjoy these gifts."

I dug carefully through the paper towel sheets and Styrofoam peanuts, setting nearly a dozen carefully wrapped items on my bed; it was quite the haul. *I bet this is all food.*

My first find was a box of imported chocolates. I held it up and breathed in deeply. My mother was from Germany and had a very fine taste for imported treats. When we were kids, she always filled our Christmas stockings with Toblerone chocolates and festive German cookies, like Lebkuchen and Pfeffernüsse. She'd add marzipan treats in the shape of pigs and foil-wrapped chocolate Santas and holiday bells, and an orange at the bottom. My siblings and I traded treats for days.

For now, I had it all to myself. Christmas in September. I surveyed the pile and could tell that my mom had gifted me items she figured I wouldn't see at Nayokpuk's General Store: dried apricots, half a loaf of German rye bread, imported crackers, a sausage, granola, and dehydrated Knorr Leek Soup. She'd added a couple of small boxes of fruit juice and an apple. The only things missing were a picnic blanket and a bottle of Chardonnay.

The last item was a strange shape and squishy. I unrolled the paper and out popped … a rubber chicken. There was a note: "Hang in your kitchen window so you fit in with the locals."

I laughed, then cried—a mix of homesickness, then joy, then frustration with teaching and then loneliness, all mixed up with my mother's sense of humor.

A chocolate might help.

I slipped one into my mouth and felt a tear roll down my cheek—this one of gratitude.

TWENTY-TWO

EGGPLANT

I was on my third chocolate when I heard Anne's footsteps. She tapped on my door.

"You in there? I'm heading to the store. Want anything?"

My mouth was filled with a lovely mass of caramel, but I managed to communicate that I didn't have any special requests. Her boots receded down the hallway and out the door, leaving the house quiet once more. When Anne returned, I would show her the rubber chicken and share some of my birthday stash. Until then, I'd take advantage of this rare opportunity to sit at the dining table undisturbed with a cup of tea and write a letter to Mia.

Dear Mia,

Thanks for your birthday gift! I loved getting "news." Very funny. You mentioned in your note that another package was coming my way. What are you sending? Candles? Socks? M&Ms? Whatever it is, thank you! I like the idea of extending my birthday since I didn't really have one this year. It passed by with a whisper. But some gifts did show up. You should have seen the box my mom sent, filled with crackers and dried fruit and a box of imported chocolates. I nearly wept with joy, then loneliness, then gratitude.

I know your birthday is coming up soon. I want to send a piece of artwork made by one of the locals, maybe a student. Marcus is getting quite accomplished with his scrimshaw on ivory walrus tusks. Or maybe you'd like a pair of rabbit-fur slippers? How about a jar of the most expensive peanut butter in the northern hemisphere?

The northern lights put on quite a show last night. At first, I thought it was a weird cloud, but then it turned kind of a luminescent sherbet green that kept moving, almost swaying in the sky. I got a neck ache watching for so long. It covered the Big Dipper and framed the North Star. When I shared my experience with my group of yearbook girls, I whistled to emphasize my meaning, and one of them got almost mad at me, telling me to never EVER whistle at the Northern Lights, or I'd get scooped up by some mysterious force and disappear into the atmosphere. She was so serious about it that I promised not to do that again, cross my heart and hope NOT to die. Have you heard of that belief before?

In other news, we recently had an unusually warm and sunny day, so I took a stroll on the beach (where else). I wonder, sometimes, how I can stay entertained walking the same terrain. But it's a different island every day with the tide changing the contours of shoreline in the morning and again at night. I bought a pair of rubber boots from Walter's and had fun sloshing through the shallow water. It was glassy and calm. There was a moment when I felt like I was walking ON the water, like Jesus.

And then the most amazing scene appeared. You would have loved it. Thousands of jellyfish had washed onto shore. Hundreds upon hundreds of palm-sized jellyfish—so many that I had to tiptoe between them. I've never seen such a thing. They looked like translucent silver dollars, glistening in the sun. I took a real close look and caught my reflection. It was like looking in a miniature fun house mirror, with my nose like Jimmy Durante's and the rest of my body sucked back in. You would think that a reflection of one's face in a jellyfish wouldn't be that clear, but I felt like I was gazing into a mirror. It happened in an instant, being pulled into that reflection and sharing jellyfish space. Do you think it was looking back?

It's one of the uncanny energetic exchanges I tend to feel up here. A seemingly insignificant object or sensation is suddenly blown into huge proportions—I feel very small and then very large, all at once. Maybe it's because of the lack of distraction or the fact that reference points are as subtle as they are vast.

School's going alright, although the days have more ups and downs than a roller coaster. Teaching is a frickin' hard ride, at least for me. With no commute to process my days, I turned to watching TV for a while, but there's only one channel and it's a haphazard array of soap operas, news, and commercials for hunting gear and Bering Air. I've turned to books instead, getting carried away to different parts of the world. Here's the latest: *Going to Extremes* (Alaska); *The Hobbit* (where in the world?); *The Well of Loneliness* (Paris, Great Britain); *As I Lay Dying* (the Midwest? I didn't enjoy that one too much); *Kate* (Hollywood, New York, Africa, Australia); *Man's Search for Himself* (an inner journey of sorts); *England, My England* (obvious); *A Grief Observed* (C.S. Lewis's marriage); *We the Living* (Russia, which is actually quite close).

I also just finished reading my last journal, the one I wrote in just before moving here. It's like from someone else's life, filled with rants about people who drove me crazy, like my boss at the campus cafeteria who fired me because I missed one shift. Remember that? I'd be mortified if anyone read about the pathetic breakup with my ex-girlfriend. Not sure what we saw in each other.

My roommate pries. She seems to sense that I'm gay, making off-the-cuff comments like, "Every woman needs the experience of marriage at least once in life." She makes marriage sound like camping. Or maybe sky diving. "Try it, you might like it." I just say "uh-huh" and joke that I'll get around to that sometime and let her know how it goes.

Spooky though—she said that one of the guy teachers was looking at me the other night at a basketball game. "He could be cultivated," she said. I almost choked on my snack bar. If she's talking about the teacher I THINK she's talking about, it makes me nauseous. He's creepy and has greasy hair.

Anne has good intentions, but it's getting harder to share the same space. Our walls are so thin, I can hear her everywhere. Like in the bathroom when she gargles with Listerine or as she shuffles around in her slippers across the sandy linoleum floors. And she talks incessantly. Half the time I don't know if she's just talking to herself or expecting a response from me. I lay low and envy teachers who live alone or with their partner.

All that said, there are times when I do enjoy my roommate's company. She can be funny at times, and if I am in the mood, a good conversationalist.

Sorry, I'm grumpy today. Some days are lonely and long. And the sun is still high, which means the kids are out. Which means a lot of screaming in the street by my bedroom window, even past curfew. Why do kids scream, and at what age do they stop?

I hope you are well in mind, body, and spirit. If you get a chance, could you send some Willa Cather from your bookshelf? The school library doesn't have her books, and I'm intrigued. ~ Love, Me

I sealed the envelope with a lick and stretched. Perhaps another cup of tea. Maybe one more chocolate? It was nice sitting at this little table. Anne was smart; it was a good spot.

But my plan to luxuriate in my own version of solitaire quickly vanished. The front door opened and in strolled Anne. In each hand she held what looked like a large purple football—a vegetable, judging by their green stems.

"Like eggplant?" She raised them above her shoulders like she was lifting weights.

"Um, no, haven't had eggplant," I replied. "At least, not that I know of."

"You're kidding! Raised in farm country and never had an eggplant?" Anne set down her prizes, lit a cigarette, and took a deep drag.

"Well, I'm gonna make you some of my famous eggplant—fried with breadcrumbs and dipped in tomato sauce. You're going to love it."

She was right. I did.

TWENTY-THREE

THE NORTH STAR

The next morning, I passed by the main office at school and heard Midge calling to me with a "Yoo-hoo!" I backed up and found her holding a plate of donuts.

"Happy birthday!" She grinned.

Principal Ken emerged from his inner office. "Yeah, what's this I hear 'bout you bein' 'nother year older an' not tellin' us?" He stepped closer to survey the plate of powdered sugar and chocolate treats with sprinkles. "Can't b'lieve you almost made me miss one-uv these."

Midge's gift surprised me, and I bumbled through an apologetic "Thanks" and "It's not a big deal."

But Midge tossed it right back. "Well, around here, it *is* a big deal!" Her face was kind, then serious. "You're so far from home. My family would go nuts if I went away, especially if I was gone for my birthday."

Midge didn't mean for her words to sting, but I suddenly felt ashamed for having left my family. But wasn't that what I was supposed to do as a young adult? Grow up, move out, and have adventures?

I shook off my self-condemnation and picked a chocolate with sprinkles. Principal Ken opted for powdered sugar and disappeared to his office.

The rest of the day went smoothly. I felt relaxed, like I'd had a good cry and could now face whatever came my way. Each period, the students were kinder than usual. During Graphic Communications class, the girls laughed and joked around like we'd been friends forever.

"Oooh, we should write more of those Dear Abby letters!"

"Yeah, and let's do more song dedications. Ask little kids what they like to listen to!"

"Maybe you can make more word finds, like with people around town!" This last comment was directed at me. The word finds with teacher and student names had been a hit. Even my sullen tenth graders got excited trying to find their names. "Ooh! Got one!" "Hey, I see yours!"

When the last class was over, I jotted down my ideas for tomorrow's lessons and skipped down the school steps. It was time for another walk. With my binoculars around my neck, camera in one pocket, and a Snickers bar in the other, I headed directly to the north-facing beach and turned right, my face to the sun.

The sea breeze was gentle today. I scanned the ocean and spotted a black dot on the horizon. What was that? How far out? Distances were difficult to gauge. The tide was out farther than I had ever seen it before, allowing me to veer away from the shoreline and stroll thirty, maybe forty yards toward the ocean's edge. The sand was rippled and hard as concrete, my shoe pacs barely making an impression. The ground was bare other than a few pieces of shell scattered about.

I stopped at the water's edge and watched the tiny curls of water lapping gently, then sinking into the sand, hardly making a sound. After a few sweeps of the horizon with my binoculars, I found the black dot. A ship. *Wow, it's way out there. Is it moving?* It was hard to tell, but I liked the idea of people on a ship on the horizon. Like company was coming. I continued a bit farther, then turned at the sound of vehicles approaching.

The rumble of engines belonged to a parade of four-wheelers and one pickup truck driving steadily on the beach near the grassy edge, and in my direction.

A few of the riders waved. All men, from what I could see. I waved back. *Strange, I wonder where they're going? There's nothing out here.*

I watched as they circled their vehicles to face the ocean and stopped in a long line. It didn't make sense to keep my distance, so I waved again and started walking toward them.

The men wore similar attire—shoe pacs, heavy workmen's pants, and parkas. I didn't look much different. Their hands were shoved deep into their coat pockets. Some had caps on, some let their jet-black hair blow in the wind. Their demeanor was calm yet alert.

"You're a teacher, right?" one of the men asked as I approached.

"Yep, high school. English, math." Maybe I'd sew a small insignia on my coat so that, from a distance, people could identify my rank and file. "What's going on?"

"Oh, *North Star*'s in. Unloading soon. Gonna take stuff back."

Seeing that I didn't understand what he meant by *North Star*, he pointed to the black dot on the horizon. "The ship out there."

My brain was still not making a connection between the ship on the horizon and the small welcoming committee. Sensing my confusion, he laughed good-naturedly.

"They unload supplies onto barges. Come to shore for the drop-off. Kinda like a D-Day invasion." He laughed again, and the other men laughed with him, nodding at his description.

"See?" he pointed again. "Take a look through them binoculars of yours."

I turned and followed the trajectory of his outstretched arm. Sure enough. Bobbing up and down in the waves, barely visible and then disappearing behind a swell, was a barge making its way to shore. It motored closer and closer, and then I heard a deep thrumming. A few men were on board, black silhouettes against the gray sky. They held on tight, steadying themselves for their last push.

Then, *whooom*! The flat-faced barge gave one last throttle and came right onto the beach, not far from where I'd been walking a few moments before. The front end fell like a door that had lost its hinges. The boat men scrambled out, and the men on the shore sprang into action, moving their vehicles to a closer rendezvous point. I stepped back, out of their way.

Another pack of men on four-wheelers approached, pulling trailers and driving fast. They joined the procession of activity, quickly unloading oil drums, wooden crates, and lumber, strapping them down and driving back to the village. I watched, fascinated with the synchrony of their movements. Few words were exchanged, yet each man knew exactly what to do.

Within minutes, the barge was empty. The boat crew pulled up the front of the craft and maneuvered out of the shallows, turning their boat toward the ship on the horizon. How many more trips would they be making? Or was that it for the day? There was no one around to ask. Maybe I could get the *Northern Lights News* girls to write a report.

I felt a shift of energy course through my body. I should feel lonely. A moment ago, I had been standing amongst a cadre of strong men rushing about to unload the barge, and now they were gone—back to the village, back to their families and friends. I had no one to go home to. But instead of feeling sorry for myself or isolated as I had so many times before, a new sensation presented itself.

I turned slowly around, feeling the wind on my face, then in my ears, and then at my back. It was just me here, with the ocean, the sand, the salty air. I turned for home and followed the urge to skip instead of trudge. My boots made skipping rather clunky, but soon I caught the rhythm from muscle memory of two hops and a step.

A giddy exuberance flooded through me, prompting me to run and twirl down the beach like Julie Andrews on her mountaintop.

"I'm free!" I shouted, stretching my arms out to the horizon. "I'm free!"

The cry of an Arctic tern answered from above. The ocean roared quietly in agreement. No one around, just me and three hundred sixty degrees of wide open nothing—yet everything—as far as the eye could see. Countless layers of grays, browns, greens, blues, and the solitary sparkle of Venus appeared in the evening sky.

A scurrying movement brought my attention in close. A little crab. It must have popped out from the sand, disoriented, and was now moving its little crabby legs as fast as it could toward the safety of the sea. I heard another Arctic tern and realized that it might be planning to make that crab its dinner. After a couple of tries, I caught the crafty crustacean by its shell and jogged to the water's edge. Its little legs flailed around wildly.

"Sorry, little crabbie. I know you're scared." I set it down, and the crab quickly reoriented, scurried to the water's edge, and disappeared into the next wave. Finding safety, finding home.

I scanned in all directions, feeling insignificant yet important in some way. It was fine for me to be here. I was in total control of what happened next. There were shells and Arctic terns. Fluid, harmonious life. No ticking clock, only my heart beating in time with what surrounded me. No worksheets, no pencils to sharpen. A kind of pressure valve opened inside, and my inner war of Me/Not Me ended.

I stretched out my arms again and ran. Then jogged. Then strolled. Utterly free from worry on a Tuesday evening, all the way home.

The next afternoon, I stopped at Walter's store and asked him about the *North Star*. "The ocean's our highway," he explained. "The ship comes once a year with oil, lumber, equipment."

The door jangled, and three men entered, nodding at Walter and then at me. I nodded back and stepped to an aisle to peruse the shelves and make space for them to chat.

Their voices were low. Unable to translate, I relaxed my effort to understand and listened to the sounds. There were clucks and quick stops, then a cascade of consonants and vowels. Easy laughter, throaty hmm-mms, and "uks."

The door flung open, and in ran a young boy and girl. They stopped at the counter and pointed at boxes of candy on the shelves behind. One of the men looked disapprovingly at the children and said something in a sharp tone. The kids looked down at their shoes for a moment, then looked up shyly and started to smile. Both were missing front teeth, either from being the age when new teeth grow in or from a candy habit, I wasn't sure. But their smiles forced the man to smile, too, which made the children giggle, which led to Walter giving them candy and waving them out the door. The men resumed their conversation, and I quietly followed the kids into the street.

The next day, I overheard one of the male teachers, Lance, talking to Principal Ken about helping villagers unload another round of supplies from the *North Star*. I joined the conversation and learned that the shipping route began as a means for traders and businessmen to travel the coast, selling wares and bartering other goods. Sometimes people hitched rides to visit relatives.

"Now, the ship brings oil drums, construction supplies, and heavy equipment," Lance added. "You've seen the Caterpillars on the south side of town, digging out the new airstrip?"

I nodded and stole a sideways glance at Principal Ken, my eyes telling him to please refrain from divulging that one of those Caterpillars pulled the school truck out of a boggy hole because of you-know-who. I knew he was aching for a good laugh, but he held his tongue.

"It's tricky," Lance continued. "The ship's gotta park several miles out on account of the shallow waters. Remember, we're standing on the Bering Land Bridge. Barges can only come a few at a time. I'll get a closer look when I go out there."

Apparently, Lance had been invited by one of the village leaders to help transfer supplies. He immediately accepted, wanting to make better connections to people in the community. "And it makes an impact on my students when they see me out there."

I felt a pang of envy mixed with frustration. *Why do the guys get to help around the village?* I'd heard that Ben, also a new teacher, had been invited to go fishing. Could I invite myself to go along, or was it more customary to be asked? I couldn't imagine myself baiting a fishhook or blasting a ptarmigan to smithereens, but I could be a gofer like I'd been at the café. Maybe I shouldn't push it. As a female, I'd more likely be invited to a sewing circle. Bad idea, as my approach to sewing was a stapler.

That afternoon, I returned to the beach and watched another barge unloading. The same smooth and mostly silent orchestration occurred—men moving swiftly to load a couple trucks and half a dozen four-wheelers. I stood farther away this time, wishing I was Lance.

The black dot on the horizon hadn't moved. "*The North Star*," I murmured to myself. "Reference point for sailors." Did they have Pilot Bread on board?

My thoughts floated back to when I was about sixteen years old, standing outside on a starry autumn night in front of the house with my brother, Todd. He was ten years younger, but we shared a lot of growing-up time together, mostly outdoors.

On that particular evening, Todd mentioned something about the Big Dipper at the dinner table, so I promised we'd go look for it when the sky grew dark enough. We lived on the outskirts of Vail in the Colorado Rockies, at an elevation of about 8,200 feet. Away from city lights and with air so clear and pure, the multitude of stars was breathtaking.

Todd and I walked down the road to get clear of the towering evergreens and aspen trees, craning our necks and gazing up. Slowly, our eyes adjusted to the darkness to make out the twinkling stars above.

"Look! There it is! The Big Dipper!" Todd pointed up.

I had already located the star formation myself but wanted him to feel that satisfaction on his own. He was only six years old but he managed to connect the stars, like dots in the sky, in the shape of a saucepan. He was ready for the next surprise.

"See the stars, how they make that shape of a pan, like a pan on the stove?" I asked. Todd nodded. "Line up the two stars on the outer edge of the pan and then go up." I moved my hand up and down slightly to indicate the angle he should follow. "Do you see that really bright star? That's the North Star, the one you use when you're in the wilderness and need to find your way home."

To be honest, I'd never had to use the North Star to find my way home, and I secretly hoped I'd never have to.

"Where's the Little Dipper?" he asked.

Surprised that my little brother even knew there was a Little Dipper, and unsure myself how to find it, I suggested we go back inside to look it up. After ten minutes with the *Encyclopedia Britannica*, we had our answer and raced back outside, craning our necks once more to get our bearings. Todd found the Big Dipper and traced the pan-edge pattern to find the North Star and then the arc of stars that led to the Little Dipper. It was a magical moment of shared understanding that I'd forgotten about until just now.

I refocused on the scene in front of me. The ocean waves curling onto shore, the men loading their trucks and four-wheelers. They were almost finished. It was too light for stargazing. Even Venus, the first star to appear in the evening sky, wasn't showing herself yet.

My stomach rumbled and I turned for home. *Did I have a North Star inside of me?* That would be cool—my own North Star to help me navigate my days here on the island, reorienting me whenever I got lost in the sea of my own teaching, guiding me to grow into the kind of teacher I wanted to become.

I picked up my pace. If there *was* a North Star inside of me, maybe I could find it. Only time would tell.

TWENTY-FOUR

TWO-POINTER

"Oh for Pete's sake!" I leaned back in my teacher chair and stared at a student's paper. It was the fourth one in a row that completely missed the mark. "All they had to do was answer five questions," I muttered.

I had intended a simple writing exercise that Lance floated to me at the copy machine a few days before, giving students in all my English classes the same passage to read and the same set of comprehension questions. Their results would establish a baseline of reading and writing skill for each grade. I should have already known to do this, but better late than never.

Lance's advice was well timed. Principal Ken was planning to conduct his first round of observations, a fundamental rite of passage through teaching territory. Observations separated the leaders from the losers, the ones to keep versus the ones to let go.

The news of this culling came unexpectedly. I had just dipped into the office before school to check for mail when I heard Principal Ken call my name. The man had a sixth sense, an uncanny ability to tell when I was near, just by the sound of my boots.

"Yes?" I leaned on the door frame, not sure if I should enter. "How's it going?" My voice sounded hopeful.

Principal Ken looked like he'd already put in a day's work. His desk was a mess of papers, and his sleeves were rolled up as if in the thick of an audit. Two coffee cups, partially filled with what was probably cold coffee, sat to the side.

"I'll be visitin' your class this week." He pulled a sheet of paper and scanned it. "Friday, third period. Tenth-grade English, right?" He looked at me over the tops of his glasses.

I hesitated, mentally flipping through the timeframes of my days, still feeling the awkwardness of what seemed to me like random start and stop times that didn't follow any logical pattern. Why couldn't classes start at the top of the hour and end fifty minutes later, with ten-minute breaks between? And why did we have to put definitive stop times on learning anyway? What if I miraculously gained momentum in Consumer Math, and the kids and I wanted to keep going? What if a student became immersed in the rhythm of learning something new or figuring out a puzzling problem? She's supposed to close her book when the big hand is on the ten? (Although, to be honest, I'd also ached for the big hand to reach the ten on multiple occasions.)

I stared at Principal Ken. *How long was a visit?*

"It's for observation." Principal Ken added, seeing my hesitation. "Y'know, just to get a sense of how things'r goin'."

I retreated to my classroom and plopped into my so-called teacher chair, heart pounding. I swiveled once around and stared at the ceiling. My student teaching stint had provided the nerve-racking experience of observations. I thought I was done with those. What would he be evaluating me on? What metric would he be using to measure my skill, or the lack thereof? Would his visit raise the curtain on my incompetence?

One of the few university lectures that made an impression on me focused on the enormous responsibility for which I was raising my right hand and swearing to uphold, so help me God. The professor lectured us long and hard about the rules for staying within the bounds of professional conduct. A teacher could be dismissed for insubordination, immoral behavior, neglecting her duty, or giving students alcohol or drugs. I wasn't particularly worried about those things. Well, other than the fact that I was a lesbian and, in some circles, that was an immoral "choice." But I doubted I'd be fired for that, not all the way up here in the Arctic. Besides, I wasn't in a relationship. I was dependable and honest, a real Girl Scout, even though I'd finished only two years of Brownie Troop.

What did worry me was losing my job due to my endless floundering—what might even be considered fraud: the misrepresentation of myself as a qualified teacher. I had that flimsy certificate from the State of Washington, but it didn't prove anything, and the naked truth of my inability to teach was going to raise its ugly head on Friday when my lesson (whatever it was going to be) would likely swim upstream like a salmon toward suicide.

What made Principal Ken's "visit" worse was that he was going to observe my lackluster tenth-grade class. Why not come during Graphic Communications? There was a lot more activity. The class was like a girls' club, run by the girls. I could easily pretend I was guiding them through our next edition of the *Northern Lights News*.

Now, it was Wednesday. I was still unclear what kind of lesson was worth observing. The tenth graders were a tough bunch; they had a code I had not yet cracked. Every day was a crapshoot. Some mornings they dragged across the threshold. On others they entered like a gang of puppies, nipping and jostling each other. And then there were the days they slid into their seats and laid down their heads in one smooth motion, as if someone had posted NAP ROOM on my door.

English class with that group was a bit more focused, but the students were still largely disinterested in working with what I'd envisioned was ... well, interesting. How did teachers navigate all this uncertainty? How did they plan a party for people they didn't really know? Why did I feel like I was the only teacher in the building just smart enough to get hired, but dumb enough to not know what to do?

I hated that feeling. It was like being stuck in a recurring dream in college, walking into a lecture hall and finding out it was Final

Exam Day, I'd forgotten to study, and my only clothing was that ridiculous miniature white towel from the fifth-grade showers.

For today's lesson, I'd copied off a short story about a rancher in Wyoming who had to hunt wolves that were killing his cattle. I figured the students would resonate with the hunting angle and have ideas for the rancher in his dilemma. Should he kill the wolves and save his cattle, and risk upsetting the delicate balance of nature that made it possible for his ranch to thrive in the wilderness? Or should he let nature take its course?

The students weren't impressed. Maybe I should have modified the story, turning the cattle into huskies, and transforming the wolves into polar bears? Even if I had thought of that, I had run out of time. The result of their disinterest meant that my students answered only a few of the questions and avoided instructions for full sentences, writing terse statements like "I don't think so," or "It depends."

More irritating were their doodles, signaling a patent dismissal of my request not to write on my one set of copies. "Other classes will use these, too," I had said. But now there were ladybugs, seagulls, little swirls with fishes, and smiling seals in the margins.

"Hey, there."

I jumped at the voice at my classroom door. It was Lance.

"Here's the basketball game schedule." He handed a sheet of paper to me. "First game's this Saturday night."

In addition to teaching Reading, Lance was the boys' basketball coach. From the sounds of squeaky sneakers on the gym floor and *bang-banging* of basketballs as they rebounded off the rims, it was clear he was working the team hard.

"Teachers take turns manning the concessions," he added. "You and Duncan are up first."

My mind went blank with the words "manning" and "Duncan." I managed to say "Oh" but wanted to scream "Noooo! I don't want to 'man' anything! And why Duncan?" But I jammed my sentiments to the back of my throat and offered a weak smile. Lance saluted and turned to leave.

"Wait!" I called after him abruptly. "I haven't manned the concessions. I don't know what to do." I paused, hoping to be excused, and then feeling embarrassed. "Where's the concession stand?"

Lance had an easy laugh. "Oh, don't worry about it. Just come to the gym at six o'clock. Duncan's done this a million times and can walk you through it."

He stooped to pick up a piece of paper that Charlie had balled up during the failed wolves and cattle story. Charlie's reluctant writing led to a lot of erasing, which led to him tearing the paper from his notebook, crumpling it, and throwing it across the room toward the trash can. He missed. And I didn't make him pick it up. I immediately sensed that it was a mistake to let Charlie get away with his behavior. His eyes weren't the only ones on me and my lack of reprimand.

I hadn't anticipated needing a policy that said, "Students may not crumple paper and throw it across the room (and then not pick it up when missing the trash can)." The rule appeared in my mind, taking flight the moment Charlie's paper whizzed through the air. The kids knew it wasn't proper; they stared at Charlie and then at me. I think they were disappointed that I didn't say anything. I admit I was disappointed, too. Something caught in my throat, a missed opportunity to prevent future shenanigans.

Lance had a different approach. With Charlie's crumpled ball of paper in hand, he jogged farther into the room, twirled, and launched it toward the metal trash can. It went in clean.

"Woo, yeah!" He pumped his arm. "Three points!"

Lance jogged back out, high fiving me as he passed. His happy-go-lucky demeanor lightened my mood. Maybe it was okay for kids to ball up their paper and throw it across the room. Maybe my hesitation to admonish Charlie wasn't off the mark. I doubted that Lance would have said anything. More likely, he would have taken the opportunity to turn his classroom into a paper-snowball-throwing frenzy.

My Inner Coach suddenly materialized, reassuring me that everything was going to be okay. *You'll figure it out like you always do!* Principal Ken would see my good intentions. I didn't need to worry about him sending me packing for Nome.

I hopped out of my chair, grabbed Charlie's paper ball from the trash can, and skipped to the other side of the room, then turned and threw it with a side arm arc. The ball ricocheted off the wall just above the can and went in. Not a three-pointer, but good enough.

TWENTY-FIVE

POWER PLAY

Friday morning came, the day of the Big Visit. My first official observation as a new teacher, Principal Ken presiding. I had to get through Consumer Math first and do whatever I could to butter up that crowd for the observation when they returned for English.

Our math textbook guided us into calculating square footage, a useful skill, but the prompts and sample problems were far removed from the reality of a remote island in the Arctic: How many bags of grass seed does Mr. Collins need for a lawn that measures sixty by eighty-five feet, if each bag will cover ten square feet? How many gallons of paint do Susie and Mike need to paint one side of their garage, measuring twelve by twenty-five feet?

The night before, I again contemplated rewriting the curriculum to fit island life. What practical examples would train my students to accurately determine the size of a space?

The answer arrived literally underfoot. I had removed my boots after a long day and noticed a hole in the heel of my wool sock. As I inspected the damage, my eyes drifted to the carpet. It was getting worn, especially under my chair.

"That's it!" I said out loud. Students would learn how to calculate square footage by measuring the classroom and pretend-ordering new carpet. Students rarely did homework, but maybe they'd be enticed to repeat the exercise at home for extended practice. I needed a tape measure—one more thing I hadn't anticipated.

Midge came to the rescue. "I've got one somewhere, I think," she rummaged in her desk drawer. "Ah, here you go." She pulled the thin metal strip to its maximum length of six feet. Shorter than I wanted, but I'd make it work.

Excited with my idea and my clever tape measure prop, I began Friday's math class with the first step in direct instruction—Demonstration—which involved me showing students how to measure the chalkboard, multiplying its width and height, and displaying the equation on the board. I was feeling confident; the students were awake and listening. I commissioned Charlie to measure the top of his own desk (Guided Practice), and he surprised everyone by mentally completing the math.

"Twenty times fifteen is, uh, three hundred." He looked at me. "Right?"

The class clapped, and suddenly I had eight kids calling out for the tape measure to calculate square footage of everything in sight—my desk, the window, the door, file cabinets, bookshelves, even Tim's head. I got them to take turns and finally swiped the tape measure back.

"Okay, that's good!" I glanced at the clock. "We've got bigger fish to fry, and I know how much y'all like fish. Have a seat."

They settled down, allowing me to explain the carpet-buying scenario, and how Principal Ken needed to know square footage of the room before placing the order. Students studied the floor and agreed that the story wasn't far-fetched.

"Let's have him order shaggy brown!" Tim suggested.

"Or pink shag!" Charlie said. The kids snickered.

I redirected. "This is going to take all of you working together, okay? No stealing the tape measure or you'll have to start over."

The students' sudden focus surprised me. They couldn't wait for my signal to get to work. I started to explain how they would need to keep track of the six-foot segments for each length of wall, but Charlie interrupted.

"We're good to go, Miss!"

And they were. In that moment, I wished more than anything that Principal Ken was observing *this* class. With no further instruction, Charlie grabbed the tape measure and started giving directions to his classmates. They worked in pairs to measure the back wall and one side, calling out numbers for a classmate to tally on the board. Anyone not measuring or calculating watched closely and demanded remeasurement if they thought something was off.

I leaned on my desk and smiled. There had been no groaning, none of the usual, "Why do we have to do this?" I hadn't seen this side of them before—a group heading for the same goal and leaving no one behind. *Oh my god. This is what teaching can feel like. Get them into something that's interesting and then get out of the way.*

"Touchdown!" Charlie yelled. He raised his arms like a referee and pointed at the board. "The room's seven hundred and twenty-eight feet!"

"You mean square feet," I corrected, and checked their math on a calculator. "You're close. Do the math again."

Tim stepped to the board and took a turn. His classmates watched in silence.

"I get seven hundred two."

Before I could point out where Tim had made his mistake, Charlie grabbed the chalk and nudged Tim to the side.

"Let's average them." He lined up the numbers and divided by two. "There," he said, playfully wiping chalk on Tim's shirt. "We need seven hundred fifteen *square* feet of carpet. Pink shag."

I knew that averaging the numbers was wildly inaccurate, but I let it go for now. The room broke into cheers, and, for the first time, my students and I had the same pulse.

The Big Visit was now in less than one hour. I would first have to get through second period English. The older students' demeanor contrasted sharply with my previous group of measuring experts. It took several minutes of coaxing to get them sitting upright and working with me to rearrange sentences that I had deliberately jumbled the night before from one of the passages in Lance's textbook.

My intention was to demonstrate how to revise a piece of writing so it flowed coherently. In general, students tended to write the same way they spoke to each other, which made their writing flit about with no discernible connection between sentences. For those who might pursue college, sentence fluency was a skill they needed to grasp, if only at a basic level.

I had been trying to get them to understand that writing is different from simply giving an opinion or recounting what you had for dinner the night before.

"Writing is a form of art," I explained, "like telling a good story or carving something out of whalebone. There's a structure. A sequence you need to follow for it to turn out right."

The mention of carving caused Joey's head to pop up. He had bags under his eyes, and his hair was smashed on one side. But he was paying attention. And having one student who paid attention was pure gold. It meant that others might follow.

"You have to be clear," I continued. "When people read your writing, they might not have you sitting next to them to explain things they don't understand. You have to help them follow your thoughts, like steppingstones in a river." I took several steps across the carpet, pretending to tiptoe on rocks across a stream.

The passage I had chosen involved pioneers rolling across a prairie in their wagons, trying to coexist with stampeding buffalo and navigating unpredictable terrain. I chose it on account of the wild animals, of course, and the similarity in environment: wide open and unpredictable. I almost divulged my drive to the dump fiasco but decided not to gamble with the momentum. So far, so good. Students were understanding the lesson's intentions.

Then the power went out.

We heard a loud *whooom*, then the lights clicked off altogether.

We froze like in a game of Red Light, Green Light. I had been standing in my Command Spot, chalk in hand, when everything went dark. Fortunately, there was just enough morning light coming through the narrow windows to make out the silhouettes of heads around the room. Will snickered. Joey mimicked Will and, one by one, I lost them. Even Daryl, who hardly ever did anything, joined in.

Henry, whom I dubbed in my attendance book as CC (Class Clown), belted out a laugh and fell out of his desk. His sidekick Caleb soon followed. They both landed face down on the floor, their entire bodies shaking with the giggles. None of this was particularly funny, but that's what made it so funny. Then I started to laugh, too. Just a little.

This was one of those moments—I had lost count how many—for which my teacher training program completely neglected to prepare me. I would have loved a class that included lessons like "How to Manage Students Who Fall Out of Their Desks" or "Tips for Teaching in the Dark."

Even if we'd had flashlights, it was clear that we wouldn't be rolling any farther with the pioneers on their journey. The clock's hands had stopped at 10:32. Thirteen minutes left.

Janice let out an involuntary burp and another round of giggling ensued. I went to my desk, unsure how to proceed. Henry and Caleb were still on the floor but had turned over—arms and legs splayed out like they were sunbathing on a beach. Darlene and Janice had been sliding progressively farther until their necks rested on the seat backs. Their eyes focused on the ceiling. Darlene blew a gum bubble and let it collapse. The rest of the students either had their heads down on crossed arms or squarely resting on their desktops. I had no game plan for this situation.

Maybe I'd put my head down too.

Principal Ken's heavy footsteps drew near, then stopped at the doorframe. He glanced at the dark figures on the floor, beckoned me with his finger, and stated the obvious. "Well, the power's gone out. Not sure why, not sure when it'll come back on." He squinted at the clock. "Why don' you dismiss in a few minutes. I'll come visit soon. Gotta git to Lance's now."

I watched Principal Ken amble down the dark hallway, his outline barely visible in the distant green light of the exit sign.

My heart sank. Unless power was restored in the next few minutes, my carefully crafted lesson might be postponed. As usual, I had prepped for it until late the night before. It took an inordinately long time because I kept sabotaging my ideas. At issue was not knowing Principal Ken's expectations. Should I continue the general sequence of lessons I'd been moving through this week or create a Special Event Lesson with multiple props?

Nearing midnight, I'd given in and decided on a textbook scenario and sentence revisions. Next up was the story of a ship captain, lost at sea. The plan was for my tenth graders to read it out loud with me, in unison. It was a strategy called "choral reading" that I found in one of the teacher manuals on my bottom shelf. Reading in unison prevented students from feeling overly shy or anxious, consequently stumbling over words. As a group, we stood a better chance of making it all the way through the passage at the same time. I chose three questions for students to reflect on and write short answers. If there was time, they would rewrite the story's ending any way they wanted.

It felt like a winning game plan last night, but as I neared time for Principal Ken's observation, I felt less sure and increasingly agitated that I hadn't thought of something else. Since the moment I got up, the idea nagged at me, prompting my Inner Coach to come to the rescue and say things like, "Look. Principal Ken is a nice man. He's not going to be hard on you! He didn't make fun of you when you typed 'Are you in?' Right? And he forgave you for driving the school's truck into a hole. He's not going to come in here and humiliate you or fire you for incompetence. He might even suggest something that'll help."

But even with periodic visits from my Inner Coach, I was still in the dark, literally and figuratively. I surveyed the scene. My students looked like a collection of Raggedy Anns and Andys. I walked to a window to get some light on my wristwatch. Five minutes to go.

A figure appeared in the doorway. This time it was Midge. She looked at the litter of bodies around the room. I thought I could see a dimple deepening in her check but couldn't be sure from that distance.

"Principal says the power's almost fixed," she started. "Got tripped somehow. Might be woodshop. Happens sometimes. You can send these lively ones to their next class."

Midge disappeared before I could verbalize the questions rising in my mind like the air bubbles in my saucepan each morning. "What am I supposed to do with the next class? Am I still getting observed? How are we going to help the sea captain lost at sea?"

Upon hearing Midge's comment about getting sent to their next class, Henry and Caleb jumped up with amazing agility. The other kids sprang into action as well.

"Hey, wait!" I jumped to the door, blocking their exit like a point guard on a basketball court. "You need to stack your notebooks on the shelf! Pencils in the cup!"

I'd recently borrowed the idea from Lance. He shared with me how he'd dedicated one shelf for student materials. Kids were dismissed only after they'd set their notebooks there and dropped borrowed pencils into a coffee can decorated with red paper and smiley face stickers. Lance was pleased. "No more excuses! No more 'I left my notebook at home!'"

That night, I cleaned out a peanut butter jar and wrapped it in blue and green construction paper, the school's colors.

Students didn't bat an eye. On their way past, they set their notebooks on the shelf and dropped their pencils into the jar. *Clink*! *Clink*!

Will nodded on his way out. "That was fun."

"Yeah," added Janice, close behind. There was a small red circle on her forehead, where she had rested it on the hard desk.

And on it went as each student left the room, smiling.

"Thanks!"

"See ya soon!"

Well, what do you know.

We didn't get the pioneers to their destination, but that didn't matter. It paled in comparison to me getting students to *my* destination of an orderly dismissal. I had survived the longest blackout so far, and my students' approval was unanimous.

TWENTY-SIX

A GRIEF OBSERVED

Several minutes later, the lights flickered on, followed by my gaggle of tenth graders returning for third period English. Charlie grabbed the measuring tape from my desk.

"Hold still," he directed Paula. "Let's see if your head's the same size as Tim's."

I chuckled lightly, knowing that the lesson for measuring three-dimensional objects would be coming soon. For now, they could play while I skimmed my lesson plan. It might be boring, but time had run out to fuss over it. I needed to commit, whether Principal Ken showed up or not. First thing, roll call.

"Hey, where's Jeremiah? He was here earlier."

Jeremiah had escaped from under my nose more than once, with no explanation for his disappearance and no apology when he returned. The kids shrugged. It was common for students to be in the building for one period but absent the next. It was also common for classmates to never divulge the whereabouts of a colleague.

All I knew was that Jeremiah's absence was going to throw things off. Exactly eight students were listed on my roster, an even number that enabled me to pair them up.

I poked my head out the door and looked both ways down the hall. No sign of Jeremiah, no sign of Principal Ken.

My heart started to beat faster. I hated this uncertainty. I began straightening papers on my desk in an effort to calm down, but thoughts ran in circles like huskies around their driftwood posts. *I can't believe Jeremiah skipped class! Seven is a prime number, and now I can't evenly divide the group! Would I have to pair up with one of them? Should I …*

My tangle of self-talk ended with the sound of heavy footsteps coming down the hall and stopping at my door. I took a deep breath as he came in.

Principal Ken's face was flushed, registering a modicum of frustration. He walked steadily along the back wall to the far side of the room without saying a word and sat down. Charlie took charge of greeting him.

"Hey, Mr. Ken! We measured the room, and you need to order seven hundred fifteen square feet of pink shag carpet!"

Tim chuckled, but the rest of the students remained quiet. They seemed a bit afraid of the principal, unsure how to address him in this moment. I had to admit feeling hesitant myself. He looked at me, one eyebrow raised.

"I'll explain later." I shrugged.

The kids followed my instructions as we began the journey of the ship captain lost at sea. They did the choral reading and politely retrieved their notebooks and pencils from the shelf. I found all of it lovely and somewhat unnerving. I was so used to tussling with them about how to properly pass out textbooks, sit up during lessons, and *not* sharpen a pencil while I was talking, that their abstinence from those behaviors was distracting. Before my eyes, the group morphed into the perfect Little House on the Prairie class. They didn't blurt out unsolicited opinions. They dutifully wrote their sentences. No groans escaped their lips when I grouped them into two pairs, with one group of three. They seemed to know that I wasn't the only person whose reputation was on the line.

I forced myself to ignore Principal Ken's watchful eyes and the periodic scratching of his pencil. I wanted to scream, "What are you seeing? Is this good or does it stink?" It was impossible to tell anything from his demeanor. His face registered nothing. I passed close by when Cathy raised her hand, but all I saw on his clipboard was a form with roughly twenty numbered items. Some were checked, but more were blank. Was it better to have more checkmarks or less?

We were about two-thirds through the lesson when Principal Ken got up and started walking out of the room. He didn't look at me, but rather at the clock. Clipboard at his side, he retraced his steps along the back wall and out the door.

That was it? Wasn't he going to stay to the end and then we'd talk? I had only been through a few observations during student teaching, and that's what my supervisor and mentor teacher had done. They stayed to the end, and we chatted about what went well and what I could improve for the future. My next period was lunch, so it would have been a no-brainer for Principal Ken to stay. His behavior baffled me.

"Well, *that* was interesting." The statement fell out of my mouth involuntarily. I didn't intend to be funny, or audible, for that matter.

Charlie giggled, then Tim. Paula and Cathy, who had been seated closest to Principal Ken, exhaled loudly, and plopped their heads onto their desks, which prompted more laughing. All of us had been holding our breath in the principal's presence, trying to pretend he wasn't in the room but unable to take our minds off the fact that he was.

"Can we do more measuring?" Charlie's question led to cheers around the room.

"Shhh!" I tried to keep a straight face and closed the door. There was a chance that Principal Ken could return. "Sure. If you finish this last part of the lesson, you can measure your little hearts out."

I skimmed students' papers during lunch. Tim had changed the captain's name from Andrews to Igor and sent the captain to an island where he met a tragic death after a run-in with a tribe of cannibals. Carol and Paula colluded on their ending. Their stapled papers revealed more kindness toward the captain, relocating him to Hawaii, where he received a magnificent feast of fish, coconuts, and pineapple. And he had a pet monkey named Alister.

With no sign of a debrief with the principal about my lesson, my Inner Coach's arch nemesis, the Voice of Doom, stepped in to fill the void. *Maybe he needs more time to type his notes before sliding them into your mailbox, attached to your Letter of Dismissal.*

I hated that voice. It was *never* helpful.

It was time for me to step into my inner Command Spot and make up my own mind. The lost sea captain lesson might have started slowly, but when the students heard they could change the ending of the story, they got excited. I just wanted them to practice sentence variation and fluency, but their creativity far exceeded my expectations.

And Principal Ken missed it.

I caught Midge in the hall. "Have you seen the principal?"

"Yep. Power outage messed up his schedule. He's catching up with observations."

So that explained it. The principal's mind had likely been miles away from where he sat in my classroom. Maybe that was a good thing.

The last period with my newspaper girls came and went. I dashed to the bathroom and returned to find Principal Ken seated in the same chair as before. His timing surprised me; this was my prep period, and it was called that for a reason. Prep period was supposed to be the teacher's time to review student work or plan ahead. It was also bathroom time, snack time, clean up one's room or swivel in one's chair time. Realistically speaking, it should have been called Recuperation Period, especially since mine was at the end of the day.

Principal Ken's sudden appearance placed my so-called "prep" on hold. He handed me a copy of his form and explained his timing.

"Goin' ta meet with ya now cuz I have 'nother meetin' in ten minutes.'"

My worst fears were confirmed. Checkmarks were better. I scored fifteen out of twenty-five. I studied the checked items closely: Lesson Introduction, Activating Prior Knowledge, Use of Materials, Formative Assessment, Command, Questions, Classroom Management—I had no idea there were so many ways to dissect a lesson. There was even one item for Appearance. Thankfully, it was checked, although I had no idea why. Was it because I showed up?

The form had no rating scale. The principal had only observed whether something was present or not. Item twenty-one was about lesson closure. It had no mark, yet Principal Ken had included it in my overall tally. Minus one for lesson closure. But he left early! He missed the students' excitement and Tim's sentencing Captain Igor to cannibals. He missed the sweetness of Carol and Paula's ending of tropical fruits and a pet monkey.

"So, how'd it go?" Principal Ken interrupted my silence.

Well, this is awkward. Isn't he *supposed to tell* me *how it went?*

I scanned the list for a starting point and ended up doing what any new teacher would do—considering only the items that weren't checked. Bad idea. Getting hung up on my deficiencies made it harder to respond to his open-ended question in a coherent way. I started feeling defensive and snarky—not only because I was losing part of my prep period, but because his assessment was incomplete and therefore inaccurate. In a court of law, I would have grounds for an appeal.

I babbled for a few minutes about how I thought the kids did a good job and worked well together, and did he want to see their creative endings to the story?

"Not this time, gotta go." He glanced at his watch. "I think you did alright. You'll improve with time."

And that was it. The scary Big Visit dissolved into the carpet as soon as he left the room.

"You've gotta be frickin' kidding me," I whispered, worried he might overhear. I couldn't believe that, after all my careful planning and fussing, "you'll improve with time" was all I got. Improve *what,* exactly? I felt like crumpling the principal's stupid observation form and attempting a three-pointer from across the room. I felt like stomping out of school. But it was too soon to exit the building without being seen. There was nowhere to go, anyway. No escape. I was trapped. Trapped with my anxiety about Principal Ken's incomplete assessment and trapped with the ceaseless nagging about what to teach next.

It was the fastest cleanup on record. I moved around the room like the Tasmanian Devil in a Looney Tunes cartoon, shoving desks back into rows and swiping up errant pieces of paper and broken pencil tips. I erased the board in a flurry, dust flying and me not caring which direction it went. Both of my erasers were thick with the chalky substance, and I mostly just smeared the board with it. *Maybe I should go outside and smack them together. I'll make a dust cloud so big this village will think a snowstorm is coming.*

"Knock knock!" I jumped at the sound of a man's voice at the door. It was Duncan, the last person I wanted to see.

"Yeah?" My tone reflected a woman on the edge.

"Don't forget, we're manning the concession stand tomorrow night. Come at six, okay?" Duncan looked like he was going to say more but thought better of it and left.

I turned back to erasing the board. My right hand looked like I'd stuck it in a bowl of powdered sugar. I finished and vigorously wiped the chalk on my pants, leaving a white smear.

Stupid observation. Stupid game. Stupid concessions.

I was in no mood to read any more papers or plan the bare bones of Monday's classes. While I knew it would have been wise to do so, I just couldn't stand the thought of sitting in this room for one more minute. I needed to get away.

My thick sleeping bag worked well to muffle my sobs. I hadn't expected to cry. I reached for my roll of toilet tissue and blew my nose. The principal's assessment wasn't fair. He had no idea how hard I'd worked to get the students prepared for that simple lesson.

He should have seen them last week when they were asleep at their desks!

Rolling onto my back, I stared at the ceiling and tried to appeal to reason. Principal Ken's comments didn't exactly signal condemnation, but they did trigger my deep-seated fear of not measuring up, of being discovered as an impostor. "You'll improve with time" was code for "We'll see if you make it."

There was a deeper ache, too. Emotional and physical. It felt like grief, like something died and I'd never get it back. *Was this me grieving the end of a career that had only just begun?*

I had wanted to be a teacher forever. It wasn't even a choice. It was a calling. The desire was bigger than me, and I desperately wanted it to keep pulling me forward.

Being told that there was nothing I could do but wait for time to pass before I felt worthy of that calling was painful. It was like unseen force had taken Darlene's arrow, stuck it back into my heart, and twisted.

I blew my nose again.

Maybe I can just quit.

The question released something inside of me, like a curl of smoke from one of Anne's cigarettes. It floated up to the light fixture, swirled around once, and disappeared.

TWENTY-SEVEN

THE CALL TO TEACH

Why did I choose this profession? That was the million-dollar question. A question that stood in front of me now, arms crossed, eyes narrowed. It wanted an answer.

My thoughts drifted back to my childhood, to the long road I had followed to get here. To a village just thirty miles shy of the Arctic Circle and lying on this bed.

For as long as I could remember, I had always loved school. I was a curious kid and got lost for hours pursuing questions like, "Who invented zippers?" and "Why do some butterflies have spots on their wings?"

Classmates called me teacher's pet, but their commentaries—while they stung—didn't last long. As far as I was concerned, they were losing out on the joy of learning and the satisfaction that came after working through a challenge.

Fifth grade was the turning point, when my teacher treated me in a way that made me feel noticed and valued. She was the one who opened the door to the teaching profession and held it as I walked straight through.

Mrs. Springer was a mix of strict but kind; firm but caring; intelligent but open to the wonders that her own students expressed through their drawings or uneven lettering on wide-ruled notepaper. She had a way of letting her pupils know they mattered. She emitted a ray of kindness, and I did all I could to get a little of it to shine on me.

As usual one day, I finished an assignment before my classmates and was mindlessly tapping my pencil out of boredom. My teacher motioned for me to report to her desk and suggested that I use my extra time to conduct research on a topic of interest. "You can create a display," she said with a hopeful smile, pointing to a blank space on the wall.

The floodgates of possibility opened. I ran home and dug through the deep pile of *National Geographic* magazines laying in a basket, searching for an idea. The winner was an issue featuring the great white shark. There was a photo on the front cover with the menacing predator coming straight at the camera, mouth open, razor teeth exposed. I wanted to study the heck out of that shark and share what I'd learned with my classmates.

I read every word and carefully cut out the photographs for my display. The magazine had no diagram of a shark, so I drew my own and labeled it, teeth to tail.

Mrs. Springer helped me prepare my display space. She took me to the teacher's workroom and showed me how to pull yellow butcher paper from the heavy roll. We carried it back together, and I held it as she stapled it to the wall. We stood back and studied our efforts.

"Hmmm. I think it needs a border," she said, and went to the storage closet for her ball of thick red yarn. Mrs. Springer loved red. She had red skirts and sweaters and scarves, and she always had on a fresh coat of red lipstick.

I'd taped up my drawings and informational notes and was nearly finished when it occurred to me that I could give my classmates a quiz at the end of my presentation.

"They can show what they learned! Would that be alright?"

"Sure, honey."

I had no idea what was going through Mrs. Springer's mind. Maybe she was amused. Maybe she wondered what kind of little teacher she had just unleashed. Maybe she was just happy not to hear me tapping my pencil.

Copy machines had yet to find their way into schools, so my quiz would be duplicated by mimeograph machine. With her hand gently guiding mine, I painted gooey blue fluid onto a large cylinder she called a drum, affixed my master copy with a clip, and cranked out multiple copies, watching in amazement as the pages of my quiz questions landed in the tray. "How long is a white shark?" And "How many teeth does a typical white shark have?"

Presentation day came, and I used Mrs. Springer's pointing stick to show my classmates all about the great white shark. When I passed out the quiz, they groaned. Their reluctance to show what they learned surprised me, but my teacher had anticipated the moment and kindly redirected the class, nodding encouragement for me to continue. The teacher in me took flight.

After that experience, my teaching aspirations went dormant for a while; my family moved to Vail, and we changed schools. But soon, I found myself in minor teaching roles, like the two summers when, as a teenager, I was hired by my tennis coach to manage a Little Players Club of six- and seven-year olds. Their tennis rackets were as big as their bodies, and they quickly tired from swinging and mostly missing the tennis balls I gently tossed in their direction. One young boy begged me to show him how to pick up a tennis ball by tapping on it. Before I knew it, all twenty of the little buggers were huddled in a corner of the tennis court, tapping Wilson tennis balls and getting nowhere. It was amusing as well as touching. The camp director came by and peered through the fence to ask what the heck I was doing.

"They're learning how to pick up balls like the pros," I explained.

"Looks like a bunch of chickens pecking in the barnyard," he replied.

I noticed some of the children's parents watching, eyebrows raised. I went back to teaching the kids how to hit a forehand.

Soon after, I headed to college, as directed by my father. "Try the Pacific Northwest," he suggested. "I think you'll like it there." I chose Western Washington University, sight unseen, only because of a photo on their brochure of a spectacular sunset over the bay. I figured that since I was heading into unknown territory, it should at least be pretty.

On my intake form, I wrote that I wanted to major in Architecture, only to find that the college had no program in that field. My college advisor suggested Industrial Design.

While I was good with project ideas and beautifully portrayed three-dimensional objects with only paper and a sharpened No. 2 pencil, I didn't feel inspired. I also became increasingly aware that I was the last woman standing in any of my design or math classes. It seemed only a matter of time before I would be weeded out. One instructor even told me I shouldn't get my hopes up. "You'll never get hired," he smirked. "You're a girl. Look around."

His horrible, lawsuit-worthy comment nearly pushed me to quit college altogether and go back to teaching little children how to pick up tennis balls. I had come too far, though, and decided to finish the last in a series of arduous math classes. Maybe passing those would lead to something employable.

But then I ran into a major issue with one Calculus teacher, whose policy was to fail any student who missed his precious final exam.

And why did I miss the final exam? It was a simple mix-up with the calendar. Spring Break was fast approaching, and my paternal grandmother, Nana, surprised me with a plane ticket to visit her in Sun City, Arizona. Grandpa Puca had recently passed away, and she wanted to spend more time with her grandchildren.

I stared in horror at the ticket's departure date. The plane would depart Bellingham on the same day as the final exam. As a matter of fact, I'd be flying right overhead, whilst my classmates were bent over their tests with Number 2 pencils. Nana had innocently misunderstood the date I'd given her, thinking that was the first day I was free, not the day I would still be held captive by a stupid test.

I tried reasoning with my professor. Couldn't he make an exception? Neither I nor my grandmother had extra money to pay for a changed ticket. Maybe he would meet me halfway, and average the unfair F with my consistent streak A's. I would pass with a grade of C.

The idea made me feel nauseous, but I was willing to cut my losses.

But my professor didn't budge. He stared at me over his thick black glasses, arms crossed on his plump chest. The answer was "No." His rule was not to be tampered with, and I would just have to live with being branded a Failure. Flunked. Finished.

I left his office, fuming and scared and sick to my stomach. Just like that, the man was going to dismiss ten weeks of hard work, and there was nothing I could do about it. Worse, I'd have to look at his frumpy face again next quarter. He was the only one who taught that particular Calculus class, and I needed it for my major.

For the next hour, I stomped around campus, hoping the movement would help me figure a way through my dilemma: staying and taking the test, or seeing my grandmother during spring break and having to take the class all over again.

Two hours of brisk walking later, the decision was clear. It would seriously delay graduation and alter the course of whatever came next, but it felt right. I thumbed my nose at Dr. Doofus (the nickname I'd assigned to him) and flew to Phoenix.

That evening, after a round of errands and chicken casserole for dinner, Nana asked how college was going. I relayed my tale about Dr. Doofus and how he'd flunked me. I didn't want her to feel bad, but I couldn't lie. She listened sympathetically, and then said in her Midwest matter-of-fact way, "I'm not sure why you're bothering with all of that. You're supposed to be a teacher."

With that proclamation, Nana opened her freezer and studied the contents. Every shelf was packed with cartons of ice cream. Orange sherbet, chocolate fudge, vanilla, and mint. Even licorice.

"What do you like to learn?" She pulled out a quart of pecan caramel-swirl.

I shrugged. "Well, I love to read and write."

"That's what you should do then." She plopped a large scoop into my bowl. "Be an English teacher."

Her words breathed life into my teacher's heart, like bellows to the flame that Mrs. Springer had lit a decade before.

With my future no longer dragging on me, Nana and I spent every waking moment together, driving her golf cart to the grocery store and to the bowling alley where we chomped fries and slurped milkshakes and watched people roll gutter balls. It was highly entertaining.

The day prior to my departure, we went to a miniature golf course. Nana, who was small in stature and typically quiet in demeanor, suddenly morphed into a spunky teenager. At the first tee, I expected her to gently tap the ball a few times until it reached the hole. But she didn't even look where the flag was.

Whack!

Her ball flew down the green felt with surprising velocity, ricocheted off some fake rocks and bounced into the surrounding landscape peppered with prickly pear cactus. Nana thought it was hilarious, and repeated the shot a few more times before we finished the 18th hole. My legs were scratched to smithereens from brushing against the sharp needles each time I volunteered to retrieve her ball.

That spring break was the best trip I'd ever had, not only because I got to spend one-on-one time with my grandmother for the first time in my life, but because she gave me a new direction for my future. Her simple phrase about being a teacher rang true. I could have quibbled about the idea, but deep down inside, where I felt strong and secure, I knew she was right. The moment I returned to the campus I changed my major to Secondary English Education.

So here I was. A teacher. On paper, at least. I had worked so hard to get to this place, yet I felt like I was in mourning. Like something had died before it got to live.

In his book *A Grief Observed*, C.S. Lewis mourned the death of his wife. He knew she had cancer, but he married her anyway and stayed with her to the end. If you ask me, that was some crazy, deep faith. What would that feel like? Could I do the same and marry someone I knew I'd lose shortly thereafter?

I was still laying on my bed. A tear slipped from one eye, and I caught it before it dripped into my ear. *But maybe I* do *know.* So far, the practice of teaching had taught me that it's a much more complicated affair than delivering lessons and collecting assignments. It demanded more than keeping students focused on a task "or else."

The work of teaching was never done, Teachers didn't clock out at night. They rarely clocked out at all. Teachers worked with human beings whose setbacks and growth spurts were unending. Students were always growing, digressing, and growing some more (hopefully). Working in all that messiness wasn't part of the job, it *was* the job.

And I was engaging with minors whose prefrontal cortex had not yet fully developed. The stakes were high. One wrong word at the wrong time could ruin a kid's life.

Teaching was serious business. It required the kind of faith that C.S. Lewis had, the kind that gave you strength to commit to a relationship that you craved with all your heart. It was an endless series of climbing fences and getting stabbed by the prickly pears of love and loss, happiness and anger, sweetness and sadness.

"You'll improve with time." Principal Ken's words echoed once more. But love could improve with time, right? Probably. Sure. Why not?

The flame in me grew brighter, and I sat up. It was time for me to let go of my impossibly high expectations. I needed to lighten up! I was just starting out, for Pete's sake. I needed to cease and desist trying to measure up to some unreasonable standard that no one but my own little Kulizuk self was setting. Principal Ken's twenty-five item checklist could never measure my effort. It would never measure how I overcame my fears, just like it would never capture the hope I had that one day I'd turn into the kind of teacher I dreamed of. The one Mrs. Springer saw in fifth grade. The one Nana knew I was meant to be.

I stood up and stretched, reflecting once more about that glorious spring break with Nana. She'd had a life of hardship and sorrow yet found happiness in small things. Even now, in her seventies, she didn't let the hard stuff linger. Nana ate ice cream and whacked golf balls and giggled like a little girl when they sailed out of bounds. That was how I wanted to live, too.

TWENTY-EIGHT

CONCESSIONS

It was Saturday, the day after the deflating, so-called observation. Burning the candle at both ends for an entire week finally caught up with me, and I rose well past my normal time, feeling a bit spacey, but free—the perfect combination for the wide-open day.

I took my coffee and a snack bar back to bed and wrote in my journal about the ups and downs of my recent week while listening to a mixtape from Mia. The Walkman was a recent technological marvel, making it possible to take one's favorite music anywhere, even as a walking woman.

But my inner peace began to crumble with the nagging reminder of tonight's "manning" of the concession stand with Duncan. *Why, oh why, out of all of the teachers, was I paired with him?* Lance was probably playing a joke on me. He'd witnessed Duncan's flirting. Poor Duncan. It was probably clear to everyone on the island that I was gay. I mean, I wore men's clothes and never talked about a boyfriend. And I had a Swiss Army knife. That was a dead giveaway.

Regardless of my romantic inclinations, there was no wriggling out of concession stand duty. I disappeared to school for the rest of the day, then returned home for a quick dinner before heading back to school again.

Anne was laying on the couch watching *Wheel of Fortune.*

"You coming to the game?" I paused to watch a blond lady in a svelte, silver-studded dress flip a panel, revealing the letter P.

"No, you idiot!" Anne yelled at the screen. "Pick E! You always start with E."

She shook her head in disgust and turned her attention to me.

"What'd you say?"

"I'm heading to the game. Gotta 'man' the concession stand," I explained, making air quotes.

"Nah, I'm gonna stay here." She turned back to the screen. "Wanna see if this fellow wins." She yelled again. "You picked J?"

I zipped my coat and stepped outside, my attention immediately drawn to the upper landing of the school only ten yards away. Dozens of eager basketball fans had already gathered, waiting for the doors to open. They lined the school steps and all the way up the street. The Shishmaref Northern Lights boys were playing a team from Savoonga, one of two villages on St. Lawrence Island, over two hundred miles to the south.

"Excuse me, excuse me, comin' through."

I inched my way through the line and up to the school doors, explaining as I went, "Helping set things up."

It was like moving through an Arctic fashion show. The women wore brightly colored jackets with floral patterns and embroidered collars, cuffs, and hems. Young girls in similar attire smiled shyly, then ducked behind pant legs. There were elderly men as well, in dark parkas and knit caps in assorted colors. They had kind eyes and rugged faces, creased by wind and sun—just like John, the interviewer who'd pointed out Shishmaref on his map. The man who knew where he was going to send someone like me and did it anyway. That seemed like a lifetime ago.

Inside the building at last, I was greeted by the aroma of fresh popcorn. I loved, loved, loved popcorn. My obsession began in Vail one winter when, at the base of the ski mountain, an ingenious person parked a bright red popcorn wagon. It was the first thing skiers saw (and smelled) as they unclipped from their bindings and started down the street. There was always a line, but it was worth the wait. One dollar bought you a bag of yummy, salty goodness. Maybe manning the concession stand wouldn't be so bad.

"Right on time," Duncan said. "This is Mable. She's in charge of the kitchen. Mable, this is Genét, new teacher."

Mable was shorter than me and a bit older. Her onyx hair was pulled back tight and held in place with a large metal clip. Narrow glasses rested on her nose. Mable had a no-nonsense air about her. She could probably run the entire lunch shift solo even if the power went out.

Duncan pointed to a countertop carnival-style popcorn machine. It had glass doors and a large silver kettle. Popcorn cascaded over the rim, landing in a large mound. He handed me a metal scoop and a stack of skinny brown bags.

"Ever worked one of these before?"

I shook my head no.

"Well, fill these up and then I'll teach you to make another batch. Or more," he added. "People go nuts for the popcorn."

He turned back to help Mable with flats of Pepsi, Coke, and Fanta Orange. Within a few minutes, I had a dozen bags filled. My concession colleagues were now setting out boxes of Milky Way bars, Snickers, and Twizzlers. Junk food heaven.

Duncan demonstrated the ratio of orange-colored oil and kernels, and soon I was on my way to becoming an official carnival popcorn chef. Halfway through my second batch, a long squeaking noise erupted behind me. Duncan was opening the metal rolling screen.

"Ready!" He called to someone by the door. In seconds, a flood of snack-loving basketball enthusiasts flowed in. I handed the popcorn to Duncan as fast as I could. People were buying two and three at a time.

For the next twenty minutes, Duncan, Mable, and I worked in concert to keep the popcorn, candy, and sodas moving. It felt like the entire village was at the game.

Finally, the last customers came through, and we heard the shrill sound of the referee's whistle. The game was on.

"Ever seen the kids play?" Duncan asked.

"No, just heard them practicing."

"Well, you should go watch for a bit. It's quite a sight."

And he was right. The gym was packed. There must have been three hundred people yelling, cheering, and shoving popcorn in their mouths. They watched each play intently and hollered at the referees whenever there was a whistle against Shishmaref. The noise was deafening, helped by a group of young children playing tag behind one of the baskets. They screamed and dispersed whenever the players came thundering down the court.

The players moved with incredible speed and grace. Their movements were breathtaking. They defied gravity, leaping huge distances in the air before making a shot.

Back and forth the teams jockeyed for position and alternating points. The ball changed hands so fast it was hard for me to keep up with who was who.

My jaw dropped when Daryl (almost always in a sour mood in class) threw a hard pass to Joey (almost always sleeping in class), who jumped in midair and banked the basketball off the glass for two points. The crowd cheered. We weren't even at halftime and the Shishmaref Northern Lights were ahead thirty-two to seventeen. I felt bad for the Savoonga team. They looked a bit dazed when their coach called a time-out.

I returned to the concession stand to help prepare for the likely rush for snacks at halftime. It was crazy. We went through just as much popcorn, soda, and candy as before the game. Beads of sweat glistened on my face, and I realized it was the first time I'd sweated since arriving in the village.

During third quarter, the popcorn-candy-soda line trickled to a near halt, and Duncan excused me once more to watch the game. I gratefully accepted and stood to one side, scanning the rows to see if I could spot anyone I knew. Sure enough, Carol, Paula, Natalie, and Darlene were clumped together, conversing and laughing, then screaming when the Northern Lights ball found the sweet spot.

Along the sidelines were the Northern Lights cheerleaders, Rianne and Fiona, pumping their pom poms and yelling, "V-I-C-T-O-R-Y, victory, victory, that's our cry!"

The heads of everyone in the room moved in unison, like at a tennis match, following the ball back and forth. Along the sideline, I spotted a toddler. He stretched out his arms to get picked up, then struggled to be set down. He had wandered a few feet into the court, but no one looked concerned. I held my breath. At the speed with which the players were running, the child would surely get run over and smacked hard to the floor.

The ball had just changed hands back to the Northern Lights, so the teams switched direction. Will sprinted down the sideline with the ball, the same one as the toddler, and—with a maneuver that once more defied gravity—pushed the ball from his chest halfway across the court to Daryl. His hands now free, Will scooped up the toddler and set him gently into a woman's arms. He took off again and assisted with a rebound to make the shot.

His fluid motion and razor-sharp focus stunned me. Maybe this was my students' true character, their true power. A power I was sadly not harnessing in my classroom.

It was clear that Shishmaref would win. The score was sixty to thirty-two, with only five minutes to go. The Savoonga team called another time-out, so I returned to the concession stand to help clean up.

There wasn't much to do, only sweeping and wiping out the popcorn machine. Mable and Duncan had already stored the soda flats and boxes of candy in a cabinet. Mable said goodnight and slipped out the door.

"How'd your observation go?" Duncan's question caught me by surprise.

"Weird," I replied. "I'm trying to forget about it."

Principal Ken's "visit" felt like it had happened a week ago. Maybe manning the concession stand had served a greater purpose. It felt good to do something that had a clear beginning, middle, and end. Progress I could measure. Popcorn kernels in, popcorn out, and popcorn into the bags. Done, done, and done. Maybe that's how my students wanted to feel, too.

"You just seemed upset when I came by ..." Duncan paused.

"Yeah, it was a crazy day, with the power going out. Kind of screwed with my nerves."

Duncan grinned sheepishly and divulged that it was his class that tripped the switch. "We had a lot of tools plugged in," he explained. "Sorry 'bout that."

It seemed innocent enough. I softened and told Duncan how Principal Ken had entered the room all flustered and just sat there making checkmarks on a form I hadn't seen.

"It was bizarre. He didn't say a word. Just checked things on his form and left before the end, which was a bummer, because that's when some good stuff happened. He came back during my prep for the debrief. Just handed me the checklist and said I'd improve with time."

Duncan and I leaned against the counter, a few feet apart. My hands were shoved into my pockets. Duncan's arms were crossed at his chest. We looked like two guys standing in a parking lot talking about going fishing.

"So that was it?" Duncan's eyebrows went up. I nodded.

"Wow. I know how you feel, sorta. It's this big buildup and you go crazy with details, and then it's over, just like that." He snapped his fingers. "The first time I got observed—that was a couple of years ago—I thought I'd be Mister Big Guy and show off the wooden sled my students and I had just finished building. You know, the kind the locals use to drag all sorts of stuff around the village?" He turned and leaned on his elbow. "Well, we took everyone out behind the school and hitched the sled to the school's sno-go. It was the first sled I'd ever built, and I hadn't tested it yet. But it seemed fine when we pulled it outside. Heavy son of a gun." Duncan started to laugh. "And you know what happened? The whole damn thing fell apart! Broke right in two."

He moved to the center of the room, mimicking riding a snow machine. "I took off real fast. *Vroom*!" He jerked a thumb into his chest. "But Mister Big Shot forgot some screws, and the sled broke in half! Kids were screaming at me to stop. By the time I turned the machine around, half of them were laying around on the snow and dying laughing."

"Oh my god!" I covered my mouth. "Really?"

"Yeah." Duncan rolled his eyes. "Then the principal says to me with this straight face, like he's trying to show concern but not lose it, too. He says, 'Good effort. You'll get the hang of it!'" Duncan shook his head. "God. What a day."

He patted my shoulder. "Don't worry about it."

But I couldn't let it go.

"The thing that got to me was all the time and energy I spent planning and second-guessing myself. But it didn't seem to matter. 'You'll improve with time, you'll get the hang of it, keep trying.'" I shook my rag in the sink. "I was hoping for a little more guidance."

"Right. But maybe the principal doesn't know any more than we do."

Duncan's enlightened comment brought on a case of giggling.

"What's so funny?" Duncan asked, wanting to join in the fun.

"Oh, god, do you know which book I just finished reading?" I wiped away a tear. "*A Grief Observed*!"

Duncan admitted that he had no idea what book I was talking about, but the title was funny enough.

We laughed until our faces hurt. Duncan ripped off a couple of pieces of paper towel for us to dry our eyes, then grabbed a can of Coke and handed it to me. The bubbles fizzed up my nose, making me cough. Duncan took a swig and belched, which sent us into another round of giggles. We were two teachers acting like teenagers and loving it. Eventually, our laughter subsided, and we got our coats to leave.

"Well, g'night." Duncan held the school door for me.

"G'night." I stepped through. "That was fun."

He followed me down the steps, then headed up the street. Such a small village, yet I had no idea where he lived. Duncan turned and called back to me.

"See you Monday!"

"Yes, you will."

TWENTY-NINE

EXPOSED

I turned the house calendar to November and studied the photo of a white ptarmigan in the snow. Its beady eyes and short black beak were all that distinguished it from the fluffy snowbank in a grove of trees. Such a sweet looking bird. I wondered what it was like to shoot one and have enough bird left to make soup, like the locals did, with rice or macaroni.

The mercury in my brother's thermometer dipped below freezing almost every day. The scale's lines were thin and hard to read, but I didn't need them to confirm that winter was coming. We'd had a few snow flurries, and patches of ice were appearing in the street. The sun was dropping lower in the sky, and the warmth from its rays no longer reached my face.

I opened my sock drawer, which had turned into a catchall for a variety of random objects, including a dozen little black canisters holding undeveloped film. Most held twenty-four pictures, a few had thirty-six. I did the math in my head—close to three-hundred photos, not counting the roll in my camera.

Since landing on this island, I had taken enough photos with my Nikon to host a modest museum exhibit. I imagined quibbling with the curator over a suitable title: "Arctic Village: An Outsider's Perspective." Or maybe "Kulizuk: The Discombobulated Life of a Novice Teacher." Perhaps "The Tundra Holes of Teaching." It was hard to figure an angle that adequately captured my experiences here. Maybe the curator and I would finally agree to tack a postcard to the wall that said *Untitled* and set out a suggestion box.

I had not intended to stockpile so many plastic containers of film, but I didn't know how to get them processed. What would have been a quick trip to the corner drugstore in my former life might take weeks of strategic planning from a place as remote as this. There was the uncertainty of planes coming and going, and the cost—half my paycheck might disappear between film processing and groceries.

My first paycheck had indeed arrived. After tax and housing deductions, I cleared just under two thousand dollars. It didn't seem like much in exchange for everything I'd invested in my job thus far, but it was more than I'd ever seen in one paycheck, enabling me to pay my debt to Walter, resolve my debt to the credit card collector, and start a savings account for things like a trip home to Vail at Christmas. Maybe I'd take the film canisters with me then.

The prospect of flying out in the dead of winter was a bit unnerving. Anne leveled a serious look at me when I mentioned flying all the way home to Colorado during winter break and went into a monologue about severe winter weather and small planes going down because of ice on their wings. "I wouldn't relish that." She shook her head and played another card.

Traveling in the dead of winter was one thing the hiring committee had neglected to mention, and Anne's comments increased my anxiety. Would I be able to make the long trek through multiple airports and into the mountains to Vail during the height of the holiday season? A lot of variables were at play: flight delays or cancellations, missing connections, and driving not once, but twice, over one hundred miles and two snowy mountain passes. And then I had to make it all the way back.

I tried to maintain a modicum of optimism and pictured myself emerging from the plane in Denver dressed like Santa Claus and carrying an enormous sack—not filled with toys for all the girls and boys, but dozens of little black canisters that, once processed, would tell the story of a young and inexperienced Smurfette, teaching English, Consumer Math, and Graphic Communications on the edge of the Chukchi Sea.

The significance of many of the photos would likely need explanation to friends and family. I had taken my fair share of the flat tundra with the village in the distance, the flat ocean, and the flat beach; those might look boring to the untrained eye. But perhaps their senses would perk up after seeing drying racks with black meat, reddish-brown fish filets, and glistening white polar bear hides. Maybe they would understand why photos of shells scattered on the sand and shimmering grass in the wind were worthy of a snap of the shutter.

I had grown to love the feel of the silver shutter button under my index finger. There was a resonance between that simple motion and my beating heart; I could *feel* the click traveling through my body. Unlike teaching, there was a finality to it. I pressed and released, and it was done—a moment in time captured in silver that would never come again. The world slowed down. Things I might have passed before and not noticed suddenly took on a new dimension.

Ice forming on Chukchi Sea

I savored those photo moments, not just for the experiences themselves, but because I knew it would be a dang long time until I saw the results. Opening the little Kodak envelope of prints was punctuated by anticipation mixed with delight and sometimes dismay depending on how things turned out. But even sloppy photos carried memories. A blurry image of mountains would bring back the feel of dirt beneath my boots and the smell of evergreen trees. Here, the memories would be permeated with scents of sand and fish and salty air.

I was still deciding which socks to wear when I heard Anne calling my name.

"Yeah?" I yelled back and stepped into the hallway. She was standing near the dining table, beckoning me to come closer.

She pointed. "You oughta see this."

I joined her at the kitchen window, both of us standing on either side of the pimply rubber chicken my mother had mailed several weeks ago. When I showed it to Anne, she laughed and quickly found some string.

"Here you go, little feller," she'd said fondly as she strung it up by its scrawny neck.

"I think it's supposed to hang by its feet," I suggested. But we left it that way.

Outside was a woman dressed in a blue poncho decorated with flowers. She was about ten yards away from our portable, behind some oil drums and a lone outboard motor. The woman brushed gray hair away from her face using the back of her hand, as if she didn't want her fingers to come near it. At her feet was something laying on the ground, like a pink bathroom carpet.

"They're cleaning seals," Anne announced, zipping up her coat. "Wanna watch?"

I was curious but also grossed out. Since my first day on the island, I had accepted, carte blanche, just about everything: deer legs, dead seals and birds, honey buckets, and all the rest. But this would be my closest encounter with butchering an animal. By the time I came along, whatever had previously inhabited the skin hanging on the rack was long gone from its body. Getting close to a carcass unsettled me. Maybe I was more of a city girl than I thought.

"Um. I think I'll watch from here."

"Suit yourself, but you really should check it out. Bring your camera."

I watched Anne as she walked by the window and caught sight of a second woman squatting over another pink carpet. *That's the inside of a sealskin.* Her arms moved back and forth in short bursts. I caught the flash of a knife in her right hand. It must have been near freezing, but she wore only a sweatshirt and jeans.

I had been a vegetarian for most of my life, trying to avoid eating other beings that had eyes, and disliking the feel of meat in my mouth. As a child, my mother would take me with her to the neighborhood German delicatessen, where I wrinkled my nose at liverwurst and beef tongue in the case.

One store near our home in Wauwatosa had a huge mural along the entire upper half of a side wall. It was impossible to ignore. No matter where I was in the store, my gaze always came back to the idyllic farm scene that was, more accurately, a story of slaughter.

Starting on the left were little piggies happily munching from a trough or lazing about in the mud outside a red barn. To the right was a line of more happy little piggies entering said barn. Then, the little piggies disappeared. At the other end of the barn, there was a farmer grinding a pink substance in a big machine that soon transformed into sausage links falling into a pile. It made me sad and mad and grossed out every time I looked at it, trying to wrap my little eight-year-old mind around the graphic nature of such violence. People ate the little piggies? I felt like Fern Arable in *Charlotte's Web*, hot and angry and flustered and scared when she found out that her father was planning to butcher the runt of the litter. I counted the piglets in the pasture: twelve innocent piggy lives. Twelve little Wilburs.

That was sixteen years and several lifetimes ago. I was no longer a child, and no one was asking me to eat a seal. Anne was right—I should check it out.

My appearance outside caught the attention of a handful of high school students hanging out on the landing by the doors of the school. I waved. They waved back and continued their conversation. How was it they were wearing such thin jackets? I zipped my parka up to my neck and walked twenty paces to join Anne, who stood at a respectable distance to observe the seal-cleaning process.

Loretta Sinnok (left) and Rachel Walliq Sinnok Stasenko, cleaning seals outside my house

Half a dozen silver and black-spotted seals lay on the ground. Most were still intact, but a few had been skinned, their blood staining several cardboard mats the women had arranged on the sand. The elderly woman was standing over the pelt of one seal, splayed open and blubber side up. In her hand was a small knife that looked like the head of a medieval axe.

"That knife is an ulu," Ann nodded toward the woman. "Short and very sharp."

The woman bent over again and angled the knife almost flat along the seal skin, making short strokes to remove the gray-pink layer of fat. It looked like hard work. The younger woman continued to squat, using her own ulu and alternating her strokes with moments of conversation in Iñupiat. Her words sounded gentle and kind.

The sky was overcast, and there wasn't much wind. The air had the feel of icy rain or maybe a snow flurry. The kids were still leaning on the school railing, enjoying lighthearted banter. Stuff was lying about everywhere: rusted oil drums, the boat motor, plywood boards, gasoline cans, and large pieces of thick, milky-white plastic sheeting. Mia had joked that she might ship some to me. "It's called Visqueen," she'd informed me. "Every self-respecting Alaskan has a stash. You can use it to build a shelter or cover equipment to keep it dry."

The women cleaning seals didn't mind our presence, but I was getting cold, and the smell of blood had wafted to where Anne and I stood, making my stomach queasy.

"Think they'd mind if I took a couple photos?" I asked Anne. She shrugged.

I walked closer to the elderly woman and pulled out my camera, pointing at it. "Would it be alright …"

She nodded, then bent down once more. I snapped a couple of photos, unsure what I was really trying to capture, then returned to Anne's side.

"Thanks for bringing me out. This is really something." I tried to catch the eye of the women to nod a silent thank you, but they were focused on their work. Judging by the number of seals left to clean, they'd be at it for a while.

As I walked back to our house, my eyes caught a piece of artwork carved out of wood and nailed to the school building. I must have walked by it a hundred times but never noticed. The image was of an Eskimo in a fur-lined, hooded parka, bending down toward a little seal. The Eskimo seemed to be coaxing the seal to come closer, not to kill it, but rather as a gesture of friendship. The seal looked up as if in agreement.

I turned back toward the women with the realization that they weren't simply skinning seals and scraping fat off the hides. They were participants in a mutual agreement with sea mammals who had given their lives for the villagers' sustenance. I was witnessing a display of coexistence between humans and animals in the cycle of life.

I stamped the sand from my boots and closed the door behind me. A cup of hot tea would be nice. Here, in the kitchen, I felt safe. Everything was familiar—my water heating up on the stove, my cup on the counter, and the silly chicken hanging by its neck. Out there, I felt exposed; I would always be an Outsider of varying degrees, living in this village at arm's length, never truly belonging. Yet the people offered access to their most sacred of acts. In that way, they were exposed, too. And so was the seal.

I felt a wisp of awareness in my heart signaling that, despite the obvious cultural distance between myself and the people of Shishmaref, the veil that initially separated us had started to dissolve. I set my camera on the counter and wondered if the photos I'd just taken had stolen the seals' souls. I'd read about that once.

"Sorry, little seals," I said quietly. "But thank you."

The teakettle whistled, and I turned back to safety, back to what I knew.

THIRTY

FUTURE PROBLEMS

One more day over with. One more day of students trudging behind as I zigzagged them up the mountain of proper conventions in the English language. Today's focus was the handy dandy semicolon, and my target audience was ninth graders. They were confident with periods but shaky with commas, using them too sparsely or inserting so many that, when I read their work out loud, it sounded like I was hyperventilating.

Punctuation was a mystery, a bona fide nuisance. "The marks get in the way!" students complained. "They slow us down."

I couldn't fault their logic. I didn't know their native tongue, but its cadence sounded brief, like a lot was said in a small space. My untrained ear heard collections of sounds, and pauses had no discernable meaning. Students also frequently omitted articles—words like the, a, and an. They said, "Going to store" instead of "I'm going to the store." And, "So boring!" instead of "This is so boring!" (Which it was.)

When I asked students to write longer sentences, they simply strung together all their fragments and added a comma wherever they thought one would appease me.

To be fair, I never learned how to teach punctuation. My college classes tested only my own skills; they didn't show me how to help others learn what I had picked up by osmosis.

It was my primary school teacher, Miss Melville, who taught me to write. Large print letters first, then cursive. During instruction in the latter, my mother sat me at the kitchen table every day after school to practice my swoops and curls.

"Just pull a book from the shelf and copy the sentences," she'd instructed.

At first, the assignment felt like punishment. My older brother didn't have to sit at the kitchen table and copy sentences, and his handwriting was worse than mine. I aired this grievance, but Mother maintained her stance and informed me that good penmanship was necessary for career advancement—and something about being female.

My complaint lessened over time, exchanged for a newfound enjoyment of reading stories of pioneers and inventors in our family's new set of Childcraft encyclopedias. And, although my handwriting didn't improve much, one hidden benefit of copying professional writing verbatim was picking up proper spelling and punctuation habits. I started developing an ear for how to write with clarity and variation. Writing became a fun way to explore both my inner and outer worlds.

It was due to that youthful enthusiasm for writing that I made the mistake of thinking my students would get excited, too. I had stayed up late the night before, chasing after what I thought was a clever idea—a worksheet with sentences that needed revision with the use of commas, semicolons, and periods. My intention was to demonstrate how easy it was to change the trajectory of written thought, simply by moving punctuation around. To help my students relax with the exercise, I wrote a couple of silly introductory sentences, followed by sentences about island life—the sea and the wind, and hunting seals and walrus. They divulged on the first day of school how much hunting and "walrusing" they did; now was their chance to elaborate.

"Punctuation marks are like tools in a toolbox," I explained. "Pliers are for grasping, hammers pound nails, and screwdrivers screw." I gestured each tool as I listed them and flinched as soon as I said the screwing part.

Sure enough, the students started giggling. I kept a straight face and moved on.

"Let's try out some examples, shall we?" *Teaching strategy #1: Deflect undesirable behavior.*

"Awwww, man! Do we hafta?"

"We did that yesterday! And the day before!"

"Yeah, class is almost over!"

I glanced at the clock. "Nice try. We've still got half an hour." I grabbed a worksheet. "I'll get you started." *Teaching Strategy #2: Model instructions before distributing worksheets.*

I copied one of the silly phrases on the board: *There are some pickles in the cupboard they are in a large jar.*

When I wrote that example last night, the word "pickles" sounded funny. Now, it just sounded absurd. Did they even know what a pickle was? I turned from the board to see several students with their heads down. Others stared out the window. My class was dead in the water.

Teaching Strategy #3: Ignore unwanted behavior.

"Jacob, please read this." I pointed at the board. Jacob's eyes moved from left to right.

I rolled my eyes. "Out loud."

"Oh," he responded innocently. Giggles traveled around the room. "So, uh, let's see." Jacob squinted and cleared his throat. "The, uh … no wait. *There* are some pickles in the cupboard they are in a large jar."

I hadn't expected Jacob to read the run-on sentence as a single sentence, but his smooth delivery was making me question the idea that he and his classmates would naturally hear the awkwardness in that statement and realize that either a period or semicolon needed to be inserted between the words "cupboard" and "they."

"Okay, good. Thank you, Jacob." *Teaching Strategy #4: Be kind when responding to students, even when they're wrong.*

"Let's see what happens when we write the sentence with proper punctuation. The mark we're focusing on today is the semicolon."

I drew a comma, a semicolon, and a period on the board, and circled the semicolon, and spent the next several minutes trying to explain how a period is like coming to a full stop at a stop sign when riding a four-wheeler around town. A comma was like slowing down at a corner but not stopping, and a semicolon was somewhere in between.

"It's not a full stop and it's not a pause," I said. "When you have two sentences that connect closely in terms of their ideas, a semicolon shows their close relationship. Like pausing at a stop sign with your blinker on and revving your motor a little."

The analogy was a good one, but I hadn't considered if people on the island used turn signals. The speed limit was only fifteen miles per hour. Did four wheelers even *have* turn signals? I could not recall ever seeing one.

The students' faces registered a combination of interest and indecision about whether they should believe the crazy teacher, whom they'd never seen drive anything (although there was a rumor she'd driven the school's truck into a hole).

"Jacob, can you read this phrase again, slowly this time, and tell us if you feel the need for a semicolon after one of the words?"

This was a direct violation of *Teaching Strategy #5: Don't ask a question when you mean to make a command.*

Jacob glared at me. He had already fulfilled his duty; it was someone else's turn to answer trivial questions! But I had the upper hand and knew that this group stayed better focused when one of their comrades was in the hot seat.

Jacob slowly lowered his head until his forehead came within a centimeter of the desktop. Then, he let it fall with a thud. His classmates chuckled.

I stood firm. "C'mon, Jacob. I know you've got this. Stay with me." I looked around the room. One by one, each student mimicked

Jacob, slowly lowering their heads and letting them fall the last centimeter. Thud. Thud. Thud.

"Guys, if you don't get through this today, you'll just have to do it tomorrow."

Uh-oh. Another violation. I had just committed the one thing I vowed I would never do as a teacher: use writing as a means of punishment. And, worse, an idle threat. But here I was.

Jacob slowly raised his head and squinted at the chalkboard again. Stella, the classmate closest to him, turned and peered at him between her bangs, then scrunched her face. This was mutiny, plain and simple, one more thing my teacher program failed to warn me about.

"Hey, if Jacob does it, and we pay attention, can we still get credit?" Curtis sat up, excited with his idea. "Like we don't have to each do a worksheet, but help Jacob and it counts for all of us?"

Other heads popped up.

I countered, "Well, if Jacob does it for all of you, how will I know what *you* learned?"

Rianne's hand shot up. "We'll learn that Jacob is the smartest and we're fine with that!" A chorus of "yeahs!" flew around the room. I was running out of ideas.

"Jacob, why don't you come to the board and one of your classmates can tell you where to place the semicolon?" *(This was both question and command.)*

I stood with the chalk just out of Jacob's reach. It was Truth or Dare time. If he took the dare, Jacob could be the hero his classmates wanted him to be.

Jacob groaned his way to the board.

"Put it after cupboard," yelled Stella.

Jacob drew a squiggly comma with a dot over it and slid back into his seat.

"Okay! That's perfect." I tried to sound encouraging. "Now, let's say you decided to use a period instead. What happens to the word after a period?" I directed my question at Jacob, keeping him in the hot seat a little longer. After all, his classmates put him there. "Jacob, when you start a new sentence, what's the rule?"

"That's not fair." He crossed his arms. "You already made me read out loud and do the semicolon thingy."

"Yes, I did." I put a hand on my heart. "My apologies, but ..."

"Oooh. Lemme do it!" Rianne jumped up, grabbed the chalk, and wrote a capital T for They, and erased the comma in Jacob's semicolon, leaving the period. She stepped back and smiled, then moved forward again and decorated the period by drawing a ladybug, making the period into the tip of one antenna.

I glanced at the clock. *Teaching Strategy #6: Don't look at the clock if they can see you looking.*

"We still have ten minutes."

The students grumbled. But I won. For the next several minutes, I heard only the sounds of pencils and an occasional eraser. I stayed at my desk, not wanting to hover. They hated it when I walked around the room and peered over their shoulders. They'd say, "Ooh, you making me nervous!"

Their concentration was lovely to witness, but then Ruben, who was frequently absent or remarkably invisible when he attended class, began staring at the clock's second hand, watching as it crept around the clock's face one tick at a time. At exactly quarter past one, he jumped up and moved toward the door with startling speed. His classmates followed, each holding out their worksheets as they passed.

"Thank you, thank you, thank you," I repeated, taking the last one and sighing in relief that I'd made it through. I plopped into my chair.

"Well, I'll be darned," I said out loud. "Giving them something to do for just ten minutes actually held their attention." It was time for lunch, and I was starving.

I had just taken a chomp into my peanut-butter-honey Pilot Bread sandwich when I heard Principal Ken's footsteps coming down the hall. The main office was only a short distance away, but the sound of his heavy boots always made the trek seem longer, like something ominous was about to happen. Our school leader weighed over two hundred pounds. At six and a half feet tall, his influence was so powerful that his body didn't need to hurry in the direction of his command. Sure enough, the footsteps ended at my door. I looked up with a tight smile.

In his hand was a packet of papers and a large manilla envelope. "You ever heard of Future Problem Solving?"

"Sorry?"

"Uh, Future. Problem. Solving," he repeated more slowly, as if trying to grasp the concept himself. "Some kind of competition."

I didn't like the sound of a competition and was hesitant to volunteer for future problem solving, given my questionable capacity to solve the problems of today.

"Says there's trainin' in Unalakleet. A weekend."

"Oh?"

A trip to the school district's office? A night in a hotel with running water? Meals in a restaurant or coffee shop? Please, oh please …

I approached, expecting him to hand the papers to me, but the principal was equally intrigued with the notion of future problem solving and seemed to want to understand more before assigning whatever it was to me.

"Sounds kinda involved. Think I'll ask Ben first. No 'fense, but he's Social Studies and this sounds more like somethin' for him." He looked at me over the tops of his glasses. "Enjoy yer lunch." He pointed to his chin, indicating that I had some food on my own. A drip of honey. I watched Principal Ken disappear down the hall, taking my dream of a hot shower and coffee shop with him.

I resumed my lunch and tried to shake off my disappointment by focusing on my next class, Graphic Communications. The girls usually had ideas for their next edition of the *Northern Lights News*, so there wasn't much to prepare. I loved having that class at the end of the day.

With no other thoughts fighting for my attention, a pesky inner voice arose. *How come Ben gets to go? Just 'cause you're the new kid on the block doesn't mean you can't figure it out. So what if Principal Ken only checked fifteen out of twenty-five items on that stupid form? I deserve a weekend in a clean, sand-free hotel room, with a hot shower ...*

The sound of Principal Ken's boots returning brought the whiny voice to an abrupt halt.

"Um. Well. Okay," he said. "Ben says he's got too much on his plate. So it's yers if you wan' it." His expression was one of resignation, as if he was stuck with the third-string quarterback to make the final play in a high-stakes game.

"I'll give it a try."

My voice feigned confidence. In truth, I was only thinking about the glorious sensation of hot water on my shoulders.

"Oh, and there's a big binder in the main office that goes with this." Principal Ken paused. "Gotta get yer plane ticket and sign up fer training. Due date's in a couple days. Lemme know what you need." He lumbered back down the hall.

I was tempted to go after the binder, but I forced myself to plan for tomorrow's ninth-grade English class. It was easier to tee up the next lesson after working with that group.

Ninth graders were tricky. They tolerated my grammar lessons for only short stints at a time. I was constantly trying to find a topic or activity that engaged them for more than a few minutes. Ninth grade had been my favorite during student teaching, so this group would be the litmus test that either confirmed or denied that I had chosen the right profession.

Maybe I should postpone the punctuation for a few days and refocus on *Romeo and Juliet*. They initially treated the story with disdain but perked up as tension mounted between the Capulet and Montague families, leading toward certain violence. We had just finished Act Three, a revenge scene where Romeo kills Tybalt, who had just killed one of Romeo's friends.

Whatever works.

I was still organizing my thoughts when my news team bounced in and announced that they wanted to go to the post office and the general store to inquire about newsworthy events.

They explained, "We need new stuff."

The four girls were dedicated, and I could trust them on an unchaperoned field trip about town. Besides, their absence would extend my planning period. I wrote a permission slip and instructed the girls to report back by the end of class. They agreed and excitedly left the room.

Before planning further with Shakespeare's play, I decided to see how my ninth graders did with their semicolon exercise.

The first paper had no name. The author had properly inserted about half of the punctuation marks and cleverly transformed each one into a tiny bug with antennae. The second paper was from Curtis. His punctuation was all over the place, but he had taken time to draw circles around most of his marks and add eight little legs. Spiders. Cute.

I flipped through the stack. Rianne had started a movement. All of them had quietly colluded to decorate their papers with bugs and spindly-legged arachnids. There were miniature suns and starbursts, spirals, and teeny tiny petaled flowers. Another student (no name, but I suspected Tyler) drew a stick of dynamite with the fuse lit, ready to blow. The students' artwork made it difficult for me to determine which punctuation marks they had inserted, but at least they were easy to find. What a bunch of knuckleheads. They probably weren't trying to spite me, but rather lighten me up.

Ten minutes before the end of the period, my news team returned.

Molly rushed in first and flopped into a desk. "We're gonna be detectives!"

"Yeah, like Cagney and Lacey!" Darlene dropped next to her, breathless from running. Cagney and Lacey, played by Sharon Gless and Tyne Daley, acted in one of the first detective shows on television that had strong women leads—smart, clever, and brash.

"Great idea!" I was caught up in their enthusiasm. "How'd you decide that?"

"Ooh, let me tell!" Natalie was too excited to sit. "We were hanging out at the Native Store and overheard that someone tried to steal the safe from City Hall!"

"We wanna interview the mayor and help solve the mystery!" Sarah crossed her arms. "We've got questions."

"Yeah," Natalie continued, "like how'd the burglars get the safe all the way down the back stairs and *outside*?" She gestured to the window, shaking her head. "It must have weighed a ton!"

The girls left the room, chatting excitedly and leaving me to reflect on the fact that I had no clue where City Hall was located. Most of the buildings in Shishmaref were nondescript, and since no one had given me a tour upon arriving, I felt like everything was off limits, except for the school, the post office, and the two grocery stores.

Alone once more, I decided to check out the big Future Problem Solving binder. Principal Ken wasn't kidding. It was four inches thick—a tome of tabbed information. What in the world was Future Problem Solving that it took a ream of paper to explain? I tucked the binder under one arm and headed home.

"What's that?" Anne glanced up from her solitaire game.

"Some kind of competition about future problems. It comes with a weekend at the school district office in Unalakleet and a night in a hotel with running water."

"Oh, yeah, heard of it." Anne studied a card, then slapped it down. "Upper grades. Critical thinking. Glad I work with the little ones. Good luck with that." She tapped her cigarette into a saucer and set it back on her lower lip.

I made a cup of peppermint tea and slathered peanut butter on a Pilot bread cracker. Unwilling to retreat to my bedroom just yet, I chose to ignore Anne's cigarette smoke, sat on the couch, and opened the binder to the "Introduction."

A fellow named Dr. E. Paul Torrance developed The Future Problem Solving Program (FPSP) in 1974. He wanted to help students build critical thinking and leadership skills by working through possible future challenges regarding the natural environment, science, or business. They'd practice brainstorming and devising solutions so that, no matter what the competition question focused on, their minds would be primed to creatively solve the issue.

Competitions for middle and high school were held at the regional level. If a team made it past those, they'd go to a national competition in Washington, D.C.

I skimmed the sample topics. Hazardous handling of waste from nuclear waste dumps. Transportation needs in high industrial areas. The challenges of equitable water distribution for agriculture versus recreation. This was going to be harder than I thought. My students were turning periods and semicolons into spiders and ladybugs.

My eyes landed on the heading, "Fuzzy Situations." I started to laugh, and got into a coughing fit when a piece of Pilot Bread lodged in my throat.

Anne looked up, concerned. "You okay?"

I washed the remnant of cracker down with a swig of tea and wiped away a tear. "This future problem solving thing involves fuzzy situations." I used air quotes and laughed again. "And that means solving problems and competing against other schools." I shook my head. "Not sure if they're up to it. Today, my ninth graders whined about using semicolons."

I felt bad for saying it. I knew my students' struggles were not entirely of their own making. The fault was more mine, and sentences about pickles weren't helping. I turned to another page.

"I'm not exactly sure how this is all supposed to work or what the timeline is."

"Hence the training in Unalakleet," Anne replied dryly. She turned over a playing card. "Ah, there we go," she smacked it down, "gotcha."

Anne took a drag on her cigarette and exhaled a stream of acrid smoke. I decided to retreat to my bedroom for the rest of the night. Whether Anne was lighting up Salems, Newports, or Marlboros, she quickly filled the house with smoke, and the ridiculous heating vents in the ceiling pushed it around the room.

I contemplated taking my studies back to my classroom but didn't feel like bundling up again. It was only thirty feet to school, but the frigid air settled into my bones and took a long time to shake off. Retreating to my bedroom was my only option.

One of the burdens of teachers is being handed new curriculum without having time to thoroughly study it. I was weary with hearing the analogy that teaching was "like building the plane while you're flying it," and wanted to ask "Why?" Why did teaching have to be like that? It made no sense—like telling a doctor she ought to be able to perform knee surgery while scanning a handbook titled "How to Operate."

My lack of experience and anemic pedagogical knowledge resulted in me either dumbing down lessons or attempting too big of a learning leap. Instead of taking students from A to B, I'd attempt A to E. My students would quit, and I'd run out of ideas.

It dawned on me that my students might not be resisting learning as much as signaling that my methods didn't match their abilities. Staring out the window and laying their heads on desks was my students' way of saying, "We don't get this. And we're embarrassed. Please don't ask us to go to the board and show you where semicolons and commas go. We don't use them. They're too small and will just fly away in the wind."

I opened the binder once more, hoping for insight as I turned methodically through the headings, quietly reading the instructions. *Break down problems, avoid jumping to conclusions, dissect possible outcomes.* And the problems would likely be futuristic, things that had not occurred yet on the planet but might happen on my students' watch.

The word "competition" appeared multiple times, as did "tests." Both unsettled me. How could I coach students through activities that I, myself, disliked?

A wave of sleepiness hit me. I set down my mug, plopped into my pillow, and pulled my sleeping bag around me, nudging the FPSP manual to the side with my feet so I could fully extend. Commas, periods, and semicolons buzzed around the room, chasing after future problems, trying to find a place to land.

Should I do this? Was it worth the likely shame if I returned from training and admitted defeat before I started recruitment? Would I have to reimburse Principal Ken for my hot shower and hotel?

The questions remained unanswered. The day's events slipped away, and I fell asleep.

Inside typical bush plane

Two weekends later, I was onboard a Bering Air flight, the only passenger on the bush plane bound for Unalakleet, a village on the eastern edge of Norton Sound. As the pilot angled the plane south, I craned my neck for a view of the little island where so much had happened in only a few months. The landscape changed from the gray-blue sea to orange-brown tundra and thousands of little permafrost holes like the one I'd driven the school's truck into. My mishap was an innocent one, but ignorant. I should have known that I wouldn't have been able to drive in a straight line without running into trouble.

For the next hour, my thoughts bumbled around: Future Problems training, teaching foibles, my eccentric roommate, Christmas vacation. I barely noticed our quick approach to Nome's runway. I thought it was a routine pit stop, but the pilot informed me that two more teachers were hitching a ride to Unalakleet, and we'd be on the tarmac for only a few minutes to load them.

Mike sat up front, and Nancy climbed into the seat next to me. We exchanged the basic information about subject areas and number of years in the bush. I was the newest and the youngest, no surprise. Mike taught math and science. Nancy was the English and social studies teacher. This was their second year.

Mike had the same easygoing, conversational air of other young male teachers I'd met so far. He wore the same attire: blue jeans and a flannel shirt, and a short beard. Nancy was quieter. She had on a long wool coat, the collar of which she kept pulling up to cover her mouth. She looked cold and tired.

We flew high over the gray-blue waters of Norton Sound, looking for whales and other signs of life, but saw nothing. Mike was chatty and took the opportunity of a captivated audience to explain how Unalakleet was home for the Bering Strait School District, which managed about fifteen schools spread out over approximately seventy-five thousand square miles.

"A little bigger than South Dakota!" Mike yelled over the loud engine noise.

I would have loved to pepper Mike and Nancy with questions about the Future Problem Solving competition, but I didn't know where to start. Mike divulged that, like my own principal, theirs was keen to have Nome High School win the event and gain notoriety.

"It's a long shot," Mike laughed, "but at least we get a hot shower out of it!"

Mike was right. The shower was divine. But I found the training terrifying. Our trainers knew their content but didn't know how to guide someone like me through it. I grew increasingly concerned with each passing hour that my hippocampus had dissolved to mush. I couldn't seem to retain anything they were saying. They led us through a flurry of flipping through the enormous Future Problem Solving binder and practicing different scenarios. I was lost. So were the two women sitting on either side of me. And we were too embarrassed to admit it. I wanted to scream, "Stop! Could someone *please* just write the step-by-step instructions on the board?"

Enough of the teachers around the room seemed to understand what to do, however, so the facilitators marched onward, while I countered my anxiety by visiting the coffee and pastries table multiple times.

I was trying on different scenarios of my own about how to break the news to Principal Ken that future problem solving was too complicated for the students (omitting me, of course), when the sound of a large binder slamming shut jolted me to attention.

"Okay, let's get out there and solve some problems!"

The room burst into claps and cheers. And that was it. Our so-called training was over. I was on my own.

After a rush of goodbyes and thank you's, teachers climbed into vans to the airport. I rode with Mike and Nancy and felt the sudden urge to change my flight plans and fly with them to Nome and hide in one of their classrooms. I'd tell Principal Ken that I didn't feel well and would return in a few days. But the thought of him being the most likely person to sub for me, and the burden of creating lesson plans I'd have to explain over the phone (when I had none) quickly brought that daydream to an end.

Sensing my consternation, Mike offered a quick hug and a pat on the shoulder before he and Nancy grabbed their bags. "You'll get the hang of it!"

I seriously doubted his optimism, but there was no way forward other than to climb aboard my own small propellor plane, this time a direct flight with me as the only passenger. The pilot added a few bags of mail and boxes of dry goods, and we were off. Post-training fatigue took over, and I fell asleep.

A midair jolt of the plane startled me back into consciousness, and I opened my eyes to see the lima-bean-shaped island and the line of waves curling into its north-facing shore. Most of the small boats had been pulled onto dry land.

So much had happened since this view first came into my life. A few months ago, I didn't know the village was on an island. I didn't know which home was mine.

I didn't know there was no coffee shop.

The village was no longer a mystery, but I still had questions. How was I going to break the news to Principal Ken that I'd failed the training? And how was I going to recruit and coach kids about something I didn't yet understand? My ideas were still up in the air when our wheels touched down.

As the plane rolled to a stop, it occurred to me that my first problem to solve was how to get home. In the hullabaloo of preparing for Unalakleet, I had neglected to arrange transportation back to my house.

Fortunately, one of the locals offered me a lift in his truck and, this time, upgraded me to First Class inside the cab. We rolled along the frozen streets in silence and came to a halt in front of my residence, no directions needed.

"Hey there." Anne glanced up from the couch. "How'd it go?"

"Okay, I guess." I didn't want to talk about it. "What's this show?"

On the screen was a tall white man in tight jeans and a button-down shirt that opened to reveal a patch of chest hair and a thick gold chain. He was leaning back on a sports car, his white cowboy hat tipped back nonchalantly. Leaning against him in intimate conversation was a blond woman whose white leather pants, halter top, and voluptuous curves left little to the imagination.

"*Dallas*," Anne said.

"Huh. Never heard of it." I continued toward my bedroom.

"You've never heard of *Dallas*?"

I changed the subject. "The training wasn't very helpful. I still don't really know what I'm supposed to do."

"Oh, I wouldn't worry too much. You'll get the hang of it."

The next afternoon, I launched my recruitment sales pitch in every class, trying to exude confidence and excitement about the wonders of the Future Problem Solving competition. I peppered my speech with motivational statements like, "It'll be cool! You'll meet kids from other villages! You can add it to your resumé!"

I said these things as if I believed them, but the students rightly sensed my trepidation and abstained in silence. I was a crappy salesperson. No one volunteered.

Principal Ken was at his desk, elbows resting on piles of paper. He didn't look up at first, but I knew he could hear me, so I cleared my throat for the concession speech I'd been rehearsing since lunch.

"So, no one's interested in Future Problem Solving. You know, the thing I went to Unalakleet for. The competition."

"What?" He peered over the tops of his glasses, a gesture I'd come to learn meant either authentic surprise or derision.

"Yeah, I tried to sell it in all my classes, but …"

"Oh! Right. That thing." He leaned back. "How was Unalakleet?"

I shrugged and explained how, in my expert opinion, the competition was better suited for kids in the Lower 48, who might have to solve dilemmas like inequitable water distribution or the negative effects of factory farming.

Principal Ken stroked his mustache thoughtfully. "Well, darn. I was hopin' we could pull a group together. Y'know, do somethin' to put this school on the map." He pushed away from his desk and stood up to stretch. "I'll chat with the middle school teachers. Maybe they can send a few kids your way. I'll let you know."

Fifteen minutes later, Principal Ken appeared at my classroom door.

"I got a teacher recruitin' for ya. He'll send some kids tomorrow after school." He winked. "Maybe I'll throw my son in the mix. God knows he needs help solvin' problems."

Then he tapped the door frame and departed, a gesture meant to say that his part of the deal was complete. The ball was back in my court.

The next day, my classes went smoothly, which was surprising, given I hadn't planned much. But I wasn't going to over-analyze. I was just opening the Future Problem Solving binder when I felt a presence in the doorway and looked up to see two young girls. They had stopped at the threshold as if an invisible force prevented crossing over to the dark side.

"Are you here for Future Problem Solving?"

Their eyebrows shot up. One girl blew a large gum bubble and popped it.

"Well, have a seat." I motioned toward the desks. "Do you know if anyone else is coming?"

They scrunched their faces and entered, pulled two desks tightly together and sat down. I stayed at my desk, mindlessly gazing at the opened binder page, catching a quote by the founder of Future Problem Solving—something about courage and creativity and having new ideas, all of which turned a person into a "minority of one." He sure nailed it.

The room was silent. The girls were calm and didn't seem bothered by sitting in an unfamiliar classroom with desks too big for their feet to reach the floor. The bubblegum girl swung her feet back and forth in cadence with her chewing.

What if this was it—two students? Maybe I could thank them for coming and say we'd try to get a larger group together next year. I felt ashamed by my lack of courage, but I was afraid that I'd be leading them down a long path of disappointment. We'd get this village on the map, alright. The headlines would read, "Shishmaref Middle Schoolers Have More Than Just Future Problems."

"Got any pop?" the non-bubblegum girl blurted out.

"How 'bout candy?" The other followed.

I resisted the urge to adjourn the meeting and send the girls back over the threshold.

"No pop or candy. Do you like Carnation Breakfast Bars?"

The girls accepted my offering, and I decided to at least conduct introductions.

"I'm Genét. I teach English and Math. What are your names?"

Bubblegum Girl responded first. "Olivia."

I shot a look at the gray wad of gum now stuck on top of her desk but held my tongue.

"Claudine," responded the other. "But I go by Chloe."

After a brief conversation, I learned two things: 1. Olivia was in fifth grade and Chloe was in sixth, and 2. Neither of them had any idea why they had been sent to my room.

This information nudged me closer to feeling okay about sending them on their way, but that plan fizzled when two more students appeared at the door: a girl I hadn't met before, and the principal's son, Mikey. His presence forced my hand. There was no way I could excuse the group and get away with it, not with Mikey going home and telling his dad how the cowardly teacher sent everyone packing, without even trying.

Thus began the Future Problem Solving Club. I explained what I knew as simply as I could, emphasizing that they'd learn useful skills for analyzing future problems. I left out references to nuclear waste and factory farming, choosing instead things like "fun" and "travel."

"Can we get out of class?" Chloe interjected.

"Yeah, or is this a trap, like with homework?" This comment came from Mikey.

Not sure myself, I fudged and said that we'd be meeting after school a couple times each week and, yes, there would be a bit of homework. Saving humanity was not for the faint of heart.

The kids looked doubtful, but I was desperate not to appear incompetent—worse, insubordinate—qualities I didn't want to add to my file in the principal's office.

I brought our meeting to a close by suggesting that the kids return tomorrow for a trial run and better snacks.

"Thanks for coming!" I called after them in a cheery voice.

God, I am going to totally suck at this.

For the next three weeks, the Future Problem Solving Club practiced asking questions about issues of concern, like how to get better lunches or more time for recess. We practiced not jumping to conclusions, instead asking more questions about our questions, then analyzing those and adding more until we were hopelessly lost in a thicket of possibilities that had no discernable end. I tried tracking the students' efforts on poster paper but, by our fourth meeting, all I had to show for our efforts was a wall filled with neurotic mind maps.

The kids were more interested in snacks.

I returned to Principal Ken's office to deliver my report.

"I'm afraid the middle schoolers are too young for solving future problems," I announced, still standing in his doorway and afraid to enter. "I've spent about fifty dollars on pop and M&Ms, but that hasn't helped."

"Yeah, I was concerned 'bout that." Principal Ken lightly tapped his pencil. "I wonder if we can still try with a different age group."

Oh my god, he's going for the kindergarten class.

"But I guess you tried. Maybe this wasn't the year." He leaned back and sighed.

"Yeah. I guess not." I tapped the door frame and left before he could respond.

Problem solved.

THIRTY-ONE

YOU GOTTA LOVE IT INTO LIFE

It was Friday night. Anne and I had just finished a rare dinner together and were cleaning up, when she remembered that there was a workshop for teachers in the morning.

"It's by Melvin Olanna, a famous carver who lives here," she said. "He's inviting teachers to learn how to carve masks. Want to go?"

I was more than ready for a diversion from lesson planning or taking walkabout number one hundred and thirty around the island. Attending a workshop might also iron out the inner wrinkles of my increasing cabin fever. The tilt of the earth in November brought only about six hours of daylight, and that was growing dimmer by the day—seven minutes, to be exact—and on a steady march to only two and a half hours by the Winter Solstice. Both ends of the school day were in the dark. I felt increasingly heavy inside, like someone had handed me a fifty-pound weight and no instructions as to when I could put it down.

"We'll have to dress warm," Anne said. "It's going to be sunny, but wicked cold."

She was right. The next day, the thermometer registered near zero. We headed up main street into a strong northern wind that made my eyes water. I was used to this and always carried a Kleenex in my pocket to dab tears from my eyes, a gesture that gave me the appearance of being perpetually upset.

The Chukchi Sea rolled into shore with more force than normal. Dark gray clouds formed a bank on the horizon, but the sky above was clear except for the usual salt haze in the air.

I tied the tassels of my new beaver hat under my chin. It was a recent, unexpected purchase at a basketball game during halftime. I was contemplating a second bag of popcorn when I was approached by an elderly woman wearing a flowery kuspuk and sealskin mukluks. A couple of white plastic shopping bags hung from each arm.

She stepped close and started pulling fur hats out of her bags, holding them up to me and smiling. The hats were handmade with corduroy cloth in browns, blues, and greens, and what looked like beaver fur. Her eyes twinkled and her eyebrows stayed in a perpetually uplifted position. I was fascinated by this involuntary interaction but unsure, at first, what was happening. Several presentations later, I realized that I was in the middle of a beaver hat buying transaction.

To be polite, I pointed at forest green. She nodded and plopped it on my head and, with the deftness of a cowgirl roping a calf, tied the tassels under my chin and stepped back to admire her handiwork. She smiled broadly, exposing a few missing front teeth.

Students gathered around.

"Ooh, you buy beaver hat?" They giggled and nodded their approval.

My face flushed from the warmth of the hat as well as from their attention.

I wasn't sure I wanted to have the remnants of a large rodent on my head, but it was a beautiful piece of handiwork. The beaver fur was the color of dark molasses, with hints of gold. It was surprisingly soft and cool to the touch, but quickly warmed my head, especially with the ear flaps (also lined with fur) hugging the sides of my face. At the end of each flap was a cord, braided with dark green and yellow yarn, which tied the flaps up or down. They were decorated with large gray fur pompoms. Maybe rabbit? The outside was finished off with dark green corduroy.

"How much?"

The woman held up three fingers.

"Thirty dollars," Molly interpreted, nodding with approval.

And, just like that, I was the proud owner of an authentic beaver hat that would help me feel more like one of the locals.

As we walked over to his workshop, Anne shared what she knew of Mr. Olanna's background.

"He's famous for his sculptures. Learned from his father, Alfred. He carves soapstone, ivory, and whalebone. Walrus bone and tusks, too, I think. He does all kinds of arctic animals. Small ones, big ones, even some pieces in museums and art galleries. He's had some health problems. One leg's a little shorter than the other. He had tuberculosis when he was young. In and out of the hospital a lot. But his work is legendary."

Melvin Olanna's house was set back from the street. We went around to a side door and knocked. Mr. Olanna opened the door himself, clad in baseball cap, a red and black flannel shirt, and jeans with suspenders. His face was kind and creased with age.

The workshop had tall wooden tables and benches. An assortment of carving tools and unfinished projects sat on the shelves. A metallic, burning smell permeated the air.

One of my students, Lyle, sat at a bench, carving a gray-white chunk of wood. Or maybe it was whale bone? I had never seen him so focused. The whir of his carving tool filled the air. It was a small, hand-held electric tool I would later learn was called a Dremel. Lyle's use of the electric device threw me off. I'd expected to see original carving tools. A stereotype popped into my mind of an old Eskimo man sitting by the light of a seal oil lamp, carving a piece of walrus tusk with a small knife fastened to a bone handle with rawhide. I knew it was a ridiculous assumption but still felt a twinge of disappointment. Using electric tools felt like cheating.

"Pretty quiet today." Melvin gestured to the near-empty space. You the only ones?" He looked back and forth between us and nodded at me. "Nice hat."

Melvin directed us back outside to find a piece of wood for carving a mask. We had the option of poking around his large woodpile or searching on the beach. Not finding anything in the woodpile, we looked at Melvin's raw materials laying on plywood tables.

"Here's a whale spine." Anne pointed at a long structure of interlocking bones. "This one's probably walrus."

I had only seen the reconstructed bones of dinosaurs from behind roped barriers in museums. Here, within arm's reach, were whale vertebrae, walrus skulls, and rib bones. Was that a pelvis? I wasn't sure. The bones were bleached white by the sun. I traced a finger along one long piece, pockmarked from exposure to the air, then placed a hand underneath to lift it. It was surprisingly heavy.

Another gust of icy wind blew across the tundra, signaling that we needed to find some wood, and fast. I retied my beaver hat tassels and followed Anne down a narrow path through the grass and toward the beach. Driftwood was surprisingly abundant in the shallow grass. It must have floated hundreds of miles up the coast before landing on this island's shore.

"Look for something this big." Anne made a circle with her hands. "About the size of a large layer cake."

I zigzagged over uneven ground, gingerly feeling along with my boots to avoid tripping on hidden pieces of wood or tufts of hard sand. Every time I thought I found a good piece, Anne told me it was either too heavy or too gnarly.

She shook her head as I presented another one. "The tool gets stuck if there's too many knots in it." Her wood carving knowledge impressed me. I didn't know much about Anne, even though we'd been sharing accommodations for almost three months.

"Hey, how about this one?" I tapped a log with my boot. "Or maybe it's too big."

"We could saw off two rounds," Anne suggested, then held out a hand. "Give me your camera. Let's get a photo of you with your kill!"

Posing with the log I chose for carving a mask. The large metal container on the beach is from the North Star ship

Carrying the heavy stump was slow going, especially on the uneven ground. After a couple of stops to catch our breath, we reached Melvin's back door. Anne went inside to find help. She emerged a moment later with one of Melvin's assistants, who expertly cut two twelve-inch rounds, three inches thick. We were ready.

Up to this point in my life, I'd had only two experiences with carving, both of which were questionable. My first was in third grade with a bar of Ivory soap and a paring knife. My attempt to carve a small turtle (my teacher's suggestion) ended in disaster. I was terrified that I'd cut my hand with the sharp blade, and I kept losing my grip on the soap. It squirted from my sweaty little hands several times and scuttled across the wood floor, getting dented and cracked. My turtle ended up being one-tenth the size of what I'd intended. I nicknamed him Stumpy and laid him to rest in an obscure place on the display table.

My second attempt with carving was in a college woodworking class when I made the acquaintance of a high-powered lathe. The idea was to carve a set of candlesticks out of two thick dowels. A few well-placed indents and curves, and—voilà! I'd have a thoughtful and elegant Christmas gift for my parents.

The lathe spun with dizzying speed and such force, I thought I'd lose an arm. But my mind was set. Determined to master just a few decorative grooves, I grasped the chisel and hung on for dear life, afraid it would fly out of my hands and impale a classmate across the room. After fifteen sweaty minutes, I reduced two twelve-inch dowels to disks the thickness of hockey pucks. I proceeded to sand and polish them, pretending that hockey puck candlesticks were exactly what I'd intended. My parents were touched by my thoughtful gift, but I never did see my creation gracing the table.

Third time's a charm, as they say.

I was timid with the Dremel at first, concerned that I'd cut too deeply into the wood and remove too much material. But Melvin countered my limiting mindset.

"Be more aggressive. You gotta love it into life."

He took my Dremel and carved a deep groove on one side of my cautious outline of a nose—so deep I thought the piece would crack in half and I'd have a Picasso on my hands. But the wood responded to his command, and he repeated the motion on the other side, reforming the flat image into a face with three dimensions that looked surprisingly lifelike.

Melvin held up the mask, studying it. "You need cheeks. I'll get you started." He steadily moved the tool back and forth to create beginning grooves for lips, which magically formed a chin and cheeks. I never realized how connected facial features were—how deepening one groove accentuated another.

Melvin had total command of the Dremel. He made it look easy, but it must have taken years to perfect. What I had considered a tool of cheating was actually an artist's best friend. Holding the Dremel correctly required considerable planning and dexterity. It was amazingly versatile and had various attachments for engraving, routing, and polishing. Carving turned out to be fun.

I worked a bit longer, wood shavings softly floating onto the table, onto my pants, and onto the floor. My hands were sore, but it was a satisfying soreness.

"Angle the tool to make little chin hairs," Melvin suggested. "Make it a little rough." He gently moved the spinning head against the wood's natural grain. "And make these," he pointed at the crow's feet forming around his own eyes and laughed. "For a happy Eskimo!"

Melvin showed me how to preserve the wood by gently rubbing oil into the grain with my fingers. I was getting to know this face, and it was getting to know me.

An hour of careful and loving mask carving later, I presented my handiwork.

"Nice." Melvin took my mask and held it over his face. "You've made it come to life."

THIRTY-TWO

COMING TO MY SENSES

That night, I dreamt that I was looking through a large kaleidoscope, so big and heavy that my hands could barely hold it. The mechanism was crafted in silver, brilliantly polished and cool to the touch. Peering through, my eye was washed with a dazzling array of deep blues and reds and purple-green flashes of color like northern lights racing across the midnight sky.

Then, the scene switched from looking through the kaleidoscope to being in it, surrounded by those vibrant colors. I knew I was asleep yet still felt the turning of the mechanism reverberating within my own body. The tumbling shapes and colors shifted into a fluid movement that coursed through my bones. I found myself in the surprising position of looking through the kaleidoscope and being in it at the same time.

The palpable sensation of becoming "one" with something forced me awake. I sat up in the cold and dark, aware that I was no longer sleeping yet still enveloped by my dream. I existed in two dimensions—not split, but more like one within the other, absorbed by an entity larger than myself. A similar sensation had passed through me on several occasions since arriving in Shishmaref, but this dream was the most potent experience thus far.

I turned on the lamp to anchor myself on the physical earth plane and tried to make sense of the time. Already nine o'clock. *What day is it?*

"Sunday" a voice whispered inside my head. I stretched, relieved that I hadn't miscalculated and slept in on a school day. Weekends should have been a time to rest, to find my own rhythm. But there was a constant pressure lurking in the background of needing to prepare lessons, to grade, to search for materials. When caught in the crosscurrents of needing to stop thinking about schoolwork, yet needing to think about it, I did what any sensible teacher would do: procrastinate.

Today's procrastination would be disguised as a healthy walk along the northwest shore, where the vastness of sky and uninterrupted landscape had a way of bringing my life into perspective. Of loosening expectations. The scenery would also help me process my mask-carving experience. Working with the wood had been both a challenging and functional activity, yet I was aware that something more expansive was occurring. Something opened inside of me. A secret latch had released, and a door had swung open. To what, I didn't know.

It was midmorning by the time I slipped out the door and into the chilly air. Metal-gray clouds mingled with my thoughts, and I found myself halfway to the southeast tip of the island, heading toward the dump. My body was tired, but I kept going. I took a deep breath of the salty air and stopped, turning my face to the wind. Closing my eyes, all I could hear were the waves coming to shore, one after the other.

They always do this, whether I am standing here or not.

Such relentless power, such constancy. The ocean advancing and then receding. The squawk of an Arctic tern opened my eyes, and I scanned the sky until I found the lone bird calmly soaring, then dipping on the wind.

Not far ahead, I spotted something white-gray laying in the sand and altered my trajectory for a closer look. It was a dead seagull, half covered by sand that waves had packed tight around its lifeless body. The head was mostly deteriorated, the legs gone.

I stood near, unsure if I should bury the carcass or leave the mass of decaying flesh and feathers exposed to the elements. Either way, it would eventually dissolve into the earth. The bird probably didn't care what I did. Its soul had flown elsewhere,.

Another squawk interrupted my thoughts. The same Arctic tern, dipping and arcing through the air, heading south. I followed its trajectory down the wet beach to the road that ran into the dump. Someone with a bulldozer had been hard at work, pushing mounds of sand on top of the trash. I had been out here quite a few times but hadn't really thought through garbage protocols on the island. Come to think of it, for most of my life, I never paid much attention to where trash went after tossing it into the can; I just appreciated the people who carried it away.

What happened to these mounds of waste? Did the villagers burn it? I'd never seen smoke. Did they just keep burying it? Maybe there was a North Star Sanitation Ship that hauled things away on occasion. I looked down the sandy road at rusted oil drums, chunks of Styrofoam, and dozens of black trash bags like the ones Anne and I used to line our honey bucket. One was torn, a disposable diaper with unicorns peeking out. So much for disposable.

"We did this."

The words flew from my mouth, startling me. But they were true. It wasn't the Native people who had introduced nonbiodegradable materials to the island, but Outsiders. People like me. We were the ones who insisted on TVs and canned soup and Carnation Breakfast Bars wrapped in plastic. And so much more. Anything that brought comfort in this harsh and often uncomfortable environment. There hadn't been much forethought about the long-term implications of those choices. No matter how much sand was piled up, almost everything I was looking at would be here for decades. The Styrofoam, forever. And now the dump had transformed from being my routine walking destination to a place of regret.

I retraced my steps and passed the dead seagull once more. It had no eyes, but I wondered if its soul was watching me, helping me watch myself. The more I walked, the more my inner eye perceived an alternate reality, prompting me to play my little game of finding shells and stones on the beach and shapeshifting them into walrus heads and seals. Maybe a polar bear.

Searching for objects was entertaining, but each step toward the village was a step toward the reality of schoolwork and its unending decisions and not knowing. The world of teaching suddenly felt very heavy.

Maybe this is how my students feel when they come to school.

I was home too soon, not wanting the ethereal quality of my walk to end. But I forced myself over the threshold and retreated to my bedroom, wanting to capture in writing the swarm of thoughts and feelings inside of me, to find the right words that might describe this string of contradictions—the lightweight soul of the seagull juxtaposed with its heavy body, the walrus head and seal stones and shells, the unicorn diaper, and pieces of Styrofoam. I wanted to hold all of it without censoring, without judgment.

My pen moved smoothly, with words like *natural* and *harmonious, free* and *dead*—the stream of consciousness filling pages in my journal for the better part of an hour. I could feel it slowing down and wrote a final line: "I am growing more in tune with all of my senses, new growth emerging, reaching into the future."

I set the pen down and watched a white cloud floating by my window. It carried my thoughts in a new direction, and the question arose: *What could I possibly teach here that mattered in the long run?* I would never truly understand my students' lives. I would always be looking through the lens of my own experience. My own kaleidoscope.

I read the last line again. It was true that I was growing more in tune with my senses and reaching for the future, but to what end? I glanced at my watch, bring my musing to an end. I could no longer delay the inevitable; the future was reaching back and telling me to get my butt to school.

Resigned to my fate, I grabbed an apple and trudged out the door. Halfway up the metal steps outside the school, I felt a wave of dizziness and grasped the railing to steady myself. It was followed by a strange sensation that raced through my chest and out the top of my head, like an electric current turning on a new level of awareness.

Generosity.

The word escaped from my lips. Where did that thought come from? It felt simple and direct. It felt true. A palpable generosity emanated from this place. The animals and people, the land, and the sea. The birds in the sky. Even the bird that died.

The people in the village had welcomed me. A stranger in their space. They didn't know if I was generous or not. But they were still kind to me, and they trusted me to contribute something of value to their children and their community. To make connections. To keep trying.

I took a deep breath, walked up the last few steps, and opened the door.

THIRTY-THREE

PIECE BY PIECE

The days passed in a blur of just-in-time lessons. It was already Friday Night—Movie Night at school—and it was my turn once more to manage the popcorn machine. The enjoyment of making popcorn was long gone; I wasn't in the mood. All I wanted to do was stay home in my bedroom and work on my puzzle.

I found it earlier in the week at Walter's store, peeking out from under some hand towels on a lower shelf. The cover depicted a field of red and yellow tulips and a weather-beaten windmill whose blades reached up to a blue sky with puffy white clouds. The image immediately transported me around the world, to a place that felt fresh and new. I craved putting that landscape together, piece by piece. It wasn't so much the desire to finish the puzzle itself as a need to experience the satisfaction that comes with completing a task, once and for all.

It had been an exhausting week in Teacher Land—especially with my tenth graders, who'd failed to appreciate my new unit on Medieval Literature. I began with what I thought was the most action-packed tale set in northern Europe that featured a fellow named Beowulf who saved the village of Heorot from Grendel, a horrible swamp monster, and upon Grendel's death, he saved the village again from Grendel's outraged swamp mother.

Beowolf was required reading in one of my college classes. I didn't like it at first but became more intrigued when my professor explained the perennial value of myths and heroes. "They exist in every culture," he said, "offering windows to their souls." That perked me up, and I expected it might do the same for my class.

I was so confident my students would love it that I made a special announcement in the *Northern Lights News*: "Students will get to hear stories and watch films about England and Germany and learn how the English language evolved to what it is today. We'll read *Beowulf*, Chaucer's *Canterbury Tales*, and the best of all—*Sir Gawain and the Green Knight*!"

My medieval unit on heroes and monsters was supposed to be finished by Halloween, but here we were, just one week from Thanksgiving and not yet finished with the first story. I should have quit after Beowulf ripped off Grendel's arm (ouch), but Beowulf was a hero. And heroes don't give up. Maybe, deep down, I wanted to be a hero, too.

I persisted with the tale of bravery, of living in harsh conditions and grappling with honor and betrayal and all the rest. My students didn't buy it. The language was too hard to translate and the storyline too far removed from their own reality. There hadn't been time for me to rework a two-hundred-fifty-page Arctic version.

I needed a new idea. Anne called it *punting*. "Like in football," she said after hearing of my frustrations. "Kick the ball and start over." But which team was I on? Probably both. I often felt like I was the one kicking the ball downfield and running like the dickens to catch it again.

One scene played back in my mind, something that had occurred a while ago, but I hadn't paid much attention to it. I'd started a school journal to reflect on what was going well in my classes versus dying on the vine (mostly the latter), as a means to sort out what to do next with the curriculum. While the students were writing about monsters, I was writing about my own.

But I started noticing on more than a few occasions that several of my surly tenth graders were coming to the pencil sharpener more often than seemed necessary. Someone had thought it was a good idea to fix the mechanism to the wall right behind the teacher's desk. The grinding drove me nuts. I was hatching a plan to remove it with my Swiss Army knife when Carol's voice made me jump. I felt her breath on my neck, followed by a waft of grape Bubblicious.

"What you writing?"

Her question prompted everyone in the class to look up.

"Just ideas." I closed the journal.

Carol popped her gum in my ear. "We have ideas."

Later that day, it occurred to me that Carol and her classmates might actually be interested in putting their ideas on paper.

I punted.

Instead of requesting that they write about Beowulf's heroism, I could invite them to write about a time in their own lives when they persisted against the odds and came through a stronger person.

The next day, I wrote the following prompt on the board: What is one of the hardest things you've ever had to do, and how did you get through it?

The blessed moment of students latching onto an idea ensued, and soon all heads were bent over paper, pencils scratching, then erasing. Their stories surprised me. Darlene wrote about a boyfriend who was playing hard to get. George and Joey wrote about pretending to hunt polar bears near the dump by shooting up pieces of trash. Not exactly life-changing events in my opinion, but who was I to say? What seemed mundane or utilitarian to me might, in fact, be a huge deal to these young teens.

The problem was, I didn't know where to go next. Beowulf was a bust and the writing prompt short lived. I had no follow-up. My punt had gone high in the air and bounced out of bounds.

Hence my puzzle addiction.

The puzzle with tulips and a windmill was my third. I had already completed one of a mountain landscape and a stable with horses, as well as a puzzle of the inside of a bookstore. Those were from the school library. I wiped off the dust and brought them home. The interview question of how I handled boredom suddenly made sense. Putting puzzles together hadn't occurred to me back then, but now it sounded like a terrific distraction. I found a card table in the school's storeroom and dragged it to my bedroom where I could work in peace.

Of course, I could only work on one puzzle at a time in my small space. When I finished the mountain landscape and horses puzzle, it occurred to me that I would have to dismantle it to make room for the one of the bookstore. Not wanting to put something together only to take it apart, I ran my hand over the puzzle's smooth surface and got an idea. I could steal a roll of contact paper from school and use it to hold all of the puzzle pieces together, thus preserving my handiwork into posters. Puzzle posters! And I could use them to decorate my bedroom.

It wasn't an easy task. The contact paper was exceptionally sticky and hard to lay flat without unplanned creasing. But I persisted. Soon, two puzzle posters adorned my private space.

My clever idea came to a screeching halt, however, when I realized that there wasn't enough contact paper left for the tulip and windmill poster. I'd have to ask Midge to order more. It bothered me, asking the school to support my habit, but Midge didn't bat an eye when I told her the truth. She just put in the order, got Principal Ken to sign, and within a week I had enough contact paper for ten more puzzles.

Midge pulled me into the hallway, out of earshot of the principal's office. "I have more puzzles, and can bring them in. My kids have outgrown them."

Soon, scenes of horses, bunnies, and boats adorned my bedroom walls. I loved the rhythm of randomness that came with looking for one piece and suddenly finding another. I could choose whatever part I felt like working on, knowing it would all get done. Sometimes it took hours to find a piece, but little by little, my eyes adjusted to subtle nuances in shapes and colors, and eventually, each piece found a home.

There were moments of frustration, to be sure, however. Like the time when I couldn't find a puzzle piece needed to finish a section of the tulip field. There was a touch of red on it, but none of the pieces on the table seemed to fit.

Where the hell is it?

I went to the kitchen for tea, then returned to my room, tired but committed to finding the darned piece before stopping for the day. I leaned back gently and then stretched down to the floor to relieve the tension in my back and spotted a flash of something red.

Good grief. It had been laying on the floor the entire time.

It pressed in, perfectly.

The puzzle wasn't yet finished, but that simple act of finding the one missing piece almost made it feel as if it were.

This is like teaching. My students and I were pieces of a puzzle, searching for ways to connect. We had no picture on a box to guide us, but maybe that was the point. We were a picture in the making.

THIRTY-FOUR

GUESS THEY CAUGHT A WHALE

I didn't know which was worse: dragging ninth graders through writing essays or trying to grade them. The students said I was "torturing" them with so much writing. If they only knew how torturous it was for me to decipher what they'd committed to paper. It was supposed to be my lunchtime, but I needed to finish reading their papers before class. I was halfway done when Stella's essay stopped me in my tracks.

Stella was what teachers called "challenging." She was often the first student to either finish her work and get off task or get off task and not finish her work. She was like a slippery fish in the lagoon, and I didn't have a net. Today, she had chosen to decorate her essay with tiny faces depicting all manner of emotion: smiles, frowns, dead, sick, cross-eyed.

I started thinking of the numerous retorts that Stella tossed at me on a regular basis to let me know precisely how she felt about my lessons. Her statements were annoying but funny. I glanced at the clock. Thirty minutes left. I could spare a few of those to start a letter to Mia, my friend and confidant in times of trouble.

Dear Mia,

Just another day in paradise. I'm trying to grade essays and finding it rather painful. My ninth graders, in particular, struggle with the concept of parallelism, where a string of verbs needs to be in the same tense. They often mix things up, like, "Billy went to the store, bought apples, and pays with a twenty-dollar bill."

I've tried so many ways to show them the correct way, but they've been in a nasty mood lately. I wish I understood the reasons for their resistance. Maybe it's just the encroaching darkness, with not much to look forward to?

Anyway, the topic for this letter is "Cracking the Code," meaning that I may have finally figured out what my students (mostly ninth graders) mean when they repeat certain words and phrases in the classroom. Here's a sampling:

SO CHEAP ~ Translation: 1) I don't want to do this; 2) This assignment has no immediate relevance to my life; 3) This pen, pencil, book, notebook, etc., is literally cheap.

SO BOOORRING ~ Translation: 1) I am bored. This sentiment is packaged in a ratio of 3:1. For every hour Yours Truly spent the night before preparing lessons and trying to make them NOT boring, students will respond with at least three SO BOOORRINGs.

WHAT TO DO? ~ Translation: 1) I wasn't listening, so I don't know what to do (followed by So Cheap and/or So Booorring; 2). I will pretend to listen to your instructions, and then ask to go to my locker so I can take a long break and return just before the end of class.

WHAT TO BRING? ~ Translation: 1) I know I was supposed to bring something to write with and something to write on to my English class where students can expect to, well … *write*. But you, Dear Teacher, didn't remind me to do so.

COME. ~ Translation: Please come to my desk, because: 1) I saw your lips moving but have no clue what you want; 2) I want someone to notice me; 3). Just kidding, I don't need anything.

I JOKES ~ No translation needed.

I set down my pen and read the list again. *These are student commands, not questions.* Interesting. And they've got me jumping up every time they utter one of those lines. I hated being pulled around like that but still could not quite trust if my students' commands were, in fact, legitimate. I couldn't yet, as one college professor explained it, "read the room." Therefore, when I managed to hold things together and received even fifty-percent compliance, I chalked it up in my grade book as a win.

I knew I needed to tighten things up and assume my Command Spot more often, inside and out. I knew I needed to trust my instincts and careful planning. But the moment students uttered, "So BOOORRing," I tended to switch tracks and jump to a different approach, confusing the heck out of them and me.

Why were they constantly trying to subvert my plans? And why did I allow them to do so?

I was in the middle of contemplating possible answers to these questions when I heard my gaggle of ninth graders coming down the hall. Lunch was over. I hadn't finished grading their papers and had forgotten to eat.

The students settled in as I did roll call from my Command Spot. I was about to launch into giving them another short essay prompt—both to give them more practice and also buy me time until I figured out what to do next—when the door flew open and slammed against the wall. It was Curtis, whom I had just marked absent. His face glistened with sweat, and his jacket was askew. He yelled something in Iñupiat, and before I could ask for a translation, an enormous wave of rotting fish smell entered my nostrils. Instinctively, I pulled my turtleneck over my nose and mouth.

The entire class jumped up in unison and ran out, leaving me in command of nothing but an empty room. A sheet of paper, lifted by the wind of the students' sudden exit, slid off a desk and gently floated to the floor. I stood with a piece of chalk in hand, dumbstruck by the swiftness of their evacuation. One minute, they were lazing in their desks, the next—and with the urgency of firefighters rushing to a four-alarm call—they'd split the scene.

I heard the school's outer doors slamming and the thumping of boots descending the steps. The building went quiet. A moment later, I heard the *clump-clump* of Principal Ken's boots in the hallway. He found me standing in the same spot, turtleneck still pulled over my mouth and nose. He surveyed the empty room, then leveled his gaze.

"Guess they caught a whale."

"A whale?" I responded through my shirt. "Is that the smell …"

He nodded. "Wanna go see it?"

I wasn't sure. The idea of suddenly having time alone to finish grading papers sounded more appealing. I lowered my shirt to test the air quality.

"Sure."

"Great. You kin ride with me in the truck. Might wanna go grab yer camera and a hat. Meet you out front in five."

I jogged home, questions swirling. *How do you catch a whale? Why was I so excited to see up-close something I had almost gagged on a few moments before?*

When I came back out of my portable, Principal Ken was already out front, engine idling. His speed surprised me. I had never seen the man move fast for anything. Even when playing pick-up basketball with the boys, his heavy body moved in slow motion, yet opponents' attempts to steal the ball failed time and time again. Left and right, the boys would bounce off his large girth and swipe only air. His shots almost always went in.

We drove up the sandy street toward the ocean, zigzagged around homes, and slipped down a narrow lane to the beach, heading south. The tide was out, the sand hard packed.

"How do you catch a whale?"

Principal Ken shrugged. "Don' have a clue. But I bet it ain't easy." Then he added, gesturing at the ocean outside my window, "It was prob'ly headin' down to Baja for warmer waters. Must've gotten too close to shore. Or maybe it was jes gettin' old."

In the distance we saw about fifty villagers on the beach, standing around an enormous black object that looked at first like a forty-foot-long boat, flipped upside down.

The people of Shishmaref had indeed caught a whale. I had never seen a whale in its entirety. In a few minutes, I'd be getting a close look at its insides as well. We rolled to a stop near a cluster of four wheelers. The wind came in hard from the north in a series of icy gusts. I pulled my parka hood over my beaver hat for added protection and followed Principal Ken as he walked toward Lance, Carrie, Duncan, and Ben. I caught the intermittent hum of voices from the various groups of watchers as they observed what was probably a rare event.

Slabs of whale several feet long and a few feet wide had been cut and set blubber-side-up on the beach, like pieces of sod. They had to be six or seven inches thick. The men took turns stepping on one of the whale's fins and climbing on top. They used long poles with curved blades to saw through the first layer of the whale's body, then lowered the pieces to men on the ground who used poles with hooks to move the slabs to the side.

I wandered away from my teacher group, wanting to get a better angle. Was it okay for me to take photos? How could I capture this scene? Would I want to share pictures of a whale's bloody carcass? Was the whale's soul looking down on me and shaking a flipper "No"?

I approached Anne.

"Think it's okay for me to take a few photos?"

"Yeah. It was okay with the seals."

I moved once more, trying to stay upwind. No such luck. The same putrid smell that Curtis had brought into my classroom flowed deep into my nose. I pulled my jacket up and took a deep breath and held it, then snapped a couple of photos, focusing on a group of women huddled over several slabs of whale. Their parkas were beautiful, an array of patterns and colors, with trimming and large hoods framed by fur that danced in the wind. No one looked at me disapprovingly, so I clicked the shutter a few more times, tucked my camera away, and turned to rejoin the teacher group only to find myself face-to-face with one of the women. Her dark eyes looked straight into mine. She grinned, and I felt the other women surrounding me, coming in so close I could feel their parkas press against mine. The first woman gestured for me to hold out my mittened hand to receive something, then placed a tiny piece of whale in it. One side had shiny black whale skin and the other was pinkish-gray blubber. I looked at her, not understanding. She mimicked popping it in her own mouth, like a gumdrop, and smiled to reassure me.

In that instant, I had to decide whether to be gracious and eat a piece of whale or hand it back in a gesture of disrespect. But what could I say? "No thank you, I don't like meat"? Even so, where did whale sushi fall on the vegetarian continuum?

The women waited.

Oh what the hell. I popped it in my mouth and brought my molars together. The expression on my face was all they needed. They laughed and chattered. One woman looped her arm around mine and squeezed it as if saying, "Way to go! You're in the club!"

The whale gumdrop was ice cold and saltier than anything I had ever tasted. I tried to chew it, but the piece kept returning to its original size of a small Superball—the kind I used to ricochet off the sides of buildings as a kid. Maybe I should have swallowed it whole.

I started to gag and feigned a cough, spitting the horrible-tasting tidbit into my mitten. The women laughed more, the voices high and cheery. Seeing that I'd survived my first piece of authentic Eskimo cuisine and wouldn't need the Heimlich maneuver, they turned back to carving up little pieces of whale. They were going to need a lot of Tupperware.

Freed from the women's focus, I walked several yards away and contemplated how to dispose of my blubber ball. Toss it in the grass? Put it in my pocket and dispose of it later? Too bad there wasn't a puppy nearby.

I heard a whistle and saw Lance signaling me to join him. On my way, I asked the whale gods for forgiveness and dropped the piece of whale on the ground, praying it wouldn't bounce.

"Yikes, did they make you try it?" Lance made a face and then laughed.

"Yeah, I didn't really have a choice." I made a face back at him. "Have you tried it?"

"What, muktuk? Nope. Never been here when they caught a whale." He gestured with his head toward the group of women I'd been with. "They took a shine to you, you know. The fact that they chose you to tease out of everyone in this crowd is a good thing."

Lance's comment surprised me. What I took to be an abject failure in cultural exchange, he observed as a success. We stood close, backs to the wind, and watched the whale slowly being transformed from a magnificent mammal to hunks on the sand that would soon be divided into smaller portions and shared with anyone who wanted some.

The sound of the truck made us turn. It was Principal Ken, ready to head back. Lance had a ride, so I hopped into the cab, relieved to be out of the icy air. I had seen enough blood and guts for one day and needed to get the taste of whale out of my mouth.

We drove in silence, and my mind turned to the whale and the life it had, swimming thousands of miles south to warmer waters in winter and then swimming all the way back.

Did having a piece of the whale in my mouth mean I had taken that journey as well, if only for an instant? The question intrigued me.

There was nothing "cheap" or "booorring" about that.

THIRTY-FIVE

DAMP VS DRY

It was late in the evening. The TV was on. Anne was asleep on the couch, snoring gently. She wouldn't notice if I reduced the volume, so I reached up to turn the knob and came face-to-face with a commercial sponsored by a council on alcohol abuse, which aired frequently.

The scene was a bright white background of nothingness and a hand holding a glass of white wine, and another hand holding a glass of red. The drinks moved in slow motion toward each other for a cheers-clink, only the "cheer" kept right on going. Liquid and shards of glass went flying everywhere. The message was clear: If you drink, you crash. If you crash, you die. All I saw was a lot of wasted wine.

In that moment, my face was closer to the TV screen than it had ever been before. I could feel its warmth and the static electricity on my cheeks. I watched in horror as the alcohol accident unfurled. *Oh my god, all that wine.* And I got that pang in my mouth—the one when my taste buds wake up—and I suddenly craved alcohol more than I had ever craved it in my life. I wanted to lick that wine, glass shards and all, right off the floor.

I had never been much of a drinker. I wasn't sure if it was the awkwardness of standing around a keg at parties where no one said much of significance, or the fact that it took a lot of beer for me to feel the desired fuzzy-happy brain. Instead of having a good time at parties, I typically ended up feeling lonely, bloated, and grumpy, leaving early to enjoy reading a good book in bed.

I drank to fit in, because—well, I didn't fit in. I was nerdy, a teacher's pet. I didn't wear cute clothes or even attempt to attract the male species. In a word, I was *booorring*! But I blew the roof off that label one evening at a Christmas party. Parties in Vail were common, especially around the holidays, and it wasn't unusual for parents to go to other parties around the town, allowing teenagers full run of the minibar. I politely declined the first round of booze, but one boy was determined to get "little book girl" drunk. He got busy at the bar and offered me a tumbler filled with ice and clear liquid.

"Here, try this." He held out a glass.

A small group of onlookers gathered. I didn't want the drink and certainly didn't want people watching me. But maybe this one time I could be cool. I tipped the glass between my pursed lips to test it, trying to be a good sport, but an impatient bystander decided it would be funny to bump my glass, which sent a good deal of the potion into my mouth at once.

The burning in my throat was sensational. It stung, making me cough. But then—*wow*. What a lovely swoosh to my brain! I wiped my chin on my sleeve, and everyone laughed. The crowd dispersed, leaving me on my own. Why not have another of whatever that was? Several shots of a variety of liquors later, I found myself at the bottom of the stairs giggling hysterically and confused as to why I couldn't stand up.

One girl whose name I didn't know managed to get me upright and said the words any teenager hates to hear: it was almost midnight. Curfew. I was inebriated but conscious enough to realize I was in no condition to ride my bike two miles home on dark country roads covered in snow. I'd likely end up in the creek or freeze to death on the golf course and not be found until the spring thaw.

She found my number in the school's family directory and held the receiver up to my ear so I could ask my father to come and give me a ride home. I thought I sounded coherent enough, but I'm sure he figured out the reason he had to throw a coat over his pajamas. When my father arrived, he didn't say a word—just opened the trunk and watched as I loaded my bike. We drove home in silence with my dad's window rolled down, even though it was frickin' cold outside. I must have reeked, not only from the alcohol, but because my party mates wanted to help "mask" the alcohol emanating from every pore of my body by spritzing me with perfume.

To his credit, my father never brought up the episode again. He knew the hangover I had coming would be punishment enough. His only reproach came as we crossed the threshold: "You should take a shower."

In Alaska, Native communities were known as "damp" or "dry." A "damp" village meant that residents could be in possession of alcohol but could not buy it locally. A "dry" village banned alcohol altogether. Shishmaref was the latter—no beer in the fridge, no bourbon in the cabinet.

When it came to non-Native people like me, the rules were less clear. I had heard that alcohol couldn't be shipped to the village or smuggled in one's luggage. Fair enough. But there seemed to be a loophole allowing people like me to *make* alcohol if they wanted to. If a person was discreet, a closet distillery was fine.

Standing on my toes in front of the television, this brutal awareness of no access to alcohol marched into my psyche and set up camp. Instead of the alcohol abuse council convincing me to steer clear of spirits, I couldn't wait to get my hands on some.

After witnessing the wine-glass-accident commercial a few more times during the week, I wrote a letter to my older brother and told him about the commercial. Close in age, André was someone with whom I could share my secrets. He also had a strong streak of sarcasm and would appreciate my I-need-a-drink predicament in a place where it wasn't allowed.

I didn't expect a response, but a week later a small box arrived with my brother's familiar scrawl. Inside were four carefully packed single-serve rum Bundt cakes and a note that said, "Skip inversion. Lop off bottom and suck."

I immediately hid the box in my closet. The cakes were so precious that I didn't want to eat them. More truthfully, I was afraid I wouldn't be able to stop.

As soon as I zipped into my sleeping bag that first night, I could think of nothing else. The night before, I'd obsessed over lesson plans; now, I was consumed by the prospect of just-one-little-bite. *Maybe it's better to eat them while they're fresh.*

André's advice backfired. The first bite was horridly bitter, and I almost spit it out.

I shifted tactics and took a bite off the non-rum top, then licked the bottom. The taste was still unpleasant, but I was desperate for a hit of whatever booze was in there.

Thus began the short tale of "Kulizuk: The Rum Cake Alcoholic." Upon waking, the little rum cakes were the first thing on my mind, and they poked at me during random moments in the school day—in the bathroom, in the copy room, and between classes. I went home during lunch and inverted the first cake so the rum would soak through evenly and be ready by four o'clock—my aprés-school libation.

But the anticipation of inebriation was short-lived. Even though I finished the cakes at the rate of one a day, they didn't deliver even a slight buzz. All I got was a metal taste in my mouth.

The last morning of Rum Cake Rumble Week, I passed the bathroom, trying to ignore Anne's daily ritual of gargling with Listerine. She spat into the sink and called after me.

"Hey, a few teachers are planning to have Thanksgiving in Nome."

I took a few steps back to look her in the eye, and she added with a cheeky grin, "Wanna come? We're goin' barhopping."

THIRTY-SIX

THROUGH THE BURLED ARCH

In the twilight of midmorning on Turkey Day itself, Anne and I stood with Tim, Lance, and Carrie at the edge of the airstrip. I knew everyone but Carrie. She was a colleague of Anne's on the elementary side of the building, a place I never had cause to visit. I found it funny that I had to leave town to meet someone who worked two minutes down the hall.

It was bone cold outside of town. We stomped our feet like a group of impatient toddlers and clapped our mittens to keep warm while the pilot finished loading. I didn't know the exact temperature; my brother's thermometer had been too frosted to read.

The pilot kept a keen eye on the horizon as he directed gear and people on board. The only predictable thing about the weather was its unpredictability. A person could be whistling "Here Comes the Sun" one minute and singing "It's Beginning to Look a Lot Like Christmas," the next.

We strapped in as the engine roared to life, and the pilot drove slowly, bumping over patches of ice and frozen sand toward the lagoon.

"Morning, folks! This is your safety check! We've got three exits—two in front, one in back." He flipped switches and turned knobs in quick succession, swinging the plane around for a north-facing takeoff.

"No smoking please, and give your seatbelts an extra cinch. Briefing cards are in front of you. Fire extinguisher is up here." He nodded to a compartment in front of Tim's knees. "In the unexpected chance we land before arriving at our destination, there's a red survival bag in the back and a red metal box with a button. One of you gals in the back will need to push it if we need to alert someone about our location." He didn't ask if we had any questions, turning instead to the most important task at hand—getting us off the ground.

The plane was larger than ones I'd flown in before. There was a propeller on each wing and ample cargo space. Still, launching skywards from the island was unnerving, at least to me. While I wanted to trust that the bolts would hold, every creak and jolt of the fuselage made it feel like the plane was going to rip apart at the seams before liftoff. We bumped and squeaked down the airstrip, going faster and faster. I watched the end of the runway approaching and said a little prayer, but our pilot had nerves of steel and kept us steady. The wheels left the ground with feet to spare, and we launched into a cloud-laden sky.

More daylight offered a commanding view of the sea ice building out from Shishmaref's shore. On the horizon was a thin line of white, signaling that another thick layer of ice was approaching from the north. In between was a dark sea with whitecaps. Winter was moving in.

The pilot came on again. "Our flight time is about an hour. Wind's not bad. Clouds are all over the place, so we'll stay below ten thousand feet today."

"I'll get us a cab when we land," Tim yelled over his shoulder. "We can check into the lodge, then hit the town!" He gave a thumbs-up, like a kid ready to step onto a whirligig ride at an amusement park.

"Tim got us teacher lodging." Anne leaned into me, her breath smelling of ash and spearmint gum. "A decent place by Nome standards."

I nodded and turned back to gazing at the endless white ground below and gray skies above, hoping I wouldn't have to push that red button. But the hour-long flight was smooth, and we landed without incident. Within minutes, we were packed into a van and rolling toward town.

The van stopped in front of a condominium, and we tumbled out, checked into our rooms, and then met by the front door, ready for whatever came next. Tim rubbed his hands together with glee. "Okay, let's get this Thanksgiving started!"

We followed him out the door. It was still before noon, but within minutes, we were ordering a round of red wine for Anne and a round of beer for the rest of us. Carrie and I played darts and followed with a game of pool against the guys. Our conversation focused mostly on teaching, but soon the stress of school fell away.

When I had first heard about the trip, I fussed about what to wear. The school's one washing machine and dryer were almost always in use, forcing me to handwash and hang dry most of the time. As a result, my clothes were growing baggier and increasingly rumpled. I looked like I was wearing the hand-me-downs of an older, oversized sibling.

My only solace was that no one cared. Teachers wore what worked; it wasn't a fashion show. Even Principal Ken wore blue jeans and sweatshirts. At first, I thought everyone looked sloppy, but it didn't take long for me to join in.

For this trip, however, I wanted to look nice, so I packed a couple of blouses, a V-neck sweater, and my one gold chain necklace for a splash of bling. I had intended to add earrings but was thwarted when I found out the holes in my ears had closed for business. I had stopped wearing earrings several weeks before; the metal was freezing in my earlobes. There was no warning except for the sharp pain that ensued when I tried to push the gold post through.

After two rounds of beer and peanuts at Bar Number One, we paid our tab and followed Tim to Front Street, a wide, snow-covered avenue that paralleled Norton Sound. It was lined with storefronts that faced away from the water, opting to forego million-dollar views for protection against the icy wind.

We plopped into a large booth, bought another round of drinks, and shared stories about our teaching successes and the lack thereof. Up to that point, I had assumed that I was the only teacher who didn't know what she was doing. It turned out that Lance and Tim had also lost track of student attendance and struggled to keep kids focused.

By now, a fair amount of alcohol had been consumed, and we needed food. We were way past lunch. Tim led us to The Board of Trade Saloon, one of Nome's few two-story structures. It had a tall facade and two sets of rounded bay windows with small panes of glass on either side of the door.

"Look at that, will ya?" Tim pointed. "Nome's Oldest Saloon Since 1900."

We eagerly stepped inside the Gold Rush décor, complete with a polished wood bar and shelves of liquor glistening in the mirrors behind it. The place was crowded, but we negotiated for a table and an odd assortment of chairs, ordered a basket of fried mozzarella sticks, and scanned the menu. I was amazed at how hungry I felt, and I almost ordered a hamburger. Almost.

"I'll have a BLT, hold the B," I said, giggling.

The waitress wasn't amused. She was the only sober person in a bar filled with tipsy patrons and a table of inebriated teachers—one of whom was not a proper meat-eating Alaskan.

The food came fast and we dug in.

"This is the place where the Iditarod ends." Lance licked ketchup from his fingers. "The finish line's right down the street. It's really cool. There's this big wooden arch all the mushers pass under ..." His voice faded as shouts broke out near the bar.

A large lumberjack of a man was shoving a fellow in the seat next to him, which caused the second man's baseball cap to fall to the floor.

"Quit it!"

The lumberjack ignored his request and shoved again. This time, the second man fell off his stool.

Oh my god, a barroom brawl, just like the Westerns I watched as a kid.

"Hey guys," the bartender moved toward them, "that's enough. Jim, Steve. Time to go."

Steve, the man on the floor, pulled himself up and tried to regain composure, but Jim gave him another shove.

"That's enough!" the bartender yelled, then nodded toward the back of the room as if signaling someone to stand at the ready.

Steve reached into his coat and pulled out a long hunting knife.

"Ima cut you." He pointed the knife in a menacing manner.

Jim stepped back, watching the blade and sobering to the possibility that he was one lunge away from needing serious medical attention to his gut.

"Hey, Steve," the bartender said in a calmer voice. "Look at me."

Steve swayed, unsure where to focus. He kept his knife pointed at Jim and looked seconds away from passing out.

Moving with the swiftness and dexterity of a cougar, the bouncer suddenly appeared behind Steve and swiped the knife out of his hand, then stepped quickly away. Steve looked down at his now empty hand, confused. Then he groped for the barstool and plopped down.

The bartender addressed the room: "Show's over." But everyone still watched while he moved Jim toward the door. The bouncer half walked, half carried Steve out the back.

Lance leaned in, crooking a finger to coax us closer. "Wonder if they'll just walk in a circle around the building and bump into each other again!"

We knew it was rude, but we giggled and snorted and kind of tried to stop. But our laughter broke loose when Lance added a quip about the men passing out under the Iditarod's arch and waking up the next morning, wondering, "Hey, man, where'd my dogs go?"

Somehow, we got ourselves back to the lodge. I was contemplating taking a shower but lay down on the bed. "Just for a few minutes," I told myself. The last thing I remembered was thinking it would be a good idea to take off my boots.

The next morning, we assembled by the front door, amazed that we were famished and even more amazed that no one had a hangover. We found a diner and dove into pancakes, eggs, and a ridiculous amount of coffee. Our waitress, Sharon, set a carafe on our table.

"Here ya go. Keep the pot. It'll save me from constantly coming over here to fill your cups," she joked. "What brings y'all to town?"

Upon hearing we were teachers, Sharon recommended the Carrie McLain Memorial Museum. "It's small, but there's interesting history stuff about Nome. Y'know, artifacts and things all teachers love." She winked.

Carrie gave a thumbs-up and took a last bite of pancake. She'd been scooting it around her plate with her fork, trying to soak up the last smears of syrup. "Oh my god," she said to no one in particular. "I think I'm gonna have to lick this plate."

"Museum's not my first choice but I guess it'll do." Tim shrugged. "I was hoping to go see White Alice, but it's too far out of town." He glanced out the window at the light flurry of snow falling and added, "It's also frickin' cold outside."

"What's a White Alice?" Carrie licked her fingers and giggled. "Sounds like that fancy drink, the what's it called …"

"You mean, a White Russian." Tim rolled his eyes.

I was starting to appreciate hanging out with teachers. They were serious, then funny, then caring, then audacious, and always filled with information that ranged from the trivial to the profound.

"White Alice," said Tim, looping his thumbs around his collar in feigned importance, "is the name of the tropospheric antennas on Anvil Mountain, just north of town, that were built during the Cold War. They're enormous, like curved outdoor theater screens. Before they were built, you couldn't make a phone call anywhere. If a person at this table wanted to call Fairbanks, only one of us could do it at a time."

Carrie pushed her plate to the side. "Why's it called White Alice?"

Tim pulled a pen from his shirt pocket and wrote ALICS on his clean napkin. "It's code for Alaska Integrated Communications System."

"And the white part?" Lance was intrigued.

Time smirked "For the snow, I guess."

Everyone groaned, and Anne stepped in to redirect us. She was the oldest and had adopted the role of den mother, so we gave in, paid the bill, and made our way to the Carrie M. McLain Memorial Museum.

It was a cluttered but fascinating place, its walls covered with murals of the gold rush that occurred between 1899 and 1909. Some bloke found gold laying all over the beach, and word got out. Thousands of gold diggers made their way north. Tools of their trade were displayed in glass cases and hung on the walls—shovels and pickaxes, tin pans and weighing scales. One placard told of a nugget weighing over eleven pounds being found in 1903 by the Pioneer Mining Company on Anvil Creek. At that time, it was worth $3276, the equivalent of well over $38,000, adjusted for inflation.

I wandered by dozens of grainy photos of men wearing wide-brimmed hats that cast shadows on their weary faces. Every man had a beard or a handlebar mustache. The ladies wore long, dark skirts and bonnets. Some of the photos showed women in saloons who had moved to Nome to make their own fortunes by entertaining the men who found gold and wanted to celebrate—or didn't find anything and needed to drown their miseries in liquor and petticoats.

The museum also honored Native Alaskan people, with photos of dogsledding teams, sealskin slippers and polar bear pants, tools for hunting, and masks and drums for ceremonies—even a sealskin-covered kayak. The Native people were clearly better suited for the harsh environment than the prospectors who dotted the landscape with tents and steel dredges, most of whom left town without recouping the cost of their adventures.

Carrie M. McLain, for whom the museum was named, came to Nome as a young girl soon after the gold rush of 1899. School was probably sparse, so she likely helped her mother with cooking and cleaning and then played outside. Maybe she entertained herself by picking up items abandoned by the miners. I imagined young Carrie coming home with her skirt and coat pockets filled with trinkets, and her mother exclaiming, "Miss Carrie McLain, where on earth are you planning to put all of those things?" And I imagined Pa McClain putting an arm around his daughter's shoulders and saying just loud enough for Ma to hear, "Don't you worry, my darlin' Carrie. How about I build you a room for your treasures?" And the Carrie M. McClain Museum was born.

After roving around in the warmth of the small museum, we finally made our way into the street. I was cold and in need of a nap. Lance put a stop to my idea by suggesting that we take a closer look at the wooden structure that marked the end of the infamous dogsled race.

It was a race like no other, and for the last several years, it featured one of Shishmaref's residents, Herbie Nayokpuk. Named the "Shishmaref Cannonball," Herbie was poised to run again in the spring. He had a reputation of being tough, smart, and kind to his dogs.

When I had confirmed that I was going on this trip, I spent an afternoon in the school library educating myself about Nome's history. It was fascinating reading. I knew there had been a dog race but had no idea dogsledding dated back thousands of years. The earliest account was from northern Canada, where some wise person got the idea to harness dogs to a sled. It was an innovation born of necessity, which changed the course of history. Dogsledding turned out to be a heckuva lot faster than trudging through deep snow with one's belongings. The sleds also made it possible to carry people and supplies when snow and ice prevented travel on rivers. Over the centuries, Native people created a network of trails throughout the entire region. When fur traders, miners, and adventurers entered the territory, they solidified the presence of those trails by building roadhouses where people could meet up, trade goods, and get some rest.

Those were the trails that made the Iditarod Dogsled Race possible—the race commemorating a daring feat of bringing medicine to disease-stricken Nome in 1925.

During that time, Nome had one doctor, Dr. Curtis Welch. He and his four nurses were starting to see an uptick in children getting sick—sore throats, coughing, and sneezing. He thought the disease might be diphtheria but had only one batch of serum. And it had expired.

Welch telegraphed colleagues for help. His caseload had grown to one hundred and fifty adults and children in a matter of weeks. Nome officials issued a quarantine, but they knew it wasn't a solution. They needed serum, but Nome's port was iced in, preventing delivery via steamship. And planes were not yet reliable under such harsh winter conditions.

The answer to Nome's dilemma was dogs. Twenty teams volunteered for The Great Race of Mercy, participating in a relay that carried the critical batch of medicine from Nenana to Nome, a distance of almost seven hundred miles. They did it in just over five days, with a Norwegian musher named Gunner Kaasan and his lead dog, Balto, the final team to slide into town. Legend had it, not a single vial broke.

That race of lifesaving medicine ultimately revitalized dogsledding in Alaska. In 1973, the Iditarod, also called "The Last Great Race on Earth," was born. Iditarod, named after a small town that had been abandoned after World War I, was the intended finish point for the competition. It's an Ingalik Indian name meaning distant place. And it was, indeed, a distant place, about four hundred and thirty miles into the wilderness, west of Anchorage, where the race begins with a ceremonial send-off. But the U.S. Army's use of the trail for training exercises encouraged the race's founders to push past Iditarod and establish the finish line in Nome.

At the time of our teacher trip, the race was a well-organized affair of forty teams of mushers and dogs that couldn't wait to get onto the snow and pull their owners and sleds over more than one thousand miles. Given the varied terrain and alternate routes every other year, the exact distance varied. Officials decided to call it good at 1,049 miles, in honor of Alaska becoming the 49th state. No matter the distance, a minimum of five furry faces were required at the finish line. With their musher, of course.

The Iditarod is a fierce race. Huskies and malamutes pull three-hundred-pound sleds filled with supplies through spruce forests and tundra, up and down hills, over mountain passes and ice-covered rivers. The final leg follows Norton Sound's northern shore. Teams endure temperatures well below zero, winds over fifty miles per hour, whiteout conditions, and the constant threat of getting dumped into a creek, running into a tree, or being attacked by moose.

Twenty checkpoints allow mushers to rest, regroup, and restock supplies flown in ahead of their journey—essential gear for each team's safety and stamina. On each sled, the mushers also pack an axe, clothes, batteries for headlamps, sled parts, extra harnesses, and booties to protect the dogs' feet on the ice. And a lot of dog food.

The goal of the race? Be the first team to slide under The Burled Arch. Doing so brings a trophy and a check for fifty thousand dollars.

Iditarod's Burled Arch

When Tim first mentioned the arch, I pictured an actual arch. But arriving on Front Street, near the side of City Hall, I discovered there was no arch at all, just a thick wooden crossbeam set across two tall wooden tripod legs. The top ends of the legs were shaped like cannonballs, making me wonder if they had anything to do with Herbie Nayokpuk's nickname.

The bottoms of the wooden legs were splayed out and fixed to a large wooden platform. Snow lightly dusted the structure, but we were able to make out the words carved into its crossbeam: END OF IDITAROD DOG RACE. In the circular parts was carved 1049 MILES, and ANCHORAGE and NOME.

"So, here we are!" Lance patted the structure. "Whaddya think?"

"Looks odd." Carrie tilted her head.

"What's up with those round balls of wood?" I asked.

"Those are burls." Lance reached up and patted one. "Unsprouted buds. Instead of growing into branches, they grow inside themselves and create these large knobby growths on the tree."

"Like an ingrown hair?" Carrie cracked up.

"Right, like that." He rolled his eyes, then traced his fingers over the wood. "But there's beautiful patterns of shapes and colors. Hard to make out in this one. It's pretty weathered."

"Wasn't there a story about Kool-Aid for a finish line?" Carrie sat on the base.

"Yeah, I heard of that," said Tim. "People claim there was so much focus on getting the first Iditarod together, folks forgot to mark where it actually ended. Someone had a jar of red Kool-Aid powder and dribbled a line across the street. I guess it worked."

Lance continued with the Iditarod trivia. "There was another story, where the mushers made fun of the finish line. Second Iditarod, I think. The last two mushers had paper plates and stuck them on their jackets." He pointed at his chest. "One of them wrote 'The' on it and the final musher behind him wrote 'End'!"

"No way." I looked at Tim and Lance, not trusting their stories.

"It's true," Anne said. "That's one of the things that prompted people to create a more permanent finish line, one that was portable. A musher named Red got wood from around Fairbanks and had this thing built. Weighs about five thousand pounds. Questionable in the portable category."

Carrie swept a line of snow from the arch's base. "Who started the Iditarod?"

"That'd be Joe Reddington," Tim said.

"And a couple of schoolteachers," added Lance. "Gleo Huck and Tom Johnson."

"There was a woman, too." Tim scratched his head. "What was her name? Began with a P." He paused. "Okay, first one who figures it out wins a drink from me tonight!"

"Dorothy Page." Anne smiled knowingly. "Mother of the Iditarod. And I'd love a glass of red wine."

"Hey!" Tim jogged under the arch, waving his arms. "Cheer me on! We're halfway through the school year!"

And we did. We cheered for ourselves and cheered for each other, taking turns jogging under the arch and clapping our hands and whistling. As I took my turn running under the arch, it occurred to me that teaching was its own kind of Iditarod, with blizzards of misunderstanding and misdirection, dogs in tangled harnesses, bone-deep fatigue, and checkpoints of principal observations.

We were indeed halfway through the school year—half done with our own personal Iditarods. I had crashed multiple times, but I hadn't given up. I hadn't scratched. There was still plenty of trail ahead, and time to prove myself through unknown terrain and finally cross the finish line, for real.

We had dinner that evening at the Nugget Inn, a building decorated with mining paraphernalia inside and out. Anne got her wine, and Tim dubbed her Honorary Mother of the Burled Arch Teacher Club—a title that suited her. In the dim lights of the tavern I caught a glimpse of a woman who'd been needing some attention, perhaps for a very long time.

The next morning, we climbed aboard a van taxi for the airport, with a pitstop at the Alaska Commercial Company, the grocery store where, only a few months prior on my way to Shishmaref, I had wandered the aisles, unsure what to purchase for a place I'd never been and could not have imagined.

I didn't feel like shopping at the moment but grabbed a box of Nature Valley Oat Bars and a small bag of apples just for show.

Back in the cab, Anne reached forward and tapped the driver's shoulder.

"Can you stop at a liquor store on the way?"

Before this trip, my roommate seemed too gruff and elderly—too set in her ways to make such an outlandish and, well, *illegal* request. It was against the law to bring liquor back to the village, even for us white folks. But the driver didn't flinch. Within minutes, he brought us to an abrupt halt in front of an unassuming storefront. Anne hopped out and Lance followed. Several minutes later, they returned, brown bags in hand. I watched Lance shove his bag into his duffel. Anne slid hers into the sleeve of a sweater, and packed other clothes around it before zipping up her bag. She caught me watching her movements.

"I'm an old broad." Her smile was sly. "No one will bother to check."

We piled into the plane, listened to another safety briefing, and tried to relax as the pilot wrestled with side winds to get the plane aloft. A few minutes of jerks and atmospheric bounces later, he steadied the plane over Norton Sound and pointed us north.

The terrain below was thick with snow, the light flat. Particles of moisture in the air dispersed the sun's rays and created a light fog that we could see through, but the effect was disorienting and made it difficult to determine how high or fast we flew. A few times, I caught the shadow of our plane on a cloud.

With not much else to focus on, I reflected on everything that we had experienced—the Thanksgiving barhopping with no turkey, mashed potatoes, or cranberry relish in sight. Not even a slice of pumpkin pie. Instead, we had the Carrie M. McLain Memorial Museum, the Burled Arch, a knife fight, and a comfortable bed and bathroom with running water. And the stop at a liquor store. I kicked myself for not having the steely nerve of my roommate. I was old enough to buy a bottle of something, but too young to try.

Deep inside, however, I knew that the grand prize of our trip wasn't the alcohol. It was seeing the Iditarod's Burled Arch and imagining Balto pulling his furry teammates and lifesaving serum into Nome. It was the sweet feeling of membership in a team of teachers and witnessing their humor, honesty, and imperfections. Their companionship encouraged me and made me believe that I would figure out how to cross the finish line of my own Iditarod—my own race to prove myself as a teacher before the year was done.

Please, oh please, god, if you're there. Help me figure it out. Let me get this.

A shudder and dip of the plane caused me to scream out loud. I grabbed Anne's arm and squeezed. She startled, then laughed.

Only two weeks to go until Christmas.

THIRTY-SEVEN

INTERIM

In December, the earth's tilt plunged the village into perpetual twilight—a shadowland with no shadows save for those under streetlamps scattered around town. The sun peeked at us from the eastern horizon, then slipped out of sight as if it had better places to go.

On the ocean side of the island, waves of heavy slush settled on top of each other, forming a shelf that extended yards out to sea. Every day, ocean ice crept closer until it crunched into the shelves in an embrace of upended slabs. Shishmaref was locked in. Winter was here.

So was winter break.

An early morning found me huddled at the airstrip once more with Carrie, Lance, and a couple of locals. The plane we planned to board for a ride to Nome would arrive soon. Vapor from everyone's breath escaped from our cluster of tunnel-vision hoods and mingled in ethereal conversation. The breath cloud was so thick, it seemed as if I could have reached up and gathered enough to make a snowball.

It was going to be a long day with multiple legs of flights, first to Nome, then Anchorage, then Seattle. Carrie and Lance were getting off there; I would continue to Denver the next day and reach Vail a few hours later. At least that was the plan.

"Wow, that's quite the trip," Anne had said when I announced my intention to go home for the holidays. "Too much work for me.

Maybe I'll go to Nome for a couple of nights. Not sure." She paused, studying her cards. "Got a son, but he's in Hawaii. No direct flights there."

Anne took a last drag on her cigarette and stamped it out in a saucer for emphasis.

I felt a little sorry for Anne. She had never mentioned having a son. Had she been married? Where was her husband? I could not recall Anne ever talking about her personal life. Like me, she had simply dropped into Shishmaref, no strings attached. I sensed a certain sadness behind her eyes. I felt bad for not having asked about her family, but she closed herself off, and I didn't want to pry.

I watched the plane come in for a neat landing, amazed that the pilot didn't skid on the ice and snow. He stopped at a safe distance, and the propellers ground to a halt. Like the rest of us, the pilot was bundled up. He also wore the largest boots I'd ever seen, like Arctic clown shoes—white and laced up to the lower parts of his calves. My man-sized Sorels were dwarfed by comparison.

It was a fast turnaround. At this time of year, pilots wanted to get in and out as fast as possible to avoid ice buildup on the wings from the plane sitting too long on the ground, exposed to the damp air. Like most Arctic villages, Shishmaref had no de-icing equipment.

Lance had explained this phenomenon earlier in the week as we stood by the coffee maker and chatted about the weather and our chances of making it out. "Propylene glycol lowers the freezing temperature of water to minus sixty degrees Fahrenheit," he said. "You spray it on the wings and the fuselage so you can fly in sub-zero temperatures. No ice buildup means that the air current isn't interrupted." He topped off my mug. "In other words, we don't fly straight into the ground."

The pilot worked quickly with a handful of locals who'd appeared in the semi-darkness on their snow machines. Boxes and bags of mail were exchanged and luggage loaded. He offered a hand to help me up and noticed me looking at his boots.

"Bunny boots." He winked. "Don't leave home without 'em."

With his cargo secured, the pilot climbed in, pulled his shoulder harness on, and set a large headset over his orange beanie.

"Morning, folks. I'm Chuck, your ground crew, flight attendant, and pilot. Should be a smooth flight to Nome. Low clouds, but we'll stay under 'em. Relax and enjoy the ride."

He made no mention of a red button to press in case of emergency, but I located it just in case. It was so cold in the plane that I could see my breath, prompting me to shove my small duffel bag between the wall and my leg to block the frigid air seeping in.

Carrie was seated next to me. I turned to make conversation, but she had disappeared into her periscope hood—for warmth or for dozing, I wasn't sure. Lance was engaged in man-talk up front, and the villagers behind me were silent. With no one to chat with, I gazed out my frosty window and traced the subtle contours in the landscape below. It was hard to tell what was land and what was sea ice. The morning's dusky light made everything look flat.

My thoughts took over, and the events of the past two weeks began to string themselves together like a beaded necklace.

The first bead was a surprise—one of those unplanned teaching moments that actually worked. It happened with my tenth graders, who had not yet been convinced that poetry was worth their time. I suddenly remembered acrostic poems, where the first letter of each line spells out a word when read vertically. And wouldn't you know it, that typically sullen group came alive. I couldn't pass out notepaper fast enough. It was teaching heaven—not cheap, not "booorring."

A few of the students asked to publish their pieces in the *Northern Lights News.* Cathy's first one was misspelled, but I didn't have the heart to point it out to her:

> ***D****ay by day*
> ***R****eal dreams and*
> ***E****ndless dreams*
> ***M****ay go on and on*
> ***S****o many of them continue.*

Her next poem was better:

> ***B****y and by*
> ***E****ach day goes by*
> ***A****ll the sand and water*
> ***C****oming to the edge of the water on a*
> ***H****ot summer day.*

Paula's recounted a more serious situation—one that made me wonder if she'd heard a rumor about some teachers spending Thanksgiving in Nome.

> ***D****rinking*
> ***R****uins*
> ***I****nnocent people's lives*
> ***N****obody wants to get hurt*
> ***K****now how to control how much you drink*
> ***S****o you won't have an accident.*

Carol struggled with finding words to spell out an acrostic poem and opted for prose:

> At thirteen, I died and was born again. For a while. I died every day. One day, when I was dying beside the sea, which ignored me, when my guts ran empty and I started sinking into that bottomless Hollow beneath the bed, I suddenly heard through the window, I heard the notes of the Appassionata calling me back into this crazy world again!

I didn't know what the Appassionata was, but it saved her from what sounded like considerable despair. Or maybe she was writing about someone else? I looked up Appassionata in the encyclopedia. It was one of Beethoven's piano sonatas.

As these memories floated together, I realized that I was seeing only a fraction of my students' true selves—only what they allowed me to see, at least in the classroom. Their diversity and depth were more multifaceted outside of the school walls.

On several occasions, I'd witnessed boys flying past me on their four-wheelers, rifles strapped to their backs and shouting, "Going hunt ducks!" And the time when I saw Fiona and Janice, usually quiet and somber, laughing boisterously with friends and elders during a basketball game. Many times I caught a glimpse into my students' inner worlds as the faint tunes of favorite songs drifted out from their new Walkman headsets—"Islands in the Stream" and "Girls Just Want to Have Fun."

A new column appeared in the *Northern Lights News*, as well, when Darlene decided to write her own version of Dear Abby. All high schoolers were encouraged to ask for relationship advice—the juicier, the better.

I wasn't sure if the letters were authentic. They could have been creative adaptations based on Darlene's projections of a classmate's romantic woes. Maybe the letters were based on her own personal teenage conundrums. No matter their source, the various inquiries and her responses provided an interesting peek into adolescents' frames of mind.

One letter, written by a girl, questioned whether to ask a guy out on a date even though he was younger and didn't have the reputation for being a "Shishmaref Wolf." Darlene's response was "Go for it!! Age doesn't matter. This is the 1980s!"

Regardless of those touching moments, I was more than ready to leave the village for a couple of weeks and regain some semblance of normalcy for my own sanity. I needed to return to what was familiar—mountains, skiing, my mother's cooking, a television with more than one channel, shops and cafés, a bed with real sheets, and long, hot, private showers in a bathroom only ten feet from my bed.

I had come close to showering and washing clothes in the Washeteria, but it was on the other side of town, and I hadn't managed to make it all the way over there. Instead, I made do with mostly sponge baths and the school's washing machine and dryer, so my basic needs for cleanliness were met. At least I didn't think I was emitting any offensive odors. I sniffed my coat. Musty, but alright.

Maybe it was the constant cold that caused people on the island not to worry about body odor. Maybe I did stink but didn't know it. Pretty much every day, students strolled into my classroom with aromas of Native cuisine clinging to their clothes. Fishy smells, sour smells, smells of salt and sand. Most of the time, I had no clue about the source of pungent odors and had to force myself to be more curious than repelled. When that didn't work, I simply held my breath.

In a figurative sense, I was holding my breath in other ways, too, stepping back from situations and shutting down. I had no place to process my emotions or my daily confusion about how to move forward—no place to absorb my loneliness. I was a flower closing in on itself, and I came face to face with that reality when I found myself acting in a way that was not … well, me.

One morning, after Anne left for school, I found myself thinking about that tall, skinny bottle she'd slipped into her bag in Nome. I never saw it in the kitchen, so the only other place she could have stashed it was her bedroom. Next thing I knew, I was tiptoeing down the hall, sliding her closet door open, and rummaging through her duffel bag on the floor.

"Frangelico," I whispered, pulling the bottle from its hiding place. *Wonder what it tastes like?* Thankfully, Anne had already opened it. I quietly unscrewed the cap, lifted the bottle to my lips, and took a tiny taste. A slightly nutty trickle of warmth graced the back of my throat.

That's when I knew I had to get out of the village. I could feel myself slipping into an unwanted, scary alternate reality, crossing an invisible threshold that might lead to behavior I'd regret. I could see myself going one step at a time, from mild awareness to coping to craving. Now, stealing. That's where I found myself, squatting oh-so-quietly in front of Anne's closet, my ears trained toward the door, ready to spring up like a deer if I heard a sound.

A jolt of the airplane snapped me back to my current setting. We were still flying between heavy cloud cover and white-gray land below. I felt similarly pressed inside, between the first half of the school year and now. It was a tight space, a liminal space—a kind of twilight in my teaching where I did not fully comprehend the value of the experiences that were behind me and had no idea how to work with what was to come.

PART FOUR

DEEP FREEZE

THIRTY-EIGHT

PARADIGM SHIFT

I had spent weeks planning and looking forward to my visit home for the holidays but found myself on multiple occasions wondering if it was worth the time and money. None of my family members or friends could relate to the stories I was sharing about my experiences in Shishmaref, and I felt lonelier than ever—between two worlds, not fitting in either one.

I said goodbye to my parents and siblings and began my long journey back from Denver through Seattle, then Anchorage and Nome. Weary but okay with my situation, I was seated at the departure gate in the Nome Airport and reading *Woman on the Edge of Time* by Marge Piercy. I'd snagged it from a free book rack in the Vail Library. Piercy's story was troublesome at the start. Lots of despair and violence against women. I almost quit reading, but the anticipation of an upcoming critical event and resonance with the title itself told me to keep going.

"Hey! Is that you?"

I turned to see Carrie, a backpack slung over one shoulder and grocery bag in hand. Her dark brown eyes twinkled with surprise. She plopped down and leaned over for a quick hug. "Your hair's cute." She tousled it with unexpected familiarity.

"Thanks." I ran my fingers through my short crop. "Got it trimmed at one of those walk-in places. The lady took one look at me and yelled, 'Who the hell's been cutting your hair?'" I chuckled. "God, I was so embarrassed. Everyone stopped talking and just stared at me. I told her that I was the one with the scissors and tried to explain how there was no Cuts-R-Us in Shishmaref. She waved her scissors in my face and said, 'Well, don't ever do that again!'"

"You're kidding!"

"No, she was serious. I didn't tell her I was returning to the village." I tucked my book in my coat pocket. "How was your break?"

"Oh, man, what a whirlwind! Feels like I've been gone for a month! There was lots of down time, lots of great food, lots of running around. Went shopping." She patted her new jeans in confirmation.

Carrie was slightly built. Her Sorels looked enormous at the end of her skinny legs. "It's probably good school's starting again. I was wearing out my folks and most of my friends. Kept dragging 'em out for coffee and going to Dick's Drive-In!"

Carrie reached into her grocery bag and pulled out a bag of coffee, bringing it to her nose and inhaling deeply. "Mmm. And then there's this. The real thing. Seattle's Best." She held it under my nose and gave it a squeeze.

"Whoa, that smells really good! Better than my instant coffee."

"Instant?" Carrie looked squarely at me. "Girl, I'll brew you a cup of this, and you'll kiss that instant stuff goodbye."

She leaned back and continued her story. "I also did a lot of laundry." She held up two fingers. "Washed my clothes two times when I got home and added some extra-scenty stuff. And I took this thing," she patted her parka, "to the poor dry cleaner guy. I didn't realize how pungent it was till my friends who picked me up at the airport were looking around inside the car, holding their noses and rolling the windows down. They kept saying, 'Something stinks!' Then we realized it was me!"

A voice on the loudspeaker interrupted our chat.

"Bering Air, departure for Shishmaref. Boarding in ten minutes."

Carrie and I looked around. We were the only people in the waiting area.

"Guess that's our cue." Carrie stood up. "Gotta run to the loo. Watch my stuff?"

Then it was my turn, and I took a moment to thank all the plumbers in the world as I rinsed my hands under a warm cascade of water that went down a drain and then down a pipe and on to wherever water goes.

A young man wearing a heavy parka with a Bering Air patch strolled up to us. "You two gals headed to Shishmaref?" We nodded. "Well, okay then." He took a quick glance at Carrie and then me, likely sizing up our weight. "We'll head out this door," he said, pointing. "Pretty cold and windy. Better zip up." We followed him outside and were immediately met with a blast of icy air.

"Oh, my bejeebers!" Carrie snatched up her parka hood to protect her face. I was already zipped and laced up, but the sudden change in temperature made my eyes water. Tears blew back along the sides of my cheeks and froze.

By now, I was familiar with the routine of small plane travel, getting sized up for where to sit, getting strapped in, hearing the pilot's protocols for staying safe or finding the distress signal box and pushing a button if we crashed. And there was always the coldness of the side of the plane that crept into whichever leg rested there.

Carrie sat up front with the pilot, pointing and asking questions about the clusters of dials. I admired her ease with conversation, her unending curiosity. No wonder she taught the younger kids. I was still nagged by the prospect that I should have done the same. The only reason I chose older kids was the belief that we'd be engaging in deep philosophical conversations. But the conversations I'd chosen hadn't caught on, at least not yet.

The plane lifted quickly, shimmying in a side wind, then straightened out.

I was alone in the second seat behind the pilot, with a rather large box strapped in beside me, addressed to Muluk Telephone

Office. I didn't mind sitting alone, glad to have the next hour to reflect on the last two weeks of Christmas vacation and perhaps try to remember what I had planned for the first week back at school.

My time in Vail had flown by. I'd had fun sliding down the slopes with my younger brother and drinking after-ski Glühwein. I enjoyed my mother's crepes and Christmas cookies and cross-country skied with my sister on New Year's Eve under a full moon.

A highlight of my trip was finally venturing into the Alaskan Shop, which I had seen all the years growing up in Vail but never felt the need to visit. This time, having lived in a genuine Alaskan village, I felt more confident chatting with the owner. He was excited to hear of my experiences in Shishmaref and how I got to carve a mask under the careful eye of Melvin Olanna, master carver.

"Oh yeah," the shopkeeper confirmed. "I've been there. Just once. Real nice people. And I have one of Melvin's here. Hard to come by." He pointed to an owl carved out of cool green-gray soapstone.

"May I pick it up?"

The store owner nodded. My fingers closed around the figurine. Its head was turned, eyes inquiring. The piece was heavy. Dense. Cool to the touch and incredibly smooth. Melvin's words returned: "You gotta love it into life."

The plane shuddered in a brief exchange of air currents, refocusing my gaze on snow-covered hills and tundra passing far below. My thoughts shifted from the weightlessness of vacation to the heaviness of teaching and the classroom I'd left behind in a disordered state. The snowflakes I taught my students to make would still be plastered all over the walls and windows, and the small fake Christmas tree my parents shipped would still be standing on top of the file cabinet, decorated with paper ornaments in the shapes of candy canes, stars, and seals.

Sophie a senior, asked if she could bring an ornament from home. "Of course," I said. The next day, she held something up to my nose.

"Sniff."

I couldn't see what it was, but I took a whiff and sneezed.

"It's the Shishmaref Star." Sophie's eyes danced. "Smells good, eh?" She dangled a small star made of seal fur and edged with tiny red and white beads. I thought back to the seals outside my portable, laying in blood on the sand. It was hard to connect that scene with the cute star Sophia turned to hang on a branch, up high.

What in the world was I going to teach next? My eyes searched the horizon, hoping a billboard would magically appear and advertise ideas. I had long since finished the poetry unit, and there was no way the kids would let me resurrect anything from medieval times.

I anticipated that most of them would remain in the village after graduation, opting out of a college degree and choosing to stay near home and family instead. A subsistence culture needed many hands. Still, I wanted each student to have a basic command of English literacy.

If only I had a full set of books, like John Steinbeck's *The Pearl* or Jack London's *To Build a Fire and Other Short Stories*. Or a textbook of selected readings with those lovely questions at the end of each chapter! I had thought many times of asking Principal Ken to order a set. But then the Voice of Doubt would reappear. *What if he orders books and the kids hate them? What if he invests in you again, like he did with Future Problem Solving, and you fail to deliver?*

I was stuck. Stuck in the middle of needing to make connections between what I had learned about teaching English and what my students needed and wanted in their lives. *Hmmm. Their own lives.*

I whispered the words, "Yes, indeed, *their* lives." My breath fogged on the window, and I traced a question mark on the cold pane.

My teaching had to connect to *their* lives. But what did I actually know about their lives, save for tentative observations—ones tainted through my own cultural framework and random song dedications in the *Northern Lights News*? I felt an opening deep inside and exhaled. Funny, I hadn't realized I was holding my breath.

The opening was barely perceptible, but familiar. It had shown up in my life many times, usually hiking alone in the mountains. It was a quiet feeling, like the time I encountered a large buck in the woods behind our house in Vail. It was huge, with antlers, and calmly drinking from a stream. Ten more steps and I could have patted him on the nose. The buck raised its head. Water dripped from its chin. We stood, frozen in each other's presence, eyes locked, trying to comprehend the unexpected meeting. The buck turned, took three jumps, and disappeared. It was a moment of shared intimacy that merged two different worlds—a thinking world and an instinctual one.

In Shishmaref, that same merged feeling appeared fleetingly, usually on the beach. I'd be strolling along, my heavy boots clumping on the sand and my mind riding a more ethereal wave of expansiveness. The result was experiencing a subtle shift in me feeling freer than the moment before, like clouds when they part, revealing a crystal-blue sky that had been there the whole time.

I was on the verge of understanding something and just needed to let my mind drift in the current. Maybe, like with the buck in the forest, I represented a distinct cognitive world, one that held only a minor connection to my students' ways of being. Their world was more instinctual, seasonal. I shook my head slightly with this realization.

I was going about this teaching thing all wrong. Even the way I talked about it hinted of self-indictment. What *I'm* teaching them. What they're learning *from me.* That perspective left no room for them to teach me, instead.

I had been given no instructions for teaching in this culture, so I kept designing activities that made sense to me, then felt like a failure when my students didn't understand. They said "Hi, Teach" when we passed in the street. But I didn't feel like a Teach. I felt like an impostor who'd be found out and kicked off the island before the spring thaw.

It seemed unfair to blame myself for everything, however. Western literacy had been around for centuries. But in Iñuit culture, the act of reading and writing was more recent, forced on Native Alaskan people by missionaries who shipped Native children away to special schools, away from their families and the only life they knew. Those authorities failed to realize that Native Alaskans had their own literacy—not only for language—but for living. It was complicated yet logical, and had enabled them to survive for centuries in conditions that would make the most stalwart Viking shiver in his boots. Their literacy came in the form of storytelling, art, and dancing. It was a literacy of the land and the seasons, something I sorely needed. How much easier my drive to the dump would have been, had I known about permafrost holes!

Pretty much everything my students lived for was different from my European background: their concept of family and extended generations; their sense of property being shared; their use of animals, of which they took great care but also killed to survive. Even competition, which was fierce when it came to basketball and wrestling, had a sportsmanship quality to it that I had not witnessed before.

One of the biggest differences I was experiencing, however, was the concept of time. My culture was enslaved by it. We spent time, killed time, gained time, lost time. We even changed the time by one hour twice a year.

It was one of the first major cultural differences I felt in Shishmaref. They had clocks on the walls, and I sometimes spotted a watch on someone's wrist. But clocks and watches were largely ornamental, simply approximating a moment when something could happen. Or not. A common joke, especially when trying to fly in or out of the village, was to hurry up and wait. Like the cardinal directions, time was relative to one's perspective.

My students ran by a different inner clock. They would miss several days of school or come late without apology, unconcerned about grades or idle threats from teachers. Principal Ken tried using his authority to scare students, and even asked my *Northern Lights News* team to add a Principal's Message in the next issue, emphasizing the importance of on-time attendance. "A day of learning lost can never be recovered," he wrote, adding that he and the student council were working on rewards as incentive. He ended his plea with "Let's put forth some individual effort. Let LEARNING motivate us to come to school!"

The girls didn't like it.

"Do we have to underline 'never'?" Darlene asked. Her eyebrows furrowed.

"Yeah," Molly said. "And does LEARNING have to be in caps?"

I shrugged, trying not to let on that I agreed with their protests. "I think the principal just wants us to put his message in there as he wrote it. He has bosses, too, and they might be enforcing the rules throughout the district. We don't really know."

The pilot's voice suddenly came over the intercom. "Okay, we're just a few minutes out."

Carrie's hood jerked up, looking right and left, and then back at me. She unzipped, revealing tousled hair, and apologized for having fallen asleep. I nodded, forgiving her and secretly thankful that her proclivity for sleeping on airplanes played in my favor on this ride.

Then, who knows where the thought came from, I remembered a song that Rachel, a ninth grader, dedicated to Curtis: "Love Will Keep Us Together" by Captain & Tennille.

Students loved dedicating songs to each other in the *Northern Lights News*. They named a song and a recipient in any grade, and it was up to the reader to figure out the gesture behind that dedication. I made some guesses, but the students never confirmed the meaning of a classmate receiving "Almost Paradise" from the movie *Footloose* or "Our House" by Crosby, Stills and Nash. Only close friends might deduce the truth of their lyrical shorthand.

As Shishmaref came into view, I started humming "Love Will Keep Us Together" while marveling at the thick carpet of ice stretching to the horizon. Did the ice stretch all the way to Russia?

Could a person walk over the North Pole and make it to Sweden? Maybe Shishmaref wasn't as isolated as I had originally thought. When I started feeling lonely again, perhaps I could think of the ice connecting me to people in other places, all as one.

We buzzed the village and circled the lagoon. The plane landed with the usual one-two bump. A short taxi brought us to the edge of a cluster of snow machines. The riders' breath and the machine exhaust comingled in the freezing air.

The song kept moving through my mind like a deep current under the surface of more tangible thoughts. As the propellers came to a halt, I made a New Year's resolution. This time, it wouldn't be focused on me, like losing weight or accomplishing some other unrealistic goal. This time, my resolution was to do a better job of connecting with students, to listen more intently and tune in more frequently to their song lyrics, and simply enjoy their teenage frivolity, quirkiness, and wisdom.

"Hey." Carrie turned to me again. "I asked Lance to come get us." She pointed at the school truck advancing slowly across the snow.

We thanked our pilot for the smooth flight and ran to the truck, throwing our bags in the bed and piling into the cozy cab as fast as we could. Lance turned toward town, maneuvering slowly over snow berms and ruts on Main Street.

"You ever get a song stuck in your head?" I tossed out the question.

"Sure," Lance said. "But I'm not sure I want to hear what's stuck in yours." He tapped the brake to absorb a large snowdrift, hard as concrete.

I started singing the refrain from Captain and Tennille's song. Carrie joined in, cranking the heat, and the three of us sang at the top of our lungs about looking in our hearts and letting love keep us together, all the way home.

THIRTY-NINE

HUMP DAY-SCHLUMP DAY

Beep-beep-beep-beep! *Beep-beep-beep-beep*!

I slammed my hand on the alarm clock. *One of these days I'm going to break this thing.* The air was cold, making me pull my arm back into my sleeping bag. My room was pitch black and quiet. No sound within the walls, no wind outside.

Wednesdays were Hump Days at school, implying a quick up and over for students and teachers alike. In other words, just get through this day and I'd be on the downhill side. But the start of Hump Day still meant there was some uphill to go. Wednesdays felt like the longest day of the week, and I often glanced at the clock more than my students.

The only way out is through. My Inner Coach prodded me out of my warm cocoon and into the kitchen for a splash of cold water from our Gatorade-sized metal canister. Water from the tap having long since dried up, we received the canister from one of the school custodians, along with a metal folding chair on which to set it. He returned moments later with large chunks of smoky white ice.

"From Serpentine River," he explained, dropping them in. "It's 'cross the lagoon, far up, so it's fresh." He patted his stomach approvingly. "Called *nilak*. Takes a while to melt, but a little goes a long way. Just turn this little spigot thingy."

I appreciated the custodian's confidence but knew I'd be boiling my water just the same. Having lived in the mountains, I knew all about the dangers of contracting giardia. I'd heard stories of unsuspecting tourists filling their bottles in sparkly mountain streams, ignorant of contamination by deer, elk, sheep, marmots, and a host of other forest animals. In the wrong place and time, drinking the water could quickly lead to stomach pains and diarrhea, even a trip to the clinic. Who knew what critters played in the Serpentine River?

School started in fifteen minutes. I had already missed my initial prep time but didn't feel rushed. With the continued darkness and frigid temperatures, students wouldn't be lined up at the door. During these winter days, students trickled in, sleepy and disheveled. They had just enough energy to give me a scrunch-face, hoping I'd have mercy and not mark them late.

"It's typical this time of year," Duncan reassured me as I made a pit stop in the copy room. "People here have lived by a seasonal clock for centuries." He poured more coffee in our mugs and added, "In summer, folks are running around all the time. In winter they're not. All you can do is welcome the kids who come and keep lessons simple so it's easy to make up if they miss a few days."

"That makes sense." I took a sip of the bitter brew. "But it's not just that. They're getting so bossy with each other. The other day, Marcus threw two pencils at Tyler and told him to shut up. I don't know what that was all about, but it wasn't normal. Marcus goofs off a lot, but he's a nice kid. I didn't say anything because it worked. Tyler shut up."

Duncan and I laughed about the wonders of peer intervention, but when I asked him if it would help kids get to school if I called their parents, he almost spit out his coffee.

"Uh, *no*." He wiped a dribble of coffee from his chin. "Think about it. A lot of the parents didn't go to school like kids do now. There's a different range of priorities, and school might not be the most important one, depending on the time of year." He took another sip. "The people here strike me as the kind who learn what they need, when they need it. They're smart, wise, resilient. You don't need twelve years of school for that."

Duncan didn't usually share his opinions about the people in Shishmaref. Sensing my surprise, he shrugged. "Just my two cents."

"I guess you're right. About contacting parents, at least. I don't have any connections with them. And, truth be told, I'm not really clear about who's who anyway. So many of the kids have the same last name. I might get an older brother or sister on the phone and be none the wiser. Besides, I get the feeling that school is *my* job, not theirs."

We sipped in silence, both lost in thought. A memory from my student teaching days flashed to awareness. It seemed minor, but the experience had scarred me. It happened after I confronted two female students—twins—to stop bullying another student. The twin sisters, who were white, kept goading the one Black girl in class. They made snide comments about her hair, her clothes, and her shyness. I told my mentor teacher how I'd pulled the twins in the hall for a private conversation on respect and civility, but they just laughed.

"Looks like you need to call their mother," my teacher said.

I remembered my hands shaking as I dialed the mother's number. Instead of apologizing, she lectured me. "You're not much of a teacher, are you? Can't even control my girls." That incident had happened one year ago, but I still felt the sting of her words.

I wanted to tell Duncan the story to get his perspective, but we'd run out of time. We clinked our mugs to wish each other Hump Day Cheer and headed to our respective classrooms.

The day wasn't exactly cheerful, but it moved along and carried me in its current. I was immersed intellectually but emotionally disconnected. I'd started calling days like this "throw-away days." Before I knew it, my prep period came and went, and school was over.

I felt the need to move around and decided to shoot a few hoops. The ball closet was locked, but I spied a ball under one of the bleachers. It needed air, but I bounced it down the court and then to the center, aimed, and ricocheted the ball off the top corner of the backboard.

I slowed to a walk and remembered how my second-grade gym teacher, Mr. Swanson, had my class bouncing those large red rubber balls around the periphery of the gym to the beat of "Stars and Stripes Forever" by John Philip Sousa. He eventually got us all bouncing in unison, but the collective vibration made the needle on the record skip. It slid across the top of the vinyl disk with an awful ear-splitting screech. Mr. Swanson said a bad word and told us to go sit down. He was probably having a Hump Day-Schlump Day like me. I marched around the gym one time in honor of Mr. Swanson, bouncing the flat basketball to the beat of Sousa's song. "Dah da-da-da-da-dah-dah-dahhh ..."

My commemorative bouncing came to an end, forcing me to think of something more exciting to do with my afternoon. Maybe I would finally venture out to the Washeteria. I could wash my overly used clothes and take a hot shower.

I caught Lance in the hall. "Hey, Lance, ever been to the Washeteria?"

"Once," he replied. "Washing machines are a couple bucks, dryers are a buck-fifty. They use tokens for the showers. Max of two for a total of six minutes." He laughed, patting his hair. "Get two. One's not enough. My hair was stiff with soap for a week."

Lance zipped his parka and headed toward the door but turned and yelled, "Take the Housing Trail, it's faster. And don't forget a towel!"

I went straight home, loaded up my pockets with quarters, and shoved my dirty clothes and my bath towel into a Hefty trash bag. The wind was calm, and the streets were quiet. I walked briskly, surprised that it took only fifteen minutes to reach the Washeteria. The low-lying building sat next to an enormous water tower the size of the school. I had no idea where the water had come from to fill such a large tank, but I was grateful for whoever did the hauling.

A young woman greeted me from behind the counter.

"Hullo!" She looked me over. "First time?"

That's when I realized I had forgotten laundry soap and shampoo.

"Not a problem," she laughed. "Everyone does that."

She poured a handful of Tide in the machine and held out a bottle of Johnson & Johnson's baby shampoo.

"This'll work on your baby fine hair. Only use a little, though. It suds like crazy!"

With two tokens in hand, I pushed through the door marked WOMEN and was immediately met with steamy air and a locker room smell of wet towels. I laid my parka on a bench and took off my boots, then stepped into a small shower space and pulled the outer curtain closed. It was the size of a phone booth, but there was enough room to undress and step past a second curtain into the shower itself.

It was the most luxurious, sweet, baby-shampoo-smelling shower I'd ever had. The hot water was heaven. Maybe I'd make this my weekly Hump Day event and get my own bottle of Johnson & Johnson's baby shampoo.

Dressed once more, I returned to the laundry room. It was steamy, too. The dryer took the last of my quarters but my clothes were still damp. I'd have to finish drying them at home. I loosely folded everything back into my Hefty bag and started for the door.

"Thank you!" I patted my head and smelled my hand. "My hair smells terrific!"

It was dark outside, and the warmth of the Washeteria was quickly replaced by icy Arctic air. My hair quickly began freezing into little icicle strands. I zipped up my periscope hood, bear-hugged my Hefty bag, and started for home.

The bag was heavy and slippery. Frost started to form on its surface from my wet clothes inside. I hugged it tighter, like a strongman carrying a boulder in a Scottish Highlands competition.

"Hey, Teach! Need a lift?"

It was one of my students, riding a sno-go. What was his name again? He didn't come to school much. It began with an H. Maybe Henry. He often skipped school or came late or left early, slipping out before I could speak with him about my concerns that his lack of attendance would lead to failing my class and not being able to graduate. Now would be the perfect time to address the issue, but the warmth of the hot shower had long left my body, and I just wanted to get home. My lecture could wait. Maybe in return for a free ride home, I would bestow upon him an honorary degree and he could get on with his life.

Henry waited patiently as I maneuvered behind him on the small sno-go seat, hoisting the Hefty bag over my shoulder like Santa Claus.

"Ready?"

Without waiting for my reply, Henry opened the throttle. We lurched forward. There being no back to the seat, I screamed and instinctively grabbed his shoulder to keep from turning Hump Day-Schlump Day into a Dump in the Snow Day.

Henry laughed, a low chuckle. Just enough to let me know he was enjoying his momentary switch in relational power. I felt the machine reduce in speed and tried to enjoy my impromptu ride over snow berms and through single-lane gullies piled high with snow. He seemed to be taking the road less traveled, through parts of Shishmaref I hadn't seen before.

Each time I felt my butt sliding off the back, I emitted a high-pitched guinea pig squeal and grabbed Henry's waist tighter, terrified that I'd fall off and my clean underwear would scatter like frisbees all over the street.

At one corner, we were momentarily blinded by the light of an oncoming snow machine.

"Hey, Henry! Hey, Teach!"

Oh, great. The story of the Squealing Teacher is going to be all over town before I even get home, and I'm going to be the target of endless teasing at school.

Maybe I would write an anonymous Dear Abby letter to Darlene, asking for advice about how to approach the possible advances of a young man (i.e., student) who offered me a ride in exchange for an A in my class. (Signed, "At a Loss.")

Henry came to a smooth stop in front of my portable. It seemed that everyone knew where I lived. I dropped my laundry bag onto the snow, and I shimmied backward to standing, patting Henry's shoulder as a gesture of thanks. He revved his engine and zoomed away.

I spent thirty minutes hanging my damp clothes on hangers and doorknobs, suddenly feeling energized. The schlump in my day had disappeared, and I was eager for entertainment.

"I'm going to grab a bite and go to the game," I said to Anne. "Want to go?"

Anne sat in her usual spot, dealing another round of solitaire. "Nah, think I'll stay where it's warm and cozy and quiet."

I threw on my parka again and stepped into the frigid air once more. Tonight, the Northern Lights girls' team was playing a team from Noatak, a village north of Shishmaref and on the mainland, along a river by the same name. The gym was only half-filled with spectators. Like Anne, people must have opted to stay home rather than venture into the dark, cold night. I would have stayed home, too, but the shouting, thumping, and cheering could be heard in my bedroom. It was less annoying to just come and have a look.

Duncan gave me a popcorn for free, and I was soon settled high in the bleachers, enjoying the panther-like prowess of both teams. Their play was more measured than the boys, but they had their own way of gracefully skidding and stopping to shoot the ball, often swishing it straight through the net. They had moments of sprinting, too, and making a clean layup. Like the boys, the girls were lightning fast, determined to outwit their opponents. They were also good-natured and intense about winning but quick to congratulate the accurate shot of an opposing team member or apologize after a foul.

During a Noatak time-out, I surveyed the room and noticed an elderly woman looking back at me. Did I know her? I glanced in the woman's direction a few minutes later. She was still watching me.

Several minutes later, Shishmaref called a time-out. I avoided looking in the woman's direction. What if she was still looking back at me? I distracted myself by watching the preschool-aged children, who were in constant motion. As on other nights, I witnessed every young child being cared for. Toddlers crawled from one lap to the next. Infants were handed around, their fat cheeks kissed and cuddled. My eyes spotted Will, cradling a baby, cooing and tickling it with his new mustache. In class, Will was sullen and quiet. Here, he was full of life. Witnessing his unexpected display of tenderness, my eyes welled up with tears.

The referee blew his whistle. The Northern Lights girls won, 25-22. The score was lower than usual, both teams making more defensive than offensive moves. As I walked toward the exit, I realized that Hump Day-Schlump Day hadn't turned out so bad after all. I had a hot shower and a room filled with damp but clean clothes. I had the crazy sno-go ride with Henry and witnessed the gentle spirit of Will. As I clomped down the school steps and across the snowy street to home, I thought about how everyone had a place here; everyone belonged. Even I was finding a place, having been pulled repeatedly through the vortex of what was possible when I let go of expectations and went with the flow.

FORTY

HOLY SMOKES

The next morning, Marcus arrived for ninth-grade English with a spring in his step and an odd smile on his face. That either meant he was up to something, or he was up to something.

"Good morning, Marcus." I looked at him directly, sending the message that I was already on to him, whatever it was.

"Good morning!" Marcus plopped into a desk and punched Tyler in the arm. Comrades through thick and thin.

"How was the Washeteria?" Marcus grinned, then looked away.

"It was lovely," I countered his teasing. "Can't wait to go back."

For the rest of the day and into the following week, I found a lighter rhythm with my teaching. I had let go of planning lessons down to the last breath and relaxed my expectations that students needed to be active every minute. In a word, I stopped being so anal. Perhaps it was the weariness of trying, especially through these dark winter months when my focus narrowed to eating and staying warm. It was so frickin' cold that I didn't want to waste energy on anything that wasn't absolutely necessary. I moved slower and used fewer words. I started communicating more with facial expressions. Eyebrows up, eyebrows down.

This shift in consciousness correlated with a passage I'd recently come across in one of my favorite grammar books, *The Elements of Style.* The authors' instructions were about conciseness. In a master painter's painting, there were no extra brush marks; in a machinist's machine, there were no extra parts. Why not apply that kind of frugality to teaching, as well? Every lesson had the potential of traveling in dozens of directions, but one strategic first step was all I needed to advance toward the objective.

Early in the year, my Graphic Communications students showed me they were perfectly capable of running the newspaper and only needed me for sideline coaching and logistical support. Why hadn't I understood this could be applied to my other classes?

These shifts with teaching created more space for learning. My habit of noting micro-movements in the margins of my lesson plans, like, "Turn around and write this on the board," gradually came to an end.

The next weekend, I took advantage of the calmer weather. The clouds were high in the stratosphere, and there was hardly any wind. I wanted to take myself on a well-deserved walk to the dump, following a well-used road that had been carved into the snow by sno-gos and the occasional truck. I'd stop short of the dump to minimize crossing paths with polar bears who might be lurking in that vicinity. I had recently joked about such a thing in the main office, when the school custodian, Kenny, countered my levity.

"You walk to the dump?" His eyebrows raised unusually high. "Watch out for nanuq!"

He dropped to his hands and knees, mimicking the movements of a polar bear ambling over the snow. His imitation was astonishing. In a few yards of carpet, he transformed from a skinny janitor in jeans to a muscled Ursus maritimus. I laughed at his antics, but Midge's stern look made me stop to reconsider the serious possibility of encountering a hungry eight-hundred-pound bear on the outskirts of town.

I decided to keep my wits about me and suited up like an Army recruit in my parka and snow pants, beaver hat, and my most recent purchase from Walter's store, a pair of snowmobiling gloves. They pulled up just short of my elbows and had sheep fleece on the top, which was handy for wiping one's nose in the frigid air. Final touches included a new set of felt liners in my boots and binoculars in my inside pocket. My camera would stay home. It was too cold to risk having it break in subzero conditions.

I stepped onto our rickety porch, which creaked from my added weight. Sparkles of icy flakes hung in the air, and smoke from nearby houses billowed up from narrow chimney pipes. Cold atmospheric pressure prevented the haze from going too far. In the distance, I heard the faint rumble of a snow machine. Other than that, the only sound was the crunch and squeak of my boots on the snow. I followed the first track, which led to another, and then I broke free of the edge of town and crunched along a primary trail. It was the same general area where I'd driven the school truck into a hole, but now it was encased in hardpacked snow and scattered with chunks of ice churned up by snow machine treads.

I settled into an easy stride, stopping and turning around periodically to measure my distance from the village. In a matter of minutes, the familiar structures shrank to little spots of color in the middle of a vast whiteness. I looked through my binoculars like a spotter in a submarine, rotating slowly to survey the scenery and—fingers crossed—nothing else. But the only thing that interrupted the landscape were willow branches that hunters cut from the mainland and stuck in the snow as guideposts for safely crossing the lagoon.

I shifted my gaze to the ocean, marveling at the size of ice slabs that pressed into each other, creating a new shoreline, like tectonic plates rearranging themselves with the changing tides.

My lens flashed over something black sticking up from the ice, like a small tree stump. *What the ...*

I focused my binoculars to their sharpest resolution and squinted. It wasn't a tree stump. That would have been ridiculous. But it was too thick to be a willow branch.

"Huh," I said out loud to myself. "Well, ain't that something. That's a seal." There was no mistaking the spots and narrow snout.

It was stuck upright in the ice, far from shore. The muffled sound of a rifle shot cracked open the stillness. Then another, confirming my discovery. Someone was out there hunting seals.

I couldn't wrap my mind around how a person managed to stick a seal upright in the snow. It must be frozen solid. I scanned for hunters but, seeing no one, panned around to the lagoon once more.

Something else was on the horizon, to the southeast of the dump. Something gray-black. Smoke? I couldn't make it out.

I looked back toward the village and shivered with cold and a bit of fear. I hadn't felt this exposed before. I couldn't run home without freezing my lungs. I kept a wary eye on the apparition, which was getting bigger, and lifted my binoculars again. It was smoke, for sure. But from what? Was there something on fire at the dump?

Then a sound. A motor? I pulled the flap of my beaver hat away from one ear. There it was. Intermittent, but definitely a motor. Intrigued, I stood still until the silhouette of a snow machine became apparent. It was moving slowly, a plume of black smoke emanating from behind. A solitary man was half standing, half kneeling on the seat. The end of a rifle poked over one shoulder. Someone was pulling something heavy, *dang* heavy.

The man waved as he approached, and called out, "Hallooo!"

"Halloo!" I replied and waved back. He was close enough now that I could make out his white parka with a fur-trimmed hood, thick snow pants, and Bunny boots. Frost clung to his eyebrows and cheeks. He'd been out here for a while.

He slowed his machine, just short of stalling out. A cigarette dangled from his lips. "Gotta keep goin'—this thing ain't going to make it much farther!"

I pointed at the bulge on his sled, tied with a canvas tarp.

"What you got there?"

"Polar bear! Shot it not far from here, just over a little ways. Thing was too big to handle in one load. Bringing it back in pieces!" He laughed. "Gonna send one of my boys for the hide."

He continued to move slowly past me. A thin red line of blood trailed behind him, staining the snow. I stood still, unsure which direction to go. If I continued to the dump, I'd be fine, right? No self-respecting polar bear would show up now, right? But what if a relative of the one who had just gotten killed wanted revenge? Did polar bears travel in groups? Would there be others following the scent of their brother's blood—the blood that led directly to the spot where I currently stood?

The decision was made for me when the man called out again, "Be careful out there!"

I looked at the pale disk of sun on the horizon, then swept my gaze toward the polar bear hides I'd first seen when I arrived on the island. They were barely perceptible against the white air and snow.

Less than an hour of daylight left. A smart Eskimo would head home. Disappointed that my walk had been cut short, I turned back toward the village, looking over my shoulder every so often and wondering about cooking a polar bear. Do you boil it? Grill it in the oven? Make a stir-fry? What did polar bear taste like?

My stomach growled with curiosity. I chuckled. This place was creating a whole new category of being vegetarian. I'd tasted moose, and there was that pot of chili Midge brought to school one day. What was in that? Some kind of meat. And now, maybe polar bear.

I followed my stomach's coaxing past my house and down the street to Walter's for a snack. At the counter was the woman who'd been looking at me when I was seated in the stands at the basketball game. She stopped her conversation with Walter upon seeing me.

"Halloo, Teacher!" Walter gestured. "I'm still waitin' on that coffee maker. It's on back order. In the meantime, have you met Ruth?"

"Not officially." I approached. "But we did see each other at the ball game." I took off my glove, and we shook hands. Ruth was small, but her hand was strong.

"Ruth's English isn't too good," Walter explained.

She was wearing mukluks, the traditional Native Alaskan boots made with seal fur and flat leather bottoms of reindeer or caribou hide. Each boot had beadwork on top, a four-petaled flower crafted with red and white beads. Softer fur, like that of my own hat's tassels, lined the boots' top edges. They went halfway up her calf.

"Those are beautiful." I pointed at her feet. Ruth nodded, then turned to Walter and said something in Iñupiat.

"She says you are welcome to visit her anytime."

Ruth said something else to Walter and headed for the door. The soles of her mukluks made a quiet shushing sound. The doorbells jangled and she was gone.

Walter laughed. "That's called the Shishmaref shuffle!" He mimicked the movement behind the store counter. "Mukluks have no tread. You need to keep your feet on the ground, or you'll slip on the ice and fall on your fanny."

I laughed at Walter's use of the word "fanny" and held up a Snickers bar. "This'll do for now."

I was almost out the door when I realized that I didn't know where Ruth lived.

"She's a few houses over." Walter jerked a thumb over his shoulder. "Look for a blue oil drum with antlers on top." His eyes twinkled, just short of a wink. "And take some cash."

"Cash?"

Walter shrugged.

"Will do." I saluted and stepped out into the cold twilight air.

FORTY-ONE

PASSION PARADOX

Icy Arctic winds whipped around the school, freezing everything in their path. It was just after lunch, and I was trying to conjure up even a smidgen of interest in poetry with my ninth graders—something more advanced than acrostic poems.

When I was in ninth grade, I didn't like poetry much but came around when my teacher shared stories of poets' lives. They became real. More accessible. Poets were people who had dreams and fears. They loved and lost. They paused long enough to recount in words the beauty of autumn sunlight through the branches of an oak tree. Their writing spoke to universal themes that captured my teenage heart; maybe they'd do the same for these teenagers, as well.

Poetry could be the powerful companion to their tendency to write in fragments. It could be the antidote to their sparseness of punctuation, a gateway that enticed them into the world of words without my usual lecture about conventions. They might even begin to comprehend the power and beauty of a perfectly placed adjective. In a way, my students were already poets in their own right. Maybe this would be the path that expanded the vocabulary of their unique experiences on the island—beyond their typical descriptors of "good" or "not good."

I had no poetry texts, so I copied about twenty poems from my own college textbook and created booklets. It took more time than I anticipated, which meant I had no time to research any poet biographies. I decided to kick off Poetry Week with a personal story about seeing Maya Angelou in person. It would give my students a window of understanding about how one person's words could change your life.

During my final year in college, I took a new class, *The African American Experience*, which included the writing of dozens of Black authors, one of whom was Maya Angelou. We read *I Know Why the Caged Bird Sings*, *Gather Together In My Name*, and poems like *And Still I Rise.* My literary life expanded into refreshing new territory that revived my deep interest in the Civil Rights Movement and all it stood for.

When I saw a poster announcing Maya Angelou's upcoming presentation at a community college, I couldn't wait to attend and got there early for a front row seat. The auditorium started to fill, and anticipation mounted. I surveyed the stage, hoping to spot Ms. Angelou as soon as she stepped into the light.

But I was looking in the wrong direction.

A hush fell over the crowd, like someone had waved a huge wand, shushing everyone to silence. People started standing up and looking toward the back of the auditorium. I stood up, too, stretching to see over their heads. But that wasn't necessary. I *felt* Maya Angelou even before I laid eyes on her royal purple turban with gold fringe. She floated down the aisle and then swept onto the stage in an equally captivating purple robe and turned to face a thousand beaming faces. She shimmered under the lights, and the room exploded in thunderous applause.

For the next two hours, Maya Angelou took the crowd on a journey of reciting poems without notes, of reading from her books and singing spirituals and folk songs in her deep, throaty voice. She was mesmerizing. Her words flowed like a waterfall into a deep lake.

This was the story I shared with my students. I waved my arms and strode like Maya Angelou across the front of the room. I showed them a picture of her toothy, smiling face.

I wasn't sure what I expected. Maybe periodic eye contact? Maybe a few smiles or head nods to show appreciation for my passionate retelling of an experience that blew open my heart?

As my story unfolded, most students laid their heads down and closed their eyes. Only Jacob continued watching me, but I could tell he was fake-listening. No one was interested.

Somehow, I had missed the boat. The passion in my heart failed to land in theirs. With no recognition of my intentions, I stopped abruptly and said, "You know what, never mind."

I sat at my desk, so tired of trying. My face was hot, and tears pooled in my eyes.

"Time to go?" A voice interrupted my sudden, awkward silence.

Something died in that moment. It went slowly, like the pilot light in my heart dimming and then—*pfft!* Snuffed out. A swell of anger rose in my chest, followed by an ache. It was the hardest few minutes I'd experienced so far. I'd taken a chance and opened my heart, but in the wrong place and at the wrong time.

I didn't know what to do, so I just sat at my desk and moved papers around in feigned busyness. The students were awake now, and I could feel them watching me. They didn't know what to do either.

I didn't look up when I spoke. "Class is dismissed. You can go."

One by one, they walked quietly out the door. I dabbed my eyes with a Kleenex and walked to the window, looking east.

"This day is so damn gray," I said to the oil tanks in the nearby field. They were always out there. Cold metal sentries, rusting in all kinds of weather. I felt like a cold metal tank, too. A gust of wind blew across the snow, swirling it up and settling it down again, a movement that brought the same unnerving questions that had been swirling inside of me for months. *Was I sure I wanted to be a teacher? If I was teaching what I loved, how come the students didn't feel the same? If this one-way passion was teaching, how long would I last?*

I moved to the chalkboard and started to erase the questions for discussion: What do you think about … and Have you ever …

They seemed irrelevant now.

The more important questions still lingered. *How could I keep my passion for writing and reading alive? How could I rekindle the fire in me after my students so nonchalantly stamped it out?*

Jack London's story "To Build a Fire" came to mind, and an odd chuckle rose in my throat. At least I wasn't that guy who froze to death in the wilderness after a clump of snow fell from a tree and extinguished his fire.

I finished erasing and wiped a hand on my trousers. My frustration and anger had dissipated. But one thing was clear—if I was going to survive to the end of the school year, I needed to find ways to better process my feelings. During student teaching, I processed my feelings during a long commute home with a stop at the Dairy Queen drive-through. In Shishmaref, my commute lasted only a minute, and the closest Dairy Queen was in Kotzebue (or so I'd heard). I wondered how far that was by sno-go.

Second, I needed to find more ways to laugh. Not just at the absurdity of the situations I found myself in, but at myself in general. Nana used to say that laughter was the best medicine. She was right, and I still needed to trust her direction to pursue a teaching career.

Where could I go for some distraction? For something new?

Then it hit me. I would go visit Ruth. The moment school ended, I turned out the lights and headed up the street to find the house with a blue oil drum and antlers on top.

It didn't take long. I stepped into the portico of a small dwelling and was about to knock when I remembered Walter's advice to bring cash. *Crap.*

I rarely carried cash. There was no need for it, except for the times when students approached me to sell pendants and earrings, the latter of which I couldn't wear on account of my pierced ears no longer being pierced. The earrings were so cute, though, and I had a hard time saying no.

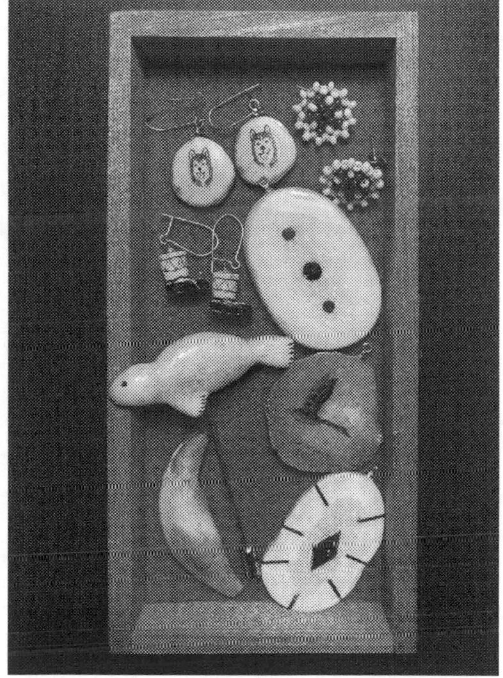

Ivory pendants and earrings that students sold to me. Ruth's tooth artifact is lower left.

The most recent pair came from Molly, who had painstakingly sewn red and white beads onto two tiny circles of leather. They were adorable. Most of the other jewelry I'd purchased was ivory, sold by boys taking a carving class at school. Some pieces were plain, others decorated with scrimshaw sketches of flowers or geese. My favorite purchase came from George, who approached me in the hall one day and shyly presented the cutest ivory earrings I had ever seen: a pair of mukluks with black soles and a crosshatch design. I paid him ten dollars on the spot.

A gust of wind whipped around the portico, lifting snow crystals to my face. I'd come this far; it seemed silly to go home. If Ruth wanted to sell something to me, I could easily return with payment.

I knocked. A moment later, it creaked open. Ruth immediately broke into a toothy smile and invited me in. Her sealskin mukluks and a pair of battered Sorels sat just inside, prompting me to remove my boots. I hooked my coat on the wall and followed her into a large room that served as a kitchen, dining space, and living room. The air was hot and stuffy and smelled like sauerkraut and burnt toast. Ruth motioned for me to sit at her dining table while she made tea. It was now my turn to experience the other side of a "visit," just like the young Bubblicious girls who had pat-patted on my door.

Ruth had a quintessential grandmother face, round and filled with creases that multiplied when she changed expression. I wondered how old she was. She could have been forty or eighty. Living on the island seemed to age people beyond their years. Some of my students' parents looked to be well over sixty years old, which I knew couldn't be right.

Every surface had something on it: pots and pans, a toaster and coffee maker, an assortment of boxes and cans of food. Pilot Bread, Kix cereal, rice, crackers, and multiple cans of soups and beans. The table where I sat had also been taken over by food items, magazines, and a plate with a piece of burnt toast and jam.

Ruth cleared a space for our tea and slid a honey bear and a spoon in my direction, nodding and smiling without a single word exchanged between us. It was curious to me that Ruth had willingly invited a stranger into her home, one who didn't speak her language. This might be the fastest visit on record.

We sipped our tea for a few minutes, and then Ruth went to a large dresser, sat down on the floor, and patted the spot next to her. *Why in the world does she want to sit on the cold linoleum floor?*

But I did as she asked and watched with curiosity as she pulled a cardboard tray from underneath the dresser. Instead of soda cans, it was filled with fragments of bones and pieces of ivory. At least that's what I thought they were. I had never seen bones or ivory in their natural state. Ruth's fingers floated, lightly touching the pieces. She said some words, apparently explaining each one. I felt like I'd been invited to a private exhibit.

This is why Walter told you to bring cash.

Ruth picked up a mushroom-shaped object the size of a thimble that looked like wood and held it to her lower lip. Seeing that I didn't understand, Ruth pointed at my ear, where the former hole was still visible.

"Oh, like pierced?"

Ruth nodded and held the object against her lower lip again. It was for a face piercing.

"Labret?"

She nodded again, pleased that I'd figured it out, and placed the piece in my palm for a closer look. I was fascinated, if a bit repulsed. I could not imagine having such a large accessory below my mouth. Didn't it press against the teeth? Ouch.

I handed it back and shook my head, indicating that I wanted to look at some of the other pieces. Ruth pulled out another cardboard flat and handed me a tooth almost as big as my pinky. It was curved and naturally yellow-brown in color. I had no idea what creature it might have come from. A fish? A walrus? Did walrus have teeth as well as tusks?

Ruth directed me to continue my shopping while she made more tea. I had no idea what I was picking through. There were dozens of tiny shells and pieces of wood or maybe ivory, but they held no significance to me in their raw state. Nonetheless, I knew it would be rude to leave without buying something. I picked up the tooth and the labret, even though I didn't want it. Maybe Ruth would accept an IOU.

Ruth returned with more tea and a saucer with shortbread cookies. I took a bite and must have made a face. It was stale and as hard as some of the artifacts. Ruth laughed and motioned to dunk the cookie in my tea, then resumed our sales transaction.

"How much?" I showed her the tooth.

She held up five fingers.

Five dollars? For a tooth? I was no archaeologist, but that seemed a bit steep. With the language barrier and the fact I had no cash on me, I decided not to haggle.

"Okay, but I don't have cash with me today."

Ruth frowned slightly.

"I can come back tomorrow, though. I'll take this, too." I picked up the labret. "How much?"

Ruth held up five fingers again.

"Sold." I smiled. "Ten dollars. Tomorrow."

Ruth slurped the last of her tea. When I did the same, we both looked at each other and burst out laughing. Two different cultures, different generations, same humor. All it took was a couple of cups of tea, a stale shortbread cookie, and some artifacts Ruth had likely found lying in the older part of the village.

In a physical sense, we had completed a simple business transaction. Ruth had invited me to visit her, and I accepted her invitation. Yet I felt conflicted. Here I was, supposedly doing her a favor while, simultaneously, representing the culture that, from what I could tell, was destroying hers. I purchased the artifacts out of a sense of moral obligation, not because I wanted them. That was my burden to bear; Ruth didn't seem bothered. She was probably just happy to have ten dollars coming her way, with the promise of more in the near future.

As I stepped onto her porch and turned to say goodbye, Ruth took my hand, cupping it with the other. Our eyes met in a surprising and intimate moment. Once again, something inside me cracked open just a little bit more.

FORTY-TWO

WHAT'S IN A (SNOW) NAME

We were now deep into winter, surrounded by snow, ice, wind, and more snow. I was no stranger to these conditions. Living in Wisconsin as a young girl had given me several seasons to experience a host of different kinds of northern hemispheric precipitation: fat snowflakes I could catch on my tongue; light snow flurries that glistened and floated in frosty air; pea-sized hail that felt like buckshot in the hurricane-force winds off Lake Michigan.

One year, when my family lived on a tall bluff above the lake, we witnessed a highly unusual temperature change. In a matter of minutes, the rain turned to sleet, and when the temperature plummeted below freezing overnight, we woke up to find every blade of grass and tree limb encased in a coating of clear ice. Our yard looked like a crystal palace.

During my teen years in Colorado, I'd skied on early winter "crud"—the locals' name for snow mixed with rocks and dirt that the first snowfalls hadn't fully covered. In the deep winter, the snow I flew over was crusted in slabs on the surface, covering light powder underneath. In spring, the surface turned to "corn snow"—the result of the sun warming the ski runs during the day and turning them to slush. Temperatures at night froze the slush into icy pebbles. I was a smart skier and usually waited until midmorning to hit the slopes, when the corn snow was softer and I wouldn't rip a hole in my pants on the pebbles' sharp edges if I fell.

Cross-country skiing happened on old snow, fresh snow, dry snow, wet snow, and icy snow—each with a different texture that required skiers to rub one kind of wax on their cross-country skis in the morning and another kind in the late afternoon. My familiarity with a variety of winter moisture likely worked in my favor during recruitment to Shishmaref, one more item the hiring committee could check off: "She knows all about snow. She's our gal!"

But what I knew about snow and ice paled in comparison with what the Iñuits knew. I'd heard that Native Alaskan people had over sixty names for their version of Winter Wonderland. They had their own rendition for fat snowflakes, slush, crud, and different kinds of ice. Such delineations were critical when traveling across unpredictable surfaces and in unexpected weather with nothing but one's own keen eye and sharp wits to negotiate challenges in the terrain. As far as I could see, there were no snowplows or tow trucks to come to your rescue.

Whether ice fishing on the lagoon or seal hunting on the ocean, knowing how to distinguish the quality of one kind of ice over another could turn what looked like a relatively easy trip on the ice into disaster.

Signs existed if a person knew how to read them. But I was naïve about Arctic snow—an ignorance that would soon be made abundantly clear.

FORTY-THREE

WHITEOUT

The school day had ended, and I was once again working late in my classroom. The building was quiet. Basketball and wrestling teams had gone home, and the gym was empty—no more muffled shouts or whistles or the shudder of basketballs off metal hoops. It was the time of day when I felt most productive: lonely but making progress with my planning and review of student work.

The deeper I got into teaching as a profession, the more I appreciated the mounds of work my own teachers must have done behind the scenes. Dozens of decisions had to be made every day and again at night. It could take hours for a new teacher like me to analyze what my students had been able to do (or not do). That information guided what made the most sense moving forward. Much of the time, I felt like Meriwether Lewis on his way to the Pacific Coast, but with no Sacajawea to warn me, "Don't go that way!"

I always started my after-school work with Consumer Math, using the sacred textbook as a map for our journey into the wilderness. Next up was banking: writing checks and calculating interest in savings accounts, all of which seemed completely irrelevant in a village with no bank. Maybe I'd take students on a field trip to Walter's.

Teaching English was the hardest. It was a puzzle with a thousand pieces and no picture on the box. It was up to me to create the design.

So far, the image seemed to be a conglomeration of Monet, M.C. Escher, and Picasso—in other words, moments of blurred beauty with stairs that led nowhere and a lot of disjointed faces.

Without a complete set of materials to work with, it was hard building momentum with reading and writing. I noticed an inverse relationship between hours spent planning and actual success the next day. The more meticulous my plan, the worse my lessons went. But there were times when I just had to go through my microscopic Virgo planning to link the steps from beginning to end. It was a tedious process that I wondered about almost daily. Would I figure this out before the end of the school year?

Such was my state of mind. For the past few hours, I had been mildly aware of the wind, which came in intermittent gusts and hit the west side of the building, far from my east-facing classroom, audible but distant.

I got up and stretched, listening more keenly this time as another wave of wind grew stronger and stronger until it reached the velocity of a runaway freight train. *Whoosh*—the wind slammed against the school. During times like this, I was grateful to have a classroom on the east-facing side. The lights flickered, but I knew the windows wouldn't get blown out.

I'd already experienced a few storms on the island, so I felt more curious than concerned. I walked to the window and cupped my face against the cold glass to look outside. Usually the lights by the oil tanks in a nearby field were visible from here. They were my personal lighthouses whose presence illuminated the direction of rain or snow and how hard it fell. This time, I couldn't see anything but my own reflection.

Well, goodness me. The window's plastered with snow!

I checked the other window. Also caked with white.

Maybe it's time to go home.

I tidied my papers and wrote a note to remind myself where to start in the morning. Just as I was contemplating taking a few more minutes to make copies while the power was still on, an even stronger gust of wind put an end to that idea. It roared around the building, then screamed as it found a crack in the doors. It whined and whistled like it was growing impatient with the obstacles in its way. The building shuddered and creaked. It was an unearthly sound that made the hairs on my arms stand up.

At least it's a short walk home.

I slid into my heavy parka and pulled the zipper to my throat, patting down the Velcro cover that kept the metal from freezing. My finger hesitated over the light switch; I was reluctant to turn it off. Regardless of my familiarity with all the school's nooks and crannies, I still got spooked at night. Once I turned off my own classroom light, the hall would be dark except for green exit signs in the hall. And that made every shadow even spookier.

Feigning confidence, I clomped loudly down to the main doors and pulled up my periscope hood. Outside the window, the streetlamp illuminated a dance of snow flying up, down, and sideways like a mess of angry hornets.

Here I am, working till ten o'clock, and there might not even be school tomorrow!

Did they even cancel school on account of the weather?

Clearly, I would have to suit up better, even for this short trek across the street. The first time I'd tried on my heavy clothing had been in the Army Navy Surplus store in Seattle during a heat wave. It felt absurd at the time, but now I was eternally grateful to the coat's designer for creating this tunnel of warmth and protection around my face.

Here goes. I pressed the metal bar to open the door. It moved slightly outward, then slammed shut, pushing me back inside. *Holy bejeebers.* The difference between the air pressure inside the building versus outside literally sucked the door shut.

Is there such a thing as a snow tornado?

Not wanting to experience my body sandwiched between the door and the doorframe, I turned and used my back to push once, then twice. Then, as if someone had pulled the door open, the wind stopped, and my heave sent me nearly sprawling onto the landing. The metal door slammed shut behind me with the precision of a guillotine.

Even with my hood zippered twelve inches out from my face, sharp ice crystals found their way down the tunnel of fur and up my nose. I turned my head, trying to get away from the snow hornets, glancing periodically toward my house to survey the situation. The wind was unrelenting. It puffed out my periscope hood and sucked it in, bringing icy pellets onto my face.

I instinctively shoved my hands into my coat pockets for protection and felt something soft. *Hallelujah. Glove liners!* I turned to face the building and pulled them on. They were pitifully thin, but better than nothing.

The school steps had disappeared under hard whips of snow. I held on to the wooden railing and gingerly took a step down. As I calculated where to step next, another gust of wind blew snow into my mouth, which I didn't realize was open. I choked and turned, realizing that the only way for me to get to the bottom without suffocating or slipping was to hold on to the railing with both hands and back down one level at a time.

One, two, three. Good grief, how many steps were there? I had climbed these stairs a hundred times. Fifteen steps? Sixteen? The snow was hard as concrete, and the drifts didn't align with the steps under them. The measure of my progress came only when the railing ran out. Soon, I was going to have to let go. I glanced up again to get my bearings and aim my boots toward home, but the snow was blowing so hard I couldn't see any part of the structure. Not the sides, not the roof.

This is ridiculous.

My mind flashed on Laura Ingalls Wilder, whose life I'd read about when I was of similar age. Entering puberty and hungry for tales of young girls surviving in precarious situations, I read the whole series, starting with *Little House in the Big Woods.*

Now, as I perched at the end of the school railing in the middle of a whomping blizzard, the book that came to mind was *The Long Winter*, in which Laura recounted her family's survival through one of the most brutal winters to ever hit the Midwest. It began in October 1880 and didn't stop until May 1881. Snow piled twenty feet high, burying houses, stables, and stores. Townspeople chiseled snow tunnels to reach each other. Supply trains couldn't get through for months, and Laura's family came close to starving.

The Ingalls were a smart bunch, though. To ensure not losing Pa when he traveled between house and barn to feed their animals, they fixed a rope to guide him there and back.

The next visit to Walter's, I'd ask if he had about thirty feet of heavy-duty rope. For now, all I needed was a glimpse of the portable through this whiteout, just one edge of the roof or a corner at its base. Then I'd make a run for it. I had walked this way countless times. How hard could it be?

I heard the voice of Laura Ingalls in my head: *Just let go, walk straight, and you'll bump right into the house. Feel your way around to the door, and you're in!*

Easy peasy.

Her advice sounded reasonable, but the snow was so thick and the wind so fierce that I was completely disoriented even as I held fast to the railing. Maybe I could throw a chunk of ice? I couldn't see, but maybe I could trust my ears to follow the sound?

I held on with one hand and knelt to grope under the steps. *Just a couple softball-sized chunks of ice will do it.*

But the ground was frozen solid.

My plan would likely fail anyway. I had a good arm, but anything I threw would be carried away in the wind. Was there something heavy in my classroom? I stomped back up the snow-encrusted steps, mentally scanning my teacher's desk. What did I have?

Maybe my stapler; it was heavy and gunmetal gray. *I bet I could hurl that sucker twenty feet and find my target.* I'd have only one shot. Was it worth it? I'd probably never find the stapler again, and Principal Ken would refuse to buy another one for me.

"You threw your stapler at your house?"

"Yes, but it saved my life!"

The school door was locked, forcing me to abandon Operation Stapler Projectile. The only option that remained was Laura's idea to aim my feet in the direction of home and run like hell. So that's what I did.

Two seconds into the void, the ground disappeared, and I pitched forward, landing hard on my stomach. Thankfully, my periscope hood cushioned what could have been a nasty blow to my face. Stunned by the sudden change in physical orientation, I lay on the cold, hard ground for a moment.

Well, isn't this *interesting.*

The snow under my body told me I was on the ground, but I was so turned aorund that I had the fleeting sensation of standing up. I patted the snow. Yup, still on the ground—an uncomfortable and precarious position if a student of mine chose this moment to take a joy ride. I pictured a front-page headline in the *Northern Lights News*: "Teacher Tragically Flattened by Sno-go Only Feet From Home."

Laura Ingalls spoke again. *You can handle getting on your knees, right?*

I pushed up to all fours.

Excellent! Now, crawl, dammit!

Crawling on my hands and knees while trying to look forward was virtually impossible. I was afraid to look up. The snow was more ice. Like steel pellets. One zing into an eyeball would blind me for life. But there was no way around it. I chanced a look. I couldn't see anything that made sense. No structures of any kind.

Okay, just turn slowly until you see the school railing again and get back to safety. This was me talking. Laura had been benched. I turned and looked up again but couldn't make out anything. I turned again. Or at least I *think* I was turning. But the school had vanished as well. This was turning into one hell of a commute, and for the first time, I felt fear.

It never occurred to me to yell for help. The wind howled so loudly that no one would hear. I had to figure this out for myself, and fast. Icy air found its way up my pant legs, and I could no longer feel my hands.

Fearing I might fall again if I stood up, I rotated on my hands and knees like a slow-moving bull in a rodeo, crawling slowly and reaching out, gently waving to see if I could find the wooden post of the school steps. Sooner than expected, I found it. *Whack*!

"Ow! Fuck!" I pulled myself up.

Now what?

The whipping wind paused, and I caught a glimpse of my house. No wonder I hadn't been able to see it. Snow and ice cloaked its sides, rendering it nearly indistinguishable from the rest of the landscape. Then I saw the short trail of my failed crossing attempt. The wind had whipped the snow around the base of the school steps into a three-foot-high curved embankment, like a bobsled course. I had fallen right over it and into the gully on the other side. Strange circular impressions remained, just a few feet away, where I'd rotated on my hands and knees, trying to get my bearings.

Maybe I can run for it now. Precious seconds ticked by as I considered this option, afraid to let go. A gust of wind blew me back into the railing. Nah. Better not take the chance of running into the house and knocking myself out. My only option was to drop and crawl again.

So that's what I did.

Like a crab running from a seagull, I scurried over the berm, crossed the street, and slapped my hand on the side of the house as if playing a game of tag. And just like Laura suggested, I groped my way to the door. My fingers were so cold that I couldn't feel the knob. Fortunately, the door wasn't completely latched, allowing me to shove it open with my shoulder. Its hinges emitted a loud squeak.

The boot room was like paradise. I cupped my hands to warm them, unzipped my periscope hood, and exhaled for the first time in twenty minutes.

Anne sat in her usual spot, playing solitaire.

"Ah, there you are," she said, eyes focused intently on the cards. "I left some soup on the stove. Tomato. Needs reheating."

She smacked down a card and looked up.

"Some storm, huh?"

FORTY-FOUR

FROZEN IN TIME

Anne's tomato soup tasted like metal and failed to warm me. I woke the next morning, still fully clothed in my parka and boots. Outside my bedroom window, I made out a black sky and a few stars. One twinkled unusually bright.

"I'll name you Endurance," I said quietly. "Or maybe One-Who-Crawled-Home-And-Lived-To-Tell-About-It."

Stars meant the storm had blown through. I glanced at the clock. *Uh-oh.* The little hands told me I'd slept in. School started in thirty minutes, and I hadn't made those copies. *Crap.*

I grunted my way out of my sleeping bag and rummaged around for clean clothes. Anne was in the kitchen, already washing out her mug.

"Morning." I yawned.

"That it is."

Outside the kitchen window the sky was completely clear. My Laura Ingalls Wilder ordeal from the night before felt like a dream. Anne set her cup in the sink and announced that it was "Constitution Time" and she'd see me later. She always called her morning bowel movements her "constitution," which was a curious and, I suppose, respectful way of describing something I didn't want to know about. It was my signal to grab some food and leave.

I threw my parka back on and shoved a banana in my coat pocket. There'd be coffee at school and maybe cookies. Teachers were always bringing in snacks to share. I turned the knob to enter the boot room, but the door banged into something hard near its bottom. I pushed again. *Thud.*

I peeked through the crack. *Oh my god. A snowdrift.*

The outer door was closed, but the gap at the threshold, which I had neglected to fix since first arriving, was big enough that snow had blown through and created a snowdrift across the boot room floor. It was about a foot high and hard as rock.

The back of the front door glistened white.

Oh my god. That's ice.

The entire door was iced shut. We were locked in our own house. I was going to be massively late to school, and we didn't even have a phone to call for help.

Before dealing with the outer door, we'd have to chip away the snow drift. My mind raced. Did we have anything in the house that was long and pointy? A fireplace poker? A screwdriver? I rummaged through the kitchen drawers.

Maybe a butter knife.

I got down on my hands and knees, pushed against the door with my shoulder, and angled the knife through the narrow opening. Progress was slow. It took five minutes to carve a small chunk and flip it away.

This was going to take a while.

By the time Anne's constitution was over, I had chipped away enough snow to squeeze into the boot room.

Anne's voice sounded behind me. "What the hell." I turned and looked up, wiping a bead of sweat from my nose.

"Yeah," I said. "Any ideas?"

We'd have to get the front door open soon, not only to get to school, but to remove the snow on the floor before it melted. There was enough to create our own miniature lagoon.

"Ice ax?" Anne snorted.

I laughed. "That wasn't on the list."

"Hair dryer?"

My roommate had lived "in the bush" for many years. She knew it was a waste of space to pack appliances. They'd break or the power would go out. But I was unaware of that fact and, even though it wasn't on the list, I packed a travel-size Conair 1600-watt hair dryer with a folding handle. It had four settings: On/Off and High/Low.

I went to my bedroom and dug it out. I had used it only once, but now, it would make up tenfold for my initial naivety. Anne grabbed a couple of old towels for mopping up, and we began Operation Door Thaw.

We worked as a team, me with the dryer and Anne stabbing with the butter knife, and chatting about how the heck this had all happened. We surmised that snow had blown under the door and melted in the warmth of the boot room, then turned to ice. Subsequent snow dustings blew on top of that and melted, and the cycle repeated, creating one heckuva sturdy snow berm. All residual moisture had attached to every surface, freezing one layer at a time until a seemingly impenetrable sheath of ice covered the back of the door. The villagers probably had a term for this situation.

I angled the hairdryer to avoid burning Anne's fingers, and she tried not to stab me with the butter knife. In short order, we transformed from the Odd Couple to the A-Team. But then a new problem presented itself: the inside door kept swinging shut. Hardly anything in the portable was plumb. Doors swung open or closed of their own accord. Bedroom doors, kitchen cabinets, it didn't matter. The house had settled in such a way that everything was askew.

The door into the boot room always swung shut—which was a good thing, except now. We needed something heavy to hold it open so warm air from the ceiling vents could find its way to us.

Anne stopped chipping and looked at me. "How 'bout that loaf of bread you baked?"

I had not been this close to her face before. It was kinder and gentler without a cigarette hanging out of her mouth.

"It's perfect," she continued, unapologetically. "You don't plan to eat it, do you?"

Anne was right. The weekend before, she'd decided to bake bread, and I wanted to try it too. But I was too aggressive with the yeast, so my loaf was half the height of Anne's and had the look and feel of a thick boot sole, not unlike the ones I wore on a daily basis. Disappointed but reluctant to throw the loaf away, I'd set it on top of the refrigerator and forgotten about it.

"Well, that'd work, I guess." I shrugged, slightly miffed by Anne's critique yet vindicated because my petrified bread loaf was the perfect solution to our current predicament. Anne's loaf might have been crunchy on the outside and soft on the inside (meaning perfect), but *my* loaf was going to save our lives.

Anne placed the loaf on the floor to prop the door open, and we started again. A few minutes later, my hair dryer overheated and clicked off. Anne lowered her knife. "Cuppa tea?"

While we waited for the hair dryer to cool, Anne and I sipped black tea with milk and honey, standing on either side of the rubber chicken and looking out the kitchen window. The sky was a brilliant blue. The little thermometer my brother had mailed to me months ago was completely encased in ice and unreadable. But it really didn't matter. We hardly looked at it anymore, knowing that it was cold, colder, or frickin' cold. I glanced at the clock on the kitchen wall. It was well past nine o'clock, yet no one had come to check on us. The door of the portable across the alley, where Bruce lived, was also closed. It didn't look like he was even trying to escape his abode.

I wondered if the snow berm that had tripped me the night before was still around the stairs of the school. Maybe it had grown even longer. It would be fun to recount my story of almost dying in a whiteout within arm's reach (almost) of home. But I decided to save it for another time. Maybe if we went on another weekend bar-hop in Nome.

It took three hair-dryer burnouts, a second cup of tea, and one round of Pilot Bread with peanut butter and honey before we were able to pry the door open. Our flushed faces were greeted by crisp, cold air. A foot-high snowdrift had built up against the front door. Even with the door pulled away, the snow stood firmly upright. With no shovel, we used our boots to kick, push, and stomp it away. We used the broom and towel for final clean up, and set the petrified loaf back on top of the fridge, just in case we needed it again in the future.

I changed out of my sweaty shirt and shoved my warmest pair of gloves into my parka pockets. Anne grabbed her coat and hat, and we went our separate ways to school.

Last night's snow mound had grown larger and was as hard as concrete. I entered the icy cold hallway, my breath perceptible only because of the green exit sign glowing at the end. Was the electricity out? And the heat?

A faint light came from the main office. I found Midge at her desk, sorting papers by the dim light of a camping lantern.

"G'morning! Some storm, heh? Principal says to tell teachers, 'No school today.'"

FORTY-FIVE

WORDS ON THE WIND

I stared at Midge, trying to process the one-hundred eighty degree turn in my day. No school? In a matter of minutes, I'd gone from iced in to free as a bird.

The only issue now was what to do with that freedom. Anne would be returning home soon, which meant spending the day in my bedroom or my classroom. Neither option sounded appealing. My bedroom was boring, and my classroom was freezing.

I headed up the street, not sure where I was going, just needing to go somewhere. After stomping over multiple snow drifts, I found myself at the crest of the bluff, contemplating a walk. I'd have to make it a short one. The weather could turn ferocious at any time.

I studied the sky. A high ceiling of clouds covered the entire expanse. Only a faint breeze blew snow crystals across the tops of my boots. There wouldn't be any gale force winds, at least for a while. At this time of year, storms came from the northwest, so if I went south and along the bluff, I'd be able to spot sudden changes in the weather and get back home to safety.

It was slow going, but I found a somewhat manageable path at the edge of the bluff where the wind had exposed tufts of grass. They were frozen and crunched underfoot. It was quiet, save for my breathing. This was turning into quite the workout.

It still shocked me to be in a place with no sounds. No motors, no jets overhead. The silence punctuated my aloneness, and I could feel the heaviness of depression lurking nearby. In moments like this, I'd found that I could improve my mood if I paused and picked three things to appreciate about the scenery.

It didn't take long.

The shoreline stretched forever, encased in slabs of gray-white ice that had pushed ashore and frozen again, stacking against each other at odd angles. The sun was shining just enough to make the top layers of fresh snow sparkle. And I was walking among dead but golden blades of grass.

That was all I needed.

Ten minutes later, the snowdrifts took over my path, preventing me from going farther. Where did all this snow come from? How far had it blown to get here? And this relentless wind—calm, insistent, or ferocious—what had it blown over and around before finally reaching me, standing here? Had it caressed the coarse hairs of a polar bear or lifted the wings of a raven?

I scanned the horizon. If there was a polar bear out there, would I see it?

Maybe this was stupid.

I slowly took in my surroundings. In moments like this, with few cues to gauge distance or orientation, a certain weightlessness entered my consciousness. It erased the sense of separateness between my body and the snow, between the blood flowing inside of me and the wind. The sense of here and not here. Grounded and groundless. I stomped my feet and flapped my arms to shake off the freaky feeling.

The snow looked so soft. I was so tired. What if I just tipped over in it? How long would it take for the wind to cover me with snow? If my boot prints were erased, could I even know I was here? If a young, blond teacher falls on the tundra, does she make a sound?

"Hallooooooooo!" I yelled loudly at the sky, then stood still and listened.

Nothing echoed back, so I turned back toward town.

Along the way, I remembered a letter I had written to Mia that I had not yet mailed. We corresponded less frequently now, both running out of interesting things to share during this time of year, when life was on autopilot. The letter sat on my dresser. I couldn't even remember what I'd written. Might as well send it anyway. Something to do.

By the time I reached home and retraced my steps toward the post office, the wind had picked up, busy once more rearranging the drifts in the street. My boot prints were long gone.

As usual, a couple of villagers clustered in the small space, catching up on the day's news, and inquiring about conditions on the ice.

"Hello, Teacher! How you today?"

It was Melvin Olanna.

"Some storm, huh?" He looked at my boots. "Been walkin'? You stay warm?"

"More or less."

The men resumed their conversation in English. Apparently, it had been wild weather for them, too, measuring minus-thirty degrees Fahrenheit, and winds gusting up to fifty miles an hour.

Melvin turned back to me. "You takin' good care of them kids in school?"

I was unsure how much to divulge. Ron beckoned me to the counter, saving me from my indecision about what to say.

"Might be a few days before this gets out." Ron pressed down a stamp and tossed my letter in the bag.

Just as I turned to leave, Melvin addressed me. "Y'know why Eskimos don't use lots of words when they talk?"

The creases around his eyes deepened. I recognized that he was delivering the first line in a joke. I shrugged, playing along. He continued.

"Well, the wind blows hard and fast, right?"

I nodded.

"Well, us Eskimos believe that words get picked up by the wind and then—*phhhttt*!" He flicked his hands. "They're gone! Who knows where they end up? So you have to be very, very careful what you say. Someone, somewhere, will hear them."

The other men nodded in agreement. All poker-faced. Mr. Olanna continued. "And you know the other reason we don't use lots of words?"

I shook my head. *Here it comes.*

"Cuz it's fuckin' *cold* out there!"

The men's laughter filled the room and followed me out the door. I picked up my pace on the icy street and didn't say one word all the way home.

FORTY-SIX

LOST THEN FOUND

The next morning before the kids arrived, Midge made the rounds. Principal Ken wanted everyone to meet in the library.

It was the first time I'd seen the entire staff, grades kindergarten through twelfth, assembled in the same space. We were a motley crew, dressed in an assortment of winter gear, alternating yawns with sips of coffee and speaking in hushed tones about why Principal Ken had called us together.

"Mornin' everyone," Principal Ken said as he entered the room. "Jes' got word there's four people gone missin' on their sno-gos b'tween here and Wales. Couple young fellas and two elders. They took off yesterday right after the storm but never arrived."

"Whoa," Duncan said. "That's like seventy miles."

Principal Ken nodded.

"They're usin' the gym to pull together a search party. Whole town'll be here shortly. No school today."

We stared at our leader and then at each other. Most people's faces registered concern about the situation, and a few of the guys asked what they could do to help. My own response danced along a continuum of worry for the missing people to relief that school had been canceled again. A twinge of guilt quickly followed. Here I was, happy that my role as Chief Classroom Management Officer had been postponed while people were stranded somewhere on that expansive and unforgiving landscape, possibly freezing to death.

Our instructions were to work in our rooms We'd get notified when to come to the gym—not to do anything, necessarily, other than to show solidarity.

"One more thing," Principal Ken said. "We don't know how long this'll last. Everyone knows everyone here. Like family, y'know? So be ready for anything."

Some teachers stayed in the library, chatting quietly about the situation. I decided to go to my classroom and stay busy. I could not imagine how cold it must be out there, with no protection from the relentless wind, at the mercy of whatever kind of weather the sea brought in. The people traveling to Wales must have known it would be a long and dangerous ride. They could run into all kinds of trouble. But they'd be prepared, right? Maybe build an igloo? I had seen some half-igloos on the lagoon, right after it iced over, and people ventured out to ice fish. Maybe the lost party had constructed a similar windbreak and were huddled behind it.

Even so, they'd be constantly exposed to weather coming off the ocean as they traveled down the coast. I couldn't imagine driving a car in those conditions, much less flying across the snow and ice on a snow machine. The seats were padded, but you had to hold on tight and use a lot of leg muscle to brace yourself over the uneven surfaces. It was a hard ride. These people were strong.

Half an hour later, Lance poked his head in my door.

"Looks like they're about to start."

I followed him, zigzagging between people to the top rows of bleachers for a seat. People spoke in hushed tones or sat silently, watching a group of men who'd assembled at center court, discussing options. Their faces registered a mix of concern and determination. Several minutes passed, and then one elderly man raised his hand for quiet and called some names. One by one, five men stepped forward and joined him, standing in a line and facing the audience. This was the search party. They looked ready to jump on their own sno-gos and head into the white unknown. None of them smiled. Leaving the island meant crossing unpredictable ice and negotiating their way over drifting snow and gullies, with no tracks to follow.

The day dragged on, then another night. Everyone in the village held a collective breath. It was hard to wait and harder not knowing what had happened. I felt aimless and numb without the routine of school.

The next morning, an answer came. Anne called my name from the entry.

"They found 'em!" she said excitedly, stomping snow off her boots. "Would you believe that? Way out there, in the middle of nowhere, they found 'em."

A knock sounded on the front door behind her. It was Lance.

"Did you hear?" He was out of breath. "Can't believe it! Two nights out there on the ice. We've been asked to come to school again. Library. Fifteen minutes. Gotta let others know."

He clomped down the porch steps and jogged past our kitchen window, his breath leaving a trail of puffs in the cold air. This was our Arctic telephone system.

The meeting in the library was short. Principal Ken announced that school would resume tomorrow, with a welcome back potluck scheduled in the gym in the afternoon. We shouldn't expect to get much done. Students would likely take advantage of potluck preparations and stay home. Our marching orders were to keep lessons short and simple.

Only half the students showed up. I tried to get a little work out of them but mostly allowed the students to chat with each other. It seemed more important for them to simply be in each other's company.

That afternoon, I found myself in a long line of villagers, holding a plate and bowl. This was a bring-your-own-dishes-and-cutlery kind of potluck. The gym was hot and stuffy, with hundreds of bodies and the aroma of unfamiliar stew. I contemplated going back home to change into lighter clothes but didn't want to lose my place. I also didn't want people to misunderstand my departure and consider me rude.

There was no telling what was in the large pot ahead. People who had already been served sat at the school's lunch tables, hunkered close, alternating between piercing large chunks of meat with their hunting knives, eating right off the blade, and drinking the broth straight from their bowls. Not a spoon in sight.

I glanced around the room, feeling nervous. Steak knife wasn't on the list of items to pack for Shishmaref, and I hadn't thought to bring my Swiss Army knife today. All I had was a butter knife, which was hardly fair game for a hunk of, well … game. And then there was my constant predicament of being a vegetarian in a meat-eating culture. How was I going to get out of eating whatever that meat was, without offending anyone?

I looked down the line and around the room for etiquette clues. How were people holding their bowls to be served? Did they say anything to the server or just nod? Did they wait for others at their table before starting to eat?

People in Shishmaref were relaxed around food protocols. They didn't make a fuss about which fork to use. Nonetheless, I wanted to make a good impression. I had never been to a potluck with mystery food and three hundred people. You never knew if someone was watching. But my fears were unfounded. Everyone's attention was on the search party and the people who'd been rescued. They were seated at the same table, laughing and enjoying their meal.

My teaching mates were scattered around the room. I tried to catch someone's eye to save me a seat. But Lance and Tim were squished together against a wall and Principal Ken sat at a table that was too full for another person to join. I couldn't find Carrie in the crowd, nor Ben and Angela. Anne was behind me. I'd be finished before she even got her turn at the pot. Maybe I would just get a small amount of food and eat standing up, then slip out.

Once at the pot, I watched, borderline horrified as the server dumped a fist-sized piece of brown meat into my bowl, followed by one ladle of broth and what looked like onion. A small piece of carrot plopped in after it.

I had no way out of this. Not only would I have to submit to being a carnivore for the next half an hour, I had to figure out how to manage that with only a butter knife. The meat looked tough, like it had come from a mean-as-britches four-legged beast. I followed the queue to the end of the table and saw a basket of sliced bread. *Thank god.* I took two slices.

I saw a flash of a hand and recognized Duncan beckoning me from across the room. Months ago, I tried my best to avoid him. Now, I could have (almost) kissed him. It was a tight spot, and I could feel the entire length of Duncan's thigh pressed against mine. He had a large Rambo-looking knife in one hand and held his bowl in the other.

"What is this?" I whispered in his ear.

"Nanuq."

I stared at him to make sure he wasn't joking, then looked more closely at my bowl. The chunk of meat sat at the bottom, like an iceberg in shallow water. There were veins of fat running through it. The smell was strong. Meaty.

"Oh, god, you're vegetarian, aren't you?" Duncan chuckled, sympathetic but amused. Droplets of soup glistened on his beard.

"This is polar bear?"

"No, I'm kidding." He stabbed his piece of meat and continued while chewing. "It's reindeer. I think."

He swallowed and looked at my bowl. "Here, I'll trade you."

Before I could answer, he flicked a teaspoon-sized remnant of meat from his bowl into mine and deftly skewered the large chunk from my bowl back to his.

"Just try that small bite there," he said. "You've come this far." He used his knife to coax the meat through his broth. "They cook this meat to smithereens. It's tough, but it's amazing. Salt and pepper help. Have some of the broth first. Dip your bread in it."

I was grateful for Duncan's coaching but growing queasier by the minute with the heat in the room and the thought of reindeer in my mouth, still hoping Duncan wasn't teasing me and I really was eating Nanuq. Images of the enormous polar bear skins flashed in my mind, along with the trail of blood from the man's sled. I took a bite of brown bread and then dipped it into the broth, which was now cold. I pulled my soup spoon from my pants pocket to scoop out more.

"Just drink it from the bowl." Duncan leaned into my shoulder. "You can wash everything down in one gulp." He tipped his bowl to show me. I raised the bowl to my lips and forced myself not to look at the meat as it slid toward my mouth. It was too big to swallow whole. To prevent myself from choking on it, I'd have to chew a little. The last thing I wanted was for Duncan to have to perform the Heimlich maneuver in front of the whole village. My teeth clamped down on the meat. It was tough all right. I scooped up the piece of potato, added that to the mush in my mouth, and swallowed hard.

"See? That wasn't so bad." Duncan winked. "Wait'll you taste Eskimo ice cream."

The room grew quiet. I looked around and laid eyes on a man who stood next to the table with the people who'd been lost, then found. His arms stretched high in a gesture to get everyone's attention. He spoke in his native language, looking back at the people at the table and then around the room. Duncan leaned in and whispered in my ear.

"I can't translate, but I heard an unexpected whiteout blew in from the coast. They got off track and ran out of gas. Ended up digging a trench in the snow and pulling a tarp over their heads to wait it out. Two cold nights, but they survived."

As I listened to Duncan's recounting of the lost party, heads around the room nodded as they listened to the same story in their own language. Hundreds of "ahhs" and "hmm-mms" reverberated in the huge room, under the mural of the polar bears playing with the moon. I wondered how many polar bears, or reindeer for that matter, it took to feed a village.

The room suddenly erupted in laughter. Duncan and I laughed along, not quite understanding. A woman sitting next to me leaned in and translated, "He said next time they'll take dogs. Dogs don't run out of gas!"

Duncan and I found this hysterically funny and had a hard time stopping our giggling. Our response seemed a mix of comic relief and also a release of the stress that had been building with schoolwork and the long winter, and the tension of the past two days and nights.

Duncan, still giggling, stood up and removed his glasses to wipe his eyes dry.

"Wanna go for gold?" He tapped my shoulder. "Let's get some of that ice cream."

I followed him to a table where a small group of women stood around some large metal bowls, scooping what looked like vanilla ice cream. My favorite ice cream was from Dairy Queen—a twist of soft vanilla and chocolate on a sugar cone. But at this moment I didn't care what flavor was being served. Anything to chase away the remnants of salty stew.

Anne appeared and cut in front of me. "Just ask for a little," she advised. "It's reindeer fat with a little sugar and berries." I stared at her. She shrugged. "Jus' sayin'."

Duncan tried to look innocent, but his ploy to make me try something even more challenging than reindeer stew had been exposed. I gave him a playful slap on the arm.

Anne stepped up and indicated to the server that she wanted just a spoonful of the substance, and I would have the same.

The locals enjoyed watching Outsiders squirm when offered a piece of dried meat dipped in seal oil or something they didn't recognize coming out of a canning jar. Just like the women on the beach during whale day, they were greatly entertained by watching an unsuspecting village newbie try a bit of muktuk and then try not to throw it up. It was all done in a good-natured way. They didn't expect someone like me to swallow, and say, "Yum!"

"Did you say reindeer fat?" I looked into my bowl and back at Anne.

"Yup." She poked at hers. "Just aim for the berries. Those are local."

Duncan had disappeared, so I followed Anne to her table and geared myself up for this next sampling of cuisine, collecting a few reddish berries onto my spoon and trying to minimize the slick white substance that held them together. It looked like frosting with a layer of vegetable oil that hadn't quite mixed in.

Anne watched my expression. "It's an acquired taste. The original version had seal oil in it, the perfect snack when you're out hunting for hours."

My stomach gurgled strangely, and I felt nauseous. Anne agreed to retrieve my soup bowl, so I excused myself and headed for the door. Along the way, I surreptitiously placed the remains of my Eskimo ice cream in a trash can and asked forgiveness from the Great Nanuq and the Reindeer Gods.

The Arctic air never felt so good.

FORTY-SEVEN

WAX AND WANE

February finally rolled in. The moon had just finished its waning phase, when it gradually disappeared from the night sky, one sliver at a time. Now it was waxing, each night growing visible in equal increments once again.

As if on cosmic cue, Principal Ken's familiar shadow appeared in my classroom door. I could feel him standing there surveying the scene. Paper snowflakes were still taped on the windows and walls. Sophie had taken her Shishmaref Star home, but I was reluctant to remove the miniature fake Christmas tree with its paper seals and angels. Spring felt impossibly far away. I was halfway through erasing the day's lesson on the handy hyphen when Principal Ken's voice confirmed his presence.

"You know anything about cross-country skiing?"

His question dumbfounded me. Sure, I'd cross-country skied before.

They did that here? In Shishmaref?

"Looks like you're the cross-country ski coach." He ignored my silence and held out a flyer. "There's a meet in Elim in March. Junior High. You should pull together a team."

It came back to me that I'd been asked about cross-country skiing during my interview. One more box for the committee to check in their search for a teacher with a wide variety of seemingly unrelated skills and mental fortitude. Their question about cross-country skiing was one that I was able to answer with a high degree of confidence. Yes! I was an avid cross-country skier! I even won first place in a competition from the top of Vail Pass to Red Cliff, a distance of about twelve miles. I'd left out the detail that only three people signed up in my age group, but it was a win just the same.

I took the flyer from Principal Ken, my eyes searching for dates.

"When did you say the meet was? And where is, um ..."

"Elim." He stroked his mustache. And winked. "South uh here."

"Yeah, just about everything's south of here," I joked back.

"I think it's on the coast," he continued, "east of Nome. Ya might get in some Iditarod action." He gestured toward the windows in my room. "Container out back has skis and stuff. Ask Midge for help with recruitment. She can get Rob or another teacher to identify some kids. And she'll handle permission slips and plane tickets." He suddenly smirked. "Lodging's included. Prob'ly means a classroom floor or somebody's couch. Take yer sleeping bag. And earplugs." Principal Ken patted my shoulder and left.

I studied the flyer: "Bering Strait School District Ski/Biathlon Championships. March 21 to 23." Four weeks away.

A strong gust of wind slammed into the building, accompanied by the clicking sound of snow and ice pellets. *This ought to be fun.*

When anyone in the Lower 48 asked me about the weather, I simply answered, "Unpredictable." That unpredictability was going to be matched by not knowing the kids who might sign up, and them not knowing me. Though maybe no one would sign up at all. Word had likely traveled through the entire middle school to avoid that blond teacher who failed to pull together a viable team for solving future problems. But maybe I could change that narrative. This time, I knew my content. I knew how to ski. Maybe the Bering Strait School District Ski/Biathlon Championship would be my redemption.

That said, snow on the ground this late in the winter season had turned to ice and rock-hard drifts, conditions that made learning how to slide consistently forward on skinny skis rather … unpredictable. The sun was the same—elusive and, even at its apex, not close enough to the earth to share its heat. What little warmth penetrated the atmosphere was quickly whisked away on the wind.

Who was I kidding? The idea of teaching cross-country skiing seemed ridiculous. My experiences with the sport were many, but I had never been faced with these kinds of conditions. In Vail, a high tax base paid for manicured trails on the golf course that allowed skiers to slide easily for hours and finish their workout with a cup of hot chocolate at the clubhouse.

In Shishmaref, we had only exposed and windswept terrain. No trails, no clubhouse.

Still, it was worth a try, right? And no matter how the kids did, a short trip to Elim might boost my spirits, especially if there was, as Principal Ken suggested, some Iditarod action. It would be so cool to see the mushers and their dogs. I wondered how far Elim was from the Iditarod's Burled Arch finish line in Nome.

Over the next few days, Midge managed to recruit five middle school students, including the principal's son, Mikey, who'd likely been volunteered. Our training window was only three weeks. *Maybe I needn't worry. Maybe the kids already know how to ski?*

At the end of the school day, a young face peered around the doorframe and into my classroom. Another appeared over her shoulder. Like most everything I had experienced as a new teacher, I wasn't ready. The metaphorical football was waiting for me to kick it, but I was scared of running forward. Sometimes I hated that the next move was up to me.

"Hi!" I greeted the two girls with forced enthusiasm. "Are you here for the cross-country ski team?"

They nodded.

"Super. Have a seat. Do you know anyone else who's coming?"

Scrunch.

A moment later, three more kids entered, jostling each other playfully. Their goofiness was for show—a likely release of nervousness, intimidated by the high school part of the building and a white teacher they didn't know. The group plopped into desks and waited expectantly.

"You got snacks?" one of the girls asked. *Darn. Of course. Snacks.* They had not yet hit the age when eating a snack was "uncool." My high schoolers never asked for snacks.

I rummaged around in my lower desk drawer. *Nope. Nada. Nothing.*

"Hang on, I'll be right back." I ran to the office and returned with the keys to the storage trailer out back, along with Sour Patch candies and plain M&Ms from Midge's secret stash.

"Before we go outside for equipment, let's do some introductions. Just tell me your name and if you've skied before." I glanced from one kid to the next, waiting for them to pause from poking through the candy and comparing colors.

"I'll start." I stood and walked to the middle of the room, hoping that taking my Command Spot would get their attention. "I'm Miss Pierce. Or you can call me 'Coach.' I learned how to ski when I was twelve years old, like you. In Colorado …"

I stopped talking, realizing that my story was falling on deaf ears. Except for Mikey, the rest probably didn't know where Colorado was, and they didn't care a lick about my experiences when I was their age.

"How about you start." I gestured to the young girl sitting closest to me.

"Ugh!" She rolled her eyes and slumped down. "Why am I always firrrrst?"

"It's cuz you looked at her." Mikey tossed an M&M in the air and caught it in his mouth.

I wasn't used to being spoken about in the third person, but he had a point. I tended to call on anyone looking at me. Was that why my own students had stopped making eye contact?

The girl gave in. "Lucy. Never skied."

"Okay. Why don't you tag someone to go next?" Kids loved playing tag.

"I tag you!" She punched Mikey's arm.

And so it went with my new recruits, punching each other one by one. Lucy, Mikey, Grace, Missy, and Edwin. No one knew how to ski. Kids in the village were active, though. They could run, drive snow machines, and play basketball. If they could walk, I could teach them to cross-country ski. I glanced out the windows. The sky was steel gray, and it would soon be dark. The temperature was below freezing, but we could at least check out the equipment.

I started putting on my parka and looked back at the group. No one had a hat. No gloves either. It was frickin' freezing outside.

"Do you guys have a hat?"

Scrunch.

"Gloves?"

Scrunch.

Their responses precipitated my first lecture as ski coach.

"You have to bring a warm hat and gloves, okay? The kind with fingers in them." I slipped on a glove and wiggled my fingers. "Mittens make it hard to hold onto your poles." I paused. They looked at me with blank expressions. "Got it? Gloves and a warm hat."

Still no confirmation.

I adopted a drill sergeant voice. "Say it back to me."

"Gloves! Warm hat!" Mikey jumped up and saluted, and the rest followed. The Sour Patches and M&Ms were kicking in.

We left the school and trudged over to the shipping container Principal Ken had pointed out earlier. It stood ten feet high and six feet across. There was hoarfrost on the padlock, but I managed to insert the key and jiggle it around until the mechanism popped open. I cleared the frost away and slid the metal bar. The kids were quiet, huddled and shivering in a clump behind me.

I pressed my gloved fingers into a gap to pry the door open, but the hinges were frozen and a small, hard drift of snow blocked the door.

"Help me stomp this snow out of the way."

The kids sprang into action, stomping on the drift and then trying to stomp on each other's feet for fun.

"Ow!" Missy jumped back.

"Sorry," said Mikey. His ears were bright pink. We needed to hurry.

In a few minutes, they had stomped and kicked away enough of the drift for me to get a workable angle on the door. I pulled hard, and it finally creaked open wide enough for me to slip inside. It was pitch black. I could barely see my hand in front of my face. I hadn't thought to bring a flashlight.

"Stand back," I said. "I'm going to push the door open from inside." They moved away, and I shoved a few times until the hinges finally gave way. The kids pushed forward to peer in.

"Ooooh. It's dark in here."

"Yep. But your eyes will adjust." I tried to sound hopeful, but my breath froze in midair, making it hard to see. The container felt empty. I blinked a few times and dabbed frosted tears from my eyes. It was frickin' cold in there, even colder than outside. The temperature had to be in the minus teens.

"Wait, I see something in the back."

I took a few Shishmaref Shuffles, not wanting to slip or stumble over something unexpected. With my luck, it'd be a reindeer leg. Placing one hand on the side of the container to steady myself, I finally reached a pile of slender sticks in one corner. I reached down and tugged. It was a cross country ski. No binding for clipping a shoe. It was coated in a thick layer of hoarfrost. So was the ski pole I reached for next. *Everything* was covered in hoarfrost. If we stayed in here much longer, we would be covered in it, too.

My eyes adjusted to the darkness, and I was able to make out a pile of wooden skis, a heap of shoes, and a tangle of bamboo poles. In short, a frozen jumble of equipment. My teeth started to chatter.

"Okay, help me get this stuff out of here."

"Cool!" Mikey yelled. He pulled two poles from the pile. "We can play swords!"

"Wait!" I yelled back. "Those'll break in half if you do that. They're like icicles." I coaxed a few more poles from under the pile. "How 'bout we form a line to the door, okay?"

My lips were so chilled, I was having a hard time forming words. *Mr. Olanna wasn't kidding about the "fucking cold."*

My recruits worked fast, and within minutes, they'd neatly lined up the gear on the snow as if preparing for a garage sale. All of it looked banged up or broken, not nearly as nice as my fiberglass skis back home in Colorado. Why didn't the hiring committee tell me I'd be doing this, and that I should bring my own set of ski equipment?

I quickly handed one set to each team member, stacking it in their arms like firewood, and told them to hurry back to school. "Warm up and wait for me!" Then I tossed all the errant pieces back into the container, revising my earlier judgment of the previous coach who had done the same. Maybe when things warmed up, I'd come back to complete a more thorough inventory and make a bonfire with the rest. I used all my body weight to shove the container door mostly closed but didn't bother with the lock. What was there to steal?

The kids had assembled in the middle of the hallway and had already put on the icy cold, hoar frosted shoes and were trying to clip into the bindings. Edwin had succeeded and was lurching around on the carpet.

"Wow," I exclaimed, trying to hide my amusement. "Good for you! But let's check your bindings to make sure they're secure. These skis have been in that trailer for a long time."

I checked their bindings, one by one, while the others played a game of bunny-hopping in the hallway. I winced each time the wood skis clacked against each other or into the walls, sure they'd splinter apart. Amazingly, everything worked fine.

The kids were quick to learn. Maybe we'd enter Phase Two: performing a binding release. I showed them how to push on the binding clip and slip their shoes out. They did remarkably well.

Time for Phase Three.

"Let's have you stand next to each other, side by side," I said. "I'm going to show you the basic arm motion. Just leave your poles on the floor."

"Why are these poles so big?" Lucy held hers up.

"The long poles help push you on flat terrain. You'll see when we go outside to practice. Lots of flat ground around here."

The kids lined up in the hallway, laughing as their skis flailed about. They looked like puppets without strings.

"Okay, copy me!" I bent my knees slightly and, staying in one spot, swung my arms back and forth, alternating them in exaggerated motions. "Swinging your arms like this helps you move forward and get more momentum."

They followed my gestures, swinging their arms awkwardly and out of sync at first, but finally in unison. We looked like a 1970s dance troupe.

Principal Ken emerged from the main office, presumably to find out who was making such a ruckus.

"Oh, hi," I said sheepishly. "Sorry. Too cold to practice outside."

He looked at the group and shook his head, then turned back to his office without a word. But I was pretty sure I caught him smile.

The next day, I wandered to my classroom windows multiple times, trying to sense if the wind would die down and the temperature would rise enough to allow the Shishmaref Junior High Cross-Country Ski Team to get their skis on the snow. At lunch and again after my last class I poked my head outside the school's front doors. The weather wasn't cooperating. There was no impending snow, but it was bone-chilling cold.

Remarkably, all five members of my team showed up. They entered the room like a pile of puppies and plopped into the desks.

"Got snacks?"

I handed out M&Ms and Fruit Roll-Ups.

"I've been watching the weather. Unfortunately, it's too cold outside to practice." The kids groaned. "I know," I said, happy with their eagerness. "But it's hard to ski when you can't feel your hands.

And I can see that most of you didn't bring a hat and gloves." I paused. "Right?"

Scrunch.

But I had a Plan B. Many months of students forgetting to bring something to write with and something to write on told me to expect that my ski team wouldn't remember their one task to bring a hat and gloves. That morning, I checked with Ben, the wrestling coach, to ask if my group could commandeer space in the gym for dryland training.

Ben and I waved to each other as I led my group to one corner and instructed them to take off their shoes.

"We're going to practice the proper gliding technique in our socks," I announced. "But first, let's get warmed up."

Ben glanced over a few times from across the room, tilting his head with curiosity over our 70s dance moves. I shrugged, indicating that I'd explain later.

For the next several minutes, the kids followed me down one side of the gym and back, swinging their arms and sliding on their socks to mimic cross-country skiing on snow.

I chanted, "Left, right, left, right."

They did remarkably well, except for Edwin, whose socks had holes, causing his heels to stick on the polyurethane-finished flooring.

"Left, right, left, right." I brought the group back after a second round.

Missy and Grace plopped down on a vacant gym mat. "We're tired!"

In a flash, the rest of the team plopped down too. They lay there, chests rising and falling, legs and arms splayed out across each other. I couldn't blame them. I could be going too fast. My train had left the station, and they were trying to keep up.

Still, I needed to keep up the pressure. I didn't know how many miles the kids would be racing, but the competition was certainly going to be longer than twice the length of the gym. If my team got this tired after ten minutes, they wouldn't stand a chance on the course.

I stood over the group with my hands on my hips, assessing what to do next. It was Friday afternoon and hard not to plop down on the mat myself.

"Okay, that's enough for today." I pulled Lucy up. Her hand was sticky with fruit roll-up residue.

The kids grabbed their shoes and started for the door.

I stopped them. "Hey, what are you going to bring to practice on Monday?"

"Gloves and a hat!" Mikey saluted.

That weekend, I inspected the equipment more closely. Despite being tossed in a heap and neglected for who knows how long, everything was in decent condition. The skis had the usual scrapes along their upper sides and bottoms. It didn't look like they'd ever been waxed, which was good; I didn't have any solvent to remove it. Only one binding needed tightening. The poles were also fine, except for one that was cracked near the bottom and missing the wrist loop—a necessary item when a skier is poling up a hill or pushing hard on the flats. Other than falling, there was nothing more annoying than pumping along on flat terrain and feeling a pole slip from one's grasp.

The shoes were also in fairly good shape, but two had cracked toe pieces, one of the pairs was mismatched by half a size, and another one needed a shoelace. It looked like the previous wearer had replaced the original with a sneaker shoelace and had to knot broken ends together. I had done that once myself, having no time to run to the ski shop for specially designed laces that were longer and had a little stretch to them.

I'd have to venture back to the shipping container and replace those pieces of equipment before Monday. I mentally ticked off the days remaining before the meet, discounting weekends, when kids took full advantage of the open-ended days to sleep in and hang out with family and friends. They were unlikely to train on their own. I also needed wax, something I doubted Walter had on his shelves.

Before leaving school, I used the school phone to call home. My younger brother picked up, surprised to hear from me.

"Hey, Bro! I have a favor to ask," I said. "Can you ship my sticks of cross-country ski wax to me, like pronto? And the cork to rub it in?"

I needed the whole pack. Blue wax helped skis grip old, dry snow. Red wax helped with gliding on slush and ice. Violet wax, used on soft snow, was probably unnecessary.

But given what I'd learned so far on the island, we needed to be ready for anything.

FORTY-EIGHT

SMALL MOVES

Dear Mia,

Here we are in March! The weather vacillates between 20 degrees one day and minus-20 the next. My classroom was so cold today, we could see our breath. I took my morning classes to the gym, so we could warm up with a little basketball.

It's been a long winter. A lot of the kids are in a funk. The day might be going well, but then one will show up in a bad mood. The other kids get moody, and then I get moody. I swear, teaching has to be one of the hardest jobs on the planet! Teachers should get emotional hazard pay. You just never know what's going to happen when you cross over the threshold.

Lately, a few kids are showing up at school chewing tobacco. They spit the excess black juice into empty pop cans. It's so gross! I tell them to get rid of it but also don't want chewed tobacco slime in my trash can. They try to sneak around. One of the teachers said I had to pick my battles. But which ones? He added that it usually takes three years to figure them out and set down rules of engagement. I'm not sure I'll last that long.

I talked to my principal about my teaching "challenges" (he told me to stop saying "problems"). And then he said that teaching here is hard, especially for a first-year teacher. Well, DUH. He assured me that most of my issues are due to the kids' upbringing. "They're not disciplined," and I ought to "take stronger measures with the kids who do a half-assed job on purpose." Like I should kick them out of class or flunk them. "It's hard being mean," he said, "but they deserve it."

I think he was in a bad mood.

I held my tongue. Only three months to go.

That said, I had one of those teaching moments you told me about—the kind that keep teachers in this crazy profession. One lesson I've had to keep repeating is the one about the difference between commas, semicolons, and periods. I was getting punchy with my grading and started drawing Mr. Yuk faces on my students' papers whenever they made a mistake (which was a lot). It was a joke to lighten things up. But one girl, Paula, suddenly got it! She said something about those punctuation marks being like direction signs in writing. "They show how to drive through your words," she said, "like they help you not get lost."

I wanted the world to stop spinning, I wanted everything to freeze around me so I could bask in the glory of having finally caught that elusive Teaching Moment, which makes me wonder why a moment is all a teacher gets.

For now, I've distracted myself with Pac-Man. I play on my school computer. It's in black and white, and I have to use direction keys instead of a joystick, but I'm getting better at it. Yesterday, I hit 40,000 points.

Write soon …

Love, Me

P.S. Some sad news, which I'm relegating to a postscript only because I don't really want to believe it's true: I just learned that my grandma, "Nana," passed away. I can't believe she is no longer here. We spoke last Christmas and she sounded good. I was going to surprise her with a phone call. Now, it's too late. Makes me realize how precious life is. Nana was the one who told me I should be a teacher. I'm so sad that I never got to prove it, if not to myself, at least to her.

I leaned back in my chair. It had been dark for hours. I was alone once more in the building. The wind whistled lightly through a gap in the front doors. It was a sound that always unsettled me, but it was also my barometer for what was happening outside, possibly warning me about what might come. When it whispered, like now, the skies were calm. If it shrilled in intermittent bursts, I needed to go home or risk another whiteout commute.

I reread my letter to Mia, my pen hovering over the postscript. I wanted to add more, but how could I sum up in words all I was feeling? I felt numb with the news of Nana's death, yet also in anguish—on the verge of tears and afraid that if I started to cry, I wouldn't be able to stop. I pictured Nana sitting with me and offering some grace. She would say not to fuss over her passing. "It happens to everyone," she'd say. "Want some ice cream?"

My face lightened. If Nana were really sitting here next to me, I'd tell her about one of the silliest things I'd experienced so far. She'd get a kick out of it.

The incident occurred just a week before, when the thermometer nudged up to an inconceivable forty degrees. I had just finished leading my cross-country ski team around town, getting them used to turning and falling and getting up again. They were getting the hang of it, mostly coaxed along by the promise of M&Ms at the end of practice. I'd learned about John B. Watson's theory of behaviorism in college and, while initially opposed to manipulating children with positive or negative reinforcement, I discovered that it worked quite well.

As I descended the school steps for home, I realized that the pleasant temperature and light of day provided the perfect opportunity for a dump run. For weeks, Anne and I had been stockpiling trash bags and honey buckets outside our door. It was gross. Someone had to dispose of it all, and that someone was me.

Fortunately, the school's sno-go was available. I grabbed the keys from Midge's top drawer and skipped outside. The wooden sled was heavy, but I managed to heave it around, latch it on, and successfully drive to the front of our house.

So far, so good.

The next step was piling on the mound of bags and honey bucket contents set inside cardboard boxes of various sizes. I stood back to survey the results of my efforts. The sled looked like it had been packed by the Grinch who stole Christmas. I didn't have his dog, Max, or any rope, but I'd wedged everything in well enough to withstand the journey if I drove slowly.

Going to the dump was a lot of work. Maybe I could make it more tolerable. Like a joy ride with snacks. I ran back inside for a Snickers bar and my Walkman. Mia had recently mailed a new cassette of songs, including one that kids were singing on a frequent basis. "We Are the World" was breaking records in the Lower 48 and now, it seemed, in the Arctic. It was a great sing-along song with many famous artists like Lionel Richie, Michael Jackson, Tina Turner, Stevie Wonder, and Diana Ross. Out on the wide-open tundra, I could sing it as loud as I wanted without a care for where the words ended up.

I plopped onto the padded seat, turned the key, and pressed the throttle. The machine hummed to life. But then I looked ahead and realized a critical error. I was pointed in the wrong direction. With the sled attached, my Grinch Mobile stretched fifteen feet—too long to turn around in the narrow street to get on the main road out of town.

Two options presented themselves: 1) unload everything, unhook the sled and turn it around, re-hitch the sled, and pile it all up again; or 2) go forward and hope that I'd find a way to weave between houses and eventually connect to the trail I needed to be on.

My Inner Coaches came out for a brief discussion. *Unload and turn around. Better safe than sorry!*

No way. You don't want to do all that! Waste of time. You can make it.

It had been a long day, and I was tired and impatient. I looked back at my strategically packed load and sighed. It would suck to do that all over again. Repositioning boxes that had you-know-what inside made me want to throw up.

Okay, Voice Number Two. Let's hope you're right.

I squared my shoulders, pushed in the go lever, and lurched forward. *Easy does it.* I pressed the lever again and began to move slowly, surveying the narrow road ahead. *No turning back now.*

The machine and I crept between houses on a narrow snow gully. I turned one corner and then another, glancing back and hoping not to see a trail of debris.

One more corner and I should break into open territory.

But around said corner, the trail disappeared. Voice Number Two was wrong. There was no straight shot to the open range. Instead, and to my horror, I was about to run smack dab into the first of two extremely large snowdrifts. They were spaced only a few yards apart, and the gully between them was at least four feet deep.

I could have stopped and thought things through. I could have asked for help to turn things around. Literally. But for some reason my instinct was to press hard on the throttle and bust through the drifts like a monster truck in a demolition derby.

I almost made it.

The first drift was like concrete, but the weight of the snowmobile broke through the top layer, and I started to sink into the loose snow underneath, thus losing traction. I clenched my teeth and leaned forward, thumb pressed hard on the throttle and hoping to keep enough momentum to get over the next drift.

If I hadn't been hauling two hundred pounds of garbage and human waste, my panicked maneuver might have worked. But right at the crest of the second drift, the machine dropped deep and tilted backward, like a horse rearing up on its hind legs. Soft snow cascaded over the skis and running boards. I lost my grip and fell flat on my back.

The snow was slippery, like fake snow made of tiny plastic shavings. I struggled back to standing, feeling its silky coldness sliding down the back of my pants and into my boots.

Oh my god, the trash.

The sled lay on its side at the crest of the first drift. Two large bags had been released into the snow behind, and the rest—including all the honey bucket boxes—were heaped in a terrifying pile in the gully. Thankfully, the boxes held together, preventing an indescribable mess. Unless there was a leak I didn't know about yet.

There I was, standing next to a stalled-out sno-go, a two-hundred-pound sled on its side, and an explosion of objectionable trash bags. I leaned on the house next to me to catch my breath. If anyone had been at the window, they could have reached out and shaken my hand.

"Wow," they'd say. "That's quite the blowout. Sucks to be you."

I kept my gaze from the windows and tried to act natural, as if I always drove that way. Like it was perfectly normal for a person to barrel into not one but *two* huge snowdrifts with an enormous load of unsecured trash.

Three options presented themselves: 1) slink away and pretend I had nothing to do with it; 2) make a tidy pile and go find Principal Ken who would, no doubt, rescue me, but then take away my driving privileges forever; or 4) get my mess cleaned up and keep going.

Option one was out of the question. No slinking away. It didn't take a Columbo to figure out that this was the school's sno-go and that the trash outside my portable was no longer there. Besides, it was totally disgusting to leave the honey buckets, and half the boxes came from Anchorage grocery orders and had my name on them.

Option two would just delay the task. And Principal Ken might forgive me, but I'd never live down future tales of my driving ineptness.

Option three it is.

I waded through the deep snow to unhitch the sled. With no shovel (not on the list), I worked for half an hour using my boots and hands to kick and paw the soft snow from under the machine's skis. I was mad, then embarrassed, then mad again. *So much for a joy ride!* A long string of expletives escaped from my mouth.

While not my best moment, the unladylike language got my blood flowing, and I didn't stop working until I had cleared away and stomped enough snow to create the foundation I needed for getting back to solid ground.

Given my work zone was only a few feet between houses, I kept stealing glances at the windows, worried I'd see a curtain move. Had anyone seen me fall? Could they hear my potty mouth? Could I be fired for this?

Twenty minutes later, all the boxes and bags were wedged together and the Grinch Mobile was on the move again. The trail widened and merged directly into the snow road I had intended to take all along. And that was it. I was in the clear. Unless I ran into a polar bear, nothing else would prevent my lovely island cruise.

I drove slowly at first, getting my nerve up, and then opened the throttle to a comfortable speed. The sun was still above the horizon, and the wind was soft, caressing my face and gently blowing my hair. No need for the Walkman. I felt light and free and secure. The sno-go rumbled beneath me and—for the first time in a long time—I felt joy.

The drive didn't last nearly long enough. I took my time with unloading the boxes and bags, stopping several times to survey the frozen ocean and reflect on the domino effect of the one wrong move I'd made at the start of this journey—the small misstep that threw such a simple task out of alignment. It was another lesson for living here, to think things through.

As I drove back to the village, I sang "We Are the World" and sang it loud, hoping the words would indeed fly on the wind and land on someone who needed to hear them.

FORTY-NINE

THE RED LANTERN

Only two days until our ski meet in Elim. I was out once more with the students, quite pleased with their progress. They could glide with momentum and had learned how to turn, fall, and get up again. The snow was sharp and unforgiving, with intermittent patches of ice as smooth and hard as marble. Ice skates would have been more appropriate. But the kids were surprisingly resilient.

Edwin slid down a shallow bluff and turned without falling. "We're like the Musketeers!"

"Yeah!" Mikey yelled back. "The *five* Musketeers!"

I wasn't sure how Musketeers related to cross-country skiing, but the name stuck, and the kids dutifully followed me around the town, yelling, "Here come the Musketeers!"

My box with ski wax had not yet arrived. The kids did amazingly well gripping the ground, but I worried they'd wreck the bottoms of their wooden skis and worried more that they'd been practicing only on one kind of snow: old and hard. Farther south, Elim's snow might be soft and harder to navigate.

Midge laid my fears to rest when she announced the next day that a package had arrived. Ski waxing class was on. My troupe huddled around me outside in the snow.

I pointed to the middle of Edwin's ski. "You only have to wax this part. It's called the kick zone. You know, where you push off?" I pressed a stub of red wax into the ski bottom.

Lucy giggled. "It's like lipstick!"

"Yeah, lipstick on our skis!" Grace sashayed and pursed her lips.

I rubbed the wax in with cork. "Let's keep this wax on the skis and not your lips, okay?"

I handed Edwin's ski back to him. "Slide around for a minute on the icier patches. Tell us if you feel a difference. Like if it's easier or not."

Edwin skied a few dozen feet away and then back.

"Feels sticky."

"Okay. Blue wax is probably better. Normally, we scrape it off before putting on a different kind, but I'm not using much. Here, Lucy, your turn to lipstick the ski."

Lucy gingerly pressed the wax into the base of Edwin's ski. "This is hard!"

"Eww," Missy giggled, "blue lipstick!"

"You've got it." I coached Lucy, guiding her hand for the right amount of pressure.

Edwin eagerly snapped into his bindings and skied another few yards. "This is easier!"

My Musketeers couldn't wait to get blue lipstick on their skis and take them out for a spin. They were as ready as they could be, from a hatless and gloveless team to a well-organized group that could handle themselves in all kinds of conditions.

Except for ski-skating. Their initial attempts were hilarious and slightly terrifying. Skating on cross-country skis is an advanced skill. The heels of cross-country ski shoes aren't fixed, allowing for a full stretch of one's legs to push and glide, like skates on ice. But that freedom also creates countless opportunities to go sprawling on one's face, skis splayed out on either side. I constantly fretted that a Musketeer would get hurt on a ski tip. Instead of "Shishmaref Cross-Country Team Wins Elim Competition!" the front page of the *Northern Lights News* would announce a more tragic tale: "Musketeer Loses Eyeball on Ice!"

Somehow, my nimble group avoided that disaster, even though they consistently went too fast, crossed their tips, and fell. But multiple spills meant ample practice for crashing safely and getting up again. It was also highly entertaining. The kids laughed at the simplest things, especially when trying to help each other stand up. If one fell, soon all five were lying on the snow and giggling until they could hardly breathe.

"You know, chances are you'll have to get up on your own power." I extended a hand to Missy. "In a race, you'll likely ski at your own pace and might not see each other all the time." I didn't want to scare them, but I wanted them to understand that cross-country races could feel lonely. "If you fall and can't get a good angle, just take off your skis and start over."

We spent part of that session with the kids pretending to faint, so I could show them how to release their shoes and get clipped in again.

Back inside the school, Principal Ken called my name as I passed the office. His habit was to begin conversations without looking at whomever he was addressing or to divide his attention with shuffling papers. At the moment, he was opening and closing desk drawers, searching for something.

"How's things with the team?" (Open, slam. Open, slam.)

"Good!" I said. "They can glide and skate and get back up when they fall."

"Well, let's hope so." He closed the lower drawer and finally looked at me. "Sorry, I keep misplacing this one file." I waited, not sure where the conversation was headed.

"There's a wicked storm near where you're goin'. Just heard the Iditarod mushers are laid up in Shaktoolik fer a bit. Wind's kickin' up fierce, way b'low zero. It's blowin' east, though. Hopefully it'll be gone before your flight, or else no one's goin' anywhere."

There was nothing I could do about the weather. I had to keep moving forward as if we were on track to leave in two days. I returned to my classroom to tidy up and found a sheet of paper on the floor. Charlie's scribbles. I scrunched it and launched the ball clean into the trash can. A torrent of thoughts began. *What if the ski meet is cancelled? What about the kids? They'll be so disappointed! Or maybe it'll just be postponed. Meaning a fresh set of sub plans. Ugh.*

As it turned out, the storm blew through. Right on schedule, one hopeful coach and her Five Musketeers boarded a seven-seater, two-prop plane. We were finally on our way to Elim, about one hundred and fifty miles southeast and at the base of Seward Peninsula.

From the air, Elim looked smaller than Shishmaref. Houses were similar in shape and size. But instead of sitting on a sandbar, they huddled between evergreen trees at the base of low hills along the coastline of Norton Sound.

"There's about two hundred people who live here," the pilot called out as we circled for landing. "These teams almost double the population!"

I was excited to meet other teachers and see a different school but was worried about the landscape. How hilly was the racecourse? Did it go through trees? My team had practiced on flat, treeless terrain, and on nothing higher in elevation than some ten-foot bluffs. At least they knew how to get up after falling. Which might happen a lot.

A couple of race officials and a teacher helped load our gear into a pickup truck. It was too full to carry us, so the teacher, who introduced herself as Susan, offered to walk with our group to the school. She and I conversed about the weather, while the Musketeers followed close behind, like ducklings after their mother.

Susan had moved to Elim from Chicago two years ago. "Weather's about the same!" she laughed. "But it's been unusually cold this spring."

We made a lot of noise with our boots crunching on the hard snow. Frosty puffs from our breath lingered in the air. *We might be using blue wax after all.*

"You can register your group over there." She pointed to a large building with a sign over the door that read Aniguiin School. "Good luck!"

We caught up with the truck and unloaded our gear, then clomped inside. I spied a thermometer fixed to the window and scratched away the frost. Ten degrees. Cold, but not bad.

After getting our group signed in, a fellow who introduced himself as Bud announced that there'd be a short orientation in half an hour. We'd learn about the racecourse and the kids would get their bibs.

"There's snacks in the next room." He pointed. "Help yourselves, but don't eat a lot. Race starts soon." I helped myself to a cup of coffee and chatted with other teachers, stealing glances at my Musketeers making friends with skiers from other villages. After all the weeks of training—from sliding on socks in the gym to sliding down bluffs—we were finally here.

Orientation was brief, mostly about safety precautions and first aid stations. Soon, we were heading outside. While race officials helped kids don their bibs, I checked bindings and poles. Then it was time for a quick huddle.

"Okay, you've done a lot to get here." I knelt on one knee. "Remember to find your own pace. When another skier passes you, don't worry. Just follow the trail, ask for help, and glide as much as you can. There might be some small hills, so bend your knees on the way down like you did on the bluffs, okay? If you fall …"

"Get up!" Mikey and Edwin shouted in unison.

"You're not coming?" Lucy looked concerned. The team and I hadn't been out of each other's sight for three weeks.

"No, coaches aren't allowed on the course."

Lucy scrunched her face, followed by equally disappointed scrunches from Missy and Grace. Edwin and Mikey didn't look as concerned.

"You'll be fine." I tried to sound encouraging. "I'll be waiting at the finish line."

We placed our hands together to say the cheer they'd been practicing—something they hoped to yell when the race was over. We knew it was a long shot, but we yelled it anyway.

"Five, four, three, two, one! The Shish'mref Musketeers have won!"

"Okay, time to line up!" a race official called out. "Skiers will begin the race in groups. When you hear your number, come to the start line!"

He looked at his clipboard. "Thirty-two, sixteen, twenty-four ..."

"That's you!" Edwin poked Mikey. "And you!" He poked Grace.

The remaining Musketeers cheered their teammates to the starting line. I watched nervously as they joined other skiers who looked much better equipped. My team had old wooden skies and wore thin winter coats and jeans. Their competitors had sleek-looking sweats and parkas and lightweight fiberglass skis.

"Ready, set, go!" The official blew his whistle.

Mikey and Grace started with easy strides to warm up, something I had taught them from the beginning. "Take your time in the beginning to get yourself sorted out," I had said. "You can sprint later."

They soon disappeared in the trees, and the official called the next set of numbers. Thankfully, Lucy, Edwin, and Missy would be lining up together. They pushed off a bit too close, clacking their ski poles. One of Missy's ski tips crossed over Edwin's, but they managed to untangle without falling.

And that was that. My Musketeers were on their own. I hated that coaches weren't allowed on the racecourse, but it was probably a wise move. The fairest races could only happen when skiers coached themselves.

I watched the last few batches of racers begin their trek, then looked around, unsure what to do. The other adults were dispersing—mostly heading back to the school for more coffee and donuts. I wanted to explore. Maybe I could nonchalantly ski into the woods and watch the course from a distance. There might be a vantage point to catch a glimpse of my team.

With no one around to object, I snapped on my skis and ventured into the woods. The snow was deep and heavy, forcing me to walk. Snowshoes would have been easier. It was slow going, but pleasant. I was breathing in the fresh pine scent of evergreen trees. The sky felt heavy with low-lying clouds, but it didn't look like more snow was coming. I continued for a while, enjoying the quiet woods and occasional cawing of crows.

A crack broke the silence. I stopped and listened. Rifle shots? Was someone hunting nearby? That would be stupid. Dozens of kids were littered throughout the forest. Then it came again. *Rat-a-tat-tat*. Then one more. *Bang*! Geez! I instinctively ducked, and headed toward one of the larger trees, looking around and trying to spot the perpetrator. I didn't see anyone. The rifle shots ceased.

Sensing the danger had passed, I continued my meandering, trying to avoid deep pockets in the snow, especially at the base of some of the larger trees. It would be a shame to fall into one, prompting another shocking headline in the *Northern Lights News*: "Shishmaref Ski Coach Suffocates in Snow Within Sight of Groomed Course."

The shots came again. I looked left and right and then down at my clothes. *Good grief, some guy with a gun's gonna think I'm a small caribou.* My coat and pants were tan, my beaver hat's flaps were up, the brown fur showing. A flash of bright orange caught my eye. I stepped forward at the edge of a clearing. In the distance were two men wearing orange vests. They stood along a row of mats on the snow, upon which lay a handful of skiers, sprawled on their stomachs and holding long rifles. They were aiming at colorful bull's-eye targets set on hay bales about forty yards away.

Oh my god. They're shooting at targets! The skiers are shooting at targets!

One word suddenly emblazoned itself across my wrinkled frontal lobes: BIATHLON. The flier said biathlon. And "bi" means two. Two events. Cross-country skiing and target practice. *Oh my god*. I had been so focused on teaching my team how to ski and dealing with paperwork and permission slips that I had completely overlooked those two vital letters. Even if I'd caught them, I didn't know how to shoot a gun.

The first group of skiers completed their shots, stood up, and pushed off again. Where were Mikey and Grace? Shouldn't they be here already? I waited behind a tree, hoping that I did blend in like a small caribou and wouldn't disqualify my Musketeers for such a flagrant violation. Technically, I wasn't on the course, but I wasn't supposed to be here, either. Fortunately, the race officials were focused on overseeing the skiers, not looking any farther than the target zone.

Minutes later, Edwin appeared at the top of a slight hill. He was moving fast, his coat flapping behind. As he approached the shooting range, Edwin dragged his poles to slow down. *Where did he learn that?* In one fluid motion, he unstrapped and dropped his poles, laid flat on the ground, took hold of the rifle resting on a wooden block, aimed, and fired. The paper target flitted, evidence that he had aimed well. Then he fired twice more. The race official took the rifle and said something to Edwin, who got up faster than I'd ever seen before, grabbed his poles, and started skating down the course without even slipping the loops over his wrists.

Of course. Those two seemingly disparate sports—skiing and shooting—were likely well known to the youth of Shishmaref. They were a combined practice of survival. Hunters had to move quickly on the ice to get close to a seal or walrus. They would have to stop and lay down, quiet their breathing, steady their aim, and pull the trigger. Mastery of those movements meant coming home with dinner or coming home empty-handed. Edwin's prowess with the rifle told me he was well on his way to providing food for his family.

I waited a few more minutes. Several skiers from other villages came and went. Then, I saw Missy. She slid down the hill at a slower pace, then pushed with her poles to the shooting range. The race official patted her on the back and pointed at the target. Missy nodded, then moved to a mat. She didn't pull the trigger right away, so the official stepped up and showed her how to brace the rifle's butt against her shoulder and cradle the muzzle with one hand. She nodded and removed her gloves, then took the gun and aimed. A few seconds later, I heard *Pop! Pop! Pop!* The paper poofed out twice. *Well, I'll be a monkey's uncle. She hit it*!

I saw the white of Missy's smile as she stood. And that, right there, was worth all the work it took to get to this competition. I exhaled. No unexpected shooting range was going to thwart my Musketeers.

The chill from standing in one place made me shiver. It was time to head back. I had reached my objective of teaching the kids to ski; they no longer needed me. In a strange way, that was the primary goal of teaching, wasn't it? Guiding students to become so self-sufficient, the teacher became obsolete. I smiled as I headed through the forest, back to the warmth of the school and a well-earned cup of coffee. And a donut with sprinkles on top.

I was just finishing my snack when the sounds of people cheering outside alerted me to quickly return to the finish line. Edwin was the first Musketeer to cross. His face was flushed. He had likely skied full-out for the entire race and was paying for it now. I snapped a photo as he pushed over the finish line and crumpled face down to the ground with a groan.

"Hey, Ed, you did great!" I reached down and patted his back. "Ed, you okay?" His muffled response confirmed he was just catching his breath.

A few minutes later, I captured photos of the other Musketeers as they slid past the banner. Lucy joined Edwin, still lying on the snow.

"Wow. Y'all did it!"

I paused, afraid to broach the subject but still wanting to know. "So … how did the shooting range thing go? That was a bit of a surprise, wasn't it?"

Mikey, who'd also dropped onto the ground, suddenly came to life.

"That was the coolest thing ever!" He unclipped his bindings and stood up, pretending to hold a rifle. "Pew! Pew! Pew! I hit the target!"

"Yeah, me too!" Edwin stepped up. "We got to shoot twice!"

"There were two shooting ranges?"

"Yeah!" Edwin and Mikey pretended to shoot into the sky. "Pew! Pew! Pew!"

I looked at the girls. They shrugged and rolled their eyes, then scooped up snow and threw it at the boys.

The awards ceremony soon followed, along with a dinner of hot chili and cornbread, and brownies for dessert. I felt horrible about missing the "bi" in biathlon, but the Musketeers didn't seem to care. They received ribbons for participating, and that, along with finishing the course and getting to shoot at targets, was reward enough.

The day's events came to a close. My team moved to a carpeted room with oversized pillows, couches, and armchairs, joining other kids as they lay about in every conceivable position, talking and laughing and watching cartoons on TV. I decided to slip outside to collect my thoughts and walk off my second brownie. Sleeping accommodations would be cramped, and I was in no hurry to lie down on a stinky wrestling mat in the school library. I had staked out my spot and just wanted to get some fresh air before turning in. It had been a big day, and tomorrow would be busy with getting the kids up, fed, and packed for the flight home.

I walked down a gentle slope toward the shoreline and turned at the sound of heavy boots crunching behind me.

"Nice evening, huh?" It was a man, an official of some kind, wearing an orange vest over his parka, thick snow pants, and a pair of Bunny boots. He had a clipboard tucked under one arm.

"Yeah, sure is." It was coming into twilight. A few stars peeked through the high clouds.

"You one of the ski coaches?"

"Yeah, Shishmaref." I paused and yawned. "Been a long day, but the kids did great."

The man nodded and extended his hand.

"I'm Dwayne. Musher checkpoint guy." He scratched his stubbled chin.

"You're looking for mushers?" *The Iditarod!* I had forgotten all about it.

"Yeah, it's been touch and go for a few days. Had to shut the race down a couple of times on account of storms." Dwayne removed his gloves and lifted his binoculars to the east. "Here comes someone now."

In the distance, a dot of light bobbed up and down. In front was a line of small black specks moving in unison—a musher's headlamp and a dog team.

We watched the entourage slowly angle up the bluff. About thirty yards below, the musher called out, "Whoa! Whoa! Arrêt!" The dogs slowed to a trot, then stopped altogether as his boot clomped on the brake. He stabbed a stake in the snow.

"Emergency brake." Dwayne nodded. "Good idea. Lots of mushers underestimate how much these dogs still want to run."

The musher collected slabs of hay from bales stacked nearby and walked down his line of dogs, sprinkling a mattress for each one. Most of the dogs had already plopped down but rearranged themselves on the straw as their owner came by.

That task complete, the man pulled a large pot and cooking stove from under the sled tarp and fired up the burner. Then he grabbed a saucepan and scooped up fresh snow, dumping each batch into the large pot. We could hear the hiss of snow as it hit the hot sides. It took a few trips, and I kept wondering why Dwayne didn't help. But soon, the musher was done; he stood quietly, warming his hands.

He looked tired. His clothes were rumpled, his hair shaggy and matted. He rolled his head a few times to stretch his neck, then reached for a large bag and poured kibble into the pot, following with handfuls of something brown out of a plastic bag. The pot steamed.

"What's that?" I asked Dwayne.

"Oh, prob'ly meat, maybe fish. The dogs need a lot of protein for energy. I've seen beef and chicken, cod and salmon. Sometimes they even get bacon or pork chops." He smiled. "They eat better than most of us out here."

Satisfied that dinner was ready, the musher rolled up one sleeve to his elbow and stuck his entire forearm into the pot, using it to stir the mush. Then he scooped up a handful of snow and washed his arm off.

Wayne chuckled. "Well, I guess that's as good as a long-handle spoon."

The musher dunked a dozen doggy bowls two at a time and served his team down the line, greeting each canine with a scritch behind an ear or pat on top of the head. I couldn't make out his words but caught the cadence of French. I'd heard him yell "Arrêt," which I knew from French classes meant "Stop!"

After each dog had been fed, the musher wiped his hands on his snow pants and turned toward us. Dwayne stepped forward and pulled out his clipboard, motioning that the musher should follow him to a building farther up the hill. They disappeared inside.

The dogs licked their bowls clean, settled once more into the hay, and closed their eyes, paws and tails tucked in. This was their chance for a nap, and they weren't going to waste it. I would have loved to learn their names and scratch their bellies. But these were working dogs, and I knew not to distract them from their goal of a short snooze before the last leg to Nome. It's what they'd trained for, what they lived for. But I could at least watch over them until their owner returned.

My role as sentry passed quickly. The lead dog's head popped up from his hay bed. His face was mostly white, with black markings around the eyes and top of the head. He looked intently at the little shack, ears twitching. Then he stood, shook, and stretched, butt high in the air, and sat down, waiting. Every muscle on alert. Within a minute, the musher emerged and clicked on his headlamp. The lead dog let out a little yelp in greeting. He knew they were on the move again.

Dwayne joined me once more, and we watched the musher check the lines and harnesses. He gathered the bowls, then started checking each dog's paws and slipping little boots on each one. I counted. Twelve dogs, four paws each. Forty-eight booties. The lead dog waited patiently, as if understanding that his role was to remain calm and steady, last in line for the ritual, but first in line when they got going again.

"That's Jacques Philip," Dwayne said. "All the way from France. His first Iditarod. Been out here almost twenty days. He's about halfway in the pack. A bunch of 'em had to scratch. Tough race this year, 'specially with that last storm." A shadow crossed his face, like he was going to say something more. But he didn't.

"I thought I caught some French," I said. "What's up with the booties?"

"Those are for the ice. The rest of the trail is mostly along the coast, and the dogs' paws can get cut pretty bad. They go through a lot of 'em, that's for sure."

The musher was fast. His sled was packed and his team was ready, when only moments before they'd appeared sound asleep. Now, they wriggled in their harnesses and barked, eager to get going again. Monsieur Philip pulled the stake out of the snow, released the brake, and yelled, "Marche!" The team lurched forward, picked up speed down the hill, and quickly disappeared from view. "Marche" sounded like "mush" to me. I wondered if there was a connection.

"How far is it to Nome?" I asked.

"Oh, 'bout hundred and twenty miles. He's gotta hit the Golovin and White Mountain checkpoints. Then Safety; that's the last one. Unless he loses the trail and has to backtrack. Hopefully the markers are all still out there. It can be hard to track at night." He paused.

"He's doin' alright for his first Iditarod—won't be the one putting out the Red Lantern."

I was about to ask what the Red Lantern was when Monsieur Philip and his dogs reappeared far below on Norton Sound. It looked lonely and cold out there. But Monsieur Philip had his loyal dogs for company. They worked together as one resolute unit of brawn and street smarts, mile after mile through territory that had no streets at all.

Dwayne scanned through his binoculars toward the east again, while my eyes followed the thin black line growing smaller on the horizon. I wondered why anyone would put themselves through such an excruciating experience—day after day with little rest, enduring freezing cold temperatures and unrelenting winds, riding and then running over unpredictable and treacherous terrain. It looked incredibly demanding. It looked amazing. It looked like the most beautiful thing in the world.

"What's the Red Lantern?"

Dwayne shifted his stance. "Imagine you're the last musher and you're crossing this ice out here and wondering if there's anyone left in Nome who's waiting to greet you at the finish," he paused and chuckled, "besides your mother." He turned toward me. "So people wait until the last musher comes through. They clap and yell like crazy to make him feel good about finishing. He deserves it, after crossing over a thousand miles of mostly wild territory. Could have faced down wolves or moose, snowstorms and all the rest. It's not for the faint of heart."

He shifted again. "There's a red lantern by the arch. Some people call it a widow's lamp. It's lit at the start of the race, and they keep it burning the whole time. The last musher to cross the finish line gets to extinguish it, and then everyone knows all the mushers are accounted for."

We stood for a few more minutes, looking at the quiet scene below.

"Well, I don't see anyone coming for a while. Nice talking with you." Dwayne gave a little salute and headed back up the hill. I still wasn't ready to go inside and decided to stroll down to see if I could spot Monsieur Philip on the ice. One hundred and twenty miles? That was farther than my hometown of Vail to Denver—a long way by car, not to mention by dog.

A spot of color in the snow caught my eye. I went over and found a turquoise bootie made of felt. It had a Velcro strap. "Bon chance, Monsieur Philip," I whispered, and tucked the bootie in my pocket. At least for me, the day was done.

The flight home was quiet. Lucy and Missy slept the whole way, their heads on each other's shoulders. Edwin and Mikey chatted, then looked out their own windows in silence. Grace sat next to me, reading a book titled *Superfudge*. I wanted to ask her about it, but she was so engrossed that I refrained.

On the ground again, families appeared one by one on their sno-gos to pick up their kids. Principal Ken rumbled down the snowy street in the school truck for Mikey and me and all the ski gear.

"Nice job over there." Principal Ken glanced over Mikey to me. The edges of a smile emerged from under his mustache. "Mikey called last night and mentioned somethin' 'bout shootin' at a target?"

"Uh, yeah. About that …"

"Well," he added before I could go further, "he also said it was the best part of the whole weekend." He playfully nudged his son. "Wasn't it?"

Mikey stayed silent, but the grin on his face told the story. A few minutes later, we pulled up to my portable.

"What about the skis?" I glanced back to the truck bed.

"We'll deal with 'em t'morrow."

"Fine with me." I slid out. Just as I reached the porch, Principal Ken lowered his window and called out. "Hey, did ya hear who won the Iditarod?"

I shook my head.

"Libby Riddles!"

"Who?"

"Libby Riddles!" Principal Ken laughed. "Wouldn't you know, she left Shaktoolik in the middle of that storm. It was so fierce. No one else dared go, and they told her not to either. But that's all she needed to hear, apparently. She jes' packed up an' left. People thought she'd never make it. Wouldn't ya know, she shows up in Nome, her team trottin' down Front Street like a Sunday stroll in the park. First ones under that arch. The first woman to win the Iditarod." He shook his head and smiled his big walrus smile. "Darnedest thing."

Principal Ken pulled away. I stood for a moment on our rickety porch, marveling at the guts of a woman who'd entered a male-dominated sport and outwitted everyone, even a brutal storm.

A couple of days later, a copy of the *Nome Nugget* newspaper appeared in the teacher's lounge. A black and white photo of Libby Riddles filled the front page. The caption read, "Dinner for twelve—Libby prepares dinner for her team while in White Mountain." The date was Wednesday, March 20, 1985. *That was the day before the Musketeers and I flew into Elim!* We had just missed her.

The image was fuzzy, but I could see that Libby wore a beaver hat like mine topped off with a large headlamp. I read quickly, eager to learn more about her harrowing journey along the northern shores of Norton Sound. Apparently, Libby spent less time at some checkpoints and gradually widened her lead. Her decisive moment came in Shaktoolik, where the winter storm Principal Ken had warned me about raged. Winds were gusting forty miles an hour. Whiteout conditions resulted in her team losing the trail a couple of times. She spent the night stranded on the ice and zipped up in her bag on the sled. She recounted trying to sleep, terrified she'd get hypothermic and stop thinking clearly—a recipe for frostbite and maybe even death. The dogs fared better. They had the perfect fur for extreme conditions and stayed warm enough even as the snow drifted over them.

I could not imagine being in her boots. My recent experience with whiteout conditions totally freaked me out, and I was only ten paces from home.

A week later, another *Nome Nugget* found its way into the teacher's lounge. On the cover was a large photo of Libby Riddles driving her team down the victory chute in Nome. This time, the headline read, "Libbymania Strikes." The article included photos of Libby and her dogs and a fuller recounting of her night on the ice, as well as the series of mishaps she endured along the trail. The story of my honey bucket ride to the dump paled in comparison.

I especially loved the photo of Libby hugging her lead dog, Duggen. He looked like he was smiling. And why not? He was the one who guided Libby and his teammates over that last incredibly demanding stretch to win the 1985 Iditarod. They did it in eighteen days and twenty minutes, resulting in a cash prize of fifty thousand dollars. And there were more awards for taking such good care of her dogs. Duggen's smile was proof.

Maybe that's what Dwayne was going to tell me when we stood on the snowy slope in Elim and watched Jacques Philip and his dog team sliding westward on the ice toward Nome.

He must have known that Libby had already won and was trying to process that news himself. Maybe he didn't quite believe a woman could win the Iditarod. Maybe he wanted women to get their own damn race, but he wasn't going to divulge his true feelings to a member of the female species, especially one wearing men's snow boots and pants, a man's parka, and a beaver hat—and looked like she might have been Libby's younger sister.

Forty mushers finished the race. Twenty-one scratched due to illness or injury. The last team into Nome was led by Monique Bene, also from France. She and her dogs had been on the trail for a little over twenty-two days.

I imagined Monique Bene being invited to extinguish the Red Lantern, likely disappointed but relieved to have made it. I bet she sent a cheeky grin in Libby's direction. Both women knew the Iditarod had been changed forever. Snuffing out the lamp wasn't the end. It was a new beginning.

FIFTY

SERPENTINE

With the biathlon complete, a pall settled over my days. I counted the weeks until the end of school and again felt stuck about the curriculum in my classes. The past few weeks of focus and frivolity with my Five Musketeers had provided momentum which temporarily spilled into my teaching and boosted my confidence. Now, that momentum was gone. I felt like I had sticky red ski wax on my boot soles and between my ears.

I reached a low point one day when Andrew and Tim, both in tenth grade English and Consumer Math classes, approached me to ask if they could bring a video to watch on Friday. I figured it couldn't hurt. I remembered watching movies in school on occasion. My mistake was not requiring that I see the video first. A few minutes after sliding the cassette into the VCR, it became apparent that the boys had chosen a horror film. The setting started out just fine, at a summer camp, but soon deteriorated with campers getting picked off one by one by some mysterious, evil force.

"Whoa, whoa, whoa." I pushed the eject button and caught the title: *Friday the 13th*.

Later that day, Duncan found me in the copy room, looking glum as I worked on math worksheets. I told him about the kids' video and my own malaise.

"I know what you mean," Duncan said. "It's like slack tide. You've got the blues and can't paddle your way out of it."

"Well, I need to get a giant frickin' paddle, because this sucks."

Duncan laughed and unwrapped a Dum-Dum sucker. "It always helps me to do something fun. Y'know—get out, relax." He sucked on the candy for a beat before adding, "Lance and I are planning a trip to Serpentine to chop ice this weekend with Lynne and Carrie. Wanna come?"

Lance and Duncan had a reputation for driving fast. I wasn't sure I wanted to travel at highway speed across the lagoon on a seat no bigger than a dinner plate. Some days, the air was bone-chilling-frickin'-cold just standing still. Left to my own devices, I could see myself zipped into my sleeping bag until spring, the arrival of which receded with each day. But the water level in our metal canister was getting low. Anne and I had been rationing this past week, unsure when the custodian would fill it again.

"Okay. Count me in."

Serpentine River. After all these months on the island, I was going to get a closer look at the place that Nora and Helen referenced during their first visit to my house—the place where they went berry picking and visited a hot spring. Duncan hadn't said anything about the hot spring. Was that part of the trip? I didn't have a suit. I was ruminating about what to say if he suggested we go skinny-dipping when I heard a knock on our door.

"Ready to go?"

Duncan was dressed in hunting gear, camouflaged head to toe. A bright orange beanie poked out from one pocket.

"Yep." I pulled on my parka. "How long are we gonna be gone? Anne wants to know."

"We'll be home before dark. We've got snacks, hot cocoa, and water, so we're good."

I stepped back inside and called out to Anne. "We'll be back before dark!" A muffled reply came through the bathroom wall. I closed the door and zipped up, then looked at the two snow machines, their engines idling. Passengers already sat on the back of both.

"Um, where am I supposed to …"

"Oh, yeah, about that." Duncan sounded apologetic. "Hope you're okay in the sled." He pointed at a pile of canvas with tips of cross-country skis poking out one end and added, "Do you have goggles?"

"Wow." I stepped closer. "Um, no." I gestured at the ski tips. "What's with the skis?"

"Figured we could slide around a little out there, so I pulled these from the trailer and guessed on shoe sizes."

"Hey, Genét!" Carrie sat on Duncan's sno-go. "Hope you don't mind riding in the sled. It's not so bad. Just gotta hang on!" She smiled encouragingly and gave me a thumbs-up.

I looked at Lance, who was mindlessly checking dials. A woman sat behind him. *Must be Lynne.* They also had a sled, with a wooden box and a couple of duffel bags strapped on.

Lance revved his motor, cutting off further discussion. The decision had been made. Such a familiar and gender-specific arrangement: Men drive, women ride. I was in the trunk.

Maybe I'd get to ride on the sno-go on the way back. Then again, maybe the group was already envisioning me holding blocks of ice on my lap. The interview committee never asked, "On a scale of one to ten, how would you feel about cradling large blocks of frozen river water while flying across the tundra in a creaky wooden sled? With no seatbelt or goggles?"

Duncan opened the layers of canvas, revealing an unzipped sleeping bag. "This is the warmest one I've got. You can sit in the middle, and I'll tuck you in." He sounded like a parent coaxing a child to bed but then added, "You might want to zip your hood all the way so ice doesn't fly into your eyes and face. Hurts like the dickens."

Roger that.

I sat down on the sled, feeling the deep cold of the bag and the hard wooden slats underneath me. Duncan zipped the bag to my waist, as high as it would go with my wide girth in snow pants and a parka.

"Lean over a bit, so I can get this under you," he said. I tried to act natural, like it was no big deal to suddenly have a man's hands under my rear. I caught Anne watching our movements from the window. She waved, looking pleased.

"Okay." Duncan finished tucking. "That ought to do it."

"Yep," I said, smirking. "Snug as a bug in a rug."

"Like a caterpillar in a chrysalis, just waitin' to become a butterfly," Duncan joked back. He tapped the side next to my leg. "Hang on to these top rails. It gets bumpy across the lagoon, but you won't fall out." He winked. "Don't worry, I tested the sled. It won't break in half."

My initial consternation about having to ride in the back of the sled dissipated with each gentle turn through the village. It was kind of fun. Duncan drove slowly, and I waved at groups of kids as we passed by. I felt like a prom queen on a float.

But when we reached the edge of the village, he stood on the runners and yelled back. "We're going to pick up speed, so hang on!"

The sled surged forward, and I grasped the side railings. Moments ago, I was riding low and seeing the village through a child's eyes. But now my Disneyland "Small World" ride had been replaced by the Arctic version of "Thunder Mountain Railroad" without the goats.

Unlike a car with shock absorbers and air in the tires, there was absolutely nothing to cushion me from sharp bumps and the jerky, swaying motion as Duncan propelled us across the lagoon. The sled runners squeaked and squealed like fingernails on a chalkboard. Small chunks of snow and ice kicked up from behind the sno-go's treads, forcing me to turn and lower my head, using my periscope hood for protection. *Great. My hands are numb, my butt's frozen, and I don't even have a view.*

We rode hard for what felt like an hour. The sled slowed.

"You okay back there?"

I raised my head and periscoped around to see who was yelling. It was Lance. He'd pulled his machine alongside.

"You okay?" He repeated, thinking I hadn't heard.

My hood nodded.

"Just a little more to go! You're doing great! We'll have some hot cocoa when we get there." He gave me a thumbs-up and I nodded in return, then took the opportunity to look at the landscape ahead. We were almost to the other side. I could see tips of brown grasses poking through the snow and a small hill in the distance.

"Hang on!" yelled Duncan.

Duncan skillfully maneuvered the machine up a small embankment, following tracks across the tundra. Small snowdrifts caught and released the sled, lurching my body back and forth. Maybe I'd tell Duncan about the wonders of blue cross-country ski wax.

My neck and shoulders were yanked around, but our slower pace made it possible for me to release the railings and pull my hands into the sleeping bag to regain feeling in my fingers.

We moved steadily over the snow, weaving around willow bushes toward a small structure. It was a cabin not more than twelve feet square. In its early days, it had been painted red. But wind and weather had beaten it down to dark rust. Pieces of sideboard had been stripped away, revealing gray wood underneath. A piece of plywood covered what used to be a window.

We pulled up, and Duncan and Lance shut down the engines.

"Here, let's get you out of this." Duncan unzipped my bag and extended a hand. My legs were like tree stumps. "There you go." He steadied me. "A little hot cocoa and you'll be all thawed out."

The cabin felt colder inside than out. A bunk bed fashioned with heavy boards was fastened to one wall. A small wood table and a couple of wooden chairs sat along another. Our breath froze in the air. A wood stove would have been nice, but what would we burn? The only viable wood around was the scant furniture or the sled. That'd be a long walk home.

Carrie poured hot cocoa into a paper cup and handed it to me. I sat down on the lower bunk bed and held the cup, waiting for its warmth to penetrate my gloved hands so I could take them off.

The other woman approached. "Hi, I'm Lynne."

The first thing I saw was her red lipstick. I would have laughed at the absurdity of lipstick out here, but I couldn't feel my face.

"That was a cold ride, huh?" She looked apologetic.

"Have you two met?" Lance walked over. "This is Lynne." He put his arm around her shoulders and gave a squeeze. "She teaches elementary." He looked back at me. "Lynne, this is Genét. She teaches high school English and Consumer Math." He paused. "And newspaper and yearbook, right?"

I nodded.

"You guys did a great job on those editions. Haven't seen one for a while, though."

My mouth had warmed enough to reply. "Yeah. Last one was in December. The news crew ran out of things to report." I took another sip. "Yearbook's up next."

"I loved those Dear Abby-like letters." Lynne laughed. "So cute!"

"Yeah, and those song dedications," Lance added. "One of my classes dedicated a song to me. What was it …" He paused and then snapped his fingers. "Oh, I know, it was 'We're Not Gonna Take It' by Twisted Sister."

"Sounds like something we ought to be singing to our students!" Lynne quipped.

While everyone thawed out from the ride, we shared stories about teaching and sang stanzas of popular songs from the students' dedications, including "Holding Out for a Hero," "Let's Hear it for the Boy," and "Almost Paradise."

The hot cocoa, snacks, and singing revived me. I could have stayed in the little cabin for the rest of the day. But the time had come to chop ice.

Lance and Lynne decided to ski down to the river. Duncan took a sno-go to survey the scene. Carrie and I volunteered to clean up.

"But first, I gotta take a little trip to the facilities," Carrie joked. "Nature calls." She slipped out the door. Of course, we both knew the facilities meant the nearest bush.

Left alone in the cabin, I took a moment to study sets of initials carved into the bunk bed: "TD was here" and "So was L.O." I ran through a mental list of students' names, but no one came to mind. Hearts and plus signs were carved into the posts. One unfinished signature simply read, "I was."

"Brrr!" Carrie startled me as she entered the cabin, laughing. "Nothing like a bare bottom squat in the snow!"

We gathered the snack remains and decided to take a quick hike up the bluff for a better view of the landscape before joining our colleagues. For the next half an hour, Carrie and I slowly angled our way up the slope, stepping carefully around willow bushes. We finally reached the base of an impassable cornice and decided to summit there.

I had spent many years in the mountains and always experienced a sense of relief with every step in elevation. High places changed my perspective on things. I loved being higher up. We were only about sixty feet above the cabin, but from this vantage point we could see the zigzag of tracks left by our snow machines as we had approached the cabin. I followed them to the west to see if the village came into view. But the tracks disappeared into a sea of white snow, all the way to the horizon.

I focused closer in and made out the tiny figures of Lance and Lynne on their skis. They'd followed a track to the edge of an ice-covered river. Duncan was already on it, walking around and stabbing his axe every few feet, testing for thickness and whatever else was needed to find the right ice vein for easy chopping.

"That's the Serpentine River, isn't it?" I pointed.

"Yep. The locals fish out here and pick berries, I think."

"Where are the hot springs?"

"They're farther inland. Never been there, but I hear it's beautiful. Bigger hills, and rock formations like spires. Something about how they formed created the hot springs. There's a bathhouse, too. The weather can be horrendous outside, but it's toasty in there." Carrie paused and shivered. "Let's go down."

We picked our way through the willows, down to the cabin, and packed up the sled. Carrie took the lead with driving and I sat behind.

"Are Lance and Lynne ..."

Carrie finished my thought. "Dating?"

"Yeah. They seem close."

"I think so. I'm a little envious." Carrie slowed to negotiate a snow berm. "It's hard out here as a woman, especially on your own. I almost quit last year. I had this awful roommate. Couldn't stand her. She was so righteous and demeaning."

Carrie slowed the sno-go again and glanced over her shoulder at me. "As a matter of fact, I think you replaced her."

My thoughts flipped back to the memory of my first days of school when students divulged how poorly the previous teacher had treated them, and how I looked just like her. She would have been a horrible roommate. Anne was quirky, but she was kind. I was probably the same for her.

"I asked around and got a small house to rent," Carrie said. "It's lonely at times, but at least I have my own space."

By the time Carrie and I reached the edge of the Serpentine River, Duncan and Lance had already carved out several large chunks of cloudy-white and blue ice. Their faces were red with exertion.

"Whew!" Duncan paused. "Someone else's turn!"

Carrie and Lynne looked at each other and laughed.

"You're doing fine," Lynne coaxed.

But I wanted to know what it felt like to chop ice on the Serpentine River, so I gave the axe a few turns. Within minutes, my face was red, too.

After we loaded up one sled, the dreaded question came.

"I hate to say this," Lance started, "but are you okay riding in the sled again?"

I shrugged, disappointed to once again be volunteered for the most uncomfortable seat. But I was the only person with a periscope hood, an essential piece of armor.

"If I need to see a chiropractor," I quipped, "I'm sending the bill to you."

I plopped into the sled and held out my arms. "Okay, pile it on." I caught Duncan's eye. "But drive slower this time."

Duncan saluted. "Aye, aye, captain."

And he did go slower. But it wasn't long before I wanted to yell, "Step on it!" Crossing the lagoon with a thirty-pound chunk of ice on my lap took forever. My body ached from bracing against the sled's lurching and unexpected turns. The first time I laid eyes on the lagoon, it didn't look so big. But now it felt like Nora had been correct all along: the Serpentine was, indeed, as far away as Utah.

The next day, I held a drinking glass under the spout of our water canister, surprised that I didn't feel the need to boil it. I knew the source and trusted it. The water was ice cold and soothing. And sweet. I wished I had asked about chopping ice earlier in the season. It might have brought relief from the doldrums of teaching and my isolation. If I had initiated the trip, maybe I would have been a driver rather than a passenger gripping the handrails over ruts and bumps and praying not to chip a tooth or lose an eyeball to flying ice.

From then on, Anne and I rationed our water or bought jugs at the store. We were coming into the Arctic spring. Warmer weather meant travel across the lagoon would be less predictable. After months of waiting, the harshness of winter was releasing its grip. Spring was on its way.

PART FIVE

SPRING THAW

FIFTY-ONE

ALOHA

Another day, another store run.

As I turned onto Main Street, I spotted a group of young girls strolling toward me—Lucy and Grace, and two more. They chattered away, absorbed in some kind of food item. It was small, round, and brown. Brown apples? Bosc pears? I couldn't make it out.

Their movements were unfamiliar: they'd take a bite as if eating an apple, then slide the skin through their teeth and toss it to the side of the street. One girl used her front teeth to chew the innards of whatever it was, made a face, spit, then wiped her chin on her sleeve.

We continued on our collision course until I blocked their way. The girls jostled to a stop.

"Hey, girls."

Lucy and Grace's eyebrows shot up.

"What you got there?"

"Not sure." Lucy frowned at the green and brown mass in her hand. "But you gotta take the skin off. It's nasty. All fuzz in your mouth." She stuck out her tongue.

"Yeah, and there's black seeds. They nasty too," added another girl I didn't recognize.

"But once you make it past that, it's good!" Lucy looked at her friends and nodded vigorously. She held out her hand, showing me the remains of a kiwifruit that looked like it had been gnawed by a squirrel. The brown fuzzy skin splayed out, revealing her timid bites into the bright green interior.

"Well, I'll be," I replied. "That's a kiwifruit!"

"A kee-weee?" Lucy looked surprised. Her friends giggled.

"Kee-weee!" Grace ran around the group with her arms outstretched like a seagull. "Kee-weeee!"

"Where'd you get kiwi?" I asked, intrigued. Fruit was not a big commodity on the island. It seemed to be flown in mostly for the white folks. Locals probably preferred their berries, picked fresh from the mainland in the fall. Aside from sturdy oranges and apples, it was uncommon for either Walter's or the Native Store to have fresh fruit. Bananas appeared on occasion but tended to arrive bruised and suitable only for pudding or bread.

"Got 'em at the store." Lucy thumbed over her shoulder toward Walter's place.

"Thanks, I'll check it out." I stood still as the gaggle of girls went on their way, flapping their arms and shouting, "Kee-weee!"

I followed the kiwi skin trail to Walter's store and felt a wave of hot air hit my face as I stepped inside. Faint tunes of a ukulele played in the background.

"Aloha!" Walter yelled from his usual perch behind the cash register. He wore a Hawaiian shirt decorated with palm trees. A lei made from plastic pink and yellow flowers hung around his neck. "Close the door or you'll let all the heat out!"

"Holy cow, what's going on?" I unzipped my parka.

"Hawaii Week!" Walter's face glistened. "A-*LO*-ha!"

He held up his palms in greeting and moved his hips like a hula dancer to the rhythm of the music.

"Well, aloha to you, too." I chuckled as my eyes adjusted to the soft lighting.

The shelf near Walter's cash register, which usually displayed canned goods and random sale items, overflowed with pineapples, mangoes, kiwifruit, and bananas. Even a couple coconuts. More plastic leis decorated the ends of shelves. It looked like he had pulled them one by one from a box and frisbeed them onto anything resembling a hook.

I plucked a kiwi from the box. "I just passed a group of young customers enjoying these. They seemed confused about what to do with the skin."

Walter waited for more explanation.

"They were biting into the fruit like an apple." I pretended to chomp into it. "Then they pulled the skin between their teeth and tossed it. They spit out the seeds as well."

Walter continued to look at me as if he couldn't understand my concern.

"But you know," I was starting to take his hint that it didn't matter how the kids ate kiwis, "it might have been a good way to eat it. Faster than peeling and slicing. They're slippery."

I changed the subject. "How much for a pineapple?"

"Pineapples are six dollars!" Walter came closer to showcase his goods. "I'll throw in a kiwi and a banana. They're going bad fast."

As he always managed to do, within minutes Walter talked me into $33.89 worth of produce and a $12 can of macadamia nuts. I didn't even like macadamia nuts.

"You've done it again, Walter." I winked. "I came to get double A batteries, but I'm walking out with a bag of groceries." I started for the door.

"Hey, you know what Hawaiians say when you leave?"

I turned, my hand on the doorknob. "Not sure, but I bet you're about to tell me."

"A-*LO*-ha!" He laughed and shimmied his hips again.

I rolled my eyes and gave the bells on the door an extra jangle on the way out, then followed the kiwi skins back up the street and headed toward home with my bag of Hawaii Week cradled in my arms. The clouds were low and heavy in the sky, and I shivered with the extreme temperature change from Walter's store to the outside world. The weather this time of year was so unpredictable. One minute, I thought spring had finally sprung, and the next minute a chill crept over the land, like dry ice on a stage, penetrating the smallest opening.

As I turned down the street next to school, a streetlamp flickered on. By the time I reached it, fat snowflakes started leisurely falling—so slowly, I was able to track one several feet overhead. It came closer and closer. I stood and waited, then caught it on my tongue.

FIFTY-TWO

MANAGING THE MIDDLE

After months of racking up bills at Walter's, I had started following the advice of other teachers to order in bulk from Anchorage—things like paper towels and packets of frozen vegetables.

Sometimes, teachers crafted a school-wide bulk order. "Hey, there's six of us getting more peanut butter. Want in?"

The irony didn't escape me. I was the Consumer Math teacher but was slow to realize consumer strategies that made life in the Arctic a little cheaper.

What I did learn, however, was that flying goods to bush communities was a complicated business, especially between winter and spring. My case of Pilot Bread from Anchorage might fly in the cargo hold to Nome, get transferred to a bush plane, and then make the trek to Shishmaref through the tiny town of Wales. Or maybe it would get flown to Unalakleet, then to St. Lawrence Island before landing in Shishmaref—unless it was returned to sender by mistake.

Cargo was a matter of priorities. It depended on weather and a host of other unexpected things, which shifted all the time. Orchestrating supplies and people across hundreds of miles of airspace seemed to require master's degrees in communication, human resource management, and meteorology. Would another shipment take precedence? Did a sudden storm require boxes of Pampers to get swapped out for medical supplies needed in another village? Did the power go out somewhere, requiring the removal of seats to shimmy in a huge generator and a technician? Anything was possible. A case of Lucky Charms cereal could easily be replaced by a water pump for a flooded village, forcing the unlucky recipient to choose between stale crackers from the back of the cupboard or paying higher prices at the local store.

Don't even get me started on underwear.

I had gotten so neurotic over the haphazard springtime shipments that I once heard a plane buzzing the village and literally froze at the chalkboard.

"Hey, was that a plane?" I blurted out to my Consumer Math class.

Carol raised her eyebrows. She had been the most focused student that day and was dutifully following my lesson on decimals.

And the moment came. The one I never thought I would deploy as a teacher with impressionable youngsters in my midst. The moment when I was going to bribe one of them to run to the airstrip to check if my box of toiletries and feminine items had arrived.

I couldn't very well run from the room and down Main Street to take care of my own business, but if I didn't pick up my box directly, it might land in someone else's house by mistake or get transferred to the school, where it would be relegated to some obscure shelf until someone noticed and handed it over to me. I didn't want to take the chance.

"Carol, since you were paying attention, I'm going to make you an offer. Five bucks if you go to the airstrip and pick up my box. I'm expecting something from Anchorage. Not sure it's coming today, but it's not heavy."

"Hey!" Charlie snapped to alertness. "That's not fair!"

"Yeah!" Tim chimed in.

I ignored their pleas and turned back to Carol, who seemed unsure about taking advantage of this sudden opportunity.

"Can I take someone with me?"

"Pick me! Pick me!" Half a dozen hands shot up. Carol looked at me for guidance.

"Sure."

As soon as the word left my mouth, I knew I was setting a terrible precedent. My students tended to forget everything I'd taught the day before, but when it came to favors, their minds were like bank vaults where they stored data in hopes of using it for a future deal.

"Well …" Carol scanned the room. "Paula."

Her choice was good. Like Carol, Paula was caught up with her work. It would be fine for her to miss class today.

"Okay, I'll tip you when you return. You'll have to split the five." I looked at the clock. "But hurry! I want you back here for your next class." I grabbed a notepad and hastily scribbled a permission slip. "Here, take this with you so people know I sent you." The two girls ran from the room. "Thank you!" I called after them.

A series of "Aww mans!" and variations in groaning and whimpering ensued. The students were going to push me on this. But I had recently learned from Lance how to redirect student energy.

"Don't apologize," he warned. "Just say what it is you're doing and then start." It was excellent advice, the kind I could have used last August.

"As I was saying, you have to move the decimal back two spaces …"

That was the first and last time I ever sent students to pick up my personal shipment. But they sure tried. Pilots didn't always fly right over the school when buzzing the village, but when they did, my students snapped to attention and yelled, "Got any packages you need picked up?"

One time I actually did have a package, but I didn't know it until I stepped into the main office after school.

Midge nodded toward a liquor-box-sized parcel. "This came for you." I read the return address on an envelope taped to the top. "United States Postal Service."

I wasn't expecting anything. The box looked strange. It had been opened and then resealed with an exceptionally large amount of strapping tape. There were water stains on the side. Midge didn't make eye contact with me, which was odd. Usually, she was excited about my packages—happy that my family hadn't abandoned me way up here in the Far North.

The box felt empty. I carried it to my classroom, pulled back the plastic seal on the top, and slipped out one sheet of paper. It was typed on official United States Postal Service stationery, addressed directly to me, and signed by the postmaster general himself.

"Dear Miss Pierce ..."

I scanned quickly, collecting the most salient words: Intoxicating Liquors. Carbonated. Exploded. Prohibited. Felony. Punishable by fine or imprisonment. And there were references to certain laws and the numbers and decimals that would direct me to said laws should I, Miss Pierce, wish to see for myself. At the bottom of the letter were the letters "cc:" and my mother's name and address.

Oh my god. My mother's involved. I opened the box. There was half a loaf of rye bread wrapped in plastic. One side was covered in mold. There was also a chunk of cheese (also moldy) and a small envelope, dimpled from dampness. I pulled out a note. The writing was blotched as well, but I made out the following from my mother's handwriting: "I hope you enjoy this bread and cheese from the German Store. I am also sending a bottle of white wine and a bottle of Martinelli's ..."

I didn't read any further. The story was clear. My mother, well-intentioned but misinformed, had shipped a bottle of wine (i.e., illegal), and the bottle of carbonated Martinelli's gave it all away. She probably didn't realize how cold it still was in the Arctic, and that carbonated beverages expand in freezing temperatures and tend to explode. Carbonated liquid in glass could be lethal.

I didn't know whether to laugh or cry. Either way, my eyes started to tear up. A chuckle came on, but then I felt sad that my mother's kind gesture had been destroyed. And then I felt sad that

I didn't get to enjoy the contents of the box, especially the wine. I sniffed it, but all I got was musty cardboard.

How many times had the postmaster written this letter? Specifically to teachers in remote communities? His wording was stern but short of indictment. Neither my mom nor I were going to be fined or hauled off to jail. Yet.

The next day, I called my mom.

"I got the same letter," she said. And then she laughed. "Can you imagine how scared those people must have been when the box exploded?"

We spent the next several minutes chuckling at possible scenarios.

Where the shipment met its untimely end would forever be a mystery. Maybe the Martinelli's met its demise en route to Wales or Gambell or Shishmaref itself and the dripping box signaled a Code Red, which led to Protocol 1-2-3-X-Y-Z, which required all illegal goods be shipped to Washington, D.C., for analysis and possible prosecution.

I imagined the postmaster general's secretary setting the offensive item on an oversized walnut desk and standing back with a salute.

"Sir, there's been another parcel incident. More illegal shenanigans by those crazy teachers in the Arctic ..."

The postmaster general likely nodded and waved his hand for the secretary to take the unsightly container from his room, then moved to the window and stared into the distance, hands clasped behind his back.

He'd reflect on what it must be like, living on the edge of the unknown. Maybe he had experienced remote island living himself or had been on the receiving end of an alcoholic libation, only to have it be rudely stolen by the physics of carbonation. Maybe he glanced behind his shoulder to make sure his secretary wasn't watching and started laughing, too.

A few days later, I bumped into Lance in the Native Store. I didn't need anything but thought it'd be fun to check out the sales rack.

"Hey." Lance walked toward me in a narrow aisle.

"Hey back. What do you think of these?" I held up a pair of red wool socks with Rudolph the Red-Nosed Reindeer heads on them. "They're on sale."

"Hmm, I think that season's come and gone." He looked at his watch. "Say, I gotta run home. Tim and I got a little experiment going on."

Tim was the science teacher and often commandeered Lance to play around in the lab.

"Oh, yeah?" I put the socks back.

"Yeah. There's a plane coming in, and I have a small box on it. Not heavy. Would you have time to run the school truck down there and pick it up?" He handed me the keys. "It's in the usual place."

"Uh, sure. Not doing much anyway." I shrugged. "A drive in the country would be nice."

It felt strange being in the driver's seat again. Since moving to Shishmaref, I could count on one hand the times that I drove any vehicle at all, and I wasn't sure if my episodes with the hole on the tundra or between the snowdrifts on my disastrous dump run counted. In truth, I was a little afraid I'd forget how to drive a stick shift when I returned to paved streets and stoplights.

I moved slowly over humps of frozen sand, patches of ice, and slush. The airstrip came too soon. No one else was around, so I pulled up at a safe distance and waited. Other than the periodic creaking of the truck as the wind blew, it was quiet. North of the airstrip, there wasn't much to look at. Just flat tundra covered with snow, all the way to Kotzebue. A flash of orange caught my eye. A windsock, attached to a pole on one side of the runway. It straightened in the wind and went limp again. The wind was blowing from the northwest, which meant the plane would approach from over the lagoon. That's how planes always seemed to come in.

The faint hum of engines broke through the silence. Sure enough, the silhouette of a plane appeared. It descended rapidly, the tail to one side, but straightening just before touching down. Unless some very short passengers were on board, the pilot was alone.

I hopped out. The air had a bite to it, colder than it had been half an hour before. I was sick of winter and zipped my parka as I watched a handful of people on snow machines and four wheelers approach. Springtime meant more options for travel, including pickup trucks. One rolled up, and the driver climbed into the truck bed to unload a rather large box, about four feet square and close to a foot high. He motioned for help to get it on the ground.

Large black lettering was visible on top. Curious, I stepped closer and made out the name of one of my students, Janice, who had flown to Anchorage on the student exchange program with another student, Sarah. They would be gone for another week. Then I read the words: DO NOT THAW! WILL STINK.

I laughed out loud. It must be frozen Eskimo food. And, if thawed, it *would* stink. Even the Native people agreed. On more than one occasion I had stepped back from a student and forced down a gag on account of the fish-or-something-else odor emanating from their breath or clothing. I knew that cod and herring, seals and walrus, whales and reindeer had been essential to their survival, and I admired that, but my nose had a hard time adjusting.

Janice must have grown tired of Western food. Sarah, too. They'd be so happy when the box arrived on the host family's doorstep. It was the kind of happiness I would have liked to experience had my mother's care package not exploded somewhere in the clouds.

I spied a small box with Lance's name. I grabbed it and drove to his house, knocked and waited, then knocked again. I left the box on his porch and drove home.

There were only a few minutes left of sunlight, but it was enough for me to take a short walk to the ocean's edge. I parked the truck at school, returned the keys, and headed out.

The sea ice was still thick, but the snow was old and dirty, filled with pockmarks from melting and freezing, then melting again.

I watched a couple of crows flying south, and my thoughts followed. This place was such a jumble of extremes, from well below zero to forty degrees Fahrenheit in a matter of hours. From the danger of stinky food thawing to beverages freezing and exploding.

Every day brought anticipation mixed with uncertainty. And there was no protocol, no predictable way to manage any of it. All that I could tell, so far, was to keep looking for ways to expand my capacity to manage the middle. Keep my head up and keep a sense of humor.

One week later, Janice and Sarah returned from their big city trip. Both had dyed their hair with streaks of purple and applied a rather heavy dose of makeup to their faces. They sashayed around the school, smiling broadly from the oohs and ahhs they received as they showed off their new city garb: black boots, tight jeans, and faux-leather jackets with silver zippers and chains. It wasn't my style, but the girls carried it well. Janice and Sarah were stunning, and they knew it.

Over the next few days, however, the girls slowly returned to wearing jeans and sweatshirts. Their hard-won city attire was no match for Shishmaref. We were coming into spring, but it was still frickin' cold enough to freeze eyelashes together if you dallied too long outside. By the end of the week, the only evidence that Janice and Sarah had traveled to Anchorage was a line of fading purple hair.

FIFTY-THREE

LOOKING INTO TOMORROW

Teachers have a code for interrupting each other. It usually starts at the threshold with a light tap on the doorframe or a "Yoo-hoo" or "Hey." This code has been one of the many unspoken yet essential features of the profession—a way of politely merging onto the highway of thoughts swirling inside the teacher's head at any given time. Teachers average fifteen hundred decisions a day. The last thing a colleague wanted to do was blow up another teacher's brains by approaching unexpectantly with a "quick question" or an unreasonable demand.

Bruce should have known this, but he worked with little kids, whose predilection to constantly interrupt adults was part of their landscape. He wasn't primed for proper high school protocol, which called for colleagues to approach each other in a calm and steady voice.

One afternoon he popped into my classroom so abruptly, I let out a squeal.

"Sorry, didn't mean to scare you," he started. "We're chartering a plane to Little Diomede! There's room for one more. We're gonna stay over in their brand new multimillion dollar school. Wanna come?"

Before I could process this torrent of opportunity, Bruce added that the "we" included himself, Carrie, and Anne, who'd heard that the district was giving teachers a Friday off to relax and do whatever teachers do when they're not working. It had been a tough winter. This was our consolation prize: Take an extra day, get your act together, and finish out your contract, please. And what better way to relax than take a trip to a tiny island in the middle of the Bering Strait?

I stared at Bruce. The gears in my brain clunked around, searching for reasons not to go. I was ridiculously behind on schoolwork. I had a do-or-die deadline looming for yearbook publication. But two nights out of town couldn't hurt. If others were taking time off, why shouldn't I?

Bruce waited. (Elementary teachers are patient people.)

The radical thought of taking a break grabbed hold, and I felt a subtle shift of energy in my chest. It was the resolute finger of Destiny reaching out and tapping me on my heart center.

"Carpe Diem," it said. "Go."

"Sure." I gave Bruce a thumbs-up. "Count me in."

The Saturday morning of our departure, Anne and I hustled to pack, then hitched a ride to the airstrip with Principal Ken. Bruce and Carrie were already there, huddled in the crisp morning light, watching the pilot performing his usual assessment of sizes, shapes, and weights of cargo and passengers.

Having heard that space would be limited, I wore half of my suitcase contents, the effect of which made me look like I weighed over two hundred pounds. Whatever that meant for defying the law of gravity, the pilot pointed at me to board the plane first and then followed as I shimmied my girth down the narrow aisle to a single seat in the plane's tail.

"Here," he held out a folded sleeping bag, "sit on this."

I tucked it under my rear and felt my head press into the ceiling.

"Maybe lose the beaver hat." He winked. "You can hold onto your duffel."

I agreed. If we crashed, the tail of the plane and my seat would separate as one unit, but at least I'd be cushioned for the ride.

Being loaded first meant that I had to sit in a cramped position for longer than anyone else, but it also meant I could engage in people-watching. Along with the teachers, a few Shishmaref locals were making the trip to visit distant relatives. I was fascinated by one elderly woman who had dressed to the nines in a fur-trimmed parka and sealskin mukluks with beadwork over the toes. Her lovely ensemble aside, she was a bit portlier than the rest of us, and I was curious how the pilot was going to pack her in. She might have been wondering the same thing as passengers entered the craft ahead of her, one by one. Only one seat remained, next to the pilot. Shotgun.

The pilot helped the woman step up and aim her bottom toward the small seat. We held our breath. The plane creaked as she dropped in. Unexpectedly, the tail, where I was sitting, shifted down. (I had no idea why, as the woman's added weight was up front.) *Cre-e-e-a-k … whomp*! I felt like I was on the end of a seesaw with a partner who had suddenly had enough of the game and dismounted. The entire back of the plane thunked onto the snow.

The pilot stepped back and looked toward the plane's tail, then looked back at the woman. She looked at him and chuckled. Then he laughed, which gave the rest of us permission to laugh as well.

"Okay, let's get you buckled in." He pulled the seat belt over her shoulder and leaned across her belly to fasten it, as if securing a toddler. She reached out and pretended to slap him on the butt. That made us laugh even harder.

The pilot backed out, his expression showing that he knew exactly what she was doing. He shook his head and closed her door, leaning hard until it clicked shut. Then he walked around the back, appeared a moment later on the other side, and climbed in. We were good to go.

"Okay, folks," the pilot yelled over his shoulder, "y'all strapped in good and tight?" More laughter ensued. We were packed in so tightly that seat belts were hardly necessary. He adjusted his headset, and his voice came over the intercom.

"I'm Jim. Welcome aboard! It's about eighty-seven miles to Little Diomede. Flight's roughly one hour. Should be a smooth ride."

I watched from my rear perch as the propellers sputtered to life, circled slowly, then rotated to a blur. The back of the plane lifted, raising me up as if my seesaw partner had returned to play. Everyone cheered. Jim taxied in a slow roll toward the lagoon, going as close as possible to the edge, then turned north and paused. I'm sure I wasn't the only one praying the runway would be long enough.

Jim increased engine power, and the wheels grabbed ground. We bumped along, passing a cluster of villagers waving goodbye. The plane's wheels rumbled on the uneven snow, and then, just before there was no more room to rumble, we lifted. Like magic, the oncoming wind caught under our wings. I leaned forward to look out the windows on my left and right. Shishmaref's shoreline zoomed by, then dropped away. The plane gradually gained altitude and arced south. We followed the coastline, visible only by the lines of sea ice that had pushed onto shore and stacked on top of each other with every movement of the ocean's current underneath.

It was a beautiful day. The sky was bright blue, and the ground sparkled white. So much white. Only occasional shadows indicated snowdrifts or blocks of ice jutting up. With no other reference point, altitude was a mystery.

No one spoke, lost in the vastness and beauty of what lay below. It was wide open, unobstructed, for hundreds of miles. Even the curvature of the earth was visible. Jim turned west, the shoreline ended, and we flew over ice-covered sea.

Several minutes later, Jim said something over the intercom, but the engines were vibrating so loud, I couldn't make it out. I tapped on Carrie's shoulder.

"What'd he say?" I yelled.

"Whales!" She pointed down to the right.

In the ink-black water of an opening in the ice were half a dozen long, ghostly-white animals.

Carrie leaned back. "Belugas!"

I had never seen a beluga whale. I didn't even know they existed. The pilot circled to give us a good look at the whales rolling and spouting. Their short flippers rotated through the Arctic air and disappeared again into the dark water. They didn't look like whales at all. Their tails were stumpy, they had no dorsal fins, and their heads looked like balloons filled with helium. God had a strange sense of humor.

There had to be hundreds, possibly thousands of miles of pack ice out here. This one opening gave the Belugas a moment to surface, rest, and breathe. When the ice closed in again, who knows how far they'd have to swim with their little flippers and bulbous heads?

Our pilot straightened the craft again and we continued our journey, the droning of propellers our only sound. Several minutes later, he reduced altitude and banked the plane again, this time to the right. His lack of warning with the sudden maneuver alarmed me, but then I saw that he was following the excited finger-pointing of his sidekick up front. I tapped Carrie's shoulder again.

"Walrus!" she said.

Holy cannoli. Resting on the bank of another opening in the ice were several walruses. They looked enormous. Their long white tusks glistened in the sun's rays.

But our viewing was cut short. The plane had startled the animals. One by one, they humped forward and slipped into the sea.

We flew for a short while longer, and then Jim slowed the plane and started to reduce altitude. Word traveled back that he thought he'd spotted polar bear tracks and was going to circle around. Once more, he expertly banked the craft and brought us lower until it felt like we were only fifty feet from the surface.

Carrie yelled over her shoulder. "Do you see 'em?" She pointed down and then away to indicate a path.

Sure enough. Round imprints in the snow. The clarity of the impressions startled me. We could see the slight drag of claws behind every other step, like the bear had been out for a lazy stroll.

The tracks continued north, but the bear was nowhere to be seen. Jim turned the plane once more to the west. I started daydreaming about trips my family had taken to the Milwaukee Zoo when I was a child, and how I'd loved to see the polar bear exhibit. One bear always entertained himself by ambling along fake rocks and diving into a large pool. He swam right past me through the viewing glass, pawing the water and twirling around. His silky, white-yellow fur billowed behind. The bear loved this circuit and did it over and over again. I could have watched for hours.

Excited gestures at the front of the plane grabbed my attention. Far in the distance, barely perceptible in the white-on-white landscape, two mountains rose above the pack ice. The one on the right, Big Diomede, was massive. On the left was Little Diomede, shaped like a gumdrop and dwarfed by comparison. Together, the two islands created breathtaking apparitions in the snowy landscape.

Right after I had given Bruce a thumbs-up about the trip, I'd gone to the school's library to research the Diomede Islands. I'd heard of Little Diomede but didn't know it was only a couple of miles away from Big Diomede, which belonged to Russia. I learned that Innuits had been living on or stopping by the islands for thousands of years. As usual, the Europeans who sailed in this hemisphere a couple centuries ago took it upon themselves to rename landforms and claim them as their own. Vitus Bering, a Danish explorer, came through the area on August 16, 1728. For some reason, he was in the service of the Russian empire, and it so happened that April 16 was the date when the Russian Orthodox Church celebrated a martyr named Saint Diomedes of Tarsus, in Greece. Why not name the islands after him? And, while he was at it, why not name the narrow stretch of water between the islands after himself.

In 1867, a treaty between the United States and Russia finalized the Alaska purchase and designated a boundary between the two nations. At that time, Little Diomede was also referred to as Krusenstern Island, after Russian explorer Adam Johann von

Krusenstern. He was the first to circumnavigate the world by sea in the early 1800s—or so he claimed.

Native people were more practical with naming places. Before the unnatural demarcation of land ownership of Russia versus the United States, they simply called the smaller of the two islands *Ignaluk*, which translates as "the other one" or "the one over there"—which meant they must have been standing on the shores of the bigger island and looking to the east. They also called the smaller island "Yesterday Isle," and the homes at its base, *Inalik*.

I didn't find a translation for that. Maybe "that which hangs on for dear life"? The black and white photos I'd found of the village showed a clump of tiny structures that looked like a cluster of barnacles at the base of a rock that could be washed away any minute.

Little Diomede, with its 40-degree slope

Conversely, people in *Inalik* called Big Diomede, across the water, "Tomorrow Land."

I was learning that naming things was a matter of perspective and whoever had the power to scribe names on a map. Big Diomede was also called Ratmanov Island or Nunarbuk. I wasn't sure what that stood for. "The bigger one of the ones over there"? I kept reading.

Little Diomede Island was sixteen miles away from the mainland of Alaska, and only 2.8 square miles in size. The only thing that seemed to make it noteworthy was its proximity to the International Dateline. Meaning Russia. Not a country to mess with during a Cold War.

What surprised me was learning that the International Dateline wasn't drawn down the middle of the 2.4-mile-wide Bering Strait; it was closer to Little Diomede, only 0.37 miles from shore. I traced the dateline with my finger over the top of the globe and landed in London. In the 1880s, British mariners used that location as the place from which to calculate their longitude. Greenwich was zero degrees. Over time, all time zones were set from that point. It was another man-made construction to help make sense of reality on a planet that still had parts unknown.

As we flew toward the village of Little Diomede, time zones and land ownership felt totally irrelevant. Muriel Rukeyser's poem, "Islands," rose up in my mind, wherein she reminds us that humans are like islands—actually connected to each other, although we may not always appear to be that way.

My poem recitation was interrupted when I realized we were flying low, almost eye level, with the village. *How are we going to land?*

A line of traffic cones came into view. I counted a dozen of the bright orange markers set twenty or thirty yards apart. They looked so small. Did anyone go out there and test the ice before a plane landed? Our vessel probably weighed several thousand pounds.

During my research, I'd learned that the Bering Strait was shallow by ocean standards, between one hundred and one hundred sixty feet. The height of a ten-story building.

Jim flew straight down the line of cones, reducing altitude and providing a vantage point that offered a spectacular view of Little

Diomede's steep hillside rising above the cluster of small houses. One much larger building sat at the north end, with dark green siding and a substantial roof. *That must be the school.* The usual water or oil tanks were visible in the village, and a few freight containers. It all looked so normal. A typical Native village, but in a radically precarious location.

Jim made another announcement. This one I heard. "Hang tight!"

I felt the back of the plane sway to the right, carrying us as if we were on a teacup carnival ride. It was an out-of-body experience. Jim conducted a maneuver that defied the law of physics—his skill was breathtaking, essentially turning the aircraft one hundred eighty degrees in midair to face the opposite direction. Jim held the controls, but it still felt like the hand of God reached down and helped with repositioning.

With the orange cones once more in sight, Jim aligned the aircraft and descended quickly. Lower and lower we went until the wheels hit the ice with a jolt, and everyone lurched forward. He turned the plane hard and taxied back to the middle of the runway, where a road to the village had been cleared on the ice.

That's when we saw them: dozens of villagers advancing down the hill. They came on snow machines and on foot. And there were kids. Lots of kids, running toward the plane as fast as their little legs could carry them.

The plane jerked to a halt and Jim cut the engines and yelled, "Sorry, I shoulda warned you 'bout that tight turn in midair! If we go into Russian airspace, they think we're lookin' to cause an international incident. It's not called the Cold Curtain for nothin'. They shoot flares sometimes. Even send out MIGS to intimidate us." He hung up his headset. "So, this is Little Diomede!" He nodded out his window. "And here comes the welcoming committee."

Jim's first order of business was to help his shotgun passenger deplane. The craft creaked when she stepped off and creaked even more from passengers unbuckling and making their way out. My left leg had fallen asleep, causing me to walk with a limp to the front of the plane. I looked like a drunken crab.

My delay in leaving the aircraft gave me time to observe the gathering outside. The Shishmaref locals laughed and spoke excitedly with Diomede villagers. About a dozen children, six or seven years old and dressed in an assortment of oversized snow gear, surrounded Carrie, Anne, and Bruce, making it impossible for them to move.

As soon as I was clear of the plane, the mob of children refocused their attention on me. One little boy broke away from the pack and ran full out. I braced for his tackle, but he surprised me with a long jump right into my chest, wrapping his little arms around my neck and squeezing hard. "Hullo! Hullo!"

"Hullo!" I tried to maintain my balance. I let him cling for a moment, then managed to pry off his little arms and set him down among the gob of kids pressed around me.

"Help," I mouthed to Carrie.

"Hey, kids!" Carrie called out, unzipping her backpack. "I brought some candy!"

In an instant, the children turned and ran toward her. She started handing out Fruit Roll-Ups as fast as she could pull them from the box. "Yikes, you guys! Calm down. Calm down. There's enough for everyone!"

Once the children were occupied, Carrie, Anne, Bruce, and I picked up our bags and glanced at Jim, who was still unloading parcels and talking to men from the village.

"Hey, Jim!" Bruce called out. "We're going to head up. Are you leaving?"

"Yeah, I gotta get going again before the ice fog starts to build. It's nice now, but it can change in a flash. I'll see y'all in two days. Stay close to the radio in the morning. I'll call in."

We thanked him and began walking toward the steep lower slope of the village. Our boots squeaked on the dry snow. We alternated between watching our step and gazing up at the peak that had no end.

Little Diomede Island is composed of Cretaceous Age granite and quartz monzonite. Most of the island was covered in snow, but bumps of dark rock lay exposed in places where the wind had blown the snow clean off. I counted about twenty houses, and above those, a scattering of small crosses. Their cemetery.

Bruce came up alongside me.

"Looks so exposed." I shifted my pack. "How many people live here?"

"I think about one hundred, maybe a bit more. And that," he looked toward the summit, "is about a thousand feet high."

We caught up to Carrie and Anne and stopped to watch the Fruit Roll-Up kids sliding on their bottoms down a steep embankment. No sleds, no inner tubes. They flew down with surprising speed, screaming and laughing the whole way.

Bruce pointed out the school and informed us that the principal agreed to meet us there. It would be a steep climb.

We started navigating the first of many shallow steps carved into the snow. Warmer spring temperatures had made them slippery, and they glistened like an ice rink after the Zamboni made a round. There wasn't a railing in sight. One misstep would mean a long, hard slide to the bottom—and another chance to meet the kids.

We followed Bruce single file and zigzagged between houses built on stilts and braced with crossbeams. Most were made with plywood, and some had a second layer of wood or metal siding. Their small windows faced the Strait and Big Diomede—humble dwellings with a million-dollar view.

The path leveled out, and we stopped to catch our breath in front of two boats resting upside down on scaffolding.

"Umiaks." Anne walked underneath. "Skin boats."

"Skin?" Carrie stepped in for a closer look.

"Yeah, walrus, I think. Maybe seal." Anne lightly touched the hull. "They use 'em for hunting or carrying supplies, even paddling to the mainland." She nodded toward Big Diomede. "Used to go back and forth between here and Big Daddy, too, visiting family.

But visits were shut down in the mid-'70s. Cold War an' all. Just military stations over there now."

I moved underneath an umiak and snapped a few photos. The wood frames and beams looked exceptionally heavy, but the villagers had taken precautions to secure the boats with thick rope. *It must get really windy through here.* I wondered how they managed to carry the massive crafts all the way up here. And how did they get them back down to shore?

View of inverted umiak (skin boat), one of several set on racks and being stored during winter

The sounds of children screaming and laughing turned our attention downhill. A man was driving a snow machine, pulling what looked like a large piece of carpet. Several kids were sitting on top; a couple tried to stand, like they were surfing. One tumbled off and screamed with delight, then ran to catch up. *Arctic inner tubing?*

"Looks like they're cleaning a polar bear skin." Anne chuckled. "Better get a photo of that." Then she gestured at something behind my boots. "And him, too."

I turned. Laying on the snow was the head of one ginormous walrus. Two long tusks protruded from its upper lip.

"You just never know what the day's going to bring," Carrie said, laughing. "Say cheese!"

Following her prompt, I snapped a photo of the walrus head, then proceeded uphill. As we approached the school, a door opened and out stepped a man, presumably the principal.

"Welcome to Little Diomede!" He shook our hands. "I'm Jake Thompson. Call me Jake."

Jake was about thirty years old and had the requisite Alaskan beard and a sweatshirt with the name *Diomede Dateliners* emblazoned on the front. He explained that the school had just been completed after years of pressure from the state's Department of Education.

"They said every kid in a bush community had to get an education, or else they'd get shipped off to boarding school." He waved his arm. "You can see what parents thought of that! They got a little more than four million dollars to build this place and keep their culture intact."

The school was remarkable, with new furniture, a well-stocked library, and a gym with smooth rubber-like flooring. The interior smelled of new carpet and paint. Jake opened a storage closet, revealing shelves filled with new pairs of roller skates.

"The kids love 'em." He chuckled. "Good exercise for the teachers, too. I've still got to work up the nerve to put a pair on."

I spied sets of brand-new cross-country skis and poles leaning in one corner. "Wow. Nice equipment." My voice carried a tinge of jealousy. "But where do you ski?"

"The kids go out on the ice. The runway's a good spot. You just gotta keep your wits about you, pay attention to sounds of the ice shifting, then sprint home."

Our tour ended in the library, where Jake informed us that only a few teachers were stationed at the school.

"Stephanie teaches elementary. She's invited you to her place for dinner."

"How many students?" Carrie asked.

"Twenty-four. Pre-K through twelfth grade."

"So, four million dollars for twenty-four kids." Bruce was quick with the math, counting on his fingers. "That's about one hundred and sixty-some thousand per kid?"

"Yep." Jake shrugged, then gestured to the far side of the room. "Bathrooms are over there. You can pull mats from the gym for sleeping here in the library. You can't beat the view!"

We spent the remainder of the afternoon settling in. I naturally gravitated to a row of *National Geographic* magazines. One had a photo of a gorilla in the Amazon Rainforest. Another sported a stunning photo of the Taj Mahal. What did the children think of those images, so far-removed from their own reality? Then again, were children in Brazil and India looking at *National Geographics* about polar bears and beluga whales?

Jake returned a short while later to inform us that we'd been invited to tea at a nearby home, after which we'd have dinner with Stephanie. He had lined up someone to escort us.

"There's no street signs or house numbers, so I've asked Sister Barat to show you the way. She presides over the small parish."

A short while later, Sister Barat came to pick us up.

"Bienvenu!"

She looked part nun and part Arctic explorer in her wool cap, snow boots, and a large parka over a long, black cassock. A patch of white cloth peeked from her throat, and her dark brown eyes twinkled in friendship.

Anne, ever the inquisitor, asked Sister Barat about her name. She shared that it was derived from Madeleine Sophie Barat, a French saint of the Catholic Church who formed the Society of the Sacred Heart. It was an important group that trained women to be in service to the church.

By her wrinkles, the sister could have been fifty or even sixty years old, but she moved with the deftness of a mountain goat over the slick paths. We followed her slight figure to a shack perched on the steep slope and supported by a crosshatch of wooden stilts. *This was someone's home? How are we all going to fit?*

My question was answered when Sister Barat pulled back a heavy curtain and beckoned us into a narrow passageway that opened into a room carved into the mountain. Two of the Shishmaref locals and a couple Diomede villagers greeted us warmly and offered Ritz crackers and jam, along with sweet, hot tea. We munched and sipped and nodded approvingly at our hosts. They spoke little English, but managed to communicate a few questions, asking us what we thought of the school and whether we liked crabbing. Their eagerness to meet teachers made me wonder if our visit was part of the principal's recruitment plan. Maybe he hoped a couple of us would join his team in their million dollar school.

We soon bid farewell and followed Sister Barat outside. She walked us back toward the school and pointed out Stephanie's house, then bowed good night. Her eyes still twinkled in the cold evening air, just like the stars that had begun to shine in the indigo sky.

Stephanie's house was cozy. She had tomato soup on the stove and was just finishing a stack of grilled cheese sandwiches. Her spectacular view of Big Diomede was blurred behind the steamy windows.

"It's my second year here." She set the platter of sandwiches on the table. "It's not for the faint of heart. But I'm a Montana girl. Snow and ice don't faze me. I love working with so many ages in one room. The kids are sweet and so eager to learn. We got to study a lot of flora and fauna before the snow and ice locked us in."

"What kinds of plants grow here?" Carrie asked.

"Oh my gosh, where do I start?" Stephanie took a slurp of soup and wiped her mouth. "Well, for fauna, there are literally thousands of birds, especially in the fall. Puffins, murres, hawks, Canadian geese …" She counted on her fingers. "And there's all kinds of foxes. Arctic, red, and blue. Even some Arctic hares. Then you've got all the water creatures—the walrus, the belugas, and bearded seals." She laughed. "It's a busy place. Did you catch the kids riding on that polar bear hide?"

I nodded, then swallowed a bite of sandwich and reminisced about my experience with Eskimo ice cream. "How about berries?"

"Sure, there's cloudberries. They're a bit hard to find. Kinda like a raspberry. Sweet and tart at the same time. Not as many seeds, though. And there are different kinds of greens—Eskimo cabbage, Eskimo potatoes …" Stephanie paused in thought. "Oh, and seaweed. They gather a lot of these things in the fall and stick 'em in seal oil to preserve them." She scrunched her face. "Still trying to appreciate that taste."

Our conversation then turned to Shishmaref and the common challenges we faced with maintaining student interest in subjects that seemed to have only a minor place in Native culture. Stephanie was sympathetic and admitted that she hadn't encountered much resistance from the younger children. They seemed eager to participate in the newness of school. Her only suggestion with older kids was to keep looking for ways to make Western curriculum relevant to the needs of Native culture.

"Speaking of which …" Stephanie stood and reached into the cupboard. "Surprise! Something from *our* culture! Betty Crocker." On the plate sat a large cake slathered with chocolate frosting. "Hope you like it!"

We most certainly did, and almost finished the entire thing. We'd used every dish and utensil in Stephanie's kitchen and insisted on staying to help her wash up before saying good night.

It was bone-chilling cold outside. The stars were magnificent. I would have loved to stay outside longer to take in the view, but I was oh-so-ready for bed and followed the puffs of exhalation from my colleagues as we tromped up the hill.

But rest was hard to come by. My gym mat was thin, and no curtains blocked the moonlight. The wind howled and whistled around the building, making it shudder and creak. I tossed and turned for what felt like hours, then finally fell into a deep and dreamless sleep.

The smell of coffee brought me back to consciousness. Nutty, delicious, mouthwatering coffee. I threw on a sweatshirt, grabbed my instant coffee (which I'd brought "just in case"), and went to investigate the light down the hall.

Carrie was in a small kitchen area, pouring boiling water into a glass carafe. Her long, dark hair was pulled back in a ponytail. She had on baggy sweats, wool socks, and an oversized wool sweater.

"Morning," I whispered.

"Morning," Carrie whispered back. "Wait a minute. What's that?" She looked with concern at the jar in my hand.

"Coffee." I held it up. "Nescafé Taster's Choice."

"Oh my lord. Nope. Sorry." She grabbed the jar and set it on the counter. "I told you I was going to make you some *real* coffee." She held the carafe under my nose. "One sip of this and you'll be hooked."

"What is that?"

"It's a French Press." Carrie looked at me, suddenly understanding I'd never seen one before. "You put your coffee in, add boiling water, and wait a few minutes. There's a mesh thingy to hold the grounds back when you pour."

The French Press had a shiny silver cap and a silver frame. It looked like more work than instant coffee, but there was an elegance to it. My jar of Nescafé suddenly looked horribly out of place.

While we waited for the coffee to steep, Carrie divulged how a friend who worked for Starbucks roasting company taught her the proper way to brew a delicious cup of coffee.

"I'm a bit of a coffee snob now." She pushed down the plunger. "But it's worth the wait."

Carrie held the carafe up to the light to examine the color.

"It's ready enough." She poured two mugs. "Cream? Sugar?"

I shook my head. Never knowing if there'd be fresh cream in the house, and not liking the taste of sugar in my cuppa Joe, I had settled on drinking my coffee black.

"Well, it'll pack a punch, compared to that stuff you've been drinking."

Before I could protest, Carrie splashed cream in my mug. "There. Try that."

She watched as I took my first sip of real coffee, my eyes growing wide with the explosion of taste.

"Oh my god. This is *dee-licious.*"

"Told ya."

Carrie and I were on our second cup when Jake arrived with a bag of breakfast goodies. We were soon enjoying scrambled eggs, toast, and wedges of juicy orange.

"Hope this is enough." He laughed. "There's no Denny's on the island. I'll stock the fridge later with some lunch things. Dinner might be crab. I asked the locals if they'd be okay with you going out to their crabbing spot and watching them pull a few in. I'll come back soon to get you pointed in the right direction."

I wasn't keen about adding crab to my compromised vegetarian status. Maybe Stephanie would sell me a can of soup. But I didn't want to miss the action. When breakfast was over, I bundled up and joined my colleagues. We headed down the hill, hugging the shoreline, with Jake in the lead. In the distance were two figures on the ice.

"That's them." Jake pointed. "Just watch your step over the ice chunks. It's hard as rock, and you'll break something or get badly bruised if you fall." He started back up the hill but turned and yelled, "And keep an ear out for moving ice. Sounds like thunder and happens fast!"

Jake was right about the precarious footing. Slabs of ice, several feet high, piled against each other. Like stratified rock in a canyon, each slab told its own story through layers of snow, gravel, and translucent sheets. Some pieces were milky blue.

It was dangerous but breathtaking. Ice crystals hovered in the air, and every surface the sun touched looked like an explosion of diamonds.

We picked our way through, helping steady each other in places. About fifty yards from shore, we finally reached flatter terrain and quietly approached the two young men, one of whom was hacking at the ice with a long pole. The other saw us and waved. As we neared, I saw that the bottom end of the one man's pole had been fitted with sharp metal tip. Chopping looked like hard work.

Our group stayed at a respectable distance. We knew that the men were in pursuit of dinner, not out here for recreation, and we didn't want to be in the way. Alaskan king crabs weren't an easy catch. The largest of their species, one crab could weigh several pounds and measure one foot at the body and over five feet from claw to claw. That's a lot of crab.

Chopping a hole in the ice to "fish" for crabs

The men beckoned us closer. The one chopping ice introduced himself as Thomas. His crabbing partner was Albert. Thomas flipped back his long, black hair and stabbed at the ice a few more times to widen the hole. "Sometimes we use an auger," he explained, "like a big drill. But this time of year, ice moves in fast." He held up his ice pick and grinned. "This is a heckuva lot easier to carry if the ice moves"

Albert grabbed a saucepan and started scooping slush out of the hole. I peered in. Where we stood, the ice was only about a foot thick.

"Gettin' ready to drop the bait." Thomas surveyed the distance between the islands, gauging our position on the ice. "Crabs like hanging out right about here."

"Ready." Albert finished scooping and stood back. Thomas wrapped a long line of string around a cluster of stones and a spark plug. Then he hooked on the bait.

"What's the bait?" Carrie peered closely.

"Codfish," he said, smiling. "Just goin' down the food chain." He lowered the bundle into the hole. "Now, we wait. And no talking."

We stood together quietly. A gentle breeze blew through my hair. The whole scene was still. Pristine. Powerful. There was potential for something monumental to occur—or nothing at all. I closed my eyes and turned my face to the sun.

A moment later, I sensed movement, and my eyes snapped open to see Thomas quickly gathering the string around a wooden spindle. His fingers flew between pulling the string out of the water and winding it up. Without a word, Albert reached his bare hand into the icy water.

He and Thomas spoke excitedly in their Native language and worked together to pull an enormous crab from its former happy place. They had to tip the crustacean sideways to clear the hole. In seconds, they had the poor thing upside down on the ice. It was orangey-brown and covered with spiky knobs that made it look like a prehistoric water creature. Its long legs flailed, in search of something to grab onto.

"Adult male." Thomas surveyed their catch. "Looks like we can take this one. Gotta set it far from the hole, though. It's a pain in the ass when they crawl back in!"

But the crab wasn't going anywhere. Its legs had started moving more slowly; the cold Arctic air would soon put it to sleep.

We watched as Thomas lowered another set of bait, this time with rocks. He had barely set the line in the water when he started pulling it back out again.

"Move back!" he yelled.

I looked across the icy landscape and blinked, suddenly feeling disoriented and trying to find a point of reference with which to steady my gaze. The ice was moving, coming straight at us. Thomas tossed the lone crab in a bucket and Albert grabbed the ice picks and his saucepan. No time to pull out their line.

The island's coastline seemed very far away. We walked briskly, like kids at a public pool, wanting to move as fast as possible but not wanting to slip and fall. I looked back and saw Thomas and Albert walking several paces behind us. Their faces registered seriousness, but they weren't panicked. I took that as a good sign.

But then I heard rumbling, followed by a large squeaking sound, like huge blocks of Styrofoam rubbing against each other. I stopped, knowing I shouldn't, but I wanted to see for myself. And there it was, the slow and steady advance of sea ice pushing against the ice that had built out from the shore. Slabs the size of garage doors slipped up and over each other, then crumpled underneath as more came in. The power of the current underneath was impossible to comprehend—something so strong that it could push tons of ice without hesitation.

"Keep going." Thomas turned me back toward safety. Albert joined, and I matched their pace.

Bruce, Carrie, and Anne had already made it back to the rocky shore. I moved faster. The creaks and rumbles made the hairs on the back of my neck stand at attention. The last thing I wanted to experience was getting run over by a ton of ice and sinking to an ocean floor filled with huge spiky crabs and a probably a hundred lost-at-sea orange traffic cones.

I turned back once more. Thomas and Albert had stopped their retreat and stood facing the ocean, as if their collective sensing could help them discern whether it was safe to venture back out again, or if one crab was going to be their only catch for the day. I watched them walk toward where their hole used to be and try to retrieve their string and bait. But the ice had cemented in place, leaving the bait for the first lucky crab to come along. They set down their pail and started hacking another hole.

The tracks of my colleagues were all that remained. They'd left me behind, which irked me at first. But then I realized I had these moments to myself to appreciate the stunning landscape. I walked slowly and breathed deeply, appreciating the rare solitude and the incomprehensible height of Little Diomede's hulk rising above me.

As I approached the village, I heard the laughter of children playing. They were at the hill again, this time sliding on garbage bags and pieces of cardboard. The snow was slick, and the kids flew with unnerving speed, screaming with delight as they crashed over hard bumps in the snow. It looked like a painful ride. But it also looked like fun.

Why not?

I didn't have anything to slide on, so I just sat down and used my hands to push, doing my best to pick up speed and hoping not to tear my snow pants apart at the seams. I may have looked ridiculous from an adult's perspective, but the kids egged me on.

I'd heard of people going to therapists for help with managing emotions or navigating a tough time. This seemed easier. It took only three trips down the hill for me to scream away my worries about teaching. With every spin-out and tumble, I felt a release of fears and frustrations, of all my not-knowing. I let go of everything I no longer wanted to hold. Most of it, anyway.

A happy moment on Little Diomede

I found my colleagues lounging in the school's library, seemingly content to stay indoors. I tried to focus on a magazine but jumped up a few minutes later, feeling antsy. Probably from the adrenaline rush of sliding down the hill.

"I'm going to take a walk," I announced. "Anyone interested?"

Bruce, Anne, and Carrie all shook their heads.

Truth be told, I knew I'd be happier on my own. I zipped up my parka again. Maybe I'd see how far I could make it up the mountain. I ambled around the houses, looking for a pathway up, retracing my steps a few times when I hit dead ends. Finally, I found open ground.

With no structures in its way, the wind had blown hard, exposing chunks of black rock covered with yellow and black lichen. I stepped carefully, aiming for patches of snow. Years of hiking above the tree line in Colorado and Washington State had taught me to avoid stomping on delicate plants. They'd worked hard to survive. I didn't want to be what killed them.

Once more the children's song arose in my mind and I half sang, half breathed the lines, "The bear went over the mountain ..." But the higher I climbed above the houses, the higher Little Diomede Island grew over my head. Stephanie had confirmed last night that the island's elevation was 1,620 feet above sea level.

"That's almost one hundred and fifty stories," she said. "I tried to reach the top once but gave up. I hear you can charter a helicopter. Maybe I'll do that someday."

Far from the protection of the houses, I felt the full force of the wind. It came in gusts that shoved my upper body like an impatient bully. My boot nicked the top of a boulder, forcing me to grab the tops of exposed rocks to keep from falling.

My Inner Coach emerged once more, whispering in one ear. "Kind of a stupid idea, don't you think, hiking here of all places?"

Before I could answer, another gust of wind flew up the slope, nearly knocking me down. My Inner Coach was right. My eyes and ears weren't trained to navigate such exposed and steep terrain. With no trees around, I had no warning of the unexpected blasts. And the patches of snow got deeper, making it harder for me to discern if the next step would plunge my foot between rocks and twist my ankle or give way entirely and render me helpless, sliding all the way back down to the village. And not, this time, screaming with delight.

I continued picking my way up, but the slope finally won. It was too steep. I sat down, braced my boots on an outcropping, and lay back to a near Lazy Boy recline.

"Okay," I said out loud. "Let's just say this is the summit." I surveyed the landscape below, and across the Bering Strait.

Was it just two days ago that I was at school and worrying about lesson plans? Ready to up and quit before the school year finished?

Maybe I needed to take a few more trips down the hill with the kids.

The wind blew over my body, and I felt a tear freeze across my cheek. A miracle—that's what I needed. Some kind of miracle telling me that trying to be a teacher of substance in Shishmaref would matter to someone, someday. I relaxed, feeling the earth under me. Mountains had a way of grounding my body and soul. This island, and the bigger one I could see from my perch, made me feel more whole. I was never going to come back here, so I let the moment seep in, wanting to lock it in my memory.

Another gust, this one icier and more menacing, told me it was time to go back down. Low clouds gathered on the horizon. A different kind of chill filled the air. I gingerly made my way around rocks and snow, crouching and traversing a more direct line down the steep slope and back toward the school. I had to calculate each movement. It was slow going.

I placed my gloved hand on a rock to steady my next move, then quickly pulled it back, startled. Right next to me was a small wooden cross, painted white, and a tiny coffin. It was a simple wooden crate set on top of the rocks and held in place with wooden stakes. I looked around. *Oh my god. I'm walking all over their graveyard.*

I glanced far below, afraid to see Sister Barat's disapproving face staring from a window. Only darkened glass looked back at me. I picked up my pace, moving with caution and praying for forgiveness every step of the way.

On our second night on Little Diomede, when the sun had long since disappeared behind a thicket of ice fog, I sat by one of the large windows and gazed across the frozen Bering Strait at Big Diomede. It rose like an enormous monolith above the ice. Snow blanketed its steep sides. An expanse of heavy snow-fog blew hard over the channel, heading south. The air was filled with ice crystals, which gave the scene a ghostly look.

Two small lights on the Russian island were all I had to anchor my view through the mist, one at the top on the north end and one at the base in the middle. Military outposts. The lights twinkled, disappeared in the fog, then reappeared again. I wondered what the military men did over there. Maybe they were playing cards. Maybe they were looking at me right now through an enormous pair of binoculars. Maybe I was under surveillance. I was someone in their Yesterday, looking into her Tomorrow, which was their Today.

Bruce appeared next to me, and we sat in silence for a while.

"I wonder if this fog will strand us here tomorrow." I took a sip of Earl Grey tea. It was more of a comment than a question.

"Depends."

"Yeah, isn't that the truth for just about everything." I twirled my tea bag.

"It's called the Venturi Effect," Bruce added. "I looked it up. When the wind comes from the north, it's squeezed between these two islands. Kinda like water when it's forced through a narrow canyon. The speed increases." He paused, as if to recount the details of his research. "So the wind rushes between the two islands and makes the pressure drop. That's what lowers the dew point and creates fog."

"Hey, people." Carrie plopped down next to Bruce. "What a trip, huh? Lazing around today was heaven! But that crabbing thing and the ice moving—that was *gnarly*.

Bruce and I nodded.

Carrie jumped up again. "Tea looks like a good idea. More hot water?"

"I'll take peppermint if you're serving. Bruce looked out the window again. "While I was researching the air currents, I came across this tidbit as well. Did you know that the Bering Strait impacts the rest of the world's ocean currents? We're sitting in front of one of the most consequential bodies of water on the planet. This water here," he gestured, "flows to the north, downhill. The strait, if I understand correctly, is a choke point between the Pacific Ocean and the Atlantic Ocean. The current we experienced today was a small reminder of what lies under the ice. It's like a ton of Mississippi Rivers flowing through."

This blew my mind. "Wow, I never thought of all the oceans being connected."

Carrie returned with her tea service, then sat down.

Bruce continued his informational lecture. "The other thing I learned was how many nutrients and phytoplankton get carried into the Arctic. There's even different levels of salt and stuff." He paused and took a sip. "And warmer water."

"That's so cool," Carrie said. "I hung out with Stephanie in her classroom this afternoon. She told me about fresh water from the Pacific Ocean and how it comes through here and helps to cap the sea ice in the Arctic. I didn't understand all of it, but there's something about the salt." She waved her hand in front of our view. "All those things make it work. Everything together."

"Look." Bruce pointed out the window. "That's about as Eskimo as you can get."

Out on the ice in the twilight, a lone hunter walked parallel to the island, moving carefully around ice slabs and drifts of old snow. Moving like a man who was meant to be there.

Dinner was Campbell's Minestrone soup and Pilot Bread with cheese. Anne cut up apples for dessert, and Carrie pulled two Cadbury chocolate bars out of her pack.

"Your sweet tooth stash never ceases to amaze me," quipped Bruce.

"Girl Scouts." She shrugged. "Always be prepared."

I slept hard the second night but had a dream that I was on an ice floe, hopping from one chunk to the next until I reached land. I kept looking forward to gauge the distance of my jumps and then looking back to where I had been. With each boot imprint, I left behind residue of something I no longer wanted. The prints started out black, but as I navigated closer to shore, the prints turned to gray. By the time I reached solid ground, there weren't any prints at all.

The next morning, Carrie slid another mug of Seattle's Best coffee with cream under my nose. We sipped in silence, taking in Big Diomede one last time. An hour later, it would be time to go.

"Plane's on its way," Jake said as he came into the room. "Don't worry about cleanup. Just get down to the landing strip. There's fog coming in, so it's going to be a fast turnaround."

We packed quickly. Carrie left a chocolate bar on the counter with a thank-you note, and we headed outside to make our way down the slippery sets of snow stairs to the wide path that led to the plane. A handful of children ran around us in circles all the way to the bottom. They patted our parkas and repeated, "Goodbye!" and "Come back soon!"

In the distance, we saw the plane approaching, just a dot in the sky. It looked fragile and insignificant. We watched the pilot make the same sharp, breathtaking turn before landing.

I looked around the group. "Where are the Shishmaref people?"

"They're staying a few more days," Anne said. "Wish I could, too."

"At least we got some crab." Bruce pointed at a box. "Dinner's at my house tonight."

My seat was more spacious this time and provided a better view of the ice below. I watched in anticipation of more walrus or beluga sightings, but they had traveled on. I cranked my neck to look one last time at the two islands—two nations living so close, yet so far apart.

If we took politics out of the equation, would the people living a mere two and a half miles away from each other really be all that different? They had migrated freely between the islands for centuries, and Bruce told me some families had been split apart, prevented from visiting anymore after the Iron Curtain shut everything down. Trust changed to suspicion, familiarity to secrecy.

I imagined that man-made separation ending one day. Strangers would find family once more, and there'd be an explosion—not of missiles—but of potlucks with crab. Lots of crab.

Muriel Rukeyser was right. The islands, with water between, presented only the illusion of separateness. Anyone brave enough to poke their head under the icy Strait would see that the islands were connected underneath. From that perspective, people on both shores were together, sharing their abundance. And orange traffic cones. Lots of those.

FIFTY-FOUR

GOLDILOCKS MOMENT

Spring had finally gotten serious about showing up. It was early April, and the tilt of the earth brought four more minutes of light each day. The unpredictable snowstorms ceased. Old snow froze overnight but turned to slush by lunchtime. The streets were an obstacle course of puddles, matted grass, and ice mounds, and the road to the dump would soon be the same. It was time for another trash run, sooner than later.

Ever since Little Diomede, I'd looked for opportunities to hang out with Carrie. She was fun, didn't have as much homework to grade, and had that French Press. I wandered over to her side of the school to see if she wanted to join me.

Carrie's classroom was an burst of color. There were posters, toys, and rows of little books on small shelves. She was at her desk. It was covered with children's drawings of Arctic animals and stick people.

"Sure!" She laughed. "Going to the dump sounds like fun. I need some fresh air."

We made a plan for me to pick Carrie up from her house in half an hour, the sled loaded and ready for travel.

"Just don't take me down that alley," she joked.

I had shared my previous debacle between snow drifts and swore Carrie to secrecy. As far as I knew, only she and Principal Ken were privy to my sorry (but funny) tale.

After grabbing the keys to the sno-go from Midge's desk drawer, I skipped down the school steps and around the corner where the machine was always parked. It hadn't been used for a while. I brushed off the snow and used my fist to break a thin coating of ice off the seat. A few pulls of the cord later, the machine rumbled to life. Hitching the sled came next. Within minutes, I was home, pointed in the right direction, and loading the sled with bags and boxes of you-know-what—this time, tied down.

"Hey, lady!" Carrie called out as I pulled up. She stuck out a hitchhiker's thumb. "Goin' my way?"

I paused and pushed up my goggles. "Nice glasses." I gestured at her face. "Those Vuarnets?"

"Not the real thing. Too expensive." She grinned and gestured back. "Nice goggles."

"Yeah, after that ride to Serpentine and back, I thought it would be a good idea to get some eye protection." I winked. "My brother mailed these to me. Yellow lenses are great for flat light, and they make every day a sunny day."

Carrie hopped on and squealed as I pulled away. We followed the well-worn snow road to the dump, singing Beatles songs: "Here Comes the Sun" and "Let It Be."

Twenty minutes later, we were tossing bags and boxes at the dump's edge. Task complete, Carrie suggested exploring the south end of the island before heading back. As I turned us that direction, she spotted a bright orange object in the distance. We went to investigate and discovered a partially decayed pumpkin. It had probably fallen off someone's sled post-Halloween and had been sitting there ever since.

"Hey, let's take photos!" Carrie plopped onto the snow and assumed a sexy pose.

After taking her picture, Carrie took mine. It was one of those silly moments in life that I knew would never come again. I mean, who else had a photo of themselves modeling with a decomposing pumpkin next to a dump in the Arctic?

On the way back, Carrie yelled over my shoulder.

"Hey, wanna come over and meet my new friend?"

"Sure!"

I expected Carrie to say more, but the identity of her friend remained a mystery up to the moment we entered her home. I was unlacing my boots when I heard, "Meew!"

"A kitten?"

"Yeah," Carrie dropped to her knees and made a kissing noise to coax the feline out of hiding. "I got her from a student whose family has a momma cat. They were looking for homes and asked if I wanted to adopt this one."

My eyes began to adjust to the dim light. Carrie's space was small. It had a kitchenette, couch and table, and a small bedroom.

"Ah, there you are!" Carrie gently picked up a tiny gray tabby with black and white stripes. It let out a high mew and yawned. "Aww, taking a nap?" She held it up to her cheek, then planted a kiss on its forehead. "Are you hungry?"

Carrie opened a can of cat food and set it on the floor.

"Oh geez, I'm such a bad hostess!" Carrie looked at me. "Coffee? Tea?"

"Coffee, of course."

For the next half hour, we talked about teaching and things we were looking forward to doing after the school year ended. I honestly didn't have any plans. My life felt as up in the air as when I'd graduated with my degree. Even though it was late afternoon, Carrie made another round of coffee, and we watched Kitten clean her paws.

"Okay, time for a little entertainment," Carrie announced. She got up and pulled a small flashlight from the drawer, then aimed the beam in front of Kitten, moving it back and forth slowly. Kitten stopped her cleaning and focused on the dot of light.

"This is one of our favorite games."

Carrie danced the light more vigorously, waiting for Kitten to pounce. It crouched, tail swishing. Then her rear end shimmied, and she jumped at the light. The light stopped on top of her paws; she froze and stared cross-eyed, uncertain what to do next.

"Oh, wait." Carrie got up again. "We need music!" She grabbed her cassette player and pressed the Play button. The first song was "Stayin' Alive" by the Bee Gees. We moved the flashlight to the steady beat and giggled like schoolgirls as Kitten tried to keep up.

"Oh, crap!" I glanced at the clock on Carrie's wall. "It's late. I need to get the sno-go back to school and finish some prep." I got up and stretched, then gave Carrie a quick hug. "Thanks a bunch. That was the best show I've been to in months."

"I know." She laughed. "Kinda pathetic! Good thing Kitten can't talk. She'd probably be calling CPS."

I slipped on my coat and boots. "What's CPS?"

"Child Protective Services. It's the federal agency you call if you suspect child abuse." She opened the door for me. "Or maybe she'd call KPS!" Carrie paused to see if I followed, then playfully nudged me onto her porch before closing it again. "Kitten Protective Services!"

I drove down the street toward the school. As I came closer, I noticed the sky was changing from light blue to amber. The sun was going down, but the day wasn't over yet. It was cold outside but not uncomfortable. Why not procrastinate a bit longer and go for a little spin? I stopped at the school and unhooked the sled. It would be easier to maneuver without dragging an extra six feet of wood behind me. There was enough daylight to safely drive to the airstrip and back. I'd take the alleys. They had more turns and ridges of snow. In other words, more fun.

No more planes would be coming today, so I drove down the runway, reliving the moment when I first landed on the island and watched Principal Ken's plane launch into the sky.

Eight months. Two-thirds of a year had seen me working diligently, groping through my first year. My college professors said that teaching was a practice, something I had to work on every day.

They were dead right about that. Teaching was a practice, not only in learning the content and skills involved with my subject area, but in observing the kids. Observing myself. And developing patience and compassion. The more I practiced those things, the more I relaxed and became present for students to do the same.

I pulled to a stop at the end of the runway and looked across the vast expanse of sea ice. What would it be like to teach like Carrie? She made it look easy. Not too hard, not too soft. Just right. She was like Goldilocks with dark hair. Of course, Goldilocks was a bit spoiled and self-serving, so the analogy wasn't a perfect fit.

Maybe teaching was more like tuning a guitar. In high school, I'd learned how to play some basic chords. My guitar teacher was always telling me to "fix the pitch and start over." In the beginning, before my ear was trained, I sometimes tuned more than I played.

The second lesson my guitar teacher taught me was how to replace strings if I tuned too tight. Once time, I wound the high E string too tight, and—*sproing*! It broke, zapping me across the cheek and leaving a thin red line that lasted for days. My friends thought it was funny. "What'd you do," they asked, "get in a fight with Zorro?"

Excited by my guitar metaphor, I opened the throttle and headed back to school. *That's it!* Teaching works best when the strings are adjusted at the right tension. I'd know a lesson's viability by listening to the tune—the one in my heart. *The one my students sing.* We could help each other adjust the strings, so to speak, until the song came out right.

Teaching isn't just about me.

It's more like a dance with multiple moves at once, between me and the content, me and my students, them with each other … there's no end to our mutual influence.

"It's resonance." I said the words out loud.

Like the resonance of my guitar. And the guitars of my students. They play, too.

I parked the sno-go at school and turned off the ignition, relieved to turn off the noise and have a moment of silence. A crow flew high overhead. I watched it circle and land on the top of an electric pole. It turned its head and blinked at me as if asking, "Terrific insights, Kulizuk, but can you put them into practice?"

"Ha ha, very funny, Mr. Crow," I said, dismounting and heading up the stairs to return the key. I felt confident, but also a bit unsteady. The crow's clever question followed me all the way inside.

FIFTY-FIVE

TURNING POINT

A rumor had flown around all morning that school was going to be canceled on Friday for annual spring reindeer herding. All teachers were invited to help. The rumor was far-fetched enough that I wasn't sure I believed it, yet realistic enough that I hoped it was true.

My encounters with reindeer on the island had involved only their legs: the one in the truck bed and the one on my porch, followed by the day I saw a puppy struggling to carry what sure looked like a deer leg. It growled when it saw me. "Don't worry," I replied. "It's all yours."

Bruce confirmed the rumor, jumping into my room and startling me once more.

"Bruce, you gotta stop doing that!"

"Sorry, it's just gonna be so cool! You're coming, right? I reserved the school sno-go and can give you a ride."

I did want to go, but Bruce's demeanor unsettled me. Ever since Little Diomede, I'd noticed his mood swinging from polite one minute to pompous the next. He hijacked conversations, pretending to be the man who always caught the bigger fish. I'd noticed this switch in behavior only when Bruce was around women. With men, he was quiet and followed their lead.

Maybe I had nothing to worry about. It was just a ride, and maybe Bruce really did know the way to the happy reindeer herding grounds.

And villagers wouldn't invite a bunch of novices if it wasn't safe to drive over the lagoon, right? We would follow their tracks and be fine.

As usual, when faced with a new adventure, the first thing I did was visit the library. I was surprised to learn that reindeer were not indigenous to Alaska. They were introduced in the late 1800s, in part by a Presbyterian minister named Sheldon Jackson.

Jackson was one of the primary individuals associated with boarding schools in Alaska, whose primary intention was to "educate" Native Alaskan children out of their cultural customs and traditions and into dominant white culture instead. He traveled all over the state and ended up making the acquaintance of a man named Captain Michael A. Healy.

Healy was the first African American man to be commissioned by the United States Revenue Cutter Service (USRC). He traveled thousands of nautical miles throughout his career, up and down the Pacific coast, south from San Francisco, and all the way north to Point Barrow. His main task was to act as a federal enforcement officer, protecting natural resources and suppressing illegal trade. Healy's ships also provided medical supplies and services, including search and rescue operations for shipwrecked sailors and miners.

On occasion, Captain Healy sailed to Siberia, an important turning point for Native people in certain parts of Alaska. During his era, whales and seals were heavily fished—not by Native people, but by everyone else. The dwindling prevalence of marine life didn't necessarily cause starvation, but the Inupiaq people along the coast were placed in the untenable position of trying to protect their primary sources for food, clothing, fuel, and countless other goods from further decline.

Captain Healy had an idea. On one of his trips to Siberia, he noticed that the Chukchi people who lived there had succeeded in domesticating reindeer for consumption. Chukchi literally means "rich in reindeer," so rather than putting a stop to the overfishing that had started this whole mess, Healy thought, "Why not ship boatloads of reindeer from Siberia to the Alaskan Territory to fill the gap?"

That's what he and Sheldon Jackson did. Over time, nearly thirteen hundred head of reindeer were rounded up, floated over, and released on the Alaskan tundra. Of course, they couldn't just run wild; they had to be cared for by the Native Alaskans from various villages. It was touch and go for a couple of decades. Caribou still roamed the territory, so there was a lot of hoof traffic on the tundra.

In the early 1920s, Shishmaref local Fred Goodhope, Sr., received a loan of fifteen hundred deer and moved them to land north of the village. He ended up selling a portion of the herd to longtime resident Clifford Weyiouanna. These were the herds our spring roundup involved, and there were close to two thousand of them.

Herding also took place in summer (for antlers) and late fall (for butchering). Now, in late spring, the focus was on moving herds to fawning areas so the mothers could give birth and raise their babies under the watchful eye of the village caretakers.

I was fascinated by this history and wished I had understood more about the breadth of animal husbandry exercised by the people of Shishmaref. Their invitation to herd reindeer would be my first chance to be immersed in their world. I hoped I'd be useful to them at the same time.

Friday morning, I emerged from my house bundled in my camel-colored winter pants and parka and sporting a bright red knit cap I'd recently purchased at Walter's. It was the perfect replacement for my beaver hat, which was starting to feel heavy and hot. Walter thought it looked terrific on me. "You look like a strawberry!"

The sputter of a snow machine rounded the corner by my house—Bruce and a second rider. *Uh-oh. It's Sophie.*

I knew it was verboten to think poorly of any student, but I rarely had a positive interaction with this particular teenager. Sophie was often absent without apology and sullen when she attended. She also loved to jockey with me for control of the classroom.

I tried to hit the reset button every time she and I crossed paths, but an underlying tension remained between us, the source of which I hadn't been able to figure out. Maybe it was me, maybe it was her.

Likely a little of both. I was several years older but felt inadequate in her presence, and her unpredictable countenance made me anxious. I had enough insecurities to manage; I didn't need an adolescent to remind me of them.

But my angst had to be tabled. Sophie and I were going to ride uncomfortably close, whether we liked it or not.

Bruce stopped the machine inches from my boots, and Sophie slipped off.

"You should wear another hat," she said bluntly. "Reindeer go crazy when they see red."

I hesitated, waiting to see if her command came with a smirk. Sophie had a sly and sometimes discourteous sense of humor. But the edges of her mouth didn't twitch. She stayed, planted in front of me like a stern mother scolding her kid.

"You're not kidding, are you?" My words came out more defensively than I'd intended, making my face flush. I felt a twinge of embarrassment and anger, like I'd suddenly transformed into that little kid who was unwilling to leave her new strawberry hat at home.

I glanced at Bruce to get his opinion, but he only shrugged.

With no choice in the matter, I went back in the house, feeling miffed about being ordered around by a teenager. Sophie was probably loving it.

I grabbed my beaver hat and clomped back out, wondering how people knew that reindeer hated the color red. Just how close were we going to get, anyway? Hopefully they'd approve of forest green and brown.

Sophie was perched on the back of the sno-go seat when I returned.

"You can sit in the middle."

I didn't argue. Sometimes it was easier to let Sophie have her way.

Bruce yelled, "Ready?"

Before I could respond, we were off and racing through the alleys and around houses, toward the lagoon with ice that I hoped was still solid. Sandwiched in the middle, I managed to zip my parka to periscope status, and I ducked my head to hide from the frigid air rushing over the sno-go's windshield. *I should have brought my sunny yellow goggles.*

The snow was rough with low, icy drifts that had been sculpted by months of ceaseless Arctic winds. I grasped the lower part of Bruce's jacket. I didn't know him well enough to impose a full embrace and also didn't want him to get any ideas.

I wondered why Sophie rode with us. Did she just need a lift out to the corral? Was she mad that the only ride she could find was with Bruce and me? But Sophie was always in a bad mood. Maybe her disposition had nothing to do with me. Maybe she had a tough home life. Maybe I didn't need to be so cynical. Maybe she came along to show us the way. Bruce said he knew, but I didn't trust that. Regardless, I couldn't feel Sophie holding onto me and had no idea how she managed to stay on the seat through Bruce's frantic pace. We hit a bump, and I grabbed his hem a little harder.

I was about to yell at Bruce to slow down when Sophie leaned forward and yelled something in my ear. We were going what felt like fifty miles per hour, and I couldn't make out her words. Sophie's body suddenly pressed into mine, which was strange. Then her right arm came over my shoulder and she hit Bruce on his.

Bruce didn't flinch. He was so intent on driving as fast as he could that he either didn't feel her fist or didn't care. But Sophie was determined to get his attention, and I wished I knew why. I also wished he would slow down. She reached out and hit his shoulder again. Even that didn't deter him. What was his problem?

Apparently, that was the last straw. Sophie launched her entire upper body over the top of my head and brought both fists down, hard, on Bruce's shoulders. She stabbed her hand near his face. "Left! Go left! Now!"

Alarmed by the tone in her voice, I peeked to the right and saw a thin black line on the ice. My eyes followed it to where we were headed. If we didn't reduce speed and turn, we'd be crossing over it in less than a minute. Bruce finally applied the brake but didn't change our trajectory.

"What?" he yelled.

Sophie jumped forward again and pulled back Bruce's hood.

"STOP!"

"STOP!" I yelled, suddenly realizing Sophie's alarm. "There's a crack in the ice!"

"Oh, god!"

Bruce realized his error and let up on the throttle so fast that Sophie and I mashed into his back. He made a cautious left and resumed at a slower pace. Sophie sat down as Bruce brought us far away from but parallel to the black line in the ice.

After a few minutes, the black line disappeared, and Sophie called out, "You can follow that track over there, but stay on it."

I unzipped my hood and pulled off my hat to get a better look at our surroundings. The cold air felt good on my face, which was hot and prickly. If I'd had a bucket of ice water, I would have stuck my head in it.

I turned toward Sophie. "Thank you."

And I meant it.

I felt her hand on my shoulder give me a little squeeze.

A student's woodblock print

We came over a small rise and there they were. Hundreds of reindeer on a gentle slope, with dozens already in a series of corrals. Their brown bodies shuffled one way, then another, moving en masse. The clacking of antlers filled the air along with the occasional snorts of confused and likely irritated animals.

We rumbled to a stop, and Bruce turned to Sophie. "Thanks for that back there."

She looked at him coldly. "You gotta slow down. Otherwise, you miss things. The old trails aren't good no more."

Bruce looked at me in an apparent attempt to gain my support. But Sophie had said all that needed saying, and I concurred. I answered Bruce with a shrug and followed Sophie up the hill, toward the corrals.

The deer were majestic and rugged looking, their fur matted in places and shedding in others. Warmer temperatures meant they would soon lose their winter coats. They moved gracefully across the uneven snow and tufts of grass, coaxed by the herders who directed them into a large corral. A few of the bigger animals grunted and snorted loudly, not keen about what was happening.

"Here," Sophie took me by the arm, "we can go in."

Oh my god, we're going in.

There would be nothing between us and the reindeer, who were growing increasingly flustered. They huffed and pranced, halted, and changed direction. I focused on their sharp antlers and pointed hooves.

"You're here!" I heard voices calling out. "Isn't this cool?"

It was my *Northern Lights News* reporters. They jogged in unison to where I stood, laughing and nudging me on account of my apparent unease.

More people entered the corral and stepped behind a cluster of reindeer that jostled along the rails for a spot as far away as possible. Everyone was lining up and distributing a wide and extremely long stretch of brown burlap. As the burlap came to me, Sophie showed me how to grab the top edge and put my arms around my neighbor's shoulders. Within minutes our long line looked like as if we were sharing one enormous beach towel.

"Now, we go fish," Sophie said softly.

Fish?

She pressed closer. I looked at her, not understanding. Her response came through a huge smile. I had never seen Sophie's smile. Her entire face sparkled with anticipation.

"Step a little." Sophie shuffled forward with the line, nudging my shoulders to follow. "Be real quiet."

A hush fell over the group. Our long line of boots, bodies, and the brown burlap inched forward, creating the illusion of a wall that decreased the size of the corral and forced the reindeer into a smaller space. One man stood on the other side of the gate, ready to swing it shut after the deer entered. From there, more handlers moved deer forward in smaller units until only one deer at a time could squeeze through the last holding pen for inspection, injections, and tagging of ears. The handler's movements were rough, maybe even brutal, but their work was necessary to preserve the herd.

A large buck with a three-foot rack of antlers decided that moving into a smaller pen was not to his liking. He took some halting steps, stopped about twenty feet in front of our section, and turned his massive antlered head left, then right. He studied the situation, trying to make sense of us. I'm sure the burlap wall was confusing. Here was a fully grown deer who had been roaming freely on the tundra for months, suddenly finding himself confronted by a moving wall. I would have been confused, too.

"It's okay," Darlene whispered at my left shoulder.

But it wasn't okay for the buck. He pawed at the ground and snorted. I still didn't understand about deer not liking red, but I could see now why Sophie told me to leave my strawberry inclinations at home. If she was right, I'd be the first person the deer aimed for. We were so close I could smell his pungent, earthy fur.

"It's okay," Darlene whispered again. "Just breathe."

I didn't know if she was saying it to herself or me, but I appreciated her reminder to stay calm. She nudged me playfully and then winked past my nose at Sophie.

In that instant, something blossomed inside of me—some energetic force. It permeated the core of my being. Or maybe it had been there this whole time and had just woken up. A soft flash of awareness distributed itself inside of me, like it was setting up home. The only confirmation of this movement within me was the look in Darlene's eyes and the simultaneous side-hug from Sophie. They were in cahoots, but in a loving way.

The buck's patience ran out. With a mere two, then three prancing steps, it ran directly at us and jumped cleanly over our heads. We ducked as its deer belly flew by. I flinched, ready to get kicked in the head, but miraculously, no collision came. We turned to watch the buck run along the metal bars of the corral, agitated, trying to figure a way out. It probably could have cleared the fence, but either didn't know that or decided not to try. *The buck stops here.* I smiled at my own joke. Harry Truman would have loved this.

The burlap wall moved again and stepped in cadence to persuade the anxious animal where the handlers wanted it to go, through the gate. It was a game of dodge and parry, and then, resigned to its fate, the deer pranced around one end of our line and into the second corral, where the handler slammed the gate closed. Everyone cheered. If a deer had fingers, I'm sure this buck would have shown us the middle one.

That was the end of "going fish" for the day. The villagers worked together to gather up the burlap. I helped, then stood to the side, observing the dozens of people talking and laughing, enjoying each other's company. This was my second visit to the mainland since arriving in Shishmaref. It was lovely. Rustic, wide open, and full of life. I could see why my students resisted the unnatural interruption of school. I would have wanted to stay out here, too.

In the ruckus of rolling up the burlap, I'd lost sight of Darlene and Sophie. They came jogging back to where I stood.

"Oh god!" Sophie laughed. "My heart was in my throat!" She gave me a side hug on one shoulder, while Darlene did the same on the other.

"You okay?" Darlene asked. "I was so scared."

I nodded, at a loss for words.

The girls departed to be with their friends and family. I looked for Bruce and a ride home.

As we bumped over the snow toward the lagoon, my thoughts returned to the last few hours and the profound experience of being with my students on their own terms—on the ice, when Sophie saved us; in the corral and face-to-face with Darlene. And that other thing—what was that? The thing that unfurled inside of me.

Whatever it was, it happened when I stood close to my students, closer than I had ever stood before, and looked into their eyes. It was like love at first sight, but not in a romantic way. More like a soul-meeting. Something clicked between us. They seemed to feel it too, like we had turned a key together and opened a door to a place we hadn't been before.

The snow machine bumped over a drift, and I instinctively reached out to grab Bruce's shoulder. He slowed our pace, and I gave him a little squeeze.

FIFTY-SIX

SEA CHANGE

The end of the school year was coming fast. A veritable sea change of projects had everyone at school thinking of the past while simultaneously planning for the future. Teachers scoured their grade books and set deadlines for missed assignments, then switched their focus to graduation and awards.

The ocean and lagoon also showed signs of seasonal tension. Ice melted and broke up, only to freeze again. Temperatures hovered near freezing, then came back up, transforming previously iced-over streets to marshes filled with gray water. The Housing Trail to the Washeteria was almost impassable, making my midweek trip an adventure of balancing on the narrow strip of sand on either side.

I felt increasing pressure to finish a last round of writing assignments, especially those written by a handful of students planning to attend college in the fall. They had applied to the University of Alaska in Fairbanks and also the campus in Anchorage. Attending college was a monumental decision. These graduates were the first in their families to pursue higher education and the rare ones willing to experience leaving home for extended periods. They would have to navigate the maze of campus life and deal with traffic and intersections, malls, and the myriad of things I took for granted—and was dying to get back to.

For most of the graduating seniors, however, college didn't make sense. At least not yet. They would live and work where they had grown up, continuing their subsistence lifestyle and raising their children. That was the reasoning behind Career Day, to help Shishmaref's youth envision a good future by wisely using what was left of their high school years.

Students listened to locals speaking about working at city hall or running the community center. They heard about the joys and challenges of managing a grocery store or becoming an artist who could make a living by selling carvings or beadwork to tourists in the big city or in the Lower 48.

A police officer from Unalakleet talked about the role of law enforcement in towns and smaller bush communities. The boys perked up with that one and talked excitedly about the prospect of chasing criminals at high speeds on a snowmobile and wearing a badge and carrying a gun.

The girls seemed to have fewer options, coaxed more into attending the presentation by a nurse from Anchorage, who highlighted the importance of her profession as a traveling health care provider. I would have liked to hear from a female pilot or a woman who served in a leadership role.

I excused myself from the event a little early, needing to inventory the remaining tasks before shipping our yearbook pages to the printer in Nome. We still needed photos of a few staff members and students. And we had to confirm basketball scores and finalize the layout.

The biggest challenge had fallen on my shoulders. As the Graphic Communications teacher, it was my job to contact businesses in Shishmaref and industries in outlying communities for ads to cover the cost of printing. When I first started the process, my list was pathetically short: Nayokpuk General Store and the Shishmaref Native Store.

"Maybe look in the book from last year," Darlene suggested.

"Yeah," Molly said. "Some airline bought a full-page ad."

"Last year's yearbook?" It had never occurred to me to even ask for one.

Fifteen minutes later, the girls returned with an armload of yearbooks, giving me the scoop about potential ad sales.

My main concern was running out of film. We had only two rolls of black and white film left for the school camera. If those got used up, I'd have to use my own supply.

My review of tasks complete, I swiveled in my chair in a playful round. Considering my meager experience with managing such a project, the yearbook was coming along well. The girls made a terrific team, following through with ideas, chasing down leads, interviewing classmates, and finishing their favorite parts of the book without prompting.

Their absolute favorite was asking the seniors to write their "wills"—short statements identifying items they intended to pass down to the classes behind them. The most common items were special writing utensils and notebooks donated to younger students who typically forgot to bring supplies to school. Their intentions made me laugh. They could donate all they wanted, but the same statements had been made by the 1983-84 graduating class, and from what I could tell, most students still showed up empty-handed.

In addition to school supplies, the seniors also promised to pass on certain character traits, like their superstar abilities in basketball or their capacity to get to school on time (also funny).

The students' other favorite part of the yearbook was "The Hall of Fame," which highlighted students' votes for the tallest and shortest students, the best dancers, the biggest flirts, and even the grouchiest. The results were spot-on, a testament to the kids' capacity to accept their classmates' teasing and revel in it.

As I skimmed those pages, it occurred to me that a survey of this tight-knit community would have been a smart way to start the school year, not end it. I surely would have learned more about my students' personalities than those silly letters I asked them to write about "what I should know about living in their village."

The other thing I would have done, had it occurred to me, was review the yearbooks from prior years to identify donors right away. From Kotzebue to Nome to Anchorage and throughout the village, everyone I contacted, albeit a bit late, was helpful and generous. Their monetary support and encouragement toward the students and even toward me would have made for a much better entry into the position. I would have learned who was who, and subsequently who to ask for curriculum ideas, especially in Consumer Math. Industries were everywhere, but my limited experience had painted my lessons into a single corner of consumerism. No wonder the students were bored. So was I.

But I had to move forward now. Next up was the Spring Carnival, slated for the upcoming weekend. From what I could tell, the Carnival was going to be quite the extravaganza. There were boxes of games and prizes piling up in the gym and banners decorating some walls. Word spread that the school staff would have carnival hats, too—the kind that Dick Van Dyke wore in Mary Poppins. I pictured teachers dancing down the hallways in their jaunty hats, minus the penguins.

Confirmation of carnival hats came early in the week. I was at my desk, deep in thought about my life as a wanna-be teacher, when Angela, who taught arts and crafts, tiptoed up behind me at my desk and plopped the hat on my head. Startled, I screamed, which made her scream.

"Oh, goodness! I'm so sorry!" Angela's eyes were almost bigger than her glasses.

"No, no. It's okay." I laughed. "What's up?"

Angela pulled a piece of paper from her apron pocket. "Oh, I need to tell you about your assignment. We didn't want to burden you, what with yearbook and all. But you're …" she scanned the page, "assigned to one shift in the kitchen and one rotation of game relief."

"Game relief?"

"Yep. When a teacher needs a break from running a game, you take over."

I offered a reluctant smile. Game relief might be fun, but kitchen duty meant only one thing: I'd smell like popcorn for days. I redirected my thoughts.

"Games? What kinds of games?"

Angela talked in a chirpy voice when she was excited, which she clearly was now. "Oh! Well, let's see. There's going to be a duck pond for the little ones, and a ball game to knock down bottles, and there's a ring toss ..." She counted on her fingers. "And we'll have a jail!"

I started to laugh. "What kind of game is jail?"

"Oh, it's not a game. It's where people go when they lose."

I decided not to pursue further questioning.

Over the next few days, a flurry of activity reverberated around school and throughout the village. The Spring Carnival was going to be a bigger event than I'd envisioned. The list of activities was impressive: half a dozen carnival games, drumming, dancing, and singing, and games of prowess and dexterity, like the High Kick and the Knuckle Hop—the latter of which sounded painful. The highlight of the weekend, at least for me, would be the dogsled race across the lagoon.

The weekend finally arrived, and the entire village descended on the school. Teachers and staff donned their hats. I ended up subbing at the duck pond and the ring toss and even got one stint as security guard at the jail. It really was a thing. Duncan built it using long wooden dowels and two-by-fours. When a participant lost a certain number of games, they were directed to jail until someone bailed them out with extra game-winning tickets.

That evening, we returned to the gym to watch dancing and singing performed by the residents of Shishmaref and people from nearby villages who had flown in for the festivities. The dancers' flowing movements mesmerized me. They arranged themselves in lines and followed a graceful choreography—arms and knees bending, bodies swaying, and thumping of soft leather soles on the gym floor.

Being a person who likes answers, it was frustrating at first to not understand what I was watching. But soon it didn't matter. Any analysis I tried to bring eventually dissolved in the soothing motions and the thrumming of large skin drums.

During one of the performances, I spotted my acquaintance, Ruth. She was on the dance floor, moving to the music. I hadn't seen her for months and made a mental note to visit soon.

The next day was bright and sunny, and the snow was hard and clean. A perfect day for dogsled racing. People gathered on the snow-covered tundra east of the school and lined up next to long ropes that served as boundaries for the start and finish. Residents from Shishmaref and other villages were everywhere, talking and laughing. Kids ran amok, wrestling each other and falling on the snow.

I meandered, taking photos for the yearbook.

"Here they come!" a kid yelled.

The dog teams approached. There were about ten teams, each with six to twelve dogs that were more than eager for a good hard run. They yipped and jumped when the mushers stopped briefly to confirm their racing order. Teams would be released across the lagoon ice one at a time to race against the clock.

The race official led the countdown and then swiped his flag. The crowd yelled, "Mush!" and the first team lurched forward to the sound of hundreds of mittens pounding and just as many boots stomping on the snow.

I spotted one of my tenth graders, Paula, approaching the start line. She rode on a small sled pulled by seven huskies. *Paula mushed?* She seemed nervous and asked for help from one of the handlers to check each dog's harness. It was a wise precaution. As soon as she stepped off the sled and walked the line, one of the dogs broke away. Several locals jumped in and helped her get things sorted. When called, Paula managed to get her dogs pointed in the same direction. The flag waved, and her team jumped forward. Paula hung on.

It would take more than half an hour for the mushers and dogs to return from the other side of the lagoon. A little half-time entertainment was in order. Enter the Rocket Club.

The Rocket Club was directed by Tim, one of the middle school teachers. He had ordered a variety of small cardboard and plastic rockets with parachutes just for this occasion.

Tim placed the first rocket on its little launchpad, lit the fuse, and asked everyone to stand back. The kids held their mittens over their ears and watched the sparks crawl along the string. But then it sputtered and died.

"Well, that happens sometimes." Tim adjusted the fuse and tried again, jumping away just as the rocket ejected from the pad. *Phffft!* It sailed out of sight. Everyone looked up, trying to find it against the clear blue sky.

One boy pointed. "I see it!" Sure enough, the rocket was coming back down. And fast.

Tim waved people back. "Look out, everyone!" The rocket's parachute wasn't opening. We watched in amazement and a little trepidation as it plummeted to earth. Then it bounced up again as though attached by a string from the heavens. The little white parachute appeared and floated the small craft safely down, so slowly that one boy caught it in his hands.

I decided to snap a few more photos to capture this lively occasion and the colorful outfits worn mostly by women. They were fashioned in the kuspuk style with its signature trimming and attached skirt. Women and girls sewed them by hand, adding ample fur around their hoods. I saw a multitude of colors and patterns—red, pink, royal blue, flowers, and polka dots. I glanced down at my drab-looking parka and wondered how I might be able to get a women's parka for myself.

A woman appeared in the crowd wearing a stunning coat fashioned with what looked to be reindeer fur and fox tails flowing from her hood all the way down to her fur mukluks. An intricate pattern of black and white geometric shapes decorated the shoulders and hem. It must have taken months to sew. I asked for permission to snap a photo. She gave me a toothy smile and posed.

Lance spotted me and walked over.

"They're something, aren't they?"

"Who's something?" I snapped one more photo of the crowd and turned to him.

"Oh, the kids, the dogs." He swept his arm around. "I get to this point in the year just before the carnival, and I think, I'm done. I'm leaving. But then I see all of this, and ... well, I love it."

"Yeah, I know what you mean. I have these back and forth conversations in my head all the time. There are days when I feel like I'm doing fine and could keep on going, and days when I want to march straight out to the airstrip and hop on the next plane. Is that a typical thing for teachers, or just in remote places like this?"

Lance was about to answer but pointed instead. "Here comes the first musher."

Spring carnival musher and team of dogs approaching the finish line.

On the horizon appeared a black dot that soon became the outline of a string of dogs and their musher. Whoever it was stood with one leg on the runner, kicking furiously with the other leg as if on a giant skateboard.

People quickly assembled behind the ropes and thumped their feet and whistled and yelled. The air was filled with their excitement, and my mind flashed back to a ski race in high school. On the course, I heard only the wind in my ears and the scrape of my ski's edges on the ice. It wasn't until I neared the finish line that the crowd's cheering became audible. Their enthusiasm gave me an extra spurt of energy. The same thing was happening here, so I screamed at the top of my lungs.

One by one, the mushers returned. Paula's team came flying back, too. I counted the dogs. She hadn't lost one. She crossed the finish in a splash of kicked-up snow and laughed, then quickly fixed the brake. A few of her dogs plopped onto the snow. The rest remained standing as if asking, "Where to next?" Ice crystals clung to their faces and chests. They looked happy.

The remaining teams came sliding into the finish and, except for the awards ceremony, the carnival was over. I helped gather up the poles and rope and picked up candy wrappers and discarded pop cans. And pull tab tickets. Hundreds of them. They littered the viewing lines like confetti.

"Pull tabs are like lottery tickets," a few of my ninth graders explained, after I said I'd never heard of them. "There's two layers of paper and you peel away the top part to see the numbers and symbols. If they match the front, you win a prize."

Note to self: Find out where to buy pull tabs.

Lance came back toward me, and I joked about needing a rake. We worked in unison, scooping up the used tabs and tossing them into a cardboard box.

"Say," he said, "there's a small party at Ben's place tonight. About seven o'clock. Just the high school teachers. Why don't you come?"

"That would be great. What should I bring?" I paused, hoping his answer would be "nothing." Anne and I had been so busy that neither of us had gone to the store in over a week. Our last two dinners consisted of canned soup, Pilot Bread, and jam.

"Nah, he's got it covered. Just bring a cup."

An hour later, I tiptoed past Anne, asleep on the couch, and slipped out the door. Ben's house was a short five-minute walk up the street and around one corner.

"You made it!" Ben pointed to a line of identical Sorel boots by the door. "Hope you don't mind wearing just your socks."

I laughed. "Maybe I should write my name in my boots?"

"I think we'll figure it out. These boots are like babies. We've been wearing them for months and ought to be able to tell them apart."

Lance jumped up from the couch. "Got your cup?"

"Yeah." I pulled a small orange plastic cup from my coat pocket. "I hope I brought the right thing?"

"That works. Follow me."

Angela, Duncan, and Tim were seated at the small dining table. Carrie and Lynne were on the couch. They weren't high school teachers but had been invited anyway. Everyone raised their cups in friendly salute as Lance and I passed by on our way to the kitchen. I was mystified by their behavior until Lance uttered the most beautiful words I'd heard all year.

"Care for a drink?"

My jaw dropped. *Oh my god.* There were two boxes sitting on the counter, one with the picture of a red wine glass, the other with white. And several dark bottles of beer. *So* that's *why this party was a secret.*

"White," I said without hesitation, and held my cup under the spout.

For the next couple of hours, through more wine and beer and potato chips, we exchanged stories from the past year, laughing uproariously at all our mistakes and the challenges of adolescent behaviors. The most common antic was students assuming that teachers didn't see what they were doing.

Ben recounted how the boys loved tying each other's shoelaces together in the locker room or hiding a teammate's towel, and Tim recounted one time when Darren brought a *Car & Driver* to class and slid it inside his large science text, thinking that Tim wouldn't see that he was paging through photos of cars instead of reading the assigned pages. Darren's attempt to ignore schoolwork imploded when Tim asked Darren why he was holding his textbook upside-down.

Duncan turned to me. "How 'bout you?"

"Oh god, I have tons of stories of wacky behavior." I paused for a sip. "It's all innocent stuff. Like the other day, I had to run to the office for staples. I couldn't have been gone more than sixty seconds."

"That's all it takes," Lance interjected.

"Right," I continued. "By the time I returned, every single one of my ninth graders had taken a Kleenex and put it over their face, like a mask. They used their eyeglasses to hold the tissue in place. When I walked in, they were sitting stone still, facing straight ahead, pretending that nothing was amiss." I started to laugh. "But then Marcus exhaled, and his Kleenex poofed out. It was the silliest thing I'd ever seen! The kids goofed off for most of the class, and I just didn't have the energy to stop them. But you know, it was actually quite refreshing."

I paused.

"Totally different topic, but how did you get beer here? I mean, the carbonation …" I hesitated to recount the story of my mother's felony package.

"Well," Lance high-fived Tim. "Turns out we're quite the Bier Meister's. We made it."

"You made it?"

"Remember when I asked you to pick up a box for me at the airstrip?"

I nodded.

"That delivery was essential for finishing our last batch." He gestured toward the bottles on the counter. "Tim and I did one round, but we had to dump it. Turned out we needed the advanced kit with more yeast and fast-priming sugar." He winked at Tim.

Tim picked up the story. "Took us a few weeks, and we had to be super chill. My clothes smelled like hops, and the kids kept pestering me. I told them it was a new kind of deodorant. Lance finally locked the beer kit in a closet. This batch is on the early end of fermentation, but we thought we'd give it a try." He raised his bottle. "Not bad! About seven percent alcohol with a medium I-B-U."

"What's an I-B-U?" Carrie burped.

"That's International Bitterness Units." Lance looked at Tim. "We've learned a lot." He took another swig. "Another couple of weeks, and this batch will be suitable for consumption." He then let out an intentional belch, which sent the room laughing once more.

"To the Bier Meisters!" Ben raised his bottle.

As more teaching stories came out, it became clear that all of us were weary with holding things together, but we also loved what we did. Teaching was such a tangled combination of precision versus befuddlement. Our students made us laugh, they impressed us unexpectedly, and they also drove us nuts.

Lance and Duncan shared more poignant moments about a couple of kids getting sick from sniffing gas. Another attempted suicide. I was shocked. I didn't know any of these things. Lance and Duncan didn't tell us the names of those students, but it left me wondering if I had missed some warning signs. I mentally ran through my rosters. Even if I had known, what was the protocol for handling such a crisis?

"The people in this village have gone through so much change in the past few decades," Ben said. "Lots of older parents and grandparents were sent to boarding schools or stayed here and had to go to the missionary school. Their names were changed to Christian names, and they were forced to learn English." He looked at me. "Not that English is a bad thing, of course. I mean, it's brought a lot of commerce and opportunities to the area. But still, I bet it can be a tough sell at times, teaching your class."

"You've got no idea." I took another sip of wine. "Things were going along alright, but then I made them read Shakespeare."

"Shakespeare!" Lance and Carrie said at the same time. Everyone started to laugh.

"Well, sure!" I felt my face flush. "But it was *The Tempest*! I thought they'd relate to the scenery. A ship at sea, the remote island." Lance and Tim and Duncan laughed so hard they almost fell on the floor.

"Here, give me that." Ben reached for my cup and headed back to the kitchen. "You deserve more."

After two plastic cups of boxed wine and more than my share of potato chips, I caught one of the yawns traveling around the room. The party was winding down.

"Okay, people, time for bed." Ben gestured toward his door. "Just don't take my boots."

As I waited to enter the boot room behind the others, I turned to Ben. "Thanks. That was generous of you to share your boxes of wine. I had no idea that existed."

"You're welcome." Ben handed over my parka. "I have a friend in Portland who says boxed wine is all the rage down there. He shipped a couple to me. The plastic pouches are great. No worries about broken glass."

Note to self.

The next week, Lance appeared in my doorway. He tapped the doorframe and glanced over one shoulder. "Busy tonight?"

"Oh gosh," I said, laughing. "Let me check my calendar!" I picked up a stack of student papers. "Oops, I almost forgot, I have to grade these."

"Girl," Lance wagged his finger, "you really need to stop assigning so much work. Remember, it's nice when they do it, but then *you* have to do it."

"So, what's tonight?"

"Tim and I are having a little get-together at our place. Come around eight."

In that moment, I decided that teachers were the coolest people in the whole world.

FIFTY-SEVEN

ANOTHER CRACK IN THE ICE

Each day, the temperature shifted higher. It ebbed and flowed like the tide under the shore ice, gradually making the landscape softer and more alive. Debris that had been covered in snow started to appear all over the village—outboard motors, defunct snow machines, scraps of lumber, and deer antlers on oil drums. The sea ice hadn't broken up yet, but everyone knew it was coming. During my walks, the cracking sounds of rifles in the distance bore testimony to the locals' increasing hunts for seals. Soon, it would be too dangerous to venture far from shore.

Returning home from Walter's store, I decided to drop by Ruth's house for a visit. Even though I knew it was perfectly acceptable to show up unexpectedly at someone's house, my hand still hesitated before knocking.

What if she's napping? What if she's washing her hair or cleaning out her honey bucket? What if she just doesn't want company?

I knocked once and waited. No answer. I was about to turn and go when the door opened. Recognizing me, Ruth smiled broadly and wiped her hands on her apron, which was decorated with bright red cherries. Before I could say a word, she waved me in.

The air was warm and steamy, like a botanical garden but with no plants in sight. I removed my boots and slid off my coat. Ruth was already at the stove, heating up water for tea.

I sat at her table and surveyed the room. The counters were still filled with boxes and bags of food. Her couch was overrun with mounds of clothes, sheets, and magazines.

For Ruth, everything was in its appointed place. Everything except her boots, which were sitting on top of her oil stove. A slight wisp of steam emanated from their leather tops. They were wrinkled and discolored, like they had been dunked in saltwater.

Ruth brought our tea to the table and chuckled when she followed my gaze. I turned back and raised my eyebrows, asking, *what happened to your boots?* She answered by first sliding a large Folgers coffee can toward me and lifting the lid. Inside was a jumble of Oreo cookies. Ruth didn't know it, but I *loved* cookies stashed in coffee cans. Nana had done the same thing. She saved coffee cans and used them to store cookies—Nutter Butter peanut butter cookies, old-fashioned iced molasses cookies, and Pecan Sandies. By the time a person was groping the last layer, any remaining cookies had taken on a subtle coffee taste. It was a delicious combination.

Ruth munched an Oreo and then decided it was time to tell her tale. She pulled the plastic liner from her trash can. It was limp, but she rounded her arms, demonstrating that it used to be full. Then she pointed to her boots and mimicked putting them on and shuffling across her linoleum floor like villagers did on the snow and ice.

"The Shishmaref Shuffle!" I started putting words to her pantomime.

Ruth nodded and pointed at her trash bag.

"You were taking out the trash?"

Ruth pointed at her feet and shuffled more cautiously, like she was getting closer to a precipice. With the trash bag still in hand, Ruth pretended to shiver. "Brrrr!" Then she squatted and patted the floor with her free hand. "Brrrr!" she repeated.

"You're outside and it's cold."

She patted the floor again and looked up at me.

"Snow?" I paused. "Ice!"

Ruth stood up, then dropped down to the floor in one swift motion.

"Sploosh!" Ruth raised her arms up high.

Now I understood. Ruth had taken her trash onto the ice and fallen through. In the old days, I'd heard that Native people set unwanted items far onto the ice-covered ocean. When the current shifted, cracks appeared, and the items dropped in. That made sense when trash was biodegradable, but Ruth had taken a plastic bag out there and had probably been doing it for decades. That was just the way things were, but I was slightly mortified by the pollution and then felt bad that I'd never thought to swing by Ruth's house on one of my dump runs.

"Are you okay?" It was a silly question, but it came out anyway.

Ruth dropped her trash bag and held her hand by her rib cage, indicating that she had fallen into icy water up to her chest.

"Woah!" My hand instinctively covered my mouth.

Ruth mimicked crawling out of the icy waters of the Chukchi Sea and dragging herself upright. Then she pointed at her boots and pretended to wring them out.

"Wet? Geez, I'd say more like totally soaked!"

Ruth nodded and started giggling, which made me giggle too. She put the trash bag back into the can and poured more hot water in my mug. I expected Ruth to pull out her cardboard trays for another session of artifact bartering, but she seemed to want to rest. We sat for a while in silence. I quietly munched another cookie, and I noticed Ruth's eyes beginning to droop.

She woke just enough to see me quietly slipping into my boots and coat.

"Thank you." I patted my stomach. "Be careful out there."

She nodded and offered a tired wave as I closed the door behind me.

Walking home, I gazed at the ocean. It still looked plenty frozen, but Ruth's incident confirmed that looks can be deceiving. I imagined her small frame dropping suddenly through a weak patch in the ice. My mind flashed to reindeer herding day and my near miss of plunging into the lagoon with Bruce and Sophie. Sophie's frantic response drove home the dangerous conditions that surrounded the people on this island. The dangerous conditions that surrounded me. Did I want to come back for another year in such a risky environment? I could die in an airplane crash, fall through the ice, get torn apart by a polar bear.

By the time I got home, my mind was a swirl of trepidation. How long before I had to decide to stay for another year, or leave?

As it turned out, not long.

FIFTY-EIGHT

TO QUIT OR NOT TO QUIT

The school day was over. I took a break from course planning and chose the easiest diversion: wandering to the library to find a title I hadn't read yet.

By this time in the year, especially without an appointed librarian, the books were in disarray. Some were pushed to the back of the shelves while others lay across the top of vertically stacked ones. I took a moment to reorganize errant books, mumbling under my breath about why I seemed to be the only one who cared about order. On the other hand, tidying could lead to an interesting discovery.

A slim book had slipped behind one row. The front cover was missing, and several pages had been creased from having been stuck in the tight space. It was a book of quotes by influential people like Martin Luther King, Jr., Eleanor Roosevelt, and Thomas Jefferson.

I could use a little inspiration.

I flipped to a random page and landed on a statement attributed to Friedrich Nietzsche—the one that says, "what doesn't kill us makes us stronger." I smiled. What had Mr. Nietzsche experienced to make him say such a thing? Maybe he'd tried teaching.

My stomach rumbled, signaling that an after-school snack might help me contemplate the philosopher's advice. I clumped down the hallway and out the door, book in hand.

Anne sat at the dining table, smoking and playing solitaire. Since learning that she hadn't been invited to the box wine and beer party, she'd given me the cold shoulder. I told her it was for high school teachers only, but she wasn't buying it.

"Carrie got to go," she said. "And Lynne."

She was right. If I'd been a defense attorney, I just lost my case. All I could do was shrug my shoulders and half-promise there'd likely be another gathering, and she could come. I didn't tell her about the beer bash at Lance and Tim's.

"Hey there." I stomped my boots in the entryway and paused. "How's it going?"

"Fine."

That being the likely extent of our conversation, I shifted gears.

"I'm going to grab a bite and head back to school."

I continued to my room to change into a lighter sweater. On my dresser lay an envelope. It had arrived in my school mailbox a few days before. Everybody had the same one, with the same return address: Bering Strait School District.

When I first unfolded the single piece of paper, my heart started beating so hard I had to sit down. Was it a letter inviting me to return to the village for a second year? An indictment of my weak teaching skills, along with a one-way ticket to the Lower 48 where I belonged? Principal Ken's words haunted me: *You'll improve with time.* Indeed, would the district give me more time to figure out this teaching life?

"Dear Miss Pierce, We are pleased to offer you …"

I audibly gasped and clamped my hand over my mouth. *No frickin' way.*

The letter provided only two options: accept or decline. Since then, and during every moment I wasn't engrossed in work, I fretted about how to respond. I was like a tiger in a cage, pacing back and forth, nowhere to go with my indecision.

I'd made a list of pros and cons on the back of the envelope. Maybe doing so would point the way.

PROS: I know my way around the village. People seem to like me. I know now to avoid medieval literature. Nana said I should be a teacher.

I contemplated the last item, then crossed it out, unsure if Nana would still feel the same way if she could see me now.

CONS: I'm lonely. There are no coffee shops, restaurants, bookstores, theaters, bike paths, trees, mountains, warm sun, running water, private toilets, or showers. I want a job where I know what to do. The kids deserve better.

The next item surprised me. It was like the underside of a huge iceberg abruptly flipping toward daylight. I felt the weight of this realization as I committed it to paper: "I represent the culture that's destroying this one."

My con list was bad. I didn't like seeing the words that expressed how I really felt. But there was more, something else churning in my psyche that rendered me incapable of checking either box on the district's letter. It took a long walk before I figured it out.

Simply put, I didn't want to quit.

I had never been a quitter, even when the stakes were high. For as long as I could remember, if there was a job to do, I stayed to the end. I didn't shy away from hard work. Whether hacking at weeds, washing windows, or creating lesson plans, I was the one who finished the job after everyone else had hung up their tools and turned out the light.

It was the same with sports. I would hit tennis balls until blisters formed on my fingers or ski down the same stretch of mountain twenty times to get the fall-line just right. People would compliment me for my tenaciousness but add the niggling critique, "Why do you work so hard?" or "You always do things the hard way." I would just look at them, not understanding their point. "It's just how I am," I tried to explain.

To decline the district's offer would be the first time in my life I quit something. It would be an indictment of the two things I really liked about myself: my dedication to a job well done and my optimistic stubbornness in the face of uncertainty.

Other questions chased me, too: To what degree would I be quitting? Just this teaching position in Shishmaref? Or quit teaching altogether?

My thoughts kept returning to Nana and her easy-going, all-knowing advice that had steered me into this profession—advice that, in my heart of hearts, I believed to be true. *I am supposed to be a teacher.* Nana knew it. Mrs. Springer knew it. If I quit Shishmaref, and especially if I quit teaching altogether, I'd also be quitting on them.

I felt like I had a millstone around my neck. I was sinking, lost in the depths of indecision, unable to find a sign telling me, *Go that way!*

The Bering Strait School District needed to know in three days whether I was returning for a second year or if they'd have to spend the time and money to interview a slew of candidates, asking questions about their fondness for camping and how they handled boredom.

Anne didn't ask about my letter, and she didn't tell me about hers. Twice, I'd walked toward Carrie's place to see if she and Kitten could help me sort things out, but I stopped short of knocking. Carrie seemed so competent; she probably wouldn't understand my indecision. She would make me a cup of coffee and give me two thumbs up. "Give it another year!" and "It's not so bad." Just like she'd done during my inaugural sled ride to Serpentine River.

Asking Principal Ken was out of the question. Normally, a person would approach their school leader for advice, but I didn't want him to know the depths of my insecurity. Besides, I'd likely need a recommendation letter for my next career bagging groceries. Principal Ken already didn't have much to say other than I "did alright" and would "improve with time." I didn't want to jeopardize that slim margin of support by giving him more reasons to doubt my competence. It had been shaky from the start.

I sat on my bed and thumbed through the small library book of inspirational quotes, hoping for a sign. What would Nietzsche say? If I stayed, would it kill me or would it make me stronger?

I pulled out my journal to see if writing might help me sort it out.

Dear Me …

What's the point of me staying? If I accept their offer and go through all the trouble to return in the fall, what's to say it won't be like this all over again?

On the other hand, I have nothing but a few boxes of stuff back in Seattle. No place to live, no job or friends waiting. And I sold my car. But if I leave, the students will have to deal with a new teacher. And then I'll be like all the other teachers who came and used up precious time and resources, and then left students hanging. That's not fair …

I paused. Outside my window, the sky was gray.

Journaling sucks. And so does this weather.

It had been gray all week. Cold, dirty. Gray. Kids ran by my window; their energy and natural optimism felt painfully foreign. I started again.

I also hate being an Outsider with a capital O. Everything that seems damaging to Native culture comes from Western culture, which is me. It's my culture, like it or not, that transplanted factory-model schools in total disregard for their seasonal way of life.

We brought foods laden with sugar and bad fats. And we brought the scourge of alcohol, bad movies, and sexualized songs. We sent generations of them to boarding schools. Every day, I try to get them to write in one language while their native tongue barely gets a nod of approval. It's like the ocean waves pounding against the sea wall; eventually, the sea finds its way through the cement and erodes the island. I'm a representative of that erosion. My simple presence here contributes to their loss. I'm an impostor, a marauder. A colonist.

My pen stopped again. *Well, this entry is certainly getting depressing.*

I got up and went to the kitchen to rustle up dinner. Anne had moved to the couch and fallen asleep. The TV flickered in the growing darkness. I left it on and took my Pilot Bread, jar of peanut butter, and an apple back to my room and ate in silence. Maybe a real letter would help. Mia would understand. There wasn't time for her to write back, but connecting with her in spirit might help me make sense of my confusion.

Dear Mia,

How are you? I haven't written since Diomede. Been busy and haven't known what to write about that you haven't already heard. I'm writing now, cuz I'm in a pickle, and don't have a private place to call you and talk on the phone.

I got a letter from the school district offering me another year here. I should be happy, but I'm in a quandary about it, not knowing whether to check the box for Accept or Decline. I can hear you saying, "trust your gut," but when I get still and listen, there's no sound. My gut's gone on vacation.

I should make these good days. And I do try. There are moments of joy with my students and some of the other teachers. But when all is said and done, I feel like I am dying up here. I feel the urge to leave – to find a place where I can start once more, but with the support of friends who can gently help me figure out how to grow more into my own skin. Do you see?

All my love, Me

The letter helped a little, but I knew I wouldn't mail it. It needed to sit another day on my dresser, next to the district's letter that was prompting these existential questions. I tucked them both deep in my sock drawer and headed back to school.

The next day, the answer about what to do was forced upon me unexpectedly during eleventh and twelfth grade English class. Sarah looked up from her work, eyebrows high.

"Miss Pierce? We heard that teachers got their letters. Are you coming back?"

It was exactly like the first day of school: a zinger of a question and nowhere to hide. No time to think of a calculated response. All eyes on me. I hesitated. They had no idea how I ached to know the answer to that question myself. *Maybe I should flip a coin and see how I feel when it lands.* Heads to stay, tails to leave with my tail between my legs.

But then the words just slipped out. "I don't think so." And I felt a release.

No one said a word.

It would have been nice to hear a little resistance—perhaps a protest. "No! You can't leave! We want you to stay!"

But they didn't say a thing. Maybe the kids had already sensed my impending departure. Maybe they were so used to being rejected that they couldn't afford to get too invested in anyone new. Who could blame them? They experienced almost one-hundred percent turnover in teachers every couple of years.

I felt my face flush. *I can't leave them hanging.*

I pulled my teacher's chair to the Command Spot and sat down, my heart in my hands.

"My leaving has nothing to do with you. It's me. I need more training on the curriculum and how to teach in a village like yours. Staying feels like a disservice. You deserve better."

The students listened, which was unnerving. They wanted more.

"What I have tried to do is help you with reading and writing, because some of you will go to college." I nodded at George and Sarah. "And many of you will stay here. But all of you," I looked around the room, "need to have the skills to protect yourselves. And one major way to do that is to know how to read and write so when people come in here and try to sell you something you don't want or try to make a deal with your land, your language, your future …" I felt a lump in my throat, "you can read the fine print and protect what you love." I paused. "And I just don't think I am the right person for that. At least not yet."

No scrunched faces, no eyebrows up. A few nodded, either agreeing with my self-assessment or accepting my decision. In my heart, what I was saying felt right. But as I stood and rolled my chair back behind my desk, my feet felt like they weighed twelve hundred pounds. Part of me wanted to hear their perspective, but I knew I'd dissolve into a puddle of tears if they uttered one word.

At the end of the day, I took a long, meandering walk, heading north to mull over my decision. A slight breeze wafted in from the ocean, carrying a salty tinge. I breathed it in and exhaled slowly, hoping the extra oxygen might restore my weary mind and help me arrive at some rational conclusion. If I didn't return, the kids might get another nasty teacher. Or maybe someone nice but as clueless as I'd been. Maybe they did stand a better chance with me. I didn't know much, but they knew me.

I walked north for an hour, creating a triangle path from north to east and then south again, cutting across tundra toward home. The house was empty. Anne wasn't there.

Good. I need to be alone.

I went to my bedroom and pulled the district's letter from the envelope, bending the creases back so it lay flat. I studied the wording again, feeling my heart beating fast in my chest. No matter which way I went, I felt bad. Guilty. Embarrassed. Like I had a knot in my neck I couldn't work out.

Ultimately, the decision to stay or to leave had to be based on the bigger picture of what felt right—what was the best "right" for all involved.

I picked up a pen.

Wait. Should I use a pencil? I might change my mind again by morning and be able to erase my mark.

No. That will only make for a restless night and prolong the inevitable. I set the pen's tip on the Decline box, exhaled, and drew an X.

It was done.

PART SIX

LEAVING

FIFTY-NINE

CHANCE MEETING

The next day was graduation rehearsal. The seniors had started skipping school, so Principal Ken sent letters home with a firm warning that any senior who didn't come to rehearsal would not be allowed to attend the ceremony and would risk not receiving their diploma.

Fortunately, all twelve came. We met in the gym and followed Principal Ken's instructions as he took us through the steps in the ceremony. He pointed out which door to enter and where to sit, then looked at me.

"Why don't you explain the awards. I hafta get back to th' office."

A few weeks before, Principal Ken had volunteered me to collect nominations from teachers for students who earned high academic scores, demonstrated strong leadership skills, or put forth the most effort. I had to create certificates of achievement and order trophies. It was the only other instance I seriously contemplated paying a kid to run to the airstrip every time I heard a plane. If Midge hadn't kept an eye out for my parcels, I would have spent at least fifty bucks for "gopher service."

With the principal no longer present, the seniors released their true feelings.

"Aww, man," whined Caleb, "we have to sit up here with everyone staring at us?"

"Yeah," George said, "and you're calling our names for an award?"

"Well, only some of you."

"If I get an award," Joey interjected, "could my cousin accept it for me?"

"Guys, this isn't the Academy Awards. You have to be here."

Sophie plopped on a wrestling mat and stretched out. "Maybe I'll skip graduation."

"It's going to be fine." I tried to reassure her. "Everyone is looking at everyone, not just at you, so all you need to do is stand up and stroll over here." I walked five feet to the podium. "Principal Ken will hand you a diploma, shake your hand, and then you sit back down." I walked back. "That's it. People will yell and scream and clap their hands. Then we'll do the awards. If you're a winner, you'll just walk over to me. I'll hand you the trophy or the certificate, and we'll shake hands."

"And people yell and scream and clap," added Joey.

"Yup." I glanced at my watch. Lunch was almost over. "Okay, it's time to get back to class. Last one for you! I'll see you back here tomorrow." None of the kids said yes, but no one said no either. With the basic details settled, I left the gym and headed for my classroom. Halfway down the hall, I heard, "Hey, Teach!"

It was Laurence, a senior. I hadn't seen him in weeks. As a matter of fact, I saw him so rarely that I'd forgotten he was a student. At the end of each quarter, I wrote "D" in my grade book and advanced his name to the next cycle, hoping he'd show up. After one quarter, I raised my concerns with Principal Ken, who looked at his records.

"Well, that 'splains it." He shook his head.

"Explains what?"

"Laurence was a senior last year, too. He just needs to pass English." Principal Ken looked over his glasses.

This was news to me. Laurence only needed to pass my class? But he rarely came, and when he did, he looked busy and then left without turning anything in. Weeks would pass before I saw him again, and the cycle repeated itself. I felt bad, but what was I supposed to do?

Laurence walked closer. He had grown a foot since I'd last seen him, and he had a definite mustache and the start of a beard.

"Hey, Laurence, how'r you doing? Where've you been?"

"Oh, been huntin', fishin'. Family. Stuff like that." He looked down for a moment, then glanced at me, then away.

I had a feeling that Laurence was proud of supporting his family. Not long before, I'd learned from Duncan that Laurence's family was large. He provided for his parents, younger siblings, and an auntie or two. It was a lot of responsibility.

Standing in front of me was an accomplished young man, but one who also seemed slightly embarrassed that he'd missed so many days of school without explaining why.

"I know," I followed. "Makes sense. How's the hunting?"

"Oh, me and my brother go out and shoot ptarmigan. It's okay. They're easier to spot now. Less snow," he explained. "They're funny. They see us comin' and just sit there like they got all day. Then, bam!" He mimicked a rifle shooting off. "Got one." He grinned.

"Well, that's good." I felt a flicker of a conflict between the reality of Laurence's life and my duty as a teacher to tell him he had flunked my class. "That's good," I repeated. "But I haven't heard from you in a long time, and now—sorry to say—you missed too many classes, which means you didn't earn enough points to get a passing grade." I paused. "And now it's too late. There's no way to bring your grade up enough to graduate."

As soon as the words flew out of my mouth, I felt terrible, like I was ruining this young man's life. I felt the need to physically move through the awkwardness, and started down the hall again, toward my classroom.

Laurence matched my pace. He reminded me of Brandon, a tenth-grade student I had during student teaching. Tough kid. Quiet. And frequently absent. He and I had no connection at all until the day he raised his hand in response to a prompt I had written on the board—my attempt to engage students emotionally with a story we were reading: What's something you enjoy doing, and why?

Snickering ensued around the room, but this kid—Brandon—raised his hand. I hesitated, not sure if I could trust him. I was afraid he might say something that would derail the entire lesson. But the look on his face was earnest, and I took the chance.

"Yes?"

"Y'all can laugh, I don't care," he began, "but you know when there's towels in the dryer and they get all warm and stuff? I love taking them out in a big pile and hugging them."

His classmates didn't say a word. It was a big reminder for all of us—never judge a book by its cover.

So it was with Laurence, this tall and solidly built young man walking next to me. I might have been older in years but felt at this moment that he was much wiser.

Yet here I was, saying he was going to be held back in Senior Purgatory because he hadn't passed my class. I felt awful, like I was handing him a Chance card in Monopoly that said, "Go to Jail. Do not pass go, do not collect two hundred dollars."

But instead of protesting or offering an excuse, Laurence gently placed an arm around me and patted my shoulder like he was trying to comfort me instead.

"That's okay." He smiled sheepishly. "I like school. If I don't graduate, I can keep coming back."

We stopped a few feet from my classroom door, and Laurence removed his arm. We watched the ninth graders file in. They called out in greeting. "Hey, Laurence! What's up?"

I knew it was my job to respond with a piece of direction or wisdom, but I didn't know how to counter Laurence's admission. What he said made sense. We walked farther down the hallway for a more private conversation. I stopped at the school doors and turned to face him.

"You're okay with that? Not graduating this year?"

"That's what I came to tell you." He said the words softly. "It's okay."

His response relaxed my concern. I nodded, then looked at the sky outside. It had been lightly overcast for the past several days. Unremarkable. Dull gray.

"Well," I started, looking back at Laurence again. "I appreciate you telling me. But I wish you had come to school more often. We could have worked something out."

I reached out my hand to shake his. Laurence seemed surprised with my formality but returned the gesture with a firm grasp.

"You can try again next year," I smiled reassuringly, "or just keep doing what you're doing. When you need a high school diploma, you can get one. There's no age limit on that."

Laurence chuckled and gave me a two-finger salute. Then he was gone. The door clicked shut, and I watched him clomp down the stairs.

Laurence was a smart young man. He knew that most of what I had to teach him probably made little sense in his world. Maybe one day it would, and he'd try again. For now, I took solace in the fact that he called me Teach. I could still feel the warmth of his strong arm across my shoulders and the weight of his presence. I might be an imperfect teacher, but I wasn't so bad that he avoided me. He had come of his own accord to say goodbye, which meant he cared on some level. Which meant he knew I cared, too.

Once more, the truth of being a teacher tapped me on the shoulder. Teaching was about connection. *This* kind of connection. Not writing, not reading, not tests. Just a meeting of hearts.

A tear rolled down my cheek. I brushed it away, exhaled, and turned back to my classroom. My ninth graders were sitting quietly. Too quietly.

Of course, suspecting I might be a few minutes late, they were up to their usual antics. Every one of them had removed their coat and put it on backwards, hoods up, creating the initial impression that they were facing the back wall.

They knew I was standing there. I waited to see who was going to blink first.

Stella's deep, throaty chuckle broke their silence and was followed by a wave of adolescent giggling around the room. It was the silliest scene—the unending giggling, the hoods bobbing in ridiculous backwards fashion. I wanted to tease my students by stepping back out of the room and disappearing but changed my mind. I knew it would be way more fun if I stayed, if only for this one last day.

SIXTY

LETTING GO

It was early morning, and I was at the airstrip. The sun was above the horizon, but the disk of light was pale, the warmth of its rays not anywhere near reaching where I stood.

This time, I would ride shotgun. Bud, the pilot, swung open the little side door and gestured me forward, then helped an elderly man into the row behind. We were the only two passengers on the plane. My companion was heading to Nome for a dentist appointment. I was heading for Juneau to spend time with Mia and figure out what to do with my life.

The seat up front was intimidating. Sitting so close to the nose of the plane reminded me of how fragile it was. The dozens of dials and buttons were a sobering testament to how complicated flying a bush plane could be. I prayed we'd make it in one piece. It would really suck if, after all the flights I'd taken, we crashed on my final tour.

I watched the pilot go through the usual motions of chatting with residents and packing in parcels and bags. His motions were fluid—talking and organizing at the same time.

It occurred to me in that moment that pilots and teachers had a lot in common. Both had their own unique style, their own sense of ease and intensity, and their own way of getting out of jams. Both had creases in their foreheads, drawn from the more serious moments that made their hearts ache or their brains worry. There were other creases as well—lines from laughing at a quick joke or one's own fallibility.

Teachers and pilots also loved to talk about what they do for a living and delighted in running into a kindred spirit in the grocery store. Conversations could last for an hour, between the shelves of Pilot Bread and kiwis. Both were professionals, constantly challenged by their own version of "flying" and (usually in hindsight) getting jazzed when unpredictable situations came their way. With both, there was joy and the occasional thrill of navigating a close call. And there were plenty of equipment failures and unruly passengers. Despite the challenges, there was also the unmistakable beauty that accompanied working alongside and supporting other souls, whether in the classroom or in the seat of a single-prop plane.

More luggage was loaded behind me, and I watched to make sure mine came too. I was bringing home most of what I'd carried with me when I first landed in Shishmaref, but lightened the load by donating most of my books to the school library. I kept my poetry anthology and Marge Piercy's *Woman on the Edge of Time,* which I had yet to finish. I had a sneaking suspicion there was a message in there, just for me.

Bud secured the passenger door, walked around to his side, and hopped in.

"Here." He reached for a second headset. "You can wear this."

I clamped the large earphones over my head and adjusted the mouthpiece. It was heavy yet made me feel secure. Maybe its weight would calm the swirl of thoughts and emotions I was experiencing in this final moment of wheels still touching Shishmaref ground.

What if I jumped out? What if, unlike when I first landed, I wanted to stay?

"Testing, testing." Bud's deep voice came through my earphones. "Can you hear me?"

"Loud and clear."

I was grateful that Bud didn't question my reason for taking this flight. Pilots usually stuck with facts and didn't ask prying questions like, "What brings you here?" Or "Why are you leaving?"

He started flicking switches and added, "We've got a good day for flying. Light winds, good visibility. About an hour to Nome."

The fuselage vibrated and buzzed to life. The propeller began to spin, lifting the tail slightly. Bud taxied us slowly toward the lagoon, and then turned around to face north, into the wind. We began the slow roll and rumble down the runway, passing clumps of gritty snow. They were all that was left of winter. The few orange traffic cones that had made it through the harshest of seasons, marked the edges on either side.

Standing alone by the tarmac was Stella. She had gotten up early with a few classmates to say goodbye. The others had giggled and laughed, a bit nervous, and then left, but Stella stayed. Such a polite thing to do. She waved at our plane, and I waved back, clenching my jaw to hold back tears.

The edge of the Chukchi Sea grew closer. Bud pulled on the yolk, and the shoreline of sand mixed with snow fell away. As we arced over the village, I fixed my eyes on familiar landmarks. The Washeteria, Walter's store, the school. Ruth's house, and then Carrie's. She had finally told me she was coming back for one more year. "Third time's a charm!" She laughed and gave me a quick hug. Then she shook her finger.

"Get a French Press! And look me up if you're ever in Seattle, okay?"

The last building I laid eyes on was the little gray-green structure next to the school. I'd probably seen it when I first flew in but didn't know it would be my home.

Anne was still down there.

"Just one more year of this, and then I'm retiring." She surprised me with a hug. Deep down, I knew Anne was a wonderful woman, but I felt a bit sorry for her next roommate, if she'd even have one. All the smoke and Solitaire.

Bud followed the coast. A long line of waves curled into the island's southern tip and washed into the lagoon. Another tide coming in or going out, I wasn't sure. Ahead, the landscape was wide open and still covered by snow.

With the instrument panel too high for me to see anything other than sky in front, I looked out my side window. Questions I had been shoving deep down finally broke through to the surface. What was the point of this adventure? What had it been about? When I first came to Shishmaref, I thought I would be making a difference in my students' lives. That's what all teachers wanted to do—make a difference, right? But what difference had I made? I'd learned much more from the students than they had learned from me.

Throughout my trial period in the village, people kept saying, "Just be yourself! You'll get the hang of it!"

I had started to get the hang of it, but not enough to overcome the paradox of daily existence where I struggled between good intentions and ignorance, friendliness and frustration, courage and being scared out of my wits. Most days, I ended up teaching far outside of my comfort zone, pretending to be someone I wasn't and spending an inordinate amount of energy trying to figure out what to teach and how to make it make sense to students who lived in a subsistence culture that was worlds away from my own.

I glanced at Bud, wondering what he would think if he could hear the conversation in my head. Maybe he'd enjoy some polite conversation. But he seemed equally occupied with his own thoughts. The gentleman behind us had already nodded off to sleep.

The plane bounced unexpectedly, jolting my melancholy toward memories that brought on a bit of a smile. Learning to play patty-cake with my first visitors. Meeting Walter and getting nicknamed Kulizuk. Driving the school's truck into a hole. Carving a mask with Melvin Olanna. Eating muktuk (sort of) and moose, then reindeer stew. Negotiating my way through a bowl of Eskimo ice cream after four villagers who'd been lost in a storm were found, and experiencing what it was like to have an entire village welcome you home.

I'd had thousands of interactions with students, and they with me. All those crazy grammar lessons, Romeo and Juliet, Sir Gawain and the Green Knight, and the *Northern Lights News*. Teaching students how to write a check.

I'd visited Little Diomede Island and seen Beluga whales, walrus, and polar bear tracks. I got to watch locals catch a crab, and I felt the massive power of sea ice as it pushed its way through the Bering Strait. I got two days of gazing across that expanse of ice, looking into tomorrow.

And there was Henry's laughter when he gave me that wild ride from the Washeteria, showing off his driving skills and making his teacher scream over snow berms and around tight turns. The trip to Elim with my Five Musketeers. Witnessing Jacques Philip and his team of dogs as they disappeared into the darkness on their way to Nome. Tea with Ruth and the tooth she sold to me for five bucks. And of course, her story of falling through the ice, Walter's Hawaii Week, and kids eating kiwis for the very first time.

Sophie, who saved Bruce and me from plunging into the lagoon's dark icy waters on reindeer day, and Darlene's reassuring arm on my shoulders, whispering "It's okay" just before the buck jumped defiantly over our heads.

Chopping ice at Serpentine. Ben's boxed wine and Lance and Tim's homemade brew. My mother's exploding care package. That one still made me laugh.

I had probably taken one hundred walks to the dump for exercise and fresh air and an abundance of self-imposed therapy. Those walks helped me process my emotions and gain a healthier perspective on most things. The relentless wind that shaped the contours of miles of sand and snow also managed to shape my own inner landscape. It taught me to choose my words carefully. It moved me toward acceptance and forgiveness, one step at a time.

For nine months, my world had been confined to those simple and sometimes profound experiences, like dots on a landscape that I tried to make sense of and connect into a larger map of meaning. Between those dots were moments of hope and laughter, disappointment and despair.

Was that it, then? My teaching career was over?

I brushed away a tear. Maybe it was, maybe it wasn't. Right now, there was nothing else to do. I squared my shoulders, fixed my eyes on the horizon, and let the plane carry me away.

SIXTY-ONE

THE CALL

Two weeks later, I was sitting on a brown plaid couch that looked suspiciously like the one in my house in Shishmaref, sipping tea and nearing the end of *Woman on the Edge of Time*. I had fallen in love with the characters and found myself rereading pages to slow my pace. I couldn't put the book down yet feared getting to the end; I wanted the story to keep going, to keep it alive inside of me.

One of Mia's friends had offered to help me find a duplex in a quiet grove of pines near the Mendenhall Glacier. The neighborhood was a calming salve after the inner turmoil that led up to my departure from the village. It didn't take long for me to find the joy in freedom from schoolwork and access to all the amenities I had missed so much. I swore I would never again take for granted hot showers, public transportation, and coffee shops. Heavenly coffee. My favorite place was on Front Street. I went so often that I didn't yet feel the need for a French Press, but I knew I'd get one soon. The coffee maker Walter had ordered never came.

I missed the warmth and quirkiness of Walter's store but was quickly falling in love with wandering aimlessly in fully stocked aisles of Juneau's Fred Meyer Super Store. I could get anything there: shoelaces, ice cream, wine. Even a dog.

It happened the day I stopped in for batteries and a bag of popcorn. A man near the entrance was giving away free puppies. He was the spitting image of Paul Bunyan, the mythical lumberjack in my childhood books. He was tall and brawny, with a bushy, brown beard, thick eyebrows, and a square jaw. The man was pure Alaskan, dressed in a red plaid shirt, blue jeans with suspenders, and heavy boots.

The free pups were in a cardboard box at his feet, snuggled together in one big gray-white fur pile. They looked just like the dogs in Shishmaref. I stooped and petted them gently.

"You look like you could use a dog." His voice was deep. "These ones are husky, shepherd, elkhound, and wolf."

"Wolf?" I raised my eyebrows. "Any males?" I didn't even know why I was asking. I guessed that, if I *did* get a puppy, and it was a male, I wouldn't be standing outside like "Paul," giving away puppies.

"That one there, with the white patch on his chest," he pointed, "only male left."

Thirty minutes later, I emerged from the store with batteries and popcorn, along with a bag of puppy chow, two puppy bowls, and a leash. The last item in my cart was my "free" puppy, actual price tag $32.87.

I introduced my chunky little furball to the yard, hoping he understood that it was his version of a honey bucket. He stepped tentatively in the newness, giving me time to study his features. He had dark gray and black fur with a white undercoat, white fur on his toes, and that cute white patch on his chest. And very bushy eyebrows, like an old man's, which gave his little puppy face an air of seriousness. He was my little protector. My knight in fuzzy armor.

"Ivanhoe," I whispered, stroking his little head. "I think you're an Ivanhoe."

Little Ivanhoe and I were enjoying a lazy morning by the wood stove, him napping and me reading, when the phone shrilled from the kitchen wall, making me jump and spill my tea.

Who the heck could that be? Hardly anyone knew me here. Ivanhoe raised his head.

"Thinking the same thing, huh?" I hoisted myself from the couch and grabbed the receiver before it rang again.

"Hello?"

"Hello, this is the operator. Will you accept a collect call from Estella-non-tokuk?"

"Say again?"

"This. Is. The. Operator. Will you accept a collect call from Estellamon-non … er, montokuk?"

The operator enunciated, but still sounded like she had marbles in her mouth.

Then it dawned on me. The caller might be Estelle Montokuk—otherwise known as Stella, my spirited ninth grade student, my Achilles heel. Stella—always finishing her work before I'd finished giving instructions. In her presence I repeatedly second-guessed myself, often falling prey to her capacity to hijack lessons with a joke or retort. She'd derail my little train to the point that no one got on and I'd forget where I was going. Stella wielded a power in the classroom I could rarely control. She was always two steps ahead, while I fell progressively behind.

Stella never missed class. She was never sick, never on vacation. I suspected that her perfect attendance was rooted in her desire to see just how far she could go, driving me nuts.

As mildly irritating as Stella was on occasion, she was also hysterically funny. She was irreverent, witty, and, at times, rather crass. And that laugh. She would start to chuckle for no reason that I could discern, and—knowing that her laugh was contagious—she would keep up a low-level "ha-ha" until the students seated nearby (which was everyone) mimicked her laugh just for the sake of doing so. In the middle of a lesson, Stella would crack a joke about a classmate or a pencil or a crow flying by and let go a full-bodied guffaw: *Hah!* And then everybody else went *Hah!* and my lesson was pretty much over.

I had to admit that Stella cracked me up, too. At times, it was all I could do to turn my head away fast enough to hide my complicity.

I'm sure she'd seen my failed attempts to keep a straight face, so she persisted.

So here was Stella, calling me collect. My mind raced. How'd she get my number? What happened? And why collect? Was she in town? Was she stranded? Did something happen up there? Could I afford this call? Was someone in her family seriously ill? Did she need me to return to the village? Would I go? Of course, I would go! But still … it was a lot to ask. I mean, I was only her teacher for one year …

The operator coughed.

Fairly sure the caller was indeed Stella, I said yes.

"Thank you." The operator sounded relieved. "Just a moment while I connect you."

I heard a couple of clicks as the connections were made across thousands of miles of wilderness, between the far reaches of Shishmaref and my home in Juneau.

"Hello?" A small female voice came through. I pressed the receiver closer to my ear.

"Hello?" I said. "Is this Stella?"

"Hello?" Girls' voices giggled in the background.

"Stella, is that you?" I repeated.

"Hi!" Two girls' voices simultaneously blurted out their greeting. "Watcha doin'?"

"I'm reading a book. What are *you* doing, and who's that with you?"

"We're calling you, that's what we're doing! And it's Cissy." More giggles. Cissy was one of Stella's younger cousins. I had seen them together a few times and noted that, whatever Stella did, Cissy copied.

"Is there anything wrong? Are you okay?" Part of me didn't want to know the answer.

"We good. Just want to visit."

Realizing that no serious illness or sudden plague stalked Stella, her family, or Shishmaref in general, I relaxed and reached down to pet Ivanhoe, who had gotten up to see what the fuss was all about. His ears twitched and his little tail swished back and forth as if anticipating that my conversation might involve him, too.

I felt myself soften. But I wasn't going to let my former student off the hook entirely. "Stella, do you know what a collect call means?"

"Sure! You taught us in class. When we want to call someone but don't have money, we call the operator and say we're calling collect."

Cissy's voice whispered in the background. "What are we collecting?" More giggling.

Just like in the classroom, I had no response at the ready. Stella was smart and must have tucked away my brief "How to make a collect call" lesson to use in the future on unsuspecting teachers. I couldn't even remember why I'd taught the kids that skill. Now, here I was, on the receiving end of it.

I stretched the phone cord to the refrigerator and pulled out a bottle of beer. It was still morning, but tea was clearly not going to be an adequate pairing for this experience.

"How are you two doing? What's been going on since school was out?"

"Ah, nothin'. So boorring! Nothing to do. We miss you! We even miss school."

More giggling. They paused. Then Stella's voice came through again, more serious. "Will you be coming back to teach us?"

My heart skipped a beat, remembering my awkward "I'm leaving" speech. It was painful and embarrassing then, and no less painful now.

"No, Stella, I'm sorry." I paused, trying to think of something better to say. "But I'm sure you will get another teacher who's good and fun, and who will teach you a lot."

My words were flat. I took a quiet sip and felt the sting of tears coming on. It would have been nice to receive some words of comfort from Stella, like, "We're so sad about you leaving. We loved having you as our teacher. We'll never have another teacher like you." But as she always seemed to do, Stella stuck a fork in my ego and popped it.

"That's okay," Stella said. "We jokes!" Then, "Okay, bye!"

"Bye, Stella, I hope—"

She hung up before I could finish.

"Bye, Stella," I repeated into the silence.

I set the receiver back on its holder and took a gulp of beer. It stung in my throat, but it felt good, like a cleansing. A washing down of something that'd been lodged there and was now set free. Ivanhoe yawned and stretched his front paws out, raising his behind in the air. He shook, jingling his collar, in anticipation of stepping outside.

A light summer rain had dampened the gravel street out front. Large pinecones littered the ground. The air smelled musty yet clean. I stood at the door and watched my new puppy do his business, then laughed as he scampered around the yard, sticking his nose in weeds and pine needles, then pouncing and chomping on a pinecone, only to jump back with surprise.

I took a few deep breaths of the green freshness I had missed so much. Shishmaref had its own kind of beauty, but I needed trees. I thought of Stella and her wonderful, unpredictable, goofy self. Who else would have had the courage to make a collect call to her departed teacher?

She had no idea how long I had agonized over whether to stay or leave. I still wondered if I'd made the right decision. I felt rotten either way.

But maybe Stella's call didn't signal the end of me as a teacher; it might be marking something new—a new beginning. Of what, I had no idea. What I *did* know was that she and her classmates, along with their families, their small island, the sea and its inhabitants—all of that had infused me like a vein of gold deep inside a mountain, waiting to be extracted at the right time.

I replayed the scene of my last interaction with Stella at the airstrip, after her classmates went home. We'd stood quietly together, watching a handful of people readying the plane. I wanted to give her a hug but wasn't sure if she'd reciprocate. Stella had never been physically demonstrative, choosing instead to keep adults at arm's length, perhaps making it easier to poke fun at them. If she got too close, it would be harder to control situations—harder to manipulate my emotions and drive me crazy. In a good-natured way, of course.

I had reached out my hand instead. Stella chuckled and offered hers. It was soft and surprisingly warm. We were caught in a moment of being together, without the usual dodge-and-parry in the classroom. And for just this moment, Stella had nothing to say.

When the pilot had motioned for me to board. I gave Stella's hand a little squeeze and said, "You take care. Don't be so hard on your teachers." A knot had formed in my throat.

Stella grinned and snickered a kind of "not-gonna-happen" reply. I quickly turned, surprised by my tears.

I was only a few yards away when I heard her call out, "Hey, Teach!"

I turned around. "Yeah?"

"Just wanted to tell you—thanks! We didn't learn much, but we sure had fun!"

As always, Stella had the last word. She laughed a big belly laugh, which made me laugh, and then so did everyone within earshot of our parting conversation.

Her words were impeccably accurate. In one short phrase, she'd summed up the entire school year. If anyone else had said those words to me, I might have been devastated. But this was Stella. Any sting of embarrassment I felt from her truth-telling was soothed by her good-natured, gotta-love-her Stella-ness. Regardless of how many times she'd kicked the tires of my teaching—whether she'd learned anything from me or not—Stella was spot-on about one thing: We *did* have fun.

"I'm going to quote you on that!" I yelled back.

And now, almost four decades later, I am.

EPILOGUE

Outside of Shishmaref High School and my little green portable home, the only place I visited more was Walter Nayokpuk's General Store. It was there that Walter welcomed me to the village and where I grew more connected each time I stepped through the small entry and jangled those bells.

Walter's store offered a constant stream of surprises. I never knew if I'd be leaving with groceries, knickknacks, a piece of wisdom, a good laugh, or all of the above.

The one surprise I'd always wondered about was the nickname Walter gave me: Kulizuk. Did it really mean brown hair?

When writing this book, I typed "kulizuk" in various Iñupiaq online dictionaries but found no such word. I tried different spellings and ran it through an online translation program, inserting "brown hair" or "dirty yellow + hair." I even tried "dishwater blonde." No such word seemed to exist.

Mystified, I emailed Rich Stasenko, one of the few Caucasian teachers still living in the village. I had already contacted him to see if I could ask random questions, and this one certainly qualified. Rich emailed back almost immediately.

"Kulizuk sounds like 'belly button,'" he wrote, adding a laughing emoji for emphasis. To be sure, he added that he'd confirm the accuracy of his translation with his wife, Rachel, a Shishmaref native.

Two days later, another email came.

"The spelling of the Inupiaq word for belly button is *qalasiq*, pronounced "kullisick."

So it was true, Walter nicknamed me "belly button."

That Walter ...

But the more I thought about it, the cuter and perhaps more profound the nickname became. Metaphorically speaking, belly buttons are a reminder of our first connection to another human being: our mother. The belly button is the critical site through which we received nourishment during our incubation, all the way through the moment we come kicking and screaming into the world. Even after our umbilical cord is cut, the connection between child and "mother" is an inescapable fact, whether close or not.

I will never know what Walter was thinking. Maybe he'd already sensed that my entry into the village was reminiscent of a baby kicking and screaming into a radical realm of newness. Maybe he knew that once I connected to some of the people in Shishmaref, there would always be a link between us, no matter how far away I travelled.

If Walter intended something else, I'll never know. He passed away a while back. But somehow it doesn't matter. I trusted Walter and can let him have (as usual) the last word.

One last thing.

I've been asked on occasion, "What ever happened to your boots?"

"You mean the Sorel Caribou Men's Nubuck upper, seam-sealed waterproof boots with the removable felt inner boot liners? The ones with the handcrafted waterproof vulcanized rubber shell and Sorel aero-trac non-loading outsole, and a heel height of one and one quarter inches? That weighed about three pounds each?"

"Yeah, I guess."

That's quite a story, but the short answer is, I wore those boots for another thirty years. We finally parted ways in the Denver International Airport, Upper Level, Concourse B.

Our sudden separation was on account of having just spent a couple of weeks in the Rocky Mountains over winter break. When I packed for my trip, I'd anticipated snow and ice, a perfectly plausible assumption for vacationing at an elevation of 8,200 feet in December. So, I brought only my shoe pacs and a pair of slippers.

That year, however, the temperature in the mountains was unseasonably warm—fifties and sixties. It was nuts. I was exhausted and hot from being forced to clomp around in those boots. To make matters worse, my flight back home to Seattle was delayed, and then delayed again. My legs ached.

I loved my boots, but I was sick of them. They might have been sick of me, too.

That's when I spied a kiosk with a sign reading "Crocs for Sale." I made a beeline for the lighter footwear and emerged fifteen minutes later with a pair of maroon-colored Crocs on my feet. It felt like I was walking on marshmallows, really fun and free.

But then I had to deal with my boots. Having no room in my carry-on bag, and being warned by flight personnel that there was "absolutely no more room for anyone or anything in the cabin," I knew the time had come.

It took a while, but I finally found a trash receptacle large enough and, when no one was looking, I said a prayer of gratitude and apology, then gently dropped my Sorels into a large trashcan.

Thud! Thud!

My plane finally departed. The flight was smooth and uneventful until we got closer to SeaTac, and the pilot announced that we were landing in a blizzard. An unexpected snowstorm. I had a window seat and looked with dismay at the flurry of big fat flakes outside, and the thickening layer of snow coating the ground. I was sure the plane was going to slide right off the tarmac and into the adjoining field.

By the time I retrieved my luggage and made it out to the curb, the snow was coming down so hard and fast that my taxi driver refused to drive me home. I finally convinced him to give it a try, greasing his wheels of reluctance with the promise of a big fat tip. He drove me almost all the way but gave up when we hit the narrow side streets.

I got out and winced with the chill of my feet sinking into a foot of snow. My luggage and I watched his taillights disappear into a world of whiteness.

Crocs have thirteen holes in them. Each.

I can still hear my boots laughing.

BIBLIOGRAPHY

Chamisso, Albert. *The Alaska Diary of Albert von Chamisso, Naturalist on the Kotzebue Voyage 1815-1818* (R. Fortuine, Trans.). Anchorage, AK: Cook Inlet Historical Society, 1986. (Original work published 1856)

Hannah, William L. Iġġiaġruk. *Fifty Miles From Tomorrow: A Memoir of Alaska and the Real People.* New York: Sarah Crichton Books, 2009.

"Indigenous Worldviews vs Western Worldviews." Indigenous Corporate Training, Inc., 2022, https://www.ictinc.ca/blog/indigenous-peoples-worldviews-vs-western-worldviews

Koutsky, Kathryn. "Early Days on Norton Sound and Bering Strait: An Overview of Historic Sites in the BSNC Region." *Anthropology and Historic Preservation, Cooperative Park Studies Unit,* vol. I, no. 4, 1981.

Marino, Elizabeth. *Fierce Climate, Sacred Ground: An Ethnography of Climate Change in Shishmaref, Alaska.* Fairbanks: University of Alaska Press, 2015.

McPhee, John. *Coming Into the Country.* New York: Farrer, Straus, and Giroux, 1976.

Niven, Jennifer. *Ada Blackjack: A True Story of Survival in the Arctic.* New York: Hachette Books, 2003.

Parker, Anne Zonne. *Stories From the Origin: Ordinary Moments in the Central Desert of Australia*. Lulu.com, 2007.

Riddles, Libby, and Tim Jones. *Race Across Alaska: First Woman to Win the Iditarod Tells Her Story*. Harrisburg, PA: Stackpole Books, 1988.

Snelling, William Joseph. *The Polar Regions of the Western Continent Explored.* Boston: W.W. Reed, 1831.

Sobelman, Sandra S. Alaska Department of Fish and Game, Division of Subsistence. "The Economics of Wild Resource Use in Shishmaref, Alaska," Technical Report 112. Fairbanks, Alaska. March 1985.

Torrance, Ellis Paul. *Education and the Creative Potential.* Minneapolis: University of Minnesota Press, 1963.

Websites for Weather / Documentaries / Other Relevant Information

Weather conditions in 1984-85: Weatherspark.com

Wind direction: https://wind.willyweather.com/ak/nome-borough/shishmaref.html

Nun's name in "Looking Into Tomorrow" chapter
https://www.britannica.com/biography/Saint-Madeleine-Sophie-Barat

France24 TV documentary on Shishmaref:
https://www.france24.com/en/20140124-revisited-shishmaref-alaska-arctic-climate-change-usa-environment-eskimos

NOVA documentary
https://www.pbs.org/wgbh/nova/video/shishmaref-alaska-community-losing-sea-ice-climate-change/

ABOUT THE AUTHOR

Genét Simone, PhD, has been a teacher and teacher educator for over thirty years. Her pedagogy highlights the importance of tending to the emotional and psychological aspects of the teaching profession. Dr. Simone has published articles in academic journals and contributed chapters to *Getting Ready for Benjamin: Preparing Teachers for Sexual Diversity; Exploring Possibility through Education; and the Handbook of Mindfulness in Education.* She is the owner of Genét Simone Educational Consulting and creator of the B.E.S.T. Formula, a system of strategies to help teachers be Brave, Effective, Self-Caring, and Transformative, so they can stay in the profession they love. She lives in Seattle, Washington. *Teaching in the Dark* is her first book.

To learn more visit www.genetsimone.com

Printed in the United States
by Baker & Taylor Publisher Services